Relax.

You've opened the right book.

Once upon a time, people were wrong. They thought the automobile was an electric death trap that would never replace the buggy, the internet was only for academic shut-ins, and people who used study guides were simply *cheaters*. Then cars stopped exploding every time you started the engine, people realized you could use computers for more than just calculating the digits of *pi*, and the "cheaters" with the study guides ... well, they started getting it. They got better grades, got into better schools, and just plain ol' got better. Times change. Rules change. *You snooze, you lose, buggy drivers.*

SparkNotes is different. We've always been thinking ahead. We were the first study guides on the internet back in 1999—you've been to SparkNotes.com haven't you? If not ... why!? You'll find busy message boards, diagnostic test prep, and all kinds of tools you'll need to get your act together and your grades up. And if your act's already together, SparkNotes will help you brutalize the competition. Or work for peace. Your call.

We're inexpensive, not cheap. Not only are our books the best bang for the buck, they're the best bang, period. Our reputation is based on staying smart and trustworthy—one step ahead, making tough topics understandable. We explain, we strategize, we translate. We get you where you want to go: smarter, better, faster than anyone else.

If you've got something to say, tell us. Your input makes us better. Found a mistake? Check www.sparknotes.com/errors. Have a comment? Go to www.sparknotes.com/comments. Did you read all the way to the bottom? Awesome. We love you. You're gonna do just fine.

SPARKNOTES™

10 PRACTICE EXAMS for the

SAT

SUBJECT TESTS

BIOLOGY E/M • CHEMISTRY
MATH LEVEL 1 • MATH LEVEL 2
U.S. HISTORY

SPARK PUBLISHING

Spark Publishing
A Division of Barnes & Noble
120 Fifth Avenue
New York, NY 10011
www.sparknotes.com

ISBN-13: 978-1-4114-9823-5
ISBN-10: 1-4114-9823-2

Please submit changes or report errors to www.sparknotes.com/errors.

Printed and bound in Canada.

1 3 5 7 9 10 8 6 4 2

CONTENTS

The SAT Math Level 1 Test . . .197

The SAT Math Level 2 Test . . .291

The SAT U.S. History Test . . . 389

HOW TO USE THIS BOOK

IF YOU WANT TO SCORE HIGH ON YOUR SAT SUBJECT TESTS, you need to know more than just the material—you need to know *how to take the test.* Practice tests are the most effective method for identifying your weaknesses and improving your score. You can use this book to:

- Simulate the real SAT Subject Test experience
- Learn important test-taking strategies
- Identify your weaknesses in a specific SAT subject and prioritize your study time
- Get more practice on specific sections or questions
- Set a target score

PRACTICING WITH PRACTICE TESTS

Studying practice tests is a powerful test-prep tool. Below we explain how to do it in four basic steps:

Step 1: Control Your Environment.

You should do everything in your power to make every practice test you take feel like the real SAT Subject Test. Simulating the actual SAT Subject Test experience as closely as possible during your study time will ensure that there will be no surprises to distract you on test day. Understanding what you're in for on test day will give you the focus and calm you'll need to reach your target score.

- Take a timed test. Don't give yourself any extra time. Be as strict as the proctor who will be administering the test. If you have to go to the bathroom, let the clock keep running. That's what'll happen on the test day.
- Take the test in a single sitting. Training yourself to endure an hour's worth of concentrated test-taking is part of your preparation.
- Take the test without distractions. Don't take the practice test in a room with lots of people walking through it. Go to a library, your bedroom, an empty classroom—anywhere quiet.

Step 2: Score Your Practice Test.

After you take your practice test, score it and see how you did. However, don't just tally up your raw score. You should also keep a list of every question you got wrong and every question you skipped. This list will be your guide for further study (see below).

The practice tests in this book come with charts that show you how to convert your raw score into a scaled score.

Step 3: Study Your Practice Test.

After grading your test, you should have a list of the questions you answered incorrectly or skipped. Studying your test involves using this list and examining each question you answered incorrectly, figuring out why you got the question wrong, and understanding what you could have done to get the question right.

The practice tests in our books were specifically designed to help you study. Each question is categorized by its major topic, such as "The Cell" in Biology or "Polynomials" in Math Level 1. The answers also provide full explanations of each question so you can identify and focus on your specific weaknesses.

Why Did You Get It Wrong?

There are four reasons why you might have gotten an individual question wrong:

1. You thought you answered the question correctly, but you actually didn't.
2. You managed to eliminate some answer choices and then guessed among the remaining answers. Sadly, you guessed wrong.
3. You knew the answer but made a careless error.
4. You left it blank.

You should know which of these reasons applies to each question you got wrong. Once you figure out why you got a question wrong, you need to figure out what you could have done to get the question right.

Reason 1: Lack of Knowledge

A question answered incorrectly for reason 1 pinpoints a void in your knowledge. Discovering this kind of error gives you the opportunity to fill that void and eliminate future errors on the same question type.

For example, if a particular math question you got wrong involves factoring a quadratic expression, don't just work out how to factor that *one* quadratic. Take the opportunity to study this topic and learn the techniques that allow you to factor *all* quadratics.

Remember: on the actual subject test, you will not see a question exactly like the question you got wrong. But you probably will see a question that covers the same topic on your practice test. For that reason, when you get a question wrong, don't just figure out the right answer to the question. Study the broader topic that the question tests.

Reason 2: Guessing Wrong

If you guessed wrong, review your guessing strategy. By thinking in a critical way about the decisions you made while taking the practice test, you can train yourself to make quicker, smarter, and better decisions.

Did you guess smartly? Did you eliminate answers you knew were wrong? Could you have eliminated more answers? If yes, why didn't you? Remember: if you can eliminate

2

even one of the five answer choices, you've reduced the number of choices from five to four and increased your odds of getting the question right.

If you took a guess and chose the incorrect answer, don't let that discourage you from guessing. Each SAT Subject Test is an entirely multiple-choice test, which means the answer is right there in front of you. If you eliminated at least one answer, you followed the right strategy by guessing even if you got the question wrong. Review the answer choices for every question, even those you answered correctly. Figuring out why certain answer choices are wrong will help you identify other wrong answers on future questions.

Reason 3: Carelessness
Here it might be tempting to say to yourself, "Oh, I made a careless error," and assure yourself you won't do that again. Unacceptable! You made that careless mistake for a reason, and you should figure out why. Getting a question wrong because you didn't know the answer reveals a weakness in your knowledge of the subject. Making a careless mistake represents a weakness in your test-taking method.

To overcome this weakness, you need to approach it in the same critical way you would approach a lack of knowledge. Study your mistake. Retrace your thought process on the problem and pinpoint the origin of your carelessness: Were you rushing? If you pin down your mistake, you are much less likely to repeat it.

Reason 4: Leaving the Question Blank
It's also a good idea to study the questions you left blank on the test, since those questions constitute a reservoir of lost points. You won't lose any points for leaving a question blank, but you don't gain yourself any points either. A blank answer results from one of two situations:

1. A total inability to answer a question
2. A lack of time

If you were totally unable to answer a question, you must either learn the material or at least try to identify a way you could have eliminated an answer choice in order to turn the guessing odds in your favor. Always guess if you can eliminate at least one answer choice.

If you left an answer blank because of time constraints, look over the question and see whether you think you could have answered it correctly. If you could have, then you know you need to speed up as much as possible without making more careless errors. If you couldn't have answered it correctly, then you've just identified a weakness waiting to be overcome.

Step 4: Talk to Yourself.
No, we haven't lost it. This is darn good advice. Here's why you should talk to yourself as you study your practice tests: as you go through the steps of a question, you should talk them out. When you verbalize something to yourself, it makes it much harder to delude yourself into thinking that you're working if you're really not. Talking out the words makes you really think about them, and taking an active grip on your studying will make all the difference between a pretty good score and a great score.

FIVE BASIC RULES FOR TAKING THE SAT SUBJECT TESTS

These five rules apply to every SAT Subject Test. They really are just commonsense guidelines, but it's amazing how the pressure and time constraints of the SAT Subject Tests can warp and mangle common sense. We list them here because you should always have these rules of test-taking resting gently in your mind as you take the test. You don't need to focus on them obsessively, but you should be sure not to forget them. They will help you save time and cut down on careless errors.

1: Know the Instructions for Each Test.

Since you'll need all the time you can get, don't waste time reading the test instructions during the actual test. Read the instructions before taking each practice test so you'll have them memorized for the actual test.

2: Use Your Test Booklet As Scratch Paper.

Some students seem to think their test booklet has to look "pretty" at the end of the test. Don't be one of those students. A pristine test booklet is a sad test booklet. On the Math Level 1 and 2 Tests, the SAT Subject Test writers even give you "scratchwork" space for drawing diagrams and writing out solutions. You should write down all your work for math problems, in case you want to return to them later to complete the question or check your answer. The Math Level 1 and 2 Tests aren't the only places where you can benefit from marginal scribbling, though. Making margin notes alongside any of the test questions can help you stay on track when answering the subsequent questions. In addition, if you want to skip a question and come back to it later, you should make a distinctive mark next to it, so you won't miss it on your second pass through the questions.

3: Don't Get Bogged Down by a Hard Question.

This rule may seem obvious, but many test-takers have a hard time letting go of a question. If you've spent a significant amount of time on a problem and haven't gotten close to answering it, just let it go. Leaving a question unfinished may seem like giving up or wasting time you've already spent, but you can come back to the problem after you've answered the easy ones. The time you spent on the problem earlier won't be wasted. When you come back to the problem, you'll already have done part of the work needed to solve it.

4: Avoid Carelessness.

There are two kinds of carelessness that threaten you as an SAT Subject test-taker. The first kind is obvious: making mistakes because you are moving too quickly through the questions. Speeding through the test can result in misinterpreting a question or missing a crucial piece of information. You should always be aware of this kind of error because the SAT Subject Test writers have written the exam with speedy test-takers in mind: they often include tempting "partial answers" among the answer choices. A partial answer is the result of some, but not all, of the steps needed to solve a problem. If you rush through a question, you may mistake a partial answer for the real answer. Students often fall into the speeding trap when they become confused, since confusion brings nervousness and fear of falling behind. But those moments of confusion are precisely the moments when you should take a second to slow down. Take a deep breath, look at the question, and make a sober decision about whether or not you can answer it. If you can, dive back in. If you can't, skip the question and go on to the next one.

The second kind of carelessness arises from frustration or lack of confidence. Don't allow yourself to assume a defeatist attitude toward questions that appear to be complex. While some of these questions may actually be complex, some of them will be fairly simple questions disguised in complex-sounding terms. You should at least skim every question to see whether you have a feasible chance of answering it. Assuming you can't answer a question is like returning a present you've never even opened.

5: Be Careful Bubbling in Your Answers.

Imagine this: you get all the right answers to the questions, but you fill in all the wrong bubbles. The scoring computer doesn't care that you did the right work; all it cares about are the blackened bubbles on the answer sheet, and the wrong answers that they indicate.

Protect yourself against this terrifying possibility with careful bubbling. An easy way to prevent slips on the SAT Subject Test answer sheet is to pay attention to the letters being bubbled. You may want to try bubbling in groups (five at a time or a page at a time) rather than answering one by one. Circle the answers in the test booklet as you go through the page, and then transfer the answers over to the answer sheet as a group. This method should increase your speed and accuracy in filling out the answer sheet. To further increase your accuracy, say the question number and the answer in your head as you fill out the grid: "Number 24, B. Number 25, E. Number 26, D."

INTRODUCTION TO THE SAT SUBJECT TESTS

THE SAT SUBJECT TESTS ARE CREATED AND ADMINISTERED by the College Board and the Educational Testing Service (ETS), the two organizations responsible for producing the dreaded SAT. The SAT Subject Tests were created to serve as complements to the SAT. Whereas the SAT tests your critical thinking skills by asking math and verbal questions, each SAT Subject Test examines your knowledge of a particular subject, such as U.S. History, Math, or Biology. The SAT is a 3-hour and 45-minute test; each SAT Subject Test is a 1-hour exam.

The SAT Subject Tests aren't necessarily "better" tests than the SAT; they're just different. Also, they aren't necessarily easier or tougher than the SAT. The difficulty of any SAT Subject Test depends on how knowledgeable you are about the subject—which translates to how diligently you've studied the subject in school and how conscientiously you've prepared for the test itself.

The Good

- Because SAT Subject Tests cover specific topics, you can study for them effectively. For example, if you don't know the structure of DNA, you can look it up and learn it. The SAT Subject Tests are therefore straightforward tests: if you know your stuff, you'll do fine.
- Often, the classes you've taken in school have already prepared you well for the SAT Subject Tests. If you've taken a biology class, you've probably covered most of the topics that are tested on the SAT Biology E/M Test. All you need is some refreshing and refocusing.

The Bad

- Because SAT Subject Tests quiz you on specific knowledge, it is much harder to "beat" or "outsmart" an SAT Subject Test than it is to outsmart the SAT. For the SAT, you can use all sorts of tricks or strategies to figure out an answer. There are far fewer strategies to help you on the SAT Subject Tests. Don't get us wrong: certain test-taking skills will help you on an SAT Subject Test, but knowing the subject will help you much, much more. In other words, to do well on the SAT Subject Tests, you can't just rely on your quick thinking and intelligence. You need to study.

COLLEGES AND THE SAT SUBJECT TESTS

We're guessing you didn't sign up to take an SAT Subject Test just for the sheer pleasure of it. You probably want to get into college and know that the only reason for taking this test is that colleges want or require you to do so.

Colleges care about SAT Subject Tests for two reasons. First, the tests demonstrate your interest, knowledge, and skill in specific subjects. Second, because SAT Subject Tests are standardized, they show how your knowledge of Biology (or History or Math) measures up to that of high school students nationwide. The grades you get in high school don't offer such a measurement to colleges: some high schools are more difficult than others, and students of equal ability might receive different grades, even in classes with a similar curriculum.

When it comes down to it, colleges like the SAT Subject Tests because the tests make their job easier. SAT Subject Tests allow colleges to easily compare you to other applicants and provide you with an excellent opportunity to shine. If you scored 93 percent on your Spanish final, and a student at another high school across the country scored 91 percent, colleges don't know how to compare the two grades. They don't know whose class was harder or whose teacher was a tougher grader. But if you score 720 on the SAT Spanish Test, and that other kid gets a 650, colleges *will* recognize the difference between your scores.

College Course Placement

Occasionally, colleges use SAT Subject Tests to determine course placement. For example, if you do very well on the SAT Chemistry Test, you might be exempted from a basic science class. It's worth finding out whether the colleges you're applying to use the SAT Subject Tests for this purpose.

SCORING THE SAT SUBJECT TESTS

There are three different versions of your SAT Subject Test score. The "raw score" is a simple score of how you did on the test, like the grade you might receive on a normal test in school. The "percentile score" compares your raw score to the raw scores of all other test-takers throughout the United States, letting you know how you did on the test in relation to your peers. The "scaled score," which ranges from 200 to 800, compares your score to the scores received by all students who have ever taken that particular SAT Subject Test.

The Raw Score

You will never know your SAT Subject Test raw score, because it is not included in the score report. But you should understand how the raw score is calculated because this knowledge can affect your strategy for approaching the test.

A student's raw score is based solely on the number of questions that the student got right, wrong, or left blank:

- You earn 1 point for every correct answer.
- You lose $1/4$ of a point for each incorrect answer on five-choice questions.
- You lose $1/3$ of a point for every incorrect answer on four-choice questions.
- You lose $1/2$ of a point for every incorrect answer on three-choice questions.
- You receive zero points for each question left blank.

Calculating the raw score is easy. First, count the number of questions answered correctly. Then multiply the number of five-choice questions you answered incorrectly by $^1/_4$; the number of four-choice questions you answered incorrectly by $^1/_3$; and the number of three-choice questions you answered incorrectly by $^1/_2$. Add these numbers together and subtract the total from the number of right answers.

$$\text{raw score} = \text{right answers} - \big[(^1/_4 \times \text{wrong five-choice answers}) $$
$$+ \ (^1/_3 \times \text{wrong four-choice answers}) $$
$$+ \ (^1/_2 \times \text{wrong three-choice answers}) \big] $$

The Percentile Score

A student's percentile is based on the percentage of the total test-takers who received a lower raw score than he or she did. Let's say, for example, you had a friend named Gregor Mendel, and he received a score that placed him in the 93rd percentile. That percentile tells Gregor that he scored better than 92 percent of the other students who took the same test; it also means that 7 percent of the students taking that test scored as well as or better than he did.

The Scaled Score

ETS takes your raw score and uses a formula to turn it into the scaled score of 200 to 800 that you've probably heard so much about.

The curve to convert raw scores to scaled scores differs from test to test. For example, a raw score of 33 on the Biology Test might scale to a 520, while the same raw score of 33 on the Chemistry Test might scale to a 560. In fact, the scaled score can even vary between different editions of the *same* test. A raw score of 33 on the February 2007 Math Level 2 Test might scale to a 710, while a 33 in June 2007 might scale to a 690. These differences in scaled scores exist to accommodate varying levels of difficulty and student performance from year to year.

WHICH SAT SUBJECT TESTS TO TAKE

There are three types of SAT Subject Tests: those you must take, those you should take, and those you shouldn't take.

- The SAT Subject Tests you *must* take are those required by the colleges you are interested in.
- The SAT Subject Tests you *should* take are tests that aren't required, but that you'll do well on, thereby impressing the colleges looking at your application.
- The SAT Subject Tests you *shouldn't* take are those that aren't required and cover a subject you don't feel confident about.

Determining Required SAT Subject Tests

You'll need to do a bit of research to find out if the colleges you're applying to require that you take a particular SAT Subject Test. Call the schools you're interested in, look at their websites, or talk to your guidance counselor. Often, colleges require you to take the following SAT Subject Tests:

- One of the two Math SAT Subject Tests (either Math Level 1 or Math Level 2)
- Another SAT Subject Test in a subject of your choice

Most colleges require you to show proficiency in different disciplines, so be careful about taking all science tests or all history tests. Instead, try to show colleges that you're a well-rounded student by taking a good mix of tests, such as Math, Biology, and U.S. History. In general, it's a good idea to take one science-based SAT Subject Test.

Deciding to Take Unrequired SAT Subject Tests

There are two rules of thumb for deciding which additional test to take:

1. **Go with what you know.** If history is your field, a strong score on the U.S. History Test will impress admissions officers far more than a bold but mediocre effort on the Latin Test.
2. **Try to show breadth.** Scoring well on similar subject tests such as Math, Physics, and Chemistry will not be as impressive as good scores in more diverse subjects, such as Math, U.S. History, and Modern Hebrew.

Of course, you also have to know what is considered a good score, and whether or not you can get that score (or higher).

Below we have included a list of the most commonly taken SAT Subject Tests and the average scaled score on each. If you feel confident that you can get a score that is above the average by at least 50 points, taking the test will probably strengthen your college application. Please note that if you are planning to attend an elite school, you might have to score significantly higher than the national average. The following table is just a general guideline. It's a good idea to call the schools that interest you or talk to a guidance counselor to get a more precise idea of what score you should be shooting for.

TEST	AVERAGE SCORE
Chemistry	620–630
Biology–Ecological	590–600
Biology–Molecular	625–635
Math Level 1	580–590
Math Level 2	665–675
U.S. History	590-600
World History	585–595
Literature	585–595
Physics	645–655

As you decide which test to take, be realistic with yourself. Don't just assume you're going to do great without at least taking a practice test and seeing where you stand.

WHEN TO TAKE AN SAT SUBJECT TEST

The best time to take an SAT Subject Test is right after you've finished a year-long class in that subject. If, for example, you take Chemistry in eleventh grade, then you should take the SAT Chemistry Test near the end of that year, when the material is still fresh in your mind. However, this rule does not apply for the Literature and the Foreign Language SAT Tests; it's best to take those after you've had as much study in the area as possible.

Unless the colleges you're applying to use the SAT Subject Tests for placement purposes, there is no point in taking any SAT Subject Test after November of your senior year, since you won't get your scores back from ETS until after the college application deadline has passed.

ETS usually sets testing dates for SAT Subject Tests in October, November, December, January, May, and June. However, not every subject test is administered in each of these months. To check when the test you want to take is being offered, visit the College Board website (www.collegeboard.com) or do some research at your school's guidance office.

REGISTERING FOR SAT SUBJECT TESTS

To register for the SAT Subject Test(s) of your choice, you have to fill out some forms and pay a registration fee. We know, we know—it's ridiculous that *you* have to pay for a test that colleges require you to take in order to make *their* jobs easier, but, sadly, there isn't anything we, or you, can do about it. (It's acceptable here for you to grumble about the unfairness of the world.)

After grumbling, however, you still have to register. There are two ways to go about it: online or by mail. To register online, go to www.collegeboard.com. To register by mail, fill out and send in the forms enclosed in the *SAT Registration Booklet*, which should be available in your high school's guidance office. You can also request a copy of the booklet by calling the College Board at (609) 771-7600, or writing to:

College Board SAT Program
P.O. Box 6200
Princeton, NJ 08541-6200

You can register to take up to three SAT Subject Tests for any given testing day. And you can even change your mind about which tests to take come test day, as long as you're not trying to take (or get out of taking) a language-listening test. You must pre-register for any listening test. Unfortunately, even if you decide to take three tests in one day, you'll still have to pay a separate registration fee for each.

GENERAL SAT SUBJECT TEST STRATEGIES

A MACHINE, NOT A PERSON, WILL SCORE YOUR SAT SUBJECT Test. The tabulating machine sees only the filled-in ovals on your answer sheet and doesn't care how you came to those answers—it cares only whether your answers are correct. A lucky guess counts in your favor just as much as an answer you give confidently. By the same token, if you accidentally fill in **B** where you meant **C**, you won't get any credit for having known what the answer was. Think of the multiple-choice test as a message to you from the ETS: "We score your answers, and not any of the work behind them." So give them right answers—as many as possible, using whatever means possible.

We'll start by discussing some general principles for test-taking that you can use for this test as well as any other test you take, then we'll move on to strategies that apply directly to the SAT Subject Tests.

THE STRATEGIES

Most of these "strategies" are common sense, and many of them you already know. The funny thing about high-pressure situations, though, is that common sense often goes out the window. If you review anything in the minutes before taking the test, review these strategies. Of course, that doesn't mean you should skip this section now. It's full of very useful hints, some of which might be new to you.

General Strategy 1: Be Calm.

The best way to do poorly on a test is to psych yourself out. If your mind starts thrashing about wildly, it will have a hard time settling on the right answers. There are a number of preventative measures you can take, beginning weeks or even months before you take the test. Buying this book was a good start: practice really does make perfect. But there are a number of other things you ought to keep in mind:

- **Study in advance.** If you've studied at regular intervals leading up to the test rather than cramming the night before, the information will sit more easily in your mind.
- **Be well rested.** Get a good night's sleep on the two nights leading up to the test. If you're frazzled or wired, you're going to have a harder time buckling down and concentrating when it really counts.

- **Come up for air.** Don't assume that the best way to take an hour-long test is to spend the full hour nose to nose with the test questions. If it feels natural for you to take breathers, don't be afraid to do so. Lift your head occasionally, look about you, and take a deep breath—you may return to the test with a clearer mind.

General Strategy 2: Set a Target Score.

You can make the job of pacing yourself much easier if you go into the test knowing how many questions you have to answer correctly to earn the score you want. What score do you want to get? Ideally, your answer should be an 800, but be realistic: consider how much you know about the subject and how well you generally do on these types of tests. You should also do a little research—talk to the admissions officers of the colleges you might want to attend, look in college guidebooks, or talk to your guidance counselor. Find out the average score of a student admitted to the schools of your choice, and set your target score above it.

Suppose the average score on the SAT U.S. History Test for the school you're interested in is 650. Set your target at about 700. To get that score, you need to get 72 questions right, while giving yourself room to get 12 wrong and leave 11 blank. As long as you have some idea of how many questions you need to answer, bearing in mind that you'll probably get some questions wrong, you can pace yourself accordingly. Taking practice tests is the best way to work on your pacing (good thing you bought this book, huh?). See how many questions you can leave blank and still get the score you want, and you'll have a better sense of what to aim at on the big day.

If you find yourself effortlessly hitting your target score when you take the practice tests, don't just pat yourself on the back. Set a higher target score and start gunning for that one. The purpose of buying this book and studying for the test is to improve your score as much as possible, so be sure to push your limits.

General Strategy 3: Grid Your Answers Carefully.

No kidding. People make mistakes while entering their answers onto the grid, and these mistakes can cost them big time. This slipup occurs most frequently if you skip a question. If you left question 43 blank and then unthinkingly put the answer to question 44 into row 43, you could be starting a long, painful chain of wrong answers. Don't do it.

You can avoid this by filling in your answer sheet five questions at a time rather than one at a time, but if you feel that's too complicated, just be careful to check the number on the answer sheet against the question number each time.

General Strategy 4: Pace Yourself.

At the very least, aim to *look* at every question on the test. You can't afford to lose points because you didn't even get to a question you could have easily answered correctly. While you can spend an average of about 50 seconds on each question, depending on the test, you'll probably breeze through some in 10 seconds and dwell on others for two minutes. Knowing how to pace yourself is a critical skill:

- **Don't dwell on any one question for too long.** If you've spent a couple of minutes laboring over the question, you might just want to circle it and move on. If you feel the answer is on the tip of your tongue, it might come more easily if you revisit it later. Not only is it demoralizing to spend five minutes on a single question, it also eats up precious time in which you might have answered a number of easier questions. Remember: you get as many points for correctly answering an easy question as a difficult one.

- **Skip the unfamiliar.** If you encounter a question you can't make heads or tails of, just circle it and move on. Don't work too hard trying to sort out what's going on. If you have time at the end, you can come back to it and see if you can make an educated guess. Your first priority should be to get all the easy questions, and your second priority should be to get through the questions you can solve with some work. Unfamiliar material should be at the bottom of your list of priorities.

- **Know where—and where not—to look for toughies.** Each subject test starts off with at least 4 or 5 pretty easy questions—definitely nothing you should consider skipping. When you come across questions grouped together in a set, these questions will probably get tougher as you go. Keep this in mind when considering which questions to skip, if any.

General Strategy 5: Read the Question.

This might sound painfully obvious, but many a point has been lost by the careless student who seizes an answer choice hastily before properly understanding the question. Take the following example from Chemistry:

> 6. Three cylinders labeled A, B, C, are all at the same temperature. The volumes of the containers are 2.0 L, 4.0 L, and 6.0 L, respectively. Cylinder A contains 0.679 grams of neon gas at a pressure of 120 mmHg, cylinder B contains 2.45 grams of nitrogen gas at a pressure of 210 mmHg, and cylinder C is completely empty at the start. If the contents of A and B were completely transferred to C (assuming ideal conditions), what would the pressure become in cylinder C?
>
> (A) 0.25 atm
> (B) 180 mmHg
> (C) 330 mmHg
> (D) 675 mmHg
> (E) 1980 mmHg

This is a fairly difficult question, but perhaps more importantly, the question is long and complicated looking. By the time the hasty student finishes reading it, he or she might have forgotten the beginning of the question and decided to simply add the pressures together and choose an incorrect answer, **C**.

To avoid situations like this, take a moment to truly *understand* the question before answering it. Read the question and then vocalize to yourself what the question is asking and what the pertinent information they give you is. Then go ahead and answer the question or solve the problem before you even look at the answer choices. This will help ensure that you aren't seduced by any of the incorrect answer choices listed. By the way, the correct answer to this question is **B**.

General Strategy 6: Know How to Guess.

ETS doesn't take off $1/4$ of a point for each wrong answer to punish you for guessing—they do it so you won't get a reward for guessing blindly. Suppose that without even glancing at any of the five-choice questions, you just randomly entered responses in the first 20 spaces on your answer sheet. Because you have a 20 percent chance of guessing correctly on any given question, odds are you would guess right for four questions and wrong for 16 questions. Your raw score for those 20 questions would then be

$$(4 \times 1) - (16 \times \sqrt[1]{4}) = 0$$

As you can see, you'd be no better or worse off blindly guessing than if you'd left those 20 spaces blank.

Now suppose that in each of the first 20 questions you are able to eliminate just one possible answer choice, so that you guess with a 25 percent chance of being right. Odds are, you'd get five questions right and 15 questions wrong, giving you a raw score of

$$(5 \times 1) - (15 \times \sqrt[1]{4}) = 1.25$$

All of a sudden, you're more than a point up. It isn't much, but every little bit helps. Here's a list of your priorities when you come to each question on an SAT Subject Test:

First priority:	Answer the question correctly.
Second priority:	If you don't know the answer, try to eliminate answer choices and then guess.
Third priority:	If you can't eliminate any answer choices, circle the question and move on to the next one. You might have time to come back to it when you've finished the other questions.

The lesson to be learned here is that blind guessing doesn't help, but educated guessing does. If you can eliminate even one of the five possible answer choices, *you must guess*. We'll discuss how to eliminate answer choices when we discuss specific test-taking strategies in the following chapters.

Guessing As Partial Credit

Some students feel that guessing is similar to cheating—that guessing correctly means getting credit where none is due. But instead of looking at guessing as an attempt to gain undeserved points, you should see it as a form of partial credit. For example, suppose you're stumped on the Chemistry question above that asks about total pressure after different gases are mixed into a new container. And suppose you're pretty sure that the answer isn't simply adding the pressures given, even though you know Dalton's law of partial pressures. You do know many gas laws but are a little unsure as to how to answer this question. You do know that the pressure will be less or at least close to the other two pressures because you have some knowledge of Boyle's law. Don't you deserve something for that extra knowledge? Well, you do get something: when you look at this question, you can throw out **C** and **E**, which leaves you with a one-in-three chance of getting the question right if you guess. Your extra knowledge gives you better odds of getting this question right, exactly as extra knowledge should.

THE SAT BIOLOGY E/M TEST

INTRODUCTION TO THE SAT BIOLOGY E/M TEST

WANT TO DO WELL ON THE SAT BIOLOGY E/M TEST? OF COURSE you do—that's why you bought this book. To do well on the test, you not only have to know your biology but also you need to know what the exam tests so that you don't waste your time cramming on the nuances of mitochondrial DNA and the physiological role of the amygdala. The SAT Biology E/M Test doesn't cover mitochondrial DNA or the amygdala.

In this chapter, we'll tell you precisely what the SAT Biology E/M Test *will* cover, how the test breaks down, and what format the questions will appear in. Take this information to heart and base your study plan around it. There's no use studying topics you won't be tested on or spending countless hours studying bacterial diversity while ignoring meiosis, which is covered far more extensively by the test.

CONTENT OF THE SAT BIOLOGY E/M TEST

The Strange Dual Nature of the SAT Biology E/M Test

The SAT Biology E/M Test has this strange name because it's actually two tests built into one. One test, the Biology-E Test, emphasizes ecology and evolution. The other test, the Biology-M Test, emphasizes molecular biology and evolution. On test day, you will take either the Biology-E or Biology-M Test. You can't take both.

The Biology-E and Biology-M Tests aren't completely dissimilar. In fact, out of a total of 80 questions, the two tests share a core of the same 60 questions. The test contains an additional 40 questions, split between the E and M specialty sections. If you decide to take the Biology-E Test, then you answer the additional section of 20 ecology and evolution questions. If you take the Biology-M version, you answer the additonal section of 20 molecular biology and evolution questions.

The SAT Biology E/M Test covers the biology topics taught in any standard American high school biology course, with particular emphasis on either ecology or molecular biology. ETS breaks the Biology-E Test down into five basic categories:

Topic	Approximate % of the Test (Biology-E)	Approximate No. of Questions (Biology-E)
Cellular and Molecular Biology Includes the cell and cell structure; biochemistry and organic chemistry; cell processes	15	12
Genetics	15	18
Evolution and Diversity Includes evolution; diversity	22	12
Organismal Biology Includes animal structure, function, and behavior; plant structure and function	25	20
Ecology	23	18

As we said, depending on which specialty section you elect to take, the total number of questions from all but one of the categories listed in the charts will vary.

While these categories are helpful, they are also very broad. For example, you may have cell structure down pat, but biochemistry throws you for a loop, and you would like to get a sense of how much of the test is devoted to these two topics. To help you out, we've broken the core of the test down even further, so that you'll know exactly where to expect to feel the squeeze. ETS breaks the Biology-M Test down into five basic categories:

Topic	Approximate % of the Test (Biology-M)	Approximate No. of Questions (Biology-M)
Cellular and Molecular Biology Includes the cell and cell structure; biochemistry and organic chemistry; cell processes	27	22
Genetics	20	16
Evolution and Diversity Includes evolution; diversity	15	12
Organismal Biology Includes animal structure, function, and behavior; plant structure and function	25	20
Ecology	13	10

Each question in the practice tests has been categorized according to these categories so that when you study your practice tests you can very precisely identify your weaknesses.

FORMAT OF THE SAT BIOLOGY E/M TEST

Whether you take the Biology-E or Biology-M, the test will last an hour and consist of 80 questions. These questions will be organized in two main groups. The 60 core questions will come first, followed by a 20-question specialty section.

Question Types

The core section of the test (and occasionally the specialty sections) contains two different types of questions. Classification questions make up approximately the first 15 questions of the core, while the rest of the questions are multiple choice.

Classification Questions

A classification question presents you with five possible answer choices and then a string of three to five test items to which those answer choices apply. The answer choices are usually the names of five related laws or concepts. Because they allow for several questions on the same topic, classification questions will ask you to exhibit a fuller understanding of the topic at hand.

The level of difficulty within any set of questions is generally pretty random: you can't expect the first question in a set to be easier than the last. However, each set of classification questions is generally a bit harder than the one that came before. In the core questions, for example, you should expect the last set of questions (e.g., 12–15) to be harder than the first set (e.g., 1–3).

Familiarize yourself with the following set of directions. Memorize them now, and save yourself some time on test day.

> Directions: Each set of lettered choices below refers to the numbered questions or statements immediately following it. Select the one lettered choice that best answers each question or best fits each statement, and then fill in the corresponding oval on the answer sheet. A choice may be used once, more than once, or not at all in each set.
>
> Questions 1–3 refer to the following organelles.
>
> (A) Chloroplast
> (B) Mitochondria
> (C) Nucleus
> (D) Cytoplasm
> (E) Cell Membrane
>
> 1. Location of cellular respiration in prokaryotes
>
> 2. Maintains proper concentrations of substances within the cell
>
> 3. Found in plant cells, but not in animal cells

You can usually answer classification questions a bit more quickly than standard multiple-choice questions, since you only need to review one set of answer choices to answer a series of questions. This example is meant mainly to show you how a classification question is formatted. If you're burning with curiosity, though, the answers to the questions are **C**, **E**, and **A**, respectively.

Standard (Ungrouped) Multiple-Choice Questions

These are the multiple-choice questions we all know and love, and the lifeblood of any multiple-choice exam. You know the drill: they ask a question and give you five possible answer choices, and you pick the best one.

> <u>Directions:</u> Each of the questions or incomplete statements below is followed by five suggested answers or completions. Some questions pertain to a set that refers to a laboratory or experimental situation. For each question, select the one choice that is the best answer to the question and then fill in the corresponding oval on the answer sheet.

As the directions imply, some five-choice questions are individual questions in which the five answer choices refer to only one question. But some are group questions, in which a set of questions all refer to the same biological scenario, figure, or experiment (we'll look at those just ahead). Here's an example of a typical individual (ungrouped) question:

> 4. Giraffes with longer necks can reach more food and are more likely to survive and have offspring. This is an example of
>
> (A) Lamarck's principle
> (B) natural selection
> (C) adaptive radiation
> (D) convergent evolution
> (E) speciation

A series of about 30 individual multiple-choice questions are found in the core section just after the classification questions. About 6–7 individual multiple-choice questions will begin each specialty section. In both the core and the specialty sections, there is a slight tendency for the questions to become progressively more difficult—although you're likely to find some toughies toward the beginning and some easier ones near the end. By the way, the answer to the example question is **B**.

Group Questions

There are actually two types of group questions. Group questions that refer to figures often test your knowledge in a very straightforward manner. For example, the test might contain a figure of a flower, with each part labeled with a number. The questions will ask you to match a function with the correct part of the flower. Group questions that deal with an experiment or scenario are usually more complicated. Some of the questions in the group may test your ability to read the data in the experiment; others may test your understanding of the experiment itself by asking you, for example, to extrapolate or make predictions based on experimental data.

In both the core and specialty sections, group questions appear after the individual multiple-choice questions. The difficulty of the questions within a group generally increases as you go. We provide examples of both kinds of group questions below.

Figure-Based Group Questions

Figure-based group questions present you with an image or graphic and ask you to identify the structures or functions being represented. The questions are all five-choice multiple-choice questions. Most of the questions dealing with figures demand only simple recognition and recall. The first two questions in the following sample fit this type: you either

22

know the name for a structure or you don't. Some figure-based questions go further, though, and ask about the major processes associated with the images you're identifying.

Questions 5–7 refer to the diagram below.

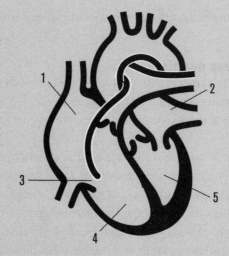

5. Oxygen-rich blood is pumped out to the body by structure

    (A) 1
    (B) 2
    (C) 3
    (D) 4
    (E) 5

6. Structure 1 is termed the

    (A) aorta
    (B) right atrium
    (C) left atrium
    (D) pulmonary artery
    (E) right ventricle

7. Which of the following muscle types are involved in circulating the blood?

            I.   skeletal
            II.   smooth
            III.   cardiac

    (A) I only
    (B) II only
    (C) III only
    (D) II and III only
    (E) I, II, and III

The third question (#7) is of this second kind: it requires you to make a leap from recognizing the heart to knowing the general characteristics of the circulatory system.

Before you start answering questions within a figure-based group, try to figure out what is being depicted and remember what biological phenomena are associated with it. For instance, if you recognize a drawing of mitochondria, chances are you'll be asked about cellular respiration. If the drawing specifies a molecule or organism, keep in mind the general characteristics of the class of molecules or organisms it represents. If you're not sure what the image or graphic in the figure group represents, you can probably pick up hints from the answer choices. Scanning the questions above and seeing the words *atrium*, *ventricle*, and *circulating the blood* provides pretty strong clues that the image shows a heart. Be careful, though: test writers love to seed misleading answers among the correct ones.

In case you're wondering, the answers to questions 5, 6, and 7 are **E**, **B**, and **E**, respectively.

Experiment-Based Group Questions

The SAT Biology E/M Test uses group questions based on experiments, biological situations, and data to measure your scientific reasoning and laboratory skills. There is no standard appearance for the experiments; the data can be presented in paragraphs, tables, and/or graphs.

These groups describe scenarios that are similar to what you've been exposed to in biology class or labs. The two main purposes of these group questions are to test how you understand scientific data and how you apply knowledge of biological principles to this data. Any unfamiliar terms or experimental techniques mentioned in the groups usually just mask simple concepts addressed by the individual questions. In fact, some questions might simply ask you to interpret the data. For these questions you won't have to think much about the concept at all.

Questions 8–10 refer to the following experiment and results obtained.

Dialysis bags are semipermeable membranes, allowing the transport of small molecules while prohibiting larger ones. In an experiment, students filled dialysis bags with different concentrations of sucrose solution and placed them in a beaker of distilled water. The bags were each weighed before being placed in the beaker. After two minutes, they were removed from the beaker, dried, and weighed again.

Contents in Dialysis Bag	Initial Mass	Final Mass
Distilled Water	25.1 g	25.3 g
0.2 M sucrose	25.9 g	28.4 g
0.4 M sucrose	26.1 g	30.0 g
0.6 M sucrose	26.3 g	30.1 g
0.8 M sucrose	25.9 g	35.6 g
1.0 M sucrose	30.7 g	37.6 g

8. Which dialysis bag experiences the largest percent change in mass?

   (A) 0.2 M sucrose
   (B) 0.4 M sucrose
   (C) 0.6 M sucrose
   (D) 0.8 M sucrose
   (E) 1.0 M sucrose

9. If the 0.6 M sucrose solution bag was left in the beaker for four minutes, all of the following occur EXCEPT:

   (A) Mass of the dialysis bag increases to more than 30.1 g.
   (B) Water travels down its concentration gradient.
   (C) Decrease in the bag's molarity of sucrose.
   (D) Sucrose leaks into the beaker.
   (E) Volume of water in the beaker decreases.

10. A glucose molecule is small enough to pass through the bag. If glucose was substituted for sucrose in the dialysis experiment above, by what process does it cross the membrane?

(A) Osmosis
(B) Active transport
(C) Simple diffusion
(D) Facilitated diffusion
(E) Transpiration

For each experiment, identify the following: what is being tested and why? What are the variables, and what factors stay the same? In this example, the mass of the dialysis bags changes with the variable of sucrose concentration. Changes in mass can only come from water entering or leaving the bags, so the question deals with osmosis.

The three sample questions are good examples of the various types of questions the SAT Biology E/M Test asks in experiment groups. You don't have to know anything about concentrations, osmosis, or membrane transport to answer the first question in this group; determining percent change in mass demands only simple data interpretation. The second question requires you to extrapolate and make predictions from the data. The third question asks you to make predictions on what would occur if the experiment were slightly modified. This last type of question goes beyond the numbers and requires knowledge of the topic. If you can identify the general biological properties of the experiment in advance, you should have no trouble answering questions of this sort. The answers to the above sample questions: **D**, **D**, and **C**, respectively.

For experiment-based questions, the test may also present data in graph form—such as a line graph, bar graph, or scatterplot graph. For graphs, make sure you know what the horizontal and vertical axes represent. Think about what relationship exists between these concepts and identify in advance any general trends you can think of. If it helps, sketch out your own tables or notes to sort the data and identify trends or exceptions. For all experiment-based questions, elimination is a helpful tool. You can eliminate answer choices that do not relate to the experiment's variables or what is being tested, or those choices that contradict your knowledge of the biological principles working in the experiment or scenario.

BASIC MATH AND THE SAT BIOLOGY E/M TEST

The writers of the SAT Biology E/M Test assume that you are able to deal with basic mathematical concepts, such as ratios and proportions. They also assume that you know the metric system. You will not be allowed to use a calculator on the test, which isn't a big deal because you won't have to do any calculations more difficult than multiplication.

SCORING THE SAT BIOLOGY E/M TEST

Scoring on the SAT Biology E/M Test is the same as scoring for all other SAT Subject Tests. For every right answer, you earn one point. For every wrong answer, you lose $^1/_4$ of a point. For each question you leave blank, you earn 0 points. These points combined equal your raw score. ETS converts your raw score to a scaled score using a curve tailored to the particular test you take. We've included a raw-to-scaled conversion chart on the next page so you can translate your raw score on a practice test into scaled scores.

This chart shows you that your score doesn't plummet with every question you can't answer confidently. You can do very well on this test without knowing or answering everything. The key to doing well on the SAT Biology E/M Test is to follow a strategy that ensures you will see and answer all the questions you can answer, while intelligently guessing on those slightly fuzzier questions. We discuss these strategies in the next section.

Raw Score	Scaled Score	Raw Score	Scaled Score	Raw Score	Scaled Score
80	800	49	600	18	420
79	800	48	590	17	410
78	790	47	590	16	410
77	780	46	580	15	400
76	770	45	580	14	390
75	770	44	570	13	390
74	760	43	560	12	380
73	760	42	560	11	370
72	750	41	550	10	360
71	740	40	550	9	360
70	740	39	540	8	350
69	730	38	540	7	350
68	730	37	530	6	340
67	720	36	520	5	340
66	710	35	520	4	330
65	700	34	510	3	330
64	700	33	500	2	320
63	690	32	500	1	320
62	680	31	490	0	310
61	680	30	490	−1	310
60	670	29	480	−2	300
59	660	28	480	−3	300
58	660	27	470	−4	290
57	650	26	470	−5	280
56	640	25	460	−6	280
55	640	24	450	−7	270
54	630	23	450	−8	270
53	620	22	440	−9	260
52	620	21	440	−10	260
51	610	20	430		
50	600	19	420		

For example, on an 80-question test, you could score:

- 800 if you answered 79 right and left 1 blank
- 750 if you answered 73 right, 4 wrong, and left 3 blank
- 700 if you answered 67 right, 8 wrong, and left 5 blank
- 650 if you answered 60 right, 12 wrong, and left 8 blank
- 600 if you answered 54 right, 16 wrong, and left 10 blank

We'll talk more about these strategies in the next chapter.

STRATEGIES FOR TAKING THE SAT BIOLOGY E/M TEST

In the previous chapter, we outlined some general test-taking strategies. These strategies will work for any and all subject tests. In this chapter, we'll cover some specific strategies for taking the SAT Biology E/M Test. Sure, some of these strategies might help you with the other SAT Subject Tests, but each and every one will help you improve your score on the SAT Biology E/M Test. Read on to see how.

Strategy 1: Know Thy Biology.

We've said it before and we'll say it again: the best way to do well on the SAT Biology E/M Test is to know your biology. There's simply no substitute for knowing the concepts, structures, results, and principles. If you're not sure what you need to focus on during your studying, take a practice test and go over your answers. Pay attention to what types of questions you got wrong, and try to figure out why you got those questions wrong. Then head to your biology textbook and study up on the missed concepts. You'll thank yourself come test day.

Studying up doesn't mean memorizing everything in your textbook. It's more important to understand the principles and ideas than to just memorize everything in chapters one through twenty. If you understand the ideas and principles behind the concepts, you'll find that everything will start to make sense. The SAT questions will become easier. Knowing your biology will help guide you to the correct answers.

The SAT Biology E/M Test evaluates your knowledge of biology in three different ways. Knowing how your knowledge may be tested should help you better prepare yourself for the exam.

Recall Questions

These questions test your basic knowledge of the fundamental facts and terminology of biology. A typical recall question might ask you to pick out the function of ribosomes, or to name the nitrogenous base that DNA and RNA do not have in common. These questions are straightforward—they're simply a matter of knowing your stuff. Some recall questions might be organized in sets around a figure, as in the example of the questions about the structure of a heart we described earlier.

Interpretation and Application Questions

These questions test your ability to digest data or biological scenarios and to extrapolate answers from that understanding. These questions often necessitate that you are able to use, in tandem, your knowledge of different topics in biology. An interpretation and application question might present a scenario in which the temperature drops and then ask you to predict how this change will affect the metabolism of a lizard and a dog. To answer this question, you have to realize, first, that a question about the change in metabolism due to temperature is asking about warm-blooded and cold-blooded animals. To get the question right, you must first recall that a dog is warm-blooded and a lizard, cold-blooded. Then you have to understand how a lowered temperature will affect each type of animal. (As temperatures decrease, the metabolism of a cold-blooded animal will slow down, while the metabolism of the warm-blooded animal will remain constant.)

Laboratory Questions

Laboratory questions describe a situation in a laboratory and often provide you with data. To answer these questions you must be able to read and understand the data, to form hypotheses and conclusions based on the data, and to be able to identify the goals and assumptions underlying the experiment.

You'll find all three types of questions all over the test, and at all different levels of difficulty. Ultimately, they all test the very same thing: whether you've grasped the basic principles of biology.

Strategy 2: Estimate and Guesstimate.

As General Strategy 5 on p. 15 states, you need to Read the Question. Do not read a question, then zoom straight into the answer choices. Take the time to figure out what the test-makers are looking for. Read the question, estimate or guesstimate an answer for yourself, and then head to the choices.

Strategy 3: Go for Clarity.

The SAT Biology E/M Test requires you to answer 80 questions in just 60 minutes. That gives you roughly 45 seconds per question—not a lot of time to work out complex definitions, equations, connections, or diagrams. If you're working on a question and you find yourself drawing a convoluted diagram or structure, chances are you've messed up somehow. Remember: the questions are designed in such a way that if you understand what's being asked, you will arrive at the answer very quickly. Convoluted is bad; clarity and simplicity are good.

Strategy 4: Write It Down.

Nobody's going to see your test book, so use the extra space to your advantage. Write down anything that might be helpful to you: mathematical equations, definitions, drawings, etc. Most important, don't forget to write down important information! Writing down all of the information may lead you to a correct answer even if you don't really understand the question. Don't be afraid to write, draw, and mark up the questions compulsively. You can even write cute little mantras to yourself. Do whatever you need to do to get the question right.

Strategy 5: Eliminate Wrong Answers.

We've already said that if you can eliminate one answer in a question, the scoring odds are in your favor, and you should guess. This means that you shouldn't skip a question just because you realize you don't know the right answer. Before skipping any question, check to see if you can at least eliminate an answer. For every question, you should go through a checklist of priorities:

- **First priority:** Answer the question correctly.
- **Second priority:** If you don't know the answer, try to eliminate answer choices and then guess.
- **Third priority:** If you can't eliminate any answer choices, move on to the next question.

On most questions, there will be at least one or two answer choices you can eliminate. There are also certain styles of questions that lend themselves to particular processes of elimination.

Classification Questions

In classification questions, the same five answer choices apply to several questions. Invariably, some of these answer choices will be tempting for some questions, but not for others. Consider, for example, the following question set:

Questions 1–3 relate to the following molecules:

- (A) phospholipid
- (B) carbohydrate
- (C) protein
- (D) DNA
- (E) RNA

1. Contains the nitrogenous base uracil

2. Acts as storage for long strings of sugars

3. One side is hydrophilic, while the other is hydrophobic

You can be pretty sure that uracil doesn't appear in protein, carbohydrates, or phospholipids, since nitrogenous bases are only found in RNA and DNA, so you can easily eliminate **A**, **B**, and **C**.

Another point that may help you guess in a pinch: in most sets of classification questions, you won't find the same answer choice being correct for two different questions. True, the directions for classification questions explicitly state that an answer choice "may be used once, more than once, or not at all," and chances are that at least one of the sets will use the same choice as the correct one more than once. But if you're trying to eliminate answers, you might want to go with the overall odds and eliminate those choices that you've already used on other questions in the same set.

For example, the answers to the above questions are 1 **E**, 2 **B**, and 3 **A**. So, if you knew the answers to questions 1 and 2 but had no clue about 3, you could use this elimination strategy to guess either **A**, **C**, or **D**.

"EXCEPT" Questions

"EXCEPT" questions are five-choice multiple-choice questions that contain a bunch of right answers and one wrong answer. The questions always contain an all-caps EXCEPT, LEAST, or some other, similar word. Even if you aren't sure of the answer (which is actually the wrong answer), you should be able to identify one or two of the answer choices as true statements and eliminate them.

> Most birds are characterized by all of the following EXCEPT
>
> (A) four-chambered heart
> (B) strong, heavy bones
> (C) powerful lungs
> (D) eggs protected by hard shells
> (E) evolved from reptiles

Perhaps you're not sure which of the five answer choices is wrong. But you should be able to identify that birds *do* lay eggs protected by shells and that they evolved from dinosaurs. Already, you've eliminated two possible answers and can make a pretty good guess from there.

The answer is **B**: the bones of birds are extremely light. Heavy bones would make flight much more difficult.

"I, II, and III" Questions

"I, II, and III" questions are multiple-choice questions that provide you with three possible answers, and the five answer choices list different combinations of those three.

> A population of animals is split in two by the formation of a river through their territory. The two populations gain different characteristics due to the different natures of their new habitats. When the river disappears, the two populations can no longer interbreed. What has occurred?
>
> I.   Natural selection
> II.   Convergent evolution
> III.   Speciation
>
> (A) I only
> (B) II only
> (C) I and III only
> (D) II and III only
> (E) I, II, and III

There's an upside and a downside to questions like this. Suppose you know that the scenario described by this question does involve speciation, but you aren't sure about natural selection or convergent evolution. The downside is that you can't get the right answer for sure. The upside is that you can eliminate **A** and **B** and significantly increase your chance of guessing the right answer. As long as you're not afraid to guess—and you should never be afraid to guess if you've eliminated an answer—these questions shouldn't be daunting. By the way, the answer is **C**: changes in organisms' characteristics due to changes in habitat are a result of natural selection, and the inability of the members of a former population to interbreed after being separated for a long time is speciation.

Now on to the practice tests!

SAT* BIOLOGY E/M PRACTICE TEST 1

SAT BIOLOGY PRACTICE TEST 1 ANSWER SHEET

1. Ⓐ Ⓑ Ⓒ Ⓓ Ⓔ	26. Ⓐ Ⓑ Ⓒ Ⓓ Ⓔ	51. Ⓐ Ⓑ Ⓒ Ⓓ Ⓔ	76. Ⓐ Ⓑ Ⓒ Ⓓ Ⓔ
2. Ⓐ Ⓑ Ⓒ Ⓓ Ⓔ	27. Ⓐ Ⓑ Ⓒ Ⓓ Ⓔ	52. Ⓐ Ⓑ Ⓒ Ⓓ Ⓔ	77. Ⓐ Ⓑ Ⓒ Ⓓ Ⓔ
3. Ⓐ Ⓑ Ⓒ Ⓓ Ⓔ	28. Ⓐ Ⓑ Ⓒ Ⓓ Ⓔ	53. Ⓐ Ⓑ Ⓒ Ⓓ Ⓔ	78. Ⓐ Ⓑ Ⓒ Ⓓ Ⓔ
4. Ⓐ Ⓑ Ⓒ Ⓓ Ⓔ	29. Ⓐ Ⓑ Ⓒ Ⓓ Ⓔ	54. Ⓐ Ⓑ Ⓒ Ⓓ Ⓔ	79. Ⓐ Ⓑ Ⓒ Ⓓ Ⓔ
5. Ⓐ Ⓑ Ⓒ Ⓓ Ⓔ	30. Ⓐ Ⓑ Ⓒ Ⓓ Ⓔ	55. Ⓐ Ⓑ Ⓒ Ⓓ Ⓔ	80. Ⓐ Ⓑ Ⓒ Ⓓ Ⓔ
6. Ⓐ Ⓑ Ⓒ Ⓓ Ⓔ	31. Ⓐ Ⓑ Ⓒ Ⓓ Ⓔ	56. Ⓐ Ⓑ Ⓒ Ⓓ Ⓔ	81. Ⓐ Ⓑ Ⓒ Ⓓ Ⓔ
7. Ⓐ Ⓑ Ⓒ Ⓓ Ⓔ	32. Ⓐ Ⓑ Ⓒ Ⓓ Ⓔ	57. Ⓐ Ⓑ Ⓒ Ⓓ Ⓔ	82. Ⓐ Ⓑ Ⓒ Ⓓ Ⓔ
8. Ⓐ Ⓑ Ⓒ Ⓓ Ⓔ	33. Ⓐ Ⓑ Ⓒ Ⓓ Ⓔ	58. Ⓐ Ⓑ Ⓒ Ⓓ Ⓔ	83. Ⓐ Ⓑ Ⓒ Ⓓ Ⓔ
9. Ⓐ Ⓑ Ⓒ Ⓓ Ⓔ	34. Ⓐ Ⓑ Ⓒ Ⓓ Ⓔ	59. Ⓐ Ⓑ Ⓒ Ⓓ Ⓔ	84. Ⓐ Ⓑ Ⓒ Ⓓ Ⓔ
10. Ⓐ Ⓑ Ⓒ Ⓓ Ⓔ	35. Ⓐ Ⓑ Ⓒ Ⓓ Ⓔ	60. Ⓐ Ⓑ Ⓒ Ⓓ Ⓔ	85. Ⓐ Ⓑ Ⓒ Ⓓ Ⓔ
11. Ⓐ Ⓑ Ⓒ Ⓓ Ⓔ	36. Ⓐ Ⓑ Ⓒ Ⓓ Ⓔ	61. Ⓐ Ⓑ Ⓒ Ⓓ Ⓔ	86. Ⓐ Ⓑ Ⓒ Ⓓ Ⓔ
12. Ⓐ Ⓑ Ⓒ Ⓓ Ⓔ	37. Ⓐ Ⓑ Ⓒ Ⓓ Ⓔ	62. Ⓐ Ⓑ Ⓒ Ⓓ Ⓔ	87. Ⓐ Ⓑ Ⓒ Ⓓ Ⓔ
13. Ⓐ Ⓑ Ⓒ Ⓓ Ⓔ	38. Ⓐ Ⓑ Ⓒ Ⓓ Ⓔ	63. Ⓐ Ⓑ Ⓒ Ⓓ Ⓔ	88. Ⓐ Ⓑ Ⓒ Ⓓ Ⓔ
14. Ⓐ Ⓑ Ⓒ Ⓓ Ⓔ	39. Ⓐ Ⓑ Ⓒ Ⓓ Ⓔ	64. Ⓐ Ⓑ Ⓒ Ⓓ Ⓔ	89. Ⓐ Ⓑ Ⓒ Ⓓ Ⓔ
15. Ⓐ Ⓑ Ⓒ Ⓓ Ⓔ	40. Ⓐ Ⓑ Ⓒ Ⓓ Ⓔ	65. Ⓐ Ⓑ Ⓒ Ⓓ Ⓔ	90. Ⓐ Ⓑ Ⓒ Ⓓ Ⓔ
16. Ⓐ Ⓑ Ⓒ Ⓓ Ⓔ	41. Ⓐ Ⓑ Ⓒ Ⓓ Ⓔ	66. Ⓐ Ⓑ Ⓒ Ⓓ Ⓔ	91. Ⓐ Ⓑ Ⓒ Ⓓ Ⓔ
17. Ⓐ Ⓑ Ⓒ Ⓓ Ⓔ	42. Ⓐ Ⓑ Ⓒ Ⓓ Ⓔ	67. Ⓐ Ⓑ Ⓒ Ⓓ Ⓔ	92. Ⓐ Ⓑ Ⓒ Ⓓ Ⓔ
18. Ⓐ Ⓑ Ⓒ Ⓓ Ⓔ	43. Ⓐ Ⓑ Ⓒ Ⓓ Ⓔ	68. Ⓐ Ⓑ Ⓒ Ⓓ Ⓔ	93. Ⓐ Ⓑ Ⓒ Ⓓ Ⓔ
19. Ⓐ Ⓑ Ⓒ Ⓓ Ⓔ	44. Ⓐ Ⓑ Ⓒ Ⓓ Ⓔ	69. Ⓐ Ⓑ Ⓒ Ⓓ Ⓔ	94. Ⓐ Ⓑ Ⓒ Ⓓ Ⓔ
20. Ⓐ Ⓑ Ⓒ Ⓓ Ⓔ	45. Ⓐ Ⓑ Ⓒ Ⓓ Ⓔ	70. Ⓐ Ⓑ Ⓒ Ⓓ Ⓔ	95. Ⓐ Ⓑ Ⓒ Ⓓ Ⓔ
21. Ⓐ Ⓑ Ⓒ Ⓓ Ⓔ	46. Ⓐ Ⓑ Ⓒ Ⓓ Ⓔ	71. Ⓐ Ⓑ Ⓒ Ⓓ Ⓔ	96. Ⓐ Ⓑ Ⓒ Ⓓ Ⓔ
22. Ⓐ Ⓑ Ⓒ Ⓓ Ⓔ	47. Ⓐ Ⓑ Ⓒ Ⓓ Ⓔ	72. Ⓐ Ⓑ Ⓒ Ⓓ Ⓔ	97. Ⓐ Ⓑ Ⓒ Ⓓ Ⓔ
23. Ⓐ Ⓑ Ⓒ Ⓓ Ⓔ	48. Ⓐ Ⓑ Ⓒ Ⓓ Ⓔ	73. Ⓐ Ⓑ Ⓒ Ⓓ Ⓔ	98. Ⓐ Ⓑ Ⓒ Ⓓ Ⓔ
24. Ⓐ Ⓑ Ⓒ Ⓓ Ⓔ	49. Ⓐ Ⓑ Ⓒ Ⓓ Ⓔ	74. Ⓐ Ⓑ Ⓒ Ⓓ Ⓔ	99. Ⓐ Ⓑ Ⓒ Ⓓ Ⓔ
25. Ⓐ Ⓑ Ⓒ Ⓓ Ⓔ	50. Ⓐ Ⓑ Ⓒ Ⓓ Ⓔ	75. Ⓐ Ⓑ Ⓒ Ⓓ Ⓔ	100. Ⓐ Ⓑ Ⓒ Ⓓ Ⓔ

SAT BIOLOGY PRACTICE TEST 1

Time—1 hour

FOR BOTH BIOLOGY-E AND BIOLOGY-M, ANSWER QUESTIONS 1–60

> **Directions:** Each set of lettered choices below refers to the numbered questions or statements immediately following it. Select the one lettered choice that best answers each question or best fits each statement and then fill in the corresponding oval on the answer sheet. A choice may be used once, more than once, or not at all in each set.

Questions 1–3 refer to members of the kingdom Plantae.

(A) Bryophytes
(B) Gymnosperms
(C) Seedless vascular plants
(D) Angiosperms
(E) Legumes

1. Divided into two subgroups—monocots and dicots

2. Include club mosses, horsetails, and ferns

3. Lack true roots, stems, and leaves

Questions 4–7

(A) Autotroph
(B) Tertiary consumer
(C) Primary consumer
(D) Saprophyte
(E) Secondary consumer

4. A carnivore that eats an herbivore

5. An organism that can use solar energy and carbon dioxide to make organic molecules

6. An organism that decomposes waste and dead material

7. An animal that eats plants

Questions 8–10

(A) Right ventricle
(B) Aorta
(C) Right atrium
(D) Pulmonary artery
(E) Atrioventricular node

8. The chamber where blood returns to the heart

9. Carries deoxygenated blood to the lungs

10. Causes the walls of the ventricles to contract

Questions 11–14 refer to the organic compounds crucial to the storage and transfer of information.

(A) Nucleic acids
(B) Steroids
(C) Phospholipids
(D) Polypeptides
(E) Polysaccharides

11. Take the form of starch or cellulose in plants

12. Form the fundamental structure of the cell membrane

13. The primary structure in hydrophobic hormones

14. Store energy in animals as glycogen

GO ON TO THE NEXT PAGE

> **Directions:** Each of the questions or incomplete statements below is followed by five suggested answers or completions. Some questions pertain to a set that refers to a laboratory or experimental situation. For each question, select the one choice that is the best answer to the question and then fill in the corresponding oval on the answer sheet.

15. If a carbon atom has 6 protons, 7 neutrons, and 6 electrons, then that carbon atom is a(n)

    (A) cation
    (B) anion
    (C) isotope
    (D) metal
    (E) electrically charged element

16. Which of the following statements is NOT true?

    (A) Prokaryotic cells are evolutionarily more advanced than eukaryotic cells.
    (B) Prokaryotic cells have no nucleus.
    (C) Plant cells are eukaryotic.
    (D) Prokaryotic cell walls are composed of peptidoglycan.
    (E) Eukaryotic cells have mitochondria.

17. A rat in a cage flinches when a burst of noise is played over a loudspeaker. The burst is played twice an hour. Otherwise, the rat is treated normally. After one day, the rat no longer flinches when the sound is played. This is an example of

    (A) sensitization
    (B) imprinting
    (C) habituation
    (D) conditioning
    (E) instinctual behavior

18. The prairie of North America and the steppe of Russia—both grasslands—are examples of the same

    (A) biome
    (B) ecosystem
    (C) biosphere
    (D) community
    (E) habitat

19. The theory that there are short periods of rapid evolution followed by long periods with little or no evolution is called

    (A) gradualism
    (B) Lamarckism
    (C) punctuated equilibrium
    (D) natural selection
    (E) random speciation

20. A lizard in the genus *Cnemidophorus* can reproduce when the female's eggs divide mitotically without being fertilized by sperm. This type of reproduction is called

    (A) sexual reproduction
    (B) parthenogenesis
    (C) regeneration
    (D) budding
    (E) hermaphrodism

21. A microscope with a 10x ocular lens and a 20x objective lens will produce a total magnification of

    (A) 10x
    (B) 20x
    (C) 30x
    (D) 200x
    (E) 2,000x

GO ON TO THE NEXT PAGE →

22. The process in which a plant loses water through its leaves is called

    (A) photosynthesis
    (B) precipitation
    (C) respiration
    (D) percolation
    (E) transpiration

23. Epinephrine and norepinephrine are the "fight-or-flight" hormones that are released by the

    (A) pituitary gland
    (B) thyroid gland
    (C) adrenal glands
    (D) hypothalamus
    (E) pancreas

24. During the Great Depression, many farmers stopped plowing their fields and abandoned them. The abandoned fields subsequently underwent ecological changes through a process known as

    (A) community rotation
    (B) population dynamics
    (C) primary succession
    (D) secondary succession
    (E) ecosystem maintenance

25. A plant in a windowsill bends toward the light. This is an example of

    (A) photoperiodism
    (B) thigmotropism
    (C) gravitropism
    (D) photorespiration
    (E) phototropism

26. The Krebs cycle takes place in the

    (A) cytoplasm of the cell
    (B) chloroplasts
    (C) matrix of the mitochondria
    (D) inner membrane of the mitochondria
    (E) thylakoid of the mitochondria

27. A scientist places three substances into three different beakers of water. The first substance dissolves, the second substance does not dissolve, and the third substance dissolves. Which of the following is the most likely identification of the components of each of the substances:

    (A) Substance 1: ionic compounds
        Substance 2: isotopes
        Substance 3: nonpinolar molecules
    (B) Substance 1: polar molecules
        Substance 2: ionic compounds
        Substance 3: molecules with hydrogen bonds
    (C) Substance 1: ionic compounds
        Substance 2: polar molecules
        Substance 3: molecules with hydrogen bonds
    (D) Substance 1: isotopes
        Substance 2: molecules with hydrogen bonds
        Substance 3: ionic compounds
    (E) Substance 1: polar molecules
        Substance 2: nonpolar molecules
        Substance 3: ionic compounds

28. In a eukaryotic cell, where can DNA be found?

    (A) Ribosomes and nucleus
    (B) Nucleus only
    (C) Nucleus and mitochondria
    (D) Golgi complex only
    (E) Cytoplasm

29. Which of the following characteristics would most likely be associated with an ocean organism that feeds exclusively on dead organic matter?

    (A) Is exclusively unicellular
    (B) Has a silicate shell
    (C) Is also autotrophic
    (D) Lives in the photic zone
    (E) Has poor eyesight

GO ON TO THE NEXT PAGE

30. When two substances are placed in a cup filled with distilled water, nothing happens. When a third substance is added to the cup, the first two substances combine, while the third remains unchanged. The third substance is a(n)

    (A) amino acid
    (B) enzyme
    (C) lipid
    (D) carbohydrate
    (E) substrate

31. In a plant cell, respiration occurs in

    (A) chloroplasts
    (B) thylakoids
    (C) ribosomes
    (D) the nucleus
    (E) mitochondria

32. The similar appearance of the wing of an insect and the wing of a bird are examples of what process?

    (A) Sympatric speciation
    (B) Adaptive radiation
    (C) Stabilizing selection
    (D) Convergent evolution
    (E) Divergent evolution

33. The substances in a leaf that absorb light are called

    (A) stomata
    (B) guard cells
    (C) thylakoids
    (D) pigments
    (E) ATP

34. Which of the following events might create a gap in the fossil record?

    I. Mass extinction
    II. Erosion
    III. Volcanic activity

    (A) I only
    (B) II only
    (C) I and III only
    (D) II and III only
    (E) I, II, and III

35. The exchange of genetic material between homologous chromosomes during the production of sperm and eggs is important because it

    (A) produces offspring that are genetically identical to the parent
    (B) increases the number of genetic combinations in the gametes
    (C) decreases the genetic variation caused by independent assortment
    (D) results in faster reproduction
    (E) creates alleles that were not present in either parent

36. Mitosis and meiosis are similar because both

    (A) result in the production of gametes in humans
    (B) involve independent assortment
    (C) result in the production of two identical daughter cells
    (D) involve replication of DNA
    (E) have two cell divisions

GO ON TO THE NEXT PAGE

37. Bile plays an important role in the digestion process because it

    (A) chemically digests starches that would otherwise be eliminated as waste
    (B) controls *E. coli* activity in the large intestine
    (C) emulsifies fat globules to increase surface area for eventual chemical digestion
    (D) protects the gall bladder from infection
    (E) enhances the absorptive power of the villi

38. Excessive acid in the stomach can result in a hole in the wall of the organ. What is this hole called?

    (A) Tumor
    (B) Cancer
    (C) Boil
    (D) Ulcer
    (E) Hemorrhoid

39. Individuals from two separate species that share an evolutionary ancestor may

    I.   have identical genetic codes
    II. be able to produce viable offspring
    III. follow similar stages of embryological development

    (A) I only
    (B) II only
    (C) III only
    (D) I and II only
    (E) I and III only

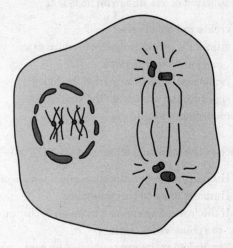

40. The homologous chromosomes in the cell pictured above are engaged in a process called

    (A) cytokinesis
    (B) substitution
    (C) replication
    (D) crossing-over
    (E) translation

41. Which of the following indicates the correct path of an electrical impulse through a neuron?

    (A) axon → dendrite → cell body
    (B) dendrite → axon → cell body
    (C) cell body → dendrite → axon
    (D) dendrite → cell body → axon
    (E) axon → cell body → dendrite

GO ON TO THE NEXT PAGE

42. The function of the sinoatrial node is to

    (A) create red blood cells
    (B) stimulate cardiac muscles to contract in a regular and controlled rhythm
    (C) remove carbon dioxide from the blood
    (D) separate the atria from the ventricles
    (E) manufacture antigens

43. Which of the following statements is NOT true?

    (A) Humans have 44 autosomes and 2 sex chromosomes.
    (B) Humans have 46 chromosomes.
    (C) If the fertilizing sperm carries an X-chromosome, the child will be male.
    (D) Sex-linked traits are controlled by genes located on sex chromosomes.
    (E) Monosomy is the absence of one copy of a chromosome.

44. Which of the following is the best example of an ecological community?

    (A) A group of prairie dogs that live in the same area and interbreed
    (B) The abiotic environment in a prairie dog town
    (C) All of the plant and animal populations that live and interact in a prairie dog town
    (D) All of the prairie dogs in North America
    (E) A group of prairie dogs and the plant species that they eat

45. Which of the following is NOT a condition for Hardy-Weinberg equilibrium?

    (A) Large population size
    (B) Non-random mating
    (C) Absence of immigration or emigration
    (D) Random reproductive success
    (E) No mutation

46. In order for germination to occur, the seed of the *Calvaria major* tree had to pass through the digestive system of a Dodo bird. When the Dodo bird became extinct, so too did the tree. This is an example of

    (A) coevolution
    (B) reciprocal competition
    (C) parasitism
    (D) niche separation
    (E) mutual dependence

47. Which of the following are true statements about cell size?

    I.   As cells grow larger, surface area increases more slowly than volume.
    II. As cells grow larger, surface area increases more rapidly than volume.
    III. Cells are small because their surface area and volume must be balanced.

    (A) I only
    (B) II only
    (C) III only
    (D) II and III only
    (E) I and III only

GO ON TO THE NEXT PAGE

Questions 48–50 refer to the dichotomous key below.

Taxonomists use dichotomous keys to identify the name of an organism. A dichotomous key has a series of two-part questions based on the characteristics of the organisms. When you answer a question, you are led to the next question and ultimately to the name of the unknown organism. The following is a dichotomous key for animals in a natural history collection.

1. ladybug   2. centipede   3. spider

4. grasshopper   5. moth

Dichotomous Key

1.	Has 6 legs . . . . go to 2
	Has more than 6 legs . . . . go to 4
2.	Hind legs are greatly enlarged. . . . . Orthoptera
	All legs are approximately the same size . . . . go to 3
3.	Has hard wings that are spotted . . . . Coleoptera
	Has soft wings that are striped . . . . Lepidoptera
4.	Has 8 legs . . . . .Arachnida
	Has more than 8 legs . . . . Chilopoda

48. Organism #1 is a(n)

(A) Orthoptera
(B) Chilopoda
(C) Lepidoptera
(D) Coleoptera
(E) Arachnida

49. All of the organisms shown are members of phylum

(A) Insecta
(B) Arthropoda
(C) Animalia
(D) Echinodermata
(E) Arachnida

50. Another example of a member of this phylum would be a(n)

(A) snail
(B) clam
(C) earthworm
(D) lobster
(E) jellyfish

GO ON TO THE NEXT PAGE

Questions 51–54 refer to the following drawing of an individual's chromosomes, arranged by size.

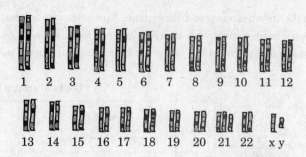

51. The above drawing is of a

    (A) pedigree
    (B) DNA helix
    (C) Punnett square
    (D) karyotype
    (E) gene sequence

52. How many individual chromosomes are shown?

    (A) 22
    (B) 23
    (C) 45
    (D) 46
    (E) 47

53. The individual whose chromosomes are shown here has a disorder called

    (A) disjunction
    (B) trisomy of chromosome 21
    (C) nondisjunction of the Y-chromosome
    (D) polyploidy
    (E) monosomy of the X-chromosome

54. This individual received a(n)

    (A) X-chromosome from the mother and a Y-chromosome from the father
    (B) Y-chromosome from the mother and an X-chromosome from the father
    (C) X- and a Y-chromosome from the mother and no sex chromosome from the father
    (D) X-chromosome from the mother and no sex chromosome from the father
    (E) X- and a Y-chromosome from both the mother and father

GO ON TO THE NEXT PAGE

<u>Questions 55–57</u> refer to the following experiment in which plant species A and B were exposed to dark and light environments for various lengths of time. The shaded areas represent "night" and the unshaded areas represent "day".

In this experiment, plants that flower only when exposed to 12 or more hours of daylight are called "long-day" plants. Plants that flower only when exposed to less than 12 hours of daylight are called "short-day" plants. Plants whose flowering patterns are not dependent on day length are called "day-neutral" plants.

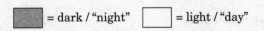

Part 1

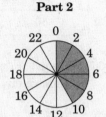

Species A – not flowering
Species B – not flowering

Part 2

Species A – not flowering
Species B – flowering

Part 3

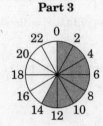

Species A – flowering
Species B – not flowering

Part 4

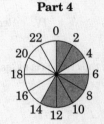

Species A – not flowering
Species B – flowering

55. Which of the following statements is correct?

(A) Plant A is a long-day plant.
(B) Plant B is a short-day plant.
(C) Plant A is a day-neutral plant.
(D) Plant A is a short-day plant.
(E) Plant B is a day-neutral plant.

56. Which of the following statements is NOT supported by the data?

(A) Plant A flowers when exposed to 14 hours of darkness.
(B) Neither plant will flower when exposed to 12 hours of light and 12 hours of darkness.
(C) Plant A will not flower if there is an interruption of exposure to darkness, even if the total hours of darkness in a full day is greater than 12 hours.
(D) Plant B will not flower if there is an interruption of exposure to darkness that causes "night" to be less than 14 hours long.
(E) Plant B flowers when exposed to 14 hours of light.

57. The plants used in this experiment are all

(A) gymnosperms
(B) angiosperms
(C) bryophytes
(D) tricots
(E) non-vascular

GO ON TO THE NEXT PAGE

Questions 58–60 refer to a breeding experiment using plants with unknown genotypes. The plant phenotypes include a plant with red flowers and a plant with white flowers.

Cross		Offspring	
		Red	White
I.	Red is self-pollinated	100	0
II.	White is self-pollinated	0	100
III.	Red is cross-pollinated with white	100	0
IV.	Red is cross-pollinated with white	50	50

58. In which of the crosses is at least one parent homozygous for red flowers?

(A) I only
(B) III only
(C) IV only
(D) I and III only
(E) I and IV only

59. If the offspring in Cross III had all been pink, then the gene for flower color would be an example of

(A) complete dominance
(B) incomplete dominance
(C) codominance
(D) complete recessiveness
(E) polygenetics

60. If the red progeny of Cross III are self-pollinated, what is the probability that an individual offspring will be red?

(A) 0%
(B) 25%
(C) 50%
(D) 75%
(E) 100%

**If you are taking the Biology-E Test, continue with questions 61–80.
If you are taking the Biology-M Test, go to question 81 now.**

BIOLOGY-E SECTION

Directions: Each of the questions or incomplete statements below is followed by five suggested answers or completions. Some questions pertain to a set that refers to a laboratory or experimental situation. For each question, select the one choice that is the best answer to the question and then fill in the corresponding oval on the answer sheet.

---

61. Evolution is defined as

    (A) a population in Hardy-Weinberg equilibrium
    (B) a change in the inhabitants of a community over time
    (C) a change in gene frequency over time
    (D) inheritance of acquired traits
    (E) survival of the fittest

62. Suppose that a botanical disease were to destroy aspen trees in Rocky Mountain National Park. What would happen with respect to the elk population that feeds on aspen trees?

    (A) The carrying capacity would decrease due to competition for space.
    (B) The carrying capacity would decrease due to competition for food.
    (C) The carrying capacity would increase due to competition for space.
    (D) The carrying capacity would increase due to predation.
    (E) The carrying capacity would increase due to disease.

63. Clusters of neurons are known as

    (A) ganglia
    (B) Nodes of Ranvier
    (C) receptors
    (D) Schwann cells
    (E) axons

64. Which of the following is NOT a characteristic of members of the kingdom Fungi?

    (A) Often live as decomposers
    (B) Are heterotrophic
    (C) Secrete enzymes to digest their food externally
    (D) Spend most of their life cycle in the haploid state
    (E) Have cell walls made of cellulose

65. In a food chain, roughly what percentage of energy is transferred from one trophic level to the next?

    (A) 100%
    (B) 80%
    (C) 50%
    (D) 10%
    (E) 1%

66. How could a farmer increase the amount of nitrogen available to his plant crops?

    I. Add nitrogen-fixing legumes to his cropfield.
    II. Add fertilizer to his cropfield.
    III. Add denitrifying bacteria to his cropfield.

    (A) I only
    (B) II only
    (C) III only
    (D) I and II only
    (E) I, II, and III

GO ON TO THE NEXT PAGE

Questions 67–69 refer to evolution in a population of turtles.

In 1940 a species of turtle was observed by scientists on a small, isolated island in the Caribbean. The scientists counted the number of turtles and measured the size of each turtle. This data is plotted on the graph in Figure 1.

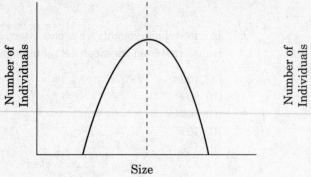

Figure 1 Turtle Size in 1940

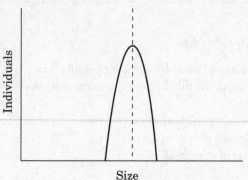

Figure 2 Turtle Size in 1990

Fifty years later, a second team of scientists came to observe the turtles. They counted the number of turtles and again measured the size of each turtle. Their observations are recorded, as shown in Figure 2.

67. Which of the following best characterizes what happened to the turtle population over time?

(A) Evolution
(B) Stabilizing selection
(C) Disruptive selection
(D) Directional selection
(E) Hardy-Weinberg equilibrium

68. A large turtle can better withstand extreme high winds than a small turtle. Which of the following graphs best represents a likely distribution of turtle size on the island if the island became subject to regular and repeated high winds for a decade or more?

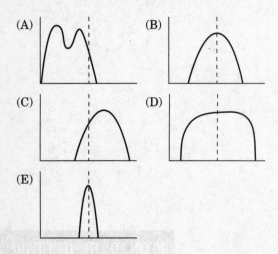

69. The population of turtles on the island grew from a few turtles that came to the island from a nearby continent. In a breeding experiment, scientists discovered that the turtles from the island can no longer breed with turtles from the continent. What has happened?

(A) Convergent evolution
(B) Hardy-Weinberg equilibrium
(C) Mutation
(D) Allopatric speciation
(E) Extinction

GO ON TO THE NEXT PAGE

BIOLOGY-E SECTION—*Continued*

<u>Questions 70–73</u> refer to the following germination experiment.

A seed cannot sprout until oxygen and water penetrate the seed coat. An experiment was conducted to determine what effect water, heat, cold, and scarification had on the germination of seeds. Scarification is the process of mechanically wearing down the seed coat. Two seed types were used in this experiment. One seed type had a very hard seed coat, and the other had a moderately soft seed coat. For 5 days prior to planting, seeds were either soaked in water, passed through the digestive system of a Guinea pig (scarification), exposed to 100°F, exposed to 30°F, or left at ambient temperatures. The seeds were then planted. Every 5 days, the number of seed sprouts from each treatment was counted.

Seeds with hard coats

Treatment	Cumulative % of Germinated Seeds				
	Day 5	Day 10	Day 15	Day 20	Day 25
Water	25%	45%	55%	65%	70%
Heat	15%	25%	45%	50%	55%
Cold	10%	20%	30%	35%	40%
Scarification	60%	75%	75%	75%	75%
Ambient temperature	15%	30%	50%	60%	60%

Seeds with soft coats

Treatment	Cumulative % of Germinated Seeds				
	Day 5	Day 10	Day 15	Day 20	Day 25
Water	5%	7%	7%	9%	10%
Heat	10%	15%	45%	65%	70%
Cold	10%	15%	35%	40%	40%
Scarification	2%	3%	3%	4%	4%
Ambient temperature	15%	30%	50%	60%	65%

GO ON TO THE NEXT PAGE

70. During which treatment did the hard-coated seeds germinate the earliest?

    (A) Water
    (B) Heat
    (C) Cold
    (D) Scarification
    (E) Ambient temperature

71. During which treatment did the greatest percentage of soft-coated seeds germinate?

    (A) Water
    (B) Heat
    (C) Cold
    (D) Scarification
    (E) Ambient temperature

72. Which treatment served as the control for this experiment?

    (A) Water
    (B) Heat
    (C) Cold
    (D) Scarification
    (E) Ambient temperature

73. Which of the following statements is the most acceptable interpretation of this data?

    (A) A seed cannot germinate unless it has been either soaked in water or exposed to high temperatures.
    (B) Exposing seeds to heat and cold increases germination by equal amounts.
    (C) Angiosperms and gymnosperms have different requirements for germination.
    (D) Monocots and dicots have different requirements for germination.
    (E) Seeds with hard coats germinated better when they were scarified, but seeds with soft coats were too damaged by scarification and didn't germinate.

GO ON TO THE NEXT PAGE

Questions 74–77 refer to the cross-section of a leaf.

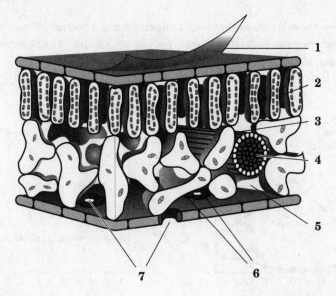

74. Gases diffuse in and out of the leaf through structure

    (A) 3
    (B) 4
    (C) 5
    (D) 6
    (E) 7

75. Which of the following would NOT be found in structure 2?

    (A) Thylakoid
    (B) Chlorophyll
    (C) Stroma
    (D) Guard cells
    (E) Granum

76. All of the following are true regarding structure 4 EXCEPT:

    (A) It is comprised of sieve elements.
    (B) It distributes the products of photosynthesis.
    (C) It is comprised of living cells.
    (D) It can carry materials both up and down the plant body.
    (E) It will become wood.

77. If structure 1 were very thick, and if structure 7 were closed during the warmest part of the day, then this plant likely lives in the

    (A) desert
    (B) taiga
    (C) rainforest
    (D) temperate deciduous forest
    (E) ocean

GO ON TO THE NEXT PAGE

Questions 78–80 refer to climatographs, as discussed below.

Climatographs are graphs that show the relationship between temperature and precipitation over the course of the year in a given geographic local. By looking at a climatograph for a given region, you can get an idea of what the environment is like, i.e., how dry or wet it is, how long the growing season lasts, how constant conditions are, and so on.

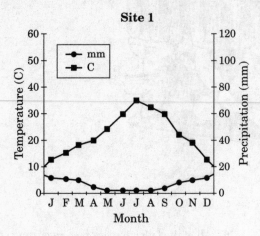

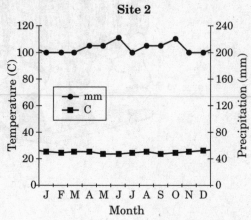

78. The average precipitation amount at Site 1 in April is

   (A) 2 mm
   (B) 3 mm
   (C) 6 mm
   (D) 20 mm
   (E) 40 mm

79. Which of the following is the LEAST accurate statement?

   (A) At Site 1, temperatures vary inversely with precipitation.
   (B) Temperature varies more during the course of the year at Site 1 than it does at Site 2.
   (C) Temperatures are consistently warmer at Site 2 than at Site 1.
   (D) At Site 1, average monthly precipitation is always below 20 mm.
   (E) At Site 2, the average monthly temperature is always above 20°C, and the average monthly precipitation is always above 100 mm.

80. Based on the climatographs, in what biomes could the two sites be found?

   (A) Site 1 – tropical rainforest
        Site 2 – arctic tundra
   (B) Site 1 – desert
        Site 2 – taiga
   (C) Site 1 – temperate deciduous forest
        Site 2 – desert
   (D) Site 1 – temperate grassland
        Site 2 – arctic tundra
   (E) Site 1 – desert
        Site 2 – tropical rainforest

S T O P

IF YOU FINISH BEFORE TIME IS CALLED, YOU MAY CHECK YOUR WORK ON THE ENTIRE BIOLOGY-E TEST ONLY. DO NOT TURN TO ANY OTHER TEST IN THIS BOOK.

BIOLOGY-M SECTION

If you are taking the Biology-M test, continue with questions 81–100.
Be sure to start this section of the test by filling in oval 81 on your answer sheet.

Directions: Each of the questions or incomplete statements below is followed by five suggested answers or completions. Some questions pertain to a set that refers to a laboratory or experimental situation. For each question, select the one choice that is the best answer to the question and then fill in the corresponding oval on the answer sheet.

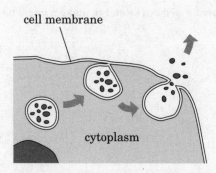

cell membrane

cytoplasm

81. The process depicted in the above picture is called

   (A) phagocytosis
   (B) cytoplasmic streaming
   (C) exocytosis
   (D) pinocytosis
   (E) osmosis

82. The number of nucleotides that are needed to code for a specific amino acid is

   (A) 1
   (B) 2
   (C) 3
   (D) 4
   (E) 6

83. Which of the following organisms is the most primitive in evolutionary terms?

   (A) Starfish
   (B) Jellyfish
   (C) Sponge
   (D) Tapeworm
   (E) Spider

84. If you want to determine whether an individual has a homozygous (BB) or a heterozygous (Bb) dominant genotype, you would perform a back cross, which involves mating the individual with another individual that is

   (A) homozygous for the dominant trait
   (B) heterozygous for the dominant trait
   (C) homozygous for the recessive trait
   (D) heterozygous for the recessive trait
   (E) absent of the trait in question

85. Prokaryotes have all of the following EXCEPT

   (A) circular DNA
   (B) cell wall
   (C) cytoplasm
   (D) ribosomes
   (E) nucleus

86. A scientist uses the rate of change in a protein called cytochrome c to calculate the point at which humans and chimpanzees last shared a common ancestor. The protein is an example of a(n)

   (A) fossil
   (B) acquired trait
   (C) vestigial structure
   (D) homologous structure
   (E) molecular clock

87. If the sequence of nucleotides in a DNA strand is CGTAAGC, the sequence of the complementary strand is

   (A) GCATTCG
   (B) CGTAAGC
   (C) CGAATGC
   (D) GCTTACG
   (E) GCAUUCG

GO ON TO THE NEXT PAGE

Questions <u>88–90</u> refer to a dialysis experiment, as discussed below.

Dialysis tubing is a semi-permeable membrane across which water and monosaccharides such as glucose and fructose can cross but across which disaccharides such as sucrose cannot.

Experiment 1: A section of dialysis tubing is filled with water and tied at the end to make a bag. The bag is submersed into a beaker containing a solution of 0.4 M fructose.

Experiment 2: A section of dialysis tubing is filled with a 0.5 M solution of sucrose and tied at the end to make a bag. The bag is submersed in a beaker of water.

88. In Experiment 1, which molecules will cross the membrane?

(A) Glucose will diffuse into the bag.
(B) Fructose will diffuse into the bag.
(C) Sucrose will diffuse into the bag.
(D) Complex sugars will diffuse into the bag.
(E) Disaccharides will diffuse out of the bag.

89. The movement of fructose across the dialysis tubing membrane

(A) requires energy
(B) is an example of active transport
(C) is an example of facilitated diffusion
(D) requires exocytosis
(E) is an example of passive diffusion

90. Which of the following is true regarding Experiment 2?

(A) The bag is hypertonic relative to the water in the beaker.
(B) The bag is isotonic relative to the water in the beaker.
(C) The bag will lose fluid.
(D) Sucrose will diffuse out of the bag.
(E) The water in the beaker is hypertonic relative to the bag.

GO ON TO THE NEXT PAGE

Questions 91–93 refer to the following experiment.

A group of five students conducted an experiment to test the effects of activity on heart rate and breathing rate. They measured their pulse rate after doing a variety of activities for 5 minutes each.

Activity	John	Maria	Beth	Steven	Oliver
Sitting still	68 beats/min 17 breaths/min	70 beats/min 18 breaths/min	68 beats/min 16 breaths/min	67 beats/min 17 breaths/min	80 beats/min 20 breaths/min
Walking	77 beats/min 22 breaths/min	85 beats/min 21 breaths/min	77 beats/min 20 breaths/min	77 beats/min 20 breaths/min	88 beats/min 22 breaths/min
Jumping rope	100 beats/min 36 breaths/min	115 beats/min 38 breaths/min	120 beats/min 38 breaths/min	130 beats/min 40 breaths/min	135 beats/min 45 breaths/min
Running	120 beats/min 45 breaths/min	100 beats/min 37 breaths/min	120 beats/min 38 breaths/min	125 beats/min 36 breaths/min	140 beats/min 47 breaths/min
Lying down	66 beats/min 16 breaths/min	68 beats/min 16 breaths/min	63 beats/min 15 breaths/min	65 beats/min 15 breaths/min	79 beats/min 19 breaths/min

91. Whose heart rate increased the most between sitting still and walking?

   (A) John
   (B) Maria
   (C) Beth
   (D) Steven
   (E) Oliver

92. For which activity did each person reach his or her maximum breathing rate?

   (A) Walking only
   (B) Lying down only
   (C) Jumping rope only
   (D) Running only
   (E) Jumping rope or running

93. Based on the data, which of the following statements is LEAST accurate?

   (A) Each person's heart rate was greater when sitting than it was when lying down.
   (B) The student with the lowest sitting pulse rate also had the lowest running pulse rate.
   (C) While sitting still, the females (Maria and Beth) had a higher average heart rate than the males (John, Steven, and Oliver).
   (D) Each person's breathing rate was greater after jumping rope than it was after walking.
   (E) Oliver had his highest pulse rate after running.

GO ON TO THE NEXT PAGE

Questions 94–96 refer to the following figures of molecules.

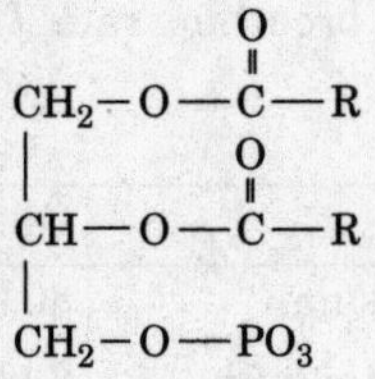

| Figure 1 | Figure 2 | Figure 3 | Figure 4 | Figure 5 |

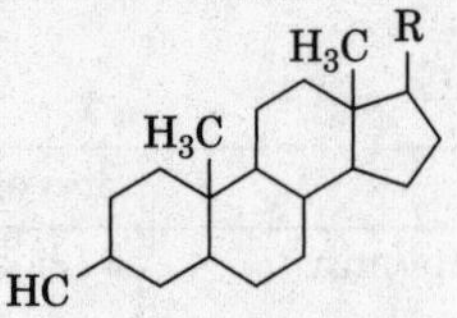

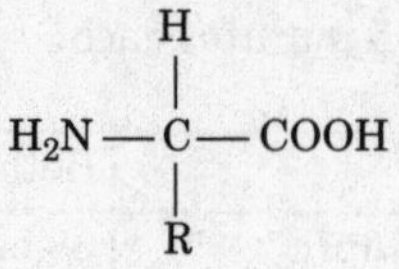

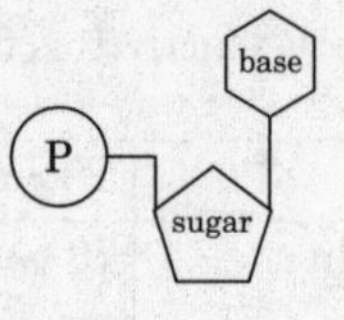

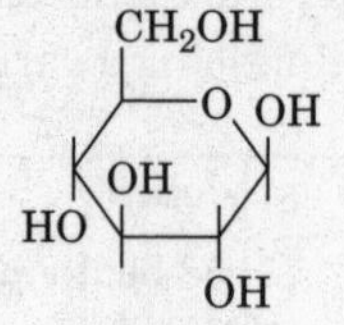

94. Which of the depicted molecules is found in DNA?

(A) 1
(B) 2
(C) 3
(D) 4
(E) 5

95. Molecule 5 is a

(A) protein
(B) monosaccharide
(C) starch
(D) lipid
(E) nucleic acid

96. Molecule 1 would most likely be found in

(A) an amino acid
(B) a cell membrane
(C) DNA
(D) a disaccharide
(E) RNA

GO ON TO THE NEXT PAGE

Questions 97–100 refer to the chromosomes depicted below.

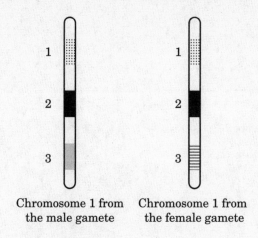

Chromosome 1 from
the male gamete

Chromosome 1 from
the female gamete

	Dominant	Recessive
1. Flower Color	Red	White
2. Height	Tall	Short
3. Seed Type	Wrinkled	Smooth

97. How many traits are coded for in the above chromosomes?

(A) 1
(B) 2
(C) 3
(D) 6
(E) 7

98. The two gametes that contain these chromosomes unite during fertilization and become part of the same zygote. What would be the individual's phenotype?

(A) Red flower, tall, smooth seeds
(B) Red flower, short, smooth seeds
(C) White flower, short, wrinkled seeds
(D) Red flower, tall, wrinkled seeds
(E) White flower, tall, wrinkled seeds

99. If the offspring resulting from the union of these original gametes were to be self-crossed, what is the likelihood of each trait appearing in this second generation?

(A) 100% white, 100% tall, 75% wrinkled, 25% smooth
(B) 100% white, 100% tall, 50% wrinkled, 50% smooth
(C) 100% white, 100% tall, 25% wrinkled, 75% smooth
(D) 50% red, 50% white, 50% tall, 50% short, 75% wrinkled, 25% smooth
(E) 50% red, 50% white, 50% tall, 50% short, 75% wrinkled, 25% smooth

100. What is the process by which these gametes were formed?

(A) Mitosis
(B) Synapsis
(C) Meiosis
(D) Fertilization
(E) Genesis

S T O P

IF YOU FINISH BEFORE TIME IS CALLED, YOU MAY CHECK YOUR WORK ON THE ENTIRE
BIOLOGY-M TEST ONLY. DO NOT TURN TO ANY OTHER TEST IN THIS BOOK.

SAT BIOLOGY E/M PRACTICE TEST 1 EXPLANATIONS

BIOLOGY PRACTICE TEST 1 ANSWERS

Question Number	Answer	Right	Wrong	Question Number	Answer	Right	Wrong
1	D	——	——	51	D	——	——
2	C	——	——	52	E	——	——
3	A	——	——	53	B	——	——
4	E	——	——	54	A	——	——
5	A	——	——	55	D	——	——
6	D	——	——	56	C	——	——
7	C	——	——	57	B	——	——
8	C	——	——	58	D	——	——
9	D	——	——	59	B	——	——
10	E	——	——	60	D	——	——
11	E	——	——	61	C	——	——
12	C	——	——	62	B	——	——
13	B	——	——	63	A	——	——
14	E	——	——	64	E	——	——
15	C	——	——	65	D	——	——
16	A	——	——	66	D	——	——
17	C	——	——	67	B	——	——
18	A	——	——	68	C	——	——
19	C	——	——	69	D	——	——
20	B	——	——	70	D	——	——
21	D	——	——	71	B	——	——
22	E	——	——	72	E	——	——
23	C	——	——	73	E	——	——
24	D	——	——	74	E	——	——
25	E	——	——	75	D	——	——
26	C	——	——	76	E	——	——
27	E	——	——	77	A	——	——
28	C	——	——	78	C	——	——
29	E	——	——	79	C	——	——
30	B	——	——	80	E	——	——
31	E	——	——	81	C	——	——
32	D	——	——	82	C	——	——
33	D	——	——	83	C	——	——
34	D	——	——	84	C	——	——
35	B	——	——	85	E	——	——
36	D	——	——	86	E	——	——
37	C	——	——	87	A	——	——
38	D	——	——	88	B	——	——
39	C	——	——	89	E	——	——
40	D	——	——	90	A	——	——
41	D	——	——	91	B	——	——
42	B	——	——	92	E	——	——
43	C	——	——	93	B	——	——
44	C	——	——	94	D	——	——
45	B	——	——	95	B	——	——
46	A	——	——	96	B	——	——
47	E	——	——	97	C	——	——
48	D	——	——	98	E	——	——
49	B	——	——	99	A	——	——
50	D	——	——	100	C	——	——

CALCULATING YOUR SCORE

Your raw score for the SAT BiologyE/M Test is calculated from the number of questions you answer correctly and incorrectly. Once you have determined your composite score, use the conversion table on page 26 of this book to calculate your scaled score. To calculate your raw score, count the number of questions you answered correctly:

_____
A

Count the number of questions you answered incorrectly, and multiply that number by $\frac{1}{4}$:

$$\underline{}_{B} \times \frac{1}{4} = \underline{}_{C}$$

Subtract the value in field C from the value in field A:

_____
D

Round the number in field D to the nearest whole number. This is your raw score:

_____
E

BIOLOGY E/M CLASSIFICATION QUESTIONS

1. D Evolution and Diversity
Angiosperms are flowering plants. Angiosperms are divided into two subgroups—monocots and dicots. Monocots have one cotyledon (seed leaf), flower parts in groups of three, and parallel venation in the leaves. Dicots have two cotyledons, flower parts in groups of four or five, and netlike venation in the leaves.

2. C Evolution and Diversity
Club mosses, horsetails, and ferns are all seedless vascular plants. They have a vascular system with both xylem and phloem. Seedless vascular plants have spores rather than seeds and require water for fertilization.

3. A Evolution and Diversity
Bryophytes are the seedless, nonvascular plants such as mosses, liverworts, and hornworts. Bryophytes have no vascular tissue (xylem and phloem) and therefore cannot have roots, stems, or leaves, which are complex structures that contain vascular tissue. Bryophytes must absorb and distribute water and nutrients by osmosis and diffusion.

4. E Ecology
A secondary consumer is always a carnivore that eats an herbivore. Primary consumers are herbivores because they eat primary producers, i.e., plants. Secondary consumers eat primary consumers. Any animal that eats another animal is a carnivore.

5. **A**   Ecology

An autotroph is an organism that can use solar energy and carbon dioxide to make organic molecules by a process called photosynthesis. Autotrophs are also called primary producers.

6. **D**   Ecology

A saprophyte or decomposer is an organism that derives its energy from feeding on dead and waste materials.

7. **C**   Ecology

Primary consumers are organisms that eat primary producers, i.e., plants.

8. **C**   Organismal Biology

The superior and inferior vena cava return deoxygenated blood from the body to the right atrium of the heart.

9. **D**   Organismal Biology

The pulmonary artery carries deoxygenated blood from the right ventricle to the lungs, where it will pick up oxygen and release carbon dioxide. The pulmonary artery is the only artery that carries deoxygenated blood.

10. **E**   Organismal Biology

The atrioventricular node fires an electrical impulse that stimulates the contraction of the ventricles. This contraction forces blood out of the heart and into the aorta and pulmonary arteries.

11. **E**   Organic and Biochemistry

Plants and animals store excess sugars as polysaccharides (3 or more monosaccharides that are linked together). The storage polysaccharide in plants is starch; in animals it is glycogen.

12. **C**   Organic and Biochemistry

Phospholipids are what give the cell membrane its "fluid" characteristics. Each phospholipid consists of a glycerol molecule with two fatty acid chains and a phosphate group attached to it. The cell membrane is a phospholipid bilayer.

13. **B**   Organic and Biochemistry

There are two major classes of hormones: steroid hormones and peptide hormones. Steroid hormones have a steroid as their fundamental unit, and because they are hydrophobic, they can easily cross cell membranes. Peptide hormones are composed of amino acids and cannot cross cell membranes. Testosterone is often used as an example of a steroid hormone. Insulin is often used as an example of a peptide hormone.

14. **E**   Organic and Biochemistry

Like plants, animals store excess sugars as polysaccharides. The storage polysaccharide in animals is glycogen.

BIOLOGY E/M SOLITARY MULTIPLE CHOICE

15. **C**   Organic and Biochemistry

An atom that has gained or lost one or more neutrons is called an isotope. Carbon-12 is the most abundant form of carbon. It has 6 protons, 6 neutrons, and 6 electrons. The example given is carbon-13, which has 6 protons, 7 neutrons, and 6 electrons.

16. **A**   The Cell

Prokaryotic cells are smaller and structurally less complex than eukaryotic cells and are therefore considered to be more primitive than eukaryotic cells.

17. **C**   Organismal Biology

Habituation occurs when a non-harmful stimulus that would normally cause an animal to respond is repeated over and over again until the animal learns to ignore it. The scenario describing the rat and the loud noise played twice an hour fits this description.

18. **A**   Ecology

A biome is a group of communities that have the same general climate and life forms. Grasslands receive 10–60 inches per year. They are too dry to support many trees but wet enough to support grass and shrub species. Common animals found in grasslands include large herbivores, small burrowing animals, birds, and insects.

19. **C**   Evolution and Diversity

The theory of punctuated equilibrium states that evolution occurs in spurts followed by long periods of little or no change. This theory is more recent than the theory of gradualism, which suggests that gradual change over time leads to the formation of new species.

20. **B**   Organismal Biology

Parthenogenesis is a type of nonsexual reproduction in which unfertilized eggs divide mitotically and the resulting offspring have genes that are identical to their mothers'. Parthenogenic populations are typically all female. Since there is no independent assortment or crossing-over involved in asexual reproduction, there is less genetic variation in parthenogenic populations. Parthenogenesis allows a population to grow quickly, but the limited variation in the offspring makes these populations very vulnerable to extreme environmental changes. Populations that use sexual reproduction grow more slowly but have more variation and are therefore more resistant to changes in the environment.

21. **D**   The Cell

In order to get the total magnification of a microscope, you must multiply the magnification of the ocular lens by the magnification of the objective lens. In this example, the ocular lens has a magnification of 10x, and the objective lens has a magnification of 20x, which yields a total magnification of 200x.

22. **E**   Organismal Biology

Transpiration is the evaporation of water from leaves or other exposed surfaces of plants.

23. C   Organismal Biology

The adrenal glands secrete hormones that help the body respond to stress. Epinephrine and norepinephrine are the "fight or flight" hormones. They cause an increase in heart and breathing rates, an increase in blood sugar, and a dilation of the pupils.

24. D   Evolution and Diversity

Succession is the progressive change in an ecological community. It occurs when current species are displaced by new immigrant species. Succession is said to lead ultimately to a stable climax community in which the essential makeup of the populations within the community will stay constant. Primary succession occurs in areas where there are no traces of plant life, such as a newly formed volcanic island. Secondary succession occurs in areas where there has been previous plant growth. An abandoned field is a classic example of a site for secondary succession.

25. E   Organismal Biology

Tropisms are hormone-mediated responses to stimuli. There are three main tropisms. Phototropism is the tendency of a plant to grow toward light. Gravitropism is the tendency of a plant to grow either with or against gravity. Thigmotropism is a reaction to touch that causes the touched part of the plant to either thicken or recoil.

26. C   Cell Processes

The Krebs cycle occurs after glycolysis, is part of aerobic cellular respiration, and takes place in the matrix of the mitochondria. The Krebs cycle produces energy-laden NADH and $FADH_2$. These two high-energy electron carriers go to the mitochondrial membrane, where the electron transport chain transfers their energy to ATP.

27. E   Organic and Biochemistry

To answer this question, you need to know how different types of compounds or molecules dissolve in water. Because the hydrogen atoms in a water molecule have a slight positive charge and the oxygen has a slight negative charge, ions and polar heads of molecules are attracted to the part of the water molecule that has a charge opposite of theirs. These attractive forces mean that polar and ionic compounds dissolve well in water while nonpolar molecules do not. Knowing that an atom is an isotope doesn't tell you whether it is polar or nonpolar and, accordingly whether it will or won't dissolve. Once you know which sorts of molecules or atoms dissolve readily in water, the question becomes simply a matter of mix-and-match. As it turns out, only the final choice, **E**, puts the substances in an order from which you are likely to get the first and third substances to dissolve, while the second substance does not dissolve.

28. C   The Cell

Eukaryotic cells house their DNA in the nucleus. However, eukaryotic cells also have mitochondria, and mitochondria have their own DNA and can make some of their own proteins. Mitochondria are thought to have originated from symbiotic primitive prokaryotes.

29. E   Ecology

Ocean scavengers that feed on dead organic matter generally live in the aphotic zone, the deepest regions of the ocean, where light can't penetrate. These organisms are often multicellular, are not autotrophic, and may or may not have silicate shells. One characteristic that most denizens of the aphotic zone share is poor eyesight. There is no evolutionary reason for an organism that lives in a region without light to have good eyesight.

30. **B**   Organic and Biochemistry

Enzymes are proteins that lower the activation energy needed for specific chemical reactions to occur. The enzymes bond to the two substrates and help bind them together. The enzymes are not themselves altered during this process. The third substance, which causes the first two substances to combine while remaining unchanged itself, is therefore an enzyme.

31. **E**   Cell Processes

Respiration occurs in the mitochondria of plant cells, just as it does in animal cells. Students often forget that plants have mitochondria as well as chloroplasts. Plants can produce carbohydrates via photosynthesis in the chloroplasts. However, plants cells also have to catabolize carbohydrates, so they must have mitochondria.

32. **D**   Evolution and Diversity

The wings of insects and birds share similar characteristics because they perform similar functions for their respective organisms—the power of flight. Because these body parts perform such similar functions, over time, they have evolved certain physical similarities. This process, in which organisms that belong to different evolutionary paths develop similar body parts because those body parts perform similar functions, is called convergent evolution.

BIOLOGY E/M GROUP MULTIPLE CHOICE

33. **D**   Cell Processes

The substances in a plant that absorb light energy are called pigments. Chlorophyll is the primary plant pigment. It absorbs blue and red light and reflects green and yellow light. There are other pigments that absorb different wavelengths of light.

34. **D**   Evolution and Diversity

Erosion can cause gaps in the fossil record, since this process eats away rock that contains fossils. Similarly, volcanic activity can disturb the fossil layer by shooting igneous rock up through sedimentary rock. This activity destroys fossils in the sedimentary rock and can cause layers of sedimentary rock to become disordered, therefore disordering the fossil record as well. Mass extinctions, however, will not affect the fossil record. What the record is recording will change when many species die out, as there will be fewer species to record. However, the record itself will not have any gaps in it, since the sedimentary layers will not be affected.

35. **B**   Genetics

Crossing-over increases the number of genetic combinations in the gametes, producing offspring with greater variability of genotype and phenotype. Greater variability allows a population to more readily adapt to shifts in the environment.

36. **D**   Genetics

Mitosis and meiosis are similar because they both involve the replication of DNA during interphase. Mitosis produces two diploid cells that are genetically identical to one another. Meiosis involves independent assortment, crossing-over, and two cell divisions. Meiosis produces four genetically distinct haploid gametes.

37. **C**   Organismal Biology

Bile is an emulsifier. Without chemically affecting the structure of fat, it breaks large fat globules into smaller globules. The greater surface area of smaller fat globules helps the enzymes that will eventually chemically digest the fats to work more quickly.

38. **D**   Organismal Biology

An ulcer is a hole or tear in the stomach lining caused by excessive acid production. Ulcers are often linked to stress.

39. **C**   Evolution and Diversity

Two individuals from separate species will never, ever share the same identical code, eliminating **A**, **D**, and **E** as possible answer choices. To decide between **B** and **C**, you need to know that the definition of a species is a population of individuals that can breed and produce viable offspring (a viable offspring is an offspring that can itself produce off-spring). According to this definition, individuals from two different species cannot inter-breed and have viable offspring.

40. **D**   Genetics

The homologous chromosomes are engaged in crossing-over, which is the exchange of corresponding pieces of DNA between the homologues. In meiosis, the DNA in one dip-loid cell is duplicated and then divided twice to make four haploid daughter cells. Cross-ing-over is a very important process because it mixes the genetic material between the two homologous chromosomes before they are divided among the four haploid daughter cells. This increases the overall genetic variation between the gametes produced, which will all be genetically distinct.

41. **D**   Organismal Biology

The correct path of an electrical impulse through a neuron is: dendrite, cell body, axon.

42. **B**   Organismal Biology

The sinoatrial node stimulates cardiac muscles to contract in a regular and controlled rhythm.

43. **C**   Genetics

Each child receives one sex chromosome from each parent. Females have the genotype XX, and males have the genotype XY. The mother can produce gametes (eggs) with only X-chromosomes, but the father can produce gametes (sperm) with either an X-chromo-some or a Y-chromosome. Since all of the eggs carry an X-chromosome, the sex of the child is determined by whether the sperm carries an X- or a Y-chromosome. If the sperm carries an X-chromosome, the baby will be female. If the sperm carries a Y-chromosome, the baby will be male.

44. C   Ecology

The best representation of a community is all of the plant and animal populations that live and interact in a prairie dog town. A community consists of all of the populations that interact in a given geographical area.

45. B   Evolution and Diversity

The Hardy-Weinberg Theorem describes a gene pool in equilibrium (i.e., a non-evolving population). Hardy-Weinberg equilibrium requires a large population size, an absence of immigration or emigration, random reproductive success, no mutation, and random mating. If mating is non-random and individuals select mates that have particular heritable traits, then there will not be random mixing of gametes, and a change in gene frequency will occur over time. Remember that the definition of evolution is "the change in the allele frequencies in the gene pool over time."

46. A   Ecology

This is an example of coevolution. Coevolution refers to the reciprocal evolutionary adjustments that take place between interacting members of an ecosystem.

47. E   The Cell

Cells are small because surface area and volume must be balanced. As a cell increases in size, its surface area does not increase as rapidly as its volume. Substances are constantly moving in and out of cells across the cell surface. If the cell's surface area–to-volume ratio is too low, substances cannot move quickly enough across the cell's surface.

48. D   Evolution and Diversity

Organism 1, a ladybug, is in the order Coleoptera. To arrive at the correct name, you had to follow the steps in the dichotomous key. The following key has the correct steps in bold print.

DICHOTOMOUS KEY		
1.	**Has 6 legs** .... **go to 2**	
	Has more than 6 legs .... go to 4	
2.	Hind legs are greatly enlarged .... Orthoptera	
	All legs are approximately the same size .... **go to 3**	
3.	**Has hard wings that are spotted** .... **Coleoptera**	
	Has soft wings that are striped .... Lepidoptera	
4.	Has 8 legs .... Arachnida	
	Has more than 8 legs .... Chilopoda	

49. B   Evolution and Diversity

All of the organisms shown are in phylum Arthropoda. Animals in this phylum have jointed feet and a hard exoskeleton made of chitin. Members of phylum Arthropoda include insects, spiders, and crustaceans.

50. D   Evolution and Diversity

The lobster is a crustacean in phylum Arthropoda. The snail and clam are both in phylum Mollusca. The earthworm is in phylum Annelida. The jellyfish belongs to phylum Cnidaria.

51. D   Genetics

A karyotype is a photo of chromosomes in which homologous chromosomes are grouped together and arranged by size.

52. E   Genetics

There are 47 chromosomes on this karyotype. There are 22 pairs of homologous autosomes and a pair of sex chromosomes (X and Y). Normally, a human cell has 46 chromosomes. This individual has an extra copy of chromosome 21.

53. B   Genetics

This individual has Down's syndrome, which results from trisomy of chromosome 21. Trisomy is a disorder caused by nondisjunction, an event in which a pair of chromosomes does not separate during meiosis. One of the daughter cells will have two copies of the chromosome, and the other daughter cell will have none. After fertilization, the embryo will have too many or too few chromosomes. If there is an extra chromosome, the disorder is called trisomy, and in most cases, the embryo cannot develop. If there is an absence of a chromosome, the disorder is called monosomy. Monosomy of the X-chromosome is the only monosomy that is compatible with life. Polyploidy occurs when there is an entire extra set of chromosomes. A human embryo with polyploidy will not develop. Polyploidy can result in viable embryos in fish and plants.

54. A   Genetics

This individual is male because he has a Y-chromosome as well as an X-chromosome (XY). Females have two X-chromosomes (XX). A mother can pass only an X-chromosome to her offspring. The father can pass either an X or a Y to his offspring. Therefore, the Y-chromosome had to have come from the father, and the X-chromosome came from the mother.

55. D   Organismal Biology

Plant A is a short-day plant because it flowers when the lengths of the days are short (< 12 hours per day).

56. C   Organismal Biology

Part 4 of the experiment shows that Plant A will not flower if there is an interruption in its exposure to darkness, even if the total duration of darkness in a day is 14 hours.

57. B   Organismal Biology or Evolution and Diversity

The plants used in this experiment are flowering plants. Angiosperms are all flowering plants. No other division of plants is capable of producing flowers.

58. D   Genetics

Based on the given data, you can see that every time a red flowered plant is crossed with another plant (red or white), some of the offspring are always red. This means that when a red plant is crossed with a white one, they do not always yield white offspring. The red allele is dominant, and the white allele is recessive. Once you know that the red allele is dominant, you can make a Punnett square for each of the crosses and guess the alleles of the gametes until you come up with the correct ratios of red and white offspring. Cross I and cross III both contain homozygous red parents.

Cross I

	R	R
R	RR	RR
R	RR	RR

100% red progeny

Cross II

	r	r
r	Rr	rr
r	Rr	rr

100% white progeny

Cross III

	R	R
r	Rr	Rr
r	Rr	Rr

100% red progeny

Cross IV

	R	r
r	Rr	rr
r	Rr	rr

50% red progeny and
50% white progeny

59. B   Genetics

The offspring in Cross III all have the genotype Rr. Since red is the dominant allele, the offspring are all red. If the offspring were all pink, then you could infer that the alleles for flower color show incomplete dominance, a condition in which two different alleles are both expressed in a heterozygote. The resulting phenotype is intermediate between the two homozygous phenotypes.

60. D   Genetics

If you self-pollinate the progeny from Cross III, the offspring would have a 75% chance of being red, as shown in the Punnett square below.

	R	r
R	RR	Rr
r	Rr	rr

75% red progeny and
25% white progeny

BIOLOGY-E SOLITARY MULTIPLE CHOICE

61. **C**   Evolution and Diversity

Evolution is defined as the change in gene frequency in a population over time.

62. **B**   Ecology

The disease reduces the amount of forage (aspen trees) that is available to the elk. The carrying capacity is reduced due to a shortage of food. Carrying capacity is the maximum number of individuals that can be supported by the available resources.

63. **A**   Organismal Biology

Clusters of neurons are called ganglia.

64. **E**   Evolution and Diversity

Fungi have cell walls made of chitin, not cellulose.

65. **D**   Ecology

In a food chain or food web, energy transfer from one trophic level to the next is not very efficient. Only 10% of the energy in a trophic level is captured by the subsequent level.

66. **D**   Ecology

Plants can only use nitrogen in the form of nitrates (NO_3^-). In order to increase the amount of nitrogen available to plants, the farmer could add nitrogen-fixing legumes, which are plants that convert atmospheric nitrogen to NO_3^-. He could also add fertilizer. Adding denitrifying bacteria would not work because they convert ammonia NH_3 from wastes and dead material into atmospheric nitrogen (N_2).

67. **B**   Evolution and Diversity

What occurred over 50 years was stabilizing selection. Stabilizing selection is when selection pressures favor the average form of a trait. The distribution of turtle sizes deviated less from the median in 1990 than it did in 1940.

68. **C**   Evolution and Diversity

Because large turtles can withstand high winds better than smaller turtles, you would expect an increase in the proportion of large turtles and a decrease in the proportion of small turtles. Directional selection would occur in favor of large individuals and against small individuals.

69. **D**   Evolution and Diversity

Allopatric speciation occurs when populations of a species are isolated from one another and evolve along different paths until they become so different that they can no longer interbreed and are considered different species. The turtles on the island were separated from the turtles on the mainland, and after many generations of evolution, the two populations could no longer be considered the same species because they could not interbreed.

BIOLOGY-E GROUP MULTIPLE CHOICE

70. **D**   Ecology
Referring to the upper table, you can see that the seeds that had been scarified germinated most quickly. After only 5 days, 60% of these seeds had germinated—far more than under any other treatment.

71. **B**   Ecology
By the end of the experiment, the group that had been exposed to heat had the highest percentage (70%) of germinated seeds.

72. **E**   Ecology
No manipulations were performed on the seeds left at ambient temperature. This was the control group.

73. **E**   Ecology
Of the hard-coated seeds that were scarified, 75% germinated. Of the soft-coated seeds that were scarified, only 4% germinated. Scarification probably helped to crack hard seed coats but damaged the material in the soft seed coats. Even if you were not immediately sure of this answer, you could have eliminated the other answer choices, which were not supported by the data.

74. **E**   Organismal Biology
Diffusion of gases occurs through structures on the underside of the leaf, called stomata, which are labeled 7 in the diagram. The opening and closing of the stomata is controlled by the guard cells.

75. **D**   Organismal Biology
Structure 2 is a chloroplast. Chloroplasts contain stacks of flattened compartments. Each compartment is a thylakoid, and a stack of thylakoids is called a granum. Chlorophyll is located within the thylakoids, and the fluid that lies outside the thylakoids is called the stroma. Guard cells are not part of the chloroplast.

76. **E**   Organismal Biology
Structure 4 is phloem. Phloem is made of living cells and is comprised of sieve elements and companion cells. The purpose of the phloem is to transport nutrients up and down the plant. Wood is made not from phloem but from xylem.

77. **A**   Organismal Biology
Structure 1 is the cuticle. Plants that live in desert climates, where water is limited, have thick cuticles to preserve water. Another adaptation for conserving water is closing the stomata (structure 7) during the hottest part of the day when evaporative demand is highest.

78. **C**   Ecology
As the legend indicates, squares denote temperature, and circles denote precipitation. Find the circle above the first A (for April) and follow it horizontally to the *y*-axis on the

right-hand side of the graph. The average precipitation amount at Site 1 in April is approximately 6 mm.

79. C Ecology

At Site 1, temperatures vary from 10°C to 35°C. At Site 2, temperatures vary only from 27°C to 30°C. During some months, temperatures at Site 1 are greater than at Site 2, while during other months the opposite is true.

80. E Ecology

At Site 1, precipitation is very low (less than 20 mm/year), and temperatures are above freezing during the winter and very hot during the summer. This climate is typical of deserts. At Site 2, the temperature is consistently between 27°C and 30°C. Because the temperatures are consistently so high, you would expect this biome to be near the equator. Precipitation is also very high (greater than 200 mm/year) at Site 2. Consistently high temperature and precipitation is characteristic of tropical rainforests.

BIOLOGY-M SOLITARY MULTIPLE CHOICE

81. C The Cell

Exocytosis is the process by which molecules are secreted from a cell. A vesicle containing fluids or particles fuses with the cell membrane and releases its contents outside of the cell.

82. C Cell Processes

A set of three nucleotides in a DNA or mRNA molecule is called a codon. The anticodon is the complement of the codon and is found on tRNA. Each codon specifies a single amino acid.

83. C Evolution and Diversity

In evolutionary terms, the sponge is the most primitive of the animals listed. Sponges are the only animals that do not have at least two of the three embryonic tissue layers (endoderm, mesoderm, and ectoderm), and the cells are not organized into specific tissues and organs. Sponges, however, do have cell recognition and slightly complex cells for reproductive and digestive purposes.

84. C Genetics

If you want to determine whether an individual has a homozygous (BB) or a heterozygous (Bb) dominant genotype, you would mate the individual with another individual that is homozygous for the recessive trait. This is called a test cross or back cross. If the individual is homozygous (BB), all of the offspring will exhibit the dominant phenotype. If the individual is heterozygous (Bb), half of the offspring will show the dominant phenotype, and the other half will show the recessive phenotype.

85. E The Cell

Prokaryotes do not have a nucleus. A prokaryotic cell is filled with cytoplasm in which circular DNA and ribosomes float. Prokaryotic cells maintain their shape with a cytoskeleton and a cell wall made of peptidoglycan.

86. **E**   Evolution and Diversity

A molecular clock is a gene or protein that has such a regular rate of change that the rate can be used to calculate the point at which two related species last shared a common ancestor.

87. **A**   Cell Processes

DNA is a double-stranded helix. The first strand is complementary to its opposing strand. DNA has four nitrogenous bases—cytosine, guanine, adenine, and thymine. Cytosine always pairs with guanine, and adenine always pairs with thymine. Therefore, if one strand has the sequence consisting of CGTAAGC, then the complementary strand will be GCATTCG.

88. **B**   The Cell

Fructose, sucrose, and water are the molecules used in Experiment 1. Sucrose is too large to cross the membrane. Fructose is a simple sugar and can cross the membrane. Because molecules tend to diffuse from an area of high concentration to an area of low concentration, fructose will diffuse into the bag.

89. **E**   The Cell

Fructose is a simple sugar and can cross the membrane. It will passively diffuse from an area of low concentration to an area of high concentration. When a molecule moves along its concentration gradient, the transport does not require energy.

90. **A**   The Cell

The terms "hypertonic," "hypotonic," and "isotonic" are relative terms. A hypertonic solution has a higher concentration of solutes than the solution to which it is being compared. A hypotonic solution has a lower concentration of solutes than the solution to which it is being compared. Isotonic solutions have equal concentrations of solutes. The bag is hypertonic because it has a higher concentration of solutes than the water in the beaker.

BIOLOGY-M GROUP MULTIPLE CHOICE

91. **B**   Organismal Biology

Oliver's heart rate was the highest after walking, but Maria's increased the most (by 15 beats per minute) between sitting still and walking.

92. **E**   Organismal Biology

Some of the subjects reached their maximum breathing rate after jumping rope, while others' peaked after running. Exertion levels varied for the people engaging in these activities.

93. **B**   Organismal Biology

Steven had the lowest sitting pulse rate (67 bpm), but Steven had the second-highest running pulse rate.

94. **D**   Organic and Biochemistry

Figure 4 is a nitrogenous base. Nitrogenous bases are the building blocks of DNA. You can recognize nitrogenous bases by their characteristic base, sugar, and phosphate-group construction.

95. **B**   Organic and Biochemistry

Figure 5 is a glucose molecule. Glucose is a monosaccharide. Monosaccharides always have a chemical formula according to the ratio $C_1H_2O_1$.

96. **B**   Organic and Biochemistry

Molecule 1 is a phospholipid, which you should be able to identify from its glycerol component (CH_2, CH, and CH_2) and also from its phosphate (PO_3). Cell membranes are composed of a phospholipid bilayer.

97. **C**   Evolution and Diversity

There are three traits coded for in the chromosomes depicted. The traits are flower color, height, and seed type.

98. **E**   Genetics

If the gametes fused, the resulting diploid individual would have a white flower, would be tall, and would have wrinkled seeds.

99. **A**   Genetics

The offspring resulting from the union of the original gametes have the following genotype: they are homozygous recessive for flower color (white phenotype), homozygous dominant for height (tall), and heterozygous for seed type (so the phenotype manifests the dominant allele: wrinkled). If two of these offspring were to unite during fertilization, *their* offspring would still have to be homozygous recessive for flower color and homozygous dominant for height. In other words, their offspring would have to be 100% white and 100% tall. **D** and **E** can therefore be quickly eliminated. Now all you have to do is make a Punnett square for seed type, the heterozygous trait.

	W	w
W	WW	Ww
w	Ww	ww

The second-generation offspring will be 25% homozygous dominant, 50% heterozygous, and 25% homozygous recessive. In terms of phenotype, this means that 75% of the second-generation offspring will have wrinkled seeds, and 25% will have smooth seeds.

100. **C**   Genetics

Meiosis is the process by which gametes form. In meiosis, a cell's genetic material is replicated and divided between two gametes. If the original cell has 2N chromosomes, each gamete will have 1N chromosomes. When the male and female gametes fuse, their resulting offspring will be 2N.

SAT* BIOLOGY E/M PRACTICE TEST 2

SAT BIOLOGY PRACTICE TEST 2 ANSWER SHEET

1. Ⓐ Ⓑ Ⓒ Ⓓ Ⓔ	26. Ⓐ Ⓑ Ⓒ Ⓓ Ⓔ	51. Ⓐ Ⓑ Ⓒ Ⓓ Ⓔ	76. Ⓐ Ⓑ Ⓒ Ⓓ Ⓔ
2. Ⓐ Ⓑ Ⓒ Ⓓ Ⓔ	27. Ⓐ Ⓑ Ⓒ Ⓓ Ⓔ	52. Ⓐ Ⓑ Ⓒ Ⓓ Ⓔ	77. Ⓐ Ⓑ Ⓒ Ⓓ Ⓔ
3. Ⓐ Ⓑ Ⓒ Ⓓ Ⓔ	28. Ⓐ Ⓑ Ⓒ Ⓓ Ⓔ	53. Ⓐ Ⓑ Ⓒ Ⓓ Ⓔ	78. Ⓐ Ⓑ Ⓒ Ⓓ Ⓔ
4. Ⓐ Ⓑ Ⓒ Ⓓ Ⓔ	29. Ⓐ Ⓑ Ⓒ Ⓓ Ⓔ	54. Ⓐ Ⓑ Ⓒ Ⓓ Ⓔ	79. Ⓐ Ⓑ Ⓒ Ⓓ Ⓔ
5. Ⓐ Ⓑ Ⓒ Ⓓ Ⓔ	30. Ⓐ Ⓑ Ⓒ Ⓓ Ⓔ	55. Ⓐ Ⓑ Ⓒ Ⓓ Ⓔ	80. Ⓐ Ⓑ Ⓒ Ⓓ Ⓔ
6. Ⓐ Ⓑ Ⓒ Ⓓ Ⓔ	31. Ⓐ Ⓑ Ⓒ Ⓓ Ⓔ	56. Ⓐ Ⓑ Ⓒ Ⓓ Ⓔ	81. Ⓐ Ⓑ Ⓒ Ⓓ Ⓔ
7. Ⓐ Ⓑ Ⓒ Ⓓ Ⓔ	32. Ⓐ Ⓑ Ⓒ Ⓓ Ⓔ	57. Ⓐ Ⓑ Ⓒ Ⓓ Ⓔ	82. Ⓐ Ⓑ Ⓒ Ⓓ Ⓔ
8. Ⓐ Ⓑ Ⓒ Ⓓ Ⓔ	33. Ⓐ Ⓑ Ⓒ Ⓓ Ⓔ	58. Ⓐ Ⓑ Ⓒ Ⓓ Ⓔ	83. Ⓐ Ⓑ Ⓒ Ⓓ Ⓔ
9. Ⓐ Ⓑ Ⓒ Ⓓ Ⓔ	34. Ⓐ Ⓑ Ⓒ Ⓓ Ⓔ	59. Ⓐ Ⓑ Ⓒ Ⓓ Ⓔ	84. Ⓐ Ⓑ Ⓒ Ⓓ Ⓔ
10. Ⓐ Ⓑ Ⓒ Ⓓ Ⓔ	35. Ⓐ Ⓑ Ⓒ Ⓓ Ⓔ	60. Ⓐ Ⓑ Ⓒ Ⓓ Ⓔ	85. Ⓐ Ⓑ Ⓒ Ⓓ Ⓔ
11. Ⓐ Ⓑ Ⓒ Ⓓ Ⓔ	36. Ⓐ Ⓑ Ⓒ Ⓓ Ⓔ	61. Ⓐ Ⓑ Ⓒ Ⓓ Ⓔ	86. Ⓐ Ⓑ Ⓒ Ⓓ Ⓔ
12. Ⓐ Ⓑ Ⓒ Ⓓ Ⓔ	37. Ⓐ Ⓑ Ⓒ Ⓓ Ⓔ	62. Ⓐ Ⓑ Ⓒ Ⓓ Ⓔ	87. Ⓐ Ⓑ Ⓒ Ⓓ Ⓔ
13. Ⓐ Ⓑ Ⓒ Ⓓ Ⓔ	38. Ⓐ Ⓑ Ⓒ Ⓓ Ⓔ	63. Ⓐ Ⓑ Ⓒ Ⓓ Ⓔ	88. Ⓐ Ⓑ Ⓒ Ⓓ Ⓔ
14. Ⓐ Ⓑ Ⓒ Ⓓ Ⓔ	39. Ⓐ Ⓑ Ⓒ Ⓓ Ⓔ	64. Ⓐ Ⓑ Ⓒ Ⓓ Ⓔ	89. Ⓐ Ⓑ Ⓒ Ⓓ Ⓔ
15. Ⓐ Ⓑ Ⓒ Ⓓ Ⓔ	40. Ⓐ Ⓑ Ⓒ Ⓓ Ⓔ	65. Ⓐ Ⓑ Ⓒ Ⓓ Ⓔ	90. Ⓐ Ⓑ Ⓒ Ⓓ Ⓔ
16. Ⓐ Ⓑ Ⓒ Ⓓ Ⓔ	41. Ⓐ Ⓑ Ⓒ Ⓓ Ⓔ	66. Ⓐ Ⓑ Ⓒ Ⓓ Ⓔ	91. Ⓐ Ⓑ Ⓒ Ⓓ Ⓔ
17. Ⓐ Ⓑ Ⓒ Ⓓ Ⓔ	42. Ⓐ Ⓑ Ⓒ Ⓓ Ⓔ	67. Ⓐ Ⓑ Ⓒ Ⓓ Ⓔ	92. Ⓐ Ⓑ Ⓒ Ⓓ Ⓔ
18. Ⓐ Ⓑ Ⓒ Ⓓ Ⓔ	43. Ⓐ Ⓑ Ⓒ Ⓓ Ⓔ	68. Ⓐ Ⓑ Ⓒ Ⓓ Ⓔ	93. Ⓐ Ⓑ Ⓒ Ⓓ Ⓔ
19. Ⓐ Ⓑ Ⓒ Ⓓ Ⓔ	44. Ⓐ Ⓑ Ⓒ Ⓓ Ⓔ	69. Ⓐ Ⓑ Ⓒ Ⓓ Ⓔ	94. Ⓐ Ⓑ Ⓒ Ⓓ Ⓔ
20. Ⓐ Ⓑ Ⓒ Ⓓ Ⓔ	45. Ⓐ Ⓑ Ⓒ Ⓓ Ⓔ	70. Ⓐ Ⓑ Ⓒ Ⓓ Ⓔ	95. Ⓐ Ⓑ Ⓒ Ⓓ Ⓔ
21. Ⓐ Ⓑ Ⓒ Ⓓ Ⓔ	46. Ⓐ Ⓑ Ⓒ Ⓓ Ⓔ	71. Ⓐ Ⓑ Ⓒ Ⓓ Ⓔ	96. Ⓐ Ⓑ Ⓒ Ⓓ Ⓔ
22. Ⓐ Ⓑ Ⓒ Ⓓ Ⓔ	47. Ⓐ Ⓑ Ⓒ Ⓓ Ⓔ	72. Ⓐ Ⓑ Ⓒ Ⓓ Ⓔ	97. Ⓐ Ⓑ Ⓒ Ⓓ Ⓔ
23. Ⓐ Ⓑ Ⓒ Ⓓ Ⓔ	48. Ⓐ Ⓑ Ⓒ Ⓓ Ⓔ	73. Ⓐ Ⓑ Ⓒ Ⓓ Ⓔ	98. Ⓐ Ⓑ Ⓒ Ⓓ Ⓔ
24. Ⓐ Ⓑ Ⓒ Ⓓ Ⓔ	49. Ⓐ Ⓑ Ⓒ Ⓓ Ⓔ	74. Ⓐ Ⓑ Ⓒ Ⓓ Ⓔ	99. Ⓐ Ⓑ Ⓒ Ⓓ Ⓔ
25. Ⓐ Ⓑ Ⓒ Ⓓ Ⓔ	50. Ⓐ Ⓑ Ⓒ Ⓓ Ⓔ	75. Ⓐ Ⓑ Ⓒ Ⓓ Ⓔ	100. Ⓐ Ⓑ Ⓒ Ⓓ Ⓔ

SAT BIOLOGY PRACTICE TEST 2

Time—1 hour

FOR BOTH BIOLOGY-E AND BIOLOGY-M, ANSWER QUESTIONS 1–60

Directions: Each set of lettered choices below refers to the numbered questions or statements immediately following it. Select the one lettered choice that best answers each question or best fits each statement and then fill in the corresponding oval on the answer sheet. A choice may be used once, more than once, or not at all in each set.

Questions 1–3

(A) Plasma
(B) Red blood cell
(C) White blood cell
(D) Hemoglobin
(E) Platelet

1. Iron-containing protein that can bind to oxygen molecules

2. Biconcave disc with no nucleus and no major organelles

3. Cell fragments that play a role in blood clotting

Questions 4–8

(A) Amino acid
(B) Hydrocarbon chain
(C) Nitrogenous base
(D) Carbohydrate
(E) Protein

4. Contains carbon, hydrogen, and oxygen atoms in a ratio of about 1:2:1

5. One of the building blocks of a nucleotide

6. Found in lipids

7. Contains elements C, H, O, and N

8. Amylase, hemoglobin, or insulin

Questions 9–11 refer to organisms of kingdom Animalia.

(A) Phylum Mollusca
(B) Phylum Cnidaria
(C) Phylum Arthropoda
(D) Phylum Annelida
(E) Phylum Echinodermata

9. Members have a foot, radula, and mantle

10. Encompasses more species than all other animal phyla combined

11. Includes sea urchins, sea cucumbers, and sea stars

Questions 12–15

(A) Phenotype
(B) Gamete
(C) Allele
(D) Homozygote
(E) Chromosome

12. One of two or more different versions of a gene

13. A haploid sex cell

14. The physical expression of a certain trait

15. Exists for a specific gene locus

GO ON TO THE NEXT PAGE

Directions: Each of the questions or incomplete statements below is followed by five suggested answers or completions. Some questions pertain to a set that refers to a laboratory or experimental situation. For each question, select the one choice that is the best answer to the question and then fill in the corresponding oval on the answer sheet.

16. A plant gets its carbon for photosynthesis by capturing

    (A) carbon monoxide from the atmosphere
    (B) elemental carbon from the soil
    (C) elemental carbon from the atmosphere
    (D) carbohydrates from the soil
    (E) carbon dioxide from the atmosphere

17. A population of mountain lions was almost completely eliminated by a forest fire 50 years ago. The lions that are currently in the area are genetically very similar to one another because they are all descendants of the few individuals that survived the fire. This is an example of

    (A) genetic drift
    (B) non-random mating
    (C) gene flow
    (D) natural selection
    (E) mutation

18. A certain blood vessel has thin walls and unidirectional valves. It must be true that this blood vessel is

    I.   an artery
    II. returning blood to the heart
    III. carrying deoxygenated blood

    (A) I only
    (B) II only
    (C) I and III only
    (D) II and III only
    (E) I, II, and III

19. If a population's growth is not limited by predation, competition, disease, or any other factor, its growth pattern will be

    (A) density-dependent
    (B) logistic
    (C) s-shaped
    (D) exponential
    (E) linear

20. How many unique gametes can be produced by an individual with the genotype XXYyZz?

    (A) 2
    (B) 4
    (C) 6
    (D) 8
    (E) 12

21. Which of the following is NOT a type of connective tissue?

    (A) Cartilage
    (B) Bone
    (C) Blood
    (D) Skeletal muscle
    (E) Tendon

22. The "tails" of the phospholipids in a phospholipid bilayer

    (A) are hydrophilic
    (B) are polar
    (C) face the cytoplasm of the cell
    (D) repel one another
    (E) are nonpolar

23. The cycling of a chemical substance between the non-living (air, water, soil) and the living components of an ecosystem is called the

    (A) Krebs cycle
    (B) biogeochemical cycle
    (C) geochemical cycle
    (D) citric acid cycle
    (E) molecular cycle

GO ON TO THE NEXT PAGE

24. Which of the following indicates the correct pathway for the elimination of urine?

   (A) kidney → ureter → bladder → urethra
   (B) kidney → bladder → ureter → urethra
   (C) bladder → ureter → kidney → urethra
   (D) bladder → urethra → kidney → ureter
   (E) ureter → kidney → bladder → urethra

25. Elephants living in the savanna of Africa feed on trees and grasses. What is true regarding the position that the elephants occupy in the food chain?

   (A) The elephant is a top consumer because it is so large.
   (B) The elephant is a carnivore because it has large, sharp tusks.
   (C) The elephant is a primary producer because it converts carbon from the trees and grasses into organic molecules.
   (D) The elephant is a top predator because no other animal preys on it.
   (E) The elephant is a primary consumer because it eats plants.

26. All of the following characteristics are shared by members of phylum Chordata EXCEPT

   (A) a dorsal, hollow nerve cord
   (B) a notochord
   (C) a four-chambered heart
   (D) gill slits present at least during embryonic development
   (E) post-anal tail present at least during embryonic development

27. If brown is the dominant allele for eye color, and blue is the recessive allele, which of the following is NOT possible?

   (A) A brown-eyed man and a brown-eyed woman have a brown-eyed child.
   (B) A brown-eyed man and a brown-eyed woman have a blue-eyed child.
   (C) A brown-eyed man and a blue-eyed woman have a blue-eyed child.
   (D) A blue-eyed man and a blue-eyed woman have a brown-eyed child.
   (E) A blue-eyed man and a brown-eyed woman have a blue-eyed child.

28. A person with a damaged larynx would NOT be able to

   (A) chew food
   (B) inhale air
   (C) hear high pitches
   (D) move food from the mouth to the stomach
   (E) speak

29. The mitotic spindle begins to form and the nuclear membrane dissolves during

   (A) interphase
   (B) prophase
   (C) metaphase
   (D) anaphase
   (E) telophase

GO ON TO THE NEXT PAGE

30. A fire destroys all the vegetation in a forest, leaving only bare rock. Over a long period of time, lichens begin to grow on the rocks, breaking them down into soil. Mosses and herbs displace the lichens and are displaced, in turn, by grasses, shrubs, poplar trees, and maple trees. As this process plays out from beginning to end, all of the following ecological changes occur EXCEPT an increase in

    (A) total biomass
    (B) total biodiversity
    (C) loss of nutrients from the system
    (D) average size of organisms
    (E) average life span of organisms

31. A fungus is growing on a piece of cake that was left in the refrigerator. What set of terms best describes the fungus?

    (A) Autotroph, saprophyte
    (B) Heterotroph, decomposer
    (C) Heterotroph, primary producer
    (D) Autotroph, primary producer
    (E) Autotroph, decomposer

32. The wings of an eagle and the flippers of a penguin are examples of

    (A) acquired traits
    (B) convergent evolution
    (C) vestigial structures
    (D) analogous structures
    (E) homologous structures

33. Which of the following is part of the stamen of a flower?

    (A) Pistil
    (B) Anther
    (C) Stigma
    (D) Ovary
    (E) Style

34. Which of the following describes the path that carbon might take in the carbon cycle?

    (A) Carbon in the soil is converted into organic plant compounds by carbon-fixing bacteria, ingested by animals, and given back to the environment through respiration of carbon dioxide.
    (B) Plants and animals take in carbon dioxide during respiration and return carbon dioxide to the air through decaying waste and, after death, decaying organic matter.
    (C) Plants take in carbon dioxide during respiration; animals ingest the carbon compounds and return carbon dioxide to the air through decaying waste and, after death, decaying organic matter.
    (D) Inert carbon in the atmosphere is taken in by plants during photosynthesis and returned to the soil as carbonate compounds when the plant dies.
    (E) Plants take in carbon dioxide during photosynthesis; animals ingest the plant carbon compounds and return carbon dioxide to the air through respiration and as decaying waste.

35. Which of the following is NOT correct?

    (A) Uracil is found in DNA but not in RNA.
    (B) Transcription occurs before translation.
    (C) A codon is a three-base sequence.
    (D) Proteins are synthesized on ribosomes.
    (E) The tRNA contains the anticodon.

GO ON TO THE NEXT PAGE

36. An island is created by a volcanic eruption. Over the next 10,000 years, the island becomes populated by plants and animals from a nearby continent.

    Which of the following is most similar to the volcanic island?

    (A) An old agricultural field that is no longer being cultivated
    (B) A forest that has been cleared of trees
    (C) An island that has been devastated by a hurricane
    (D) An area where a glacier has recently receded and exposed bare rock
    (E) A grassland that has recently caught on fire

37. Movement first evolved in which phylum of kingdom Animalia?

    (A) Porifera
    (B) Mollusca
    (C) Cnidaria
    (D) Arthropoda
    (E) Annelida

38. Stomach fluid has a pH of 2. The fluid in the stomach

    (A) is basic
    (B) has a low hydrogen ion concentration
    (C) has a high hydrogen ion concentration
    (D) has the same pH as water
    (E) is neutral

39. A pesticide production plant accidentally dumps DDT into the bay. The average amount of DDT found in a forage fish is 2 parts per million, while the average amount found in a fish-eating predator is 10 parts per million. This is an example of

    (A) amplification
    (B) biomagnification
    (C) energy loss
    (D) chemosynthesis
    (E) biodampening

40. A scientist isolates a single strand of DNA that had bonded with an mRNA strand and analyzes the proportions of nitrogenous bases in the bonded string. Which of the following could be the proportions discovered by the scientist?

    (A) 20% adenine, 30% cytosine, 30% guanine, 20% thymine
    (B) 20% adenine, 30% cytosine, 30% guanine, 20% uracil
    (C) 20% adenine, 20% cytosine, 20% guanine, 20% thymine, 20% uracil
    (D) 20% adenine, 30% cytosine, 30% guanine, 10% thymine, 10% uracil
    (E) 40% adenine, 20% cytosine, 10% guanine, 15% thymine, 15% uracil

41. When a rabbit eats a flower, the flower's carbon matter

    (A) remains entirely in the rabbit until it dies and decomposes
    (B) partially remains in the rabbit until death, and partially is given off as waste
    (C) is eliminated by the rabbit through waste
    (D) is given off into the atmosphere via respiration
    (E) is processed by bacteria that release the carbon as carbon dioxide

GO ON TO THE NEXT PAGE

42. Which of the following is true regarding the genotype of an individual organism?

    I.   The genotype depends on the phenotype.
    II. The genotype is acquired during an individual's lifetime.
    III. The genotype can be homozygous or heterozygous.
    IV. The genotype determines the phenotype.

    (A) I only
    (B) I and II only
    (C) III and IV only
    (D) II, III, IV only
    (E) I and III only

43. All of the following characteristics differentiate between monocots and dicots EXCEPT for

    (A) the number of petals on the flowers
    (B) whether or not the plant has vascular tissue
    (C) the venation pattern of the leaves
    (D) the arrangement of the vascular bundles
    (E) the number of cotyledons that the plant has during embryonic development

44. An enzyme-aided reaction occurs in a solution. If the solution is already saturated with substrates, what could be done to speed the reaction's progress?

    (A) Reduce the temperature of the solution to 0°C.
    (B) Add more substrate to the solution.
    (C) Increase the temperature of the solution to 120°C.
    (D) Add an allosteric inhibitor to the solution.
    (E) Add more enzymes to the solution.

45. Rank the biomes in order from lowest to highest latitude.

    (A) Tundra, taiga, temperate deciduous forest, rainforest
    (B) Taiga, tundra, temperate deciduous forest, rainforest
    (C) Rainforest, temperate deciduous forest, tundra, taiga
    (D) Rainforest, temperate deciduous forest, taiga, tundra
    (E) Rainforest, taiga, tundra, temperate deciduous forest

46. The kangaroo rat is a mammal. What might be some of the adaptations that help it to conserve water?

    I.   Nocturnal lifestyle
    II. Exceptionally long loops of Henle in the kidney
    III. A waxy exoskeleton
    IV. An amniotic egg

    (A) I and II only
    (B) III and IV only
    (C) I, II, III only
    (D) I, II, IV only
    (E) I, II, III, and IV

GO ON TO THE NEXT PAGE

<u>Questions 47–50</u> refer to experiments performed on a population of fleas.

Common fleas, *Siphonaptera,* were allowed to breed in a large culture. After many generations, students removed three groups of fleas and placed each group into a separate canister. The fleas in each canister were exposed to different concentrations of pesticide. Group A was exposed to 0.3% concentration of pesticide, Group B was exposed to a pesticide concentration of 0.5%, and Group C was exposed to a pesticide concentration of 0.7%. After a day, the students counted the percentage of surviving fleas in each group, as shown in Figure 1. The three groups of surviving fleas were kept separate and allowed to produce offspring. The offspring in each group were then exposed to a pesticide concentration of 0.5% and the percentage of survivors in each group was determined, as shown in Figure 2.

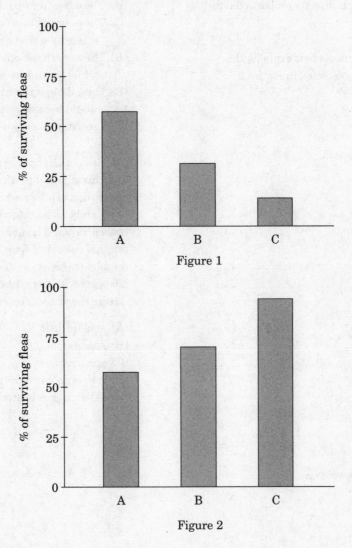

Figure 1

Figure 2

GO ON TO THE NEXT PAGE

47. From the data in Figure 1, it can be inferred that

    (A) pesticides are becoming increasingly ineffective
    (B) pesticides must be used more than once over every twenty-four-hour period in order for it to be effective
    (C) temperature can affect pesticides' effectiveness
    (D) pesticides' effectiveness is indirectly proportional to the size of the flea population
    (E) pesticides' effectiveness is directly proportional to concentration

48. What of the following phenomena best explains the results of the experiment, as depicted in Figure 2?

    (A) Mutation
    (B) Selection
    (C) Adaptive radiation
    (D) Hardy-Weinberg equilibrium
    (E) Habituation

49. Scientists perform a series of crosses and discover that resistance to the pesticide in the fleas is a recessive trait. What would happen if a population of fleas that were resistant to the pesticide were bred over a series of generations, along with a population of fleas that were NOT resistant?

    (A) All of the offspring would be resistant to the pesticide.
    (B) The offspring would develop fatal mutations.
    (C) The majority of offspring would be resistant, while a minority would not be resistant.
    (D) The majority of offspring would not be resistant, while a minority would be resistant.
    (E) Even though the trait is recessive, the offspring would become increasingly resistant since only the resistant fleas would survive to produce offspring.

50. The fleas in Group C are treated with higher and higher concentrations of pesticide during each successive generation of offspring. After a year, the fleas are completely resistant to the pesticide, regardless of its concentration. The fleas are then returned to the original culture of fleas, and scientists notice that the completely resistant fleas can only produce viable offspring with each other. The process that occurred during the year of the experiment is called

    (A) genetic drift
    (B) succession
    (C) speciation
    (D) convergent evolution
    (E) stabilizing selection

GO ON TO THE NEXT PAGE

Questions 51–54 refer to a genetic disease.

A man and woman are both heterozygous for a disease called phenylketonuria (PKU), which affects a person's ability to metabolize an amino acid called phenylalanine. The man and woman are both phenotypically normal and do not have any symptoms of the disease. Men and woman are equally likely to have the disease.

51. This disease is

    (A) autosomal recessive
    (B) autosomal dominant
    (C) sex-linked recessive
    (D) sex-linked dominant
    (E) X-linked

52. The man and woman are both carriers of PKU. Therefore:

    I.   The man and woman could pass the disease on to their offspring.
    II. The man and woman will die from the disease.
    III. At least one of the man's parents was a carrier of the disease.

    (A) I only
    (B) II only
    (C) I and II only
    (D) I and III only
    (E) II and III only

53. What is the probability that a child born to the couple will be a heterozygous carrier of the disease?

    (A) 0%
    (B) 25%
    (C) 50%
    (D) 75%
    (E) 100%

54. The couple has had three phenotypically normal children. What is the probability that their fourth child will have the disease?

    (A) 0%
    (B) 25%
    (C) 50%
    (D) 75%
    (E) 100%

GO ON TO THE NEXT PAGE

Questions 55–57 refer to cellular organelles.

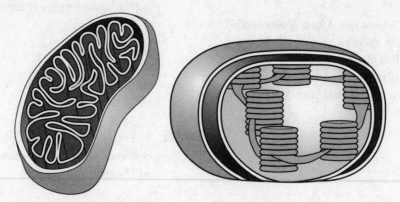

Structure 1   Structure 2

55. The two organelles pictured above are found in

    (A) monerans
    (B) bacteria
    (C) prokaryotes
    (D) plants
    (E) viruses

56. Structure 2 is required for

    (A) glycolysis
    (B) photosynthesis
    (C) DNA replication
    (D) aerobic respiration
    (E) protein synthesis

57. What do these structures have in common?

    (A) Both contain chlorophyll.
    (B) Both are thought to have originated from
         endosymbiotic bacteria.
    (C) Both are found in animal cells.
    (D) Both have only one membrane.
    (E) Both contain DNA housed in a nucleus.

GO ON TO THE NEXT PAGE

<u>Questions 58–60</u> refer to the following nutrition-related experiment.

A dietician prepares four different lunch menus for forty students. The students are divided into four groups of ten, and each group eats a different meal at noon. The students have their blood sugar levels monitored throughout the day.

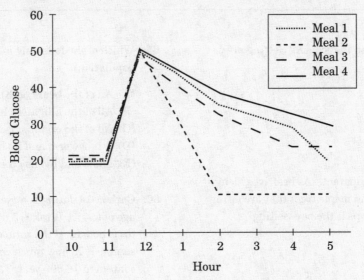

58. What chemical is released directly after the meals are eaten?

    (A) Prolactin
    (B) Glucagon
    (C) Oxytocin
    (D) Insulin
    (E) Creatine

59. From highest to lowest, rank the meals according to the blood glucose levels of the students at 3:00 p.m.

    (A) 2, 3, 1, 4
    (B) 4, 3, 2, 1
    (C) 4, 1, 3, 2
    (D) 1, 2, 3, 4
    (E) 4, 2, 3, 1

60. Which meal probably contains the highest simple sugar-to-protein ratio?

    (A) 1
    (B) 2
    (C) 3
    (D) 4
    (E) It cannot be determined from the data.

If you are taking the Biology-E Test, continue with questions 61–80.
If you are taking the Biology-M Test, go to question 81 now.

BIOLOGY-E SECTION

Directions: Each of the questions or incomplete statements below is followed by five suggested answers or completions. Some questions pertain to a set that refers to a laboratory or experimental situation. For each question, select the one choice that is the best answer to the question and then fill in the corresponding oval on the answer sheet.

---

61. The components of the blood that control clotting are

    (A) white blood cells
    (B) hemoglobin molecules
    (C) platelets
    (D) plasma
    (E) red blood cells

62. A boy goes to visit his grandparents. As he drives along, he sees many birch, oak, and maple trees that are losing their leaves. What biome type is the boy visiting?

    (A) Tropical rainforest
    (B) Desert
    (C) Taiga
    (D) Temperate deciduous forest
    (E) Savanna

63. Which of the following is more advanced, in evolutionary terms, than an amphibian but more primitive than a bird?

    (A) Frog
    (B) Polar bear
    (C) Hagfish
    (D) Lizard
    (E) Chicken

64. Which of the following is NOT a mechanism by which an animal might deal with cold?

    (A) Secretion of epinephrine
    (B) Hibernation
    (C) Vasoconstriction
    (D) Shivering
    (E) Panting

65. Which of the following is the best example of a population?

    (A) All of the bears on Kodiak Island
    (B) All of the alligators in the world
    (C) All of the organisms that live in the rainforest
    (D) A tapeworm and its human host
    (E) Lions and hyenas coexisting in a savanna

66. Carbon-14 dating is a method used to approximate the age of fossils. It takes 5,600 years for carbon-14 to decay to carbon-12. If the ratio of carbon-14 to carbon-12 in a sample is X, how much carbon-14 will the sample contain in 16,800 years?

    (A) X
    (B) $\frac{X}{2}$
    (C) $\frac{X}{3}$
    (D) $\frac{X}{4}$
    (E) $\frac{X}{8}$

67. Exposure to carbon monoxide is extremely dangerous for aerobic organisms, because

    (A) carbon monoxide destroys hemoglobin in red blood cells
    (B) carbon monoxide causes the lungs to secrete too much mucous
    (C) carbon monoxide displaces oxygen molecules on hemoglobin, and the body becomes oxygen deprived
    (D) carbon monoxide combines with carbon dioxide to create a poisonous chemical
    (E) carbon monoxide paralyzes the diaphragm

GO ON TO THE NEXT PAGE

Questions 68–70 refer to the life cycle of a plant.

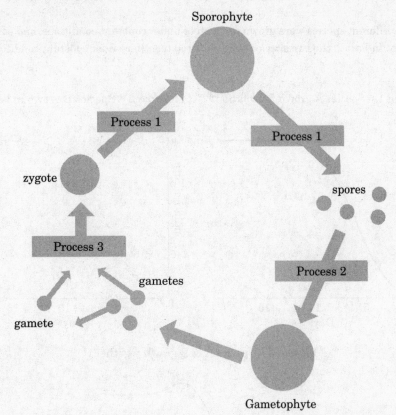

68. What is the name of the process labeled 3?

    (A) Meiosis
    (B) Mitosis
    (C) Fertilization
    (D) Asexual reproduction
    (E) Duplication

69. Which of the following elements of the plant life cycle is incorrectly matched with a description of its chromosomes?

    (A) Spores – diploid
    (B) Gametophyte – haploid
    (C) Zygote – diploid
    (D) Gametes – haploid
    (E) Sporophyte – diploid

70. The type of life cycle depicted is common in plants and is called

    (A) alternation of generations
    (B) parthenogenesis
    (C) budding
    (D) pedogenesis
    (E) dominance of the diploid

GO ON TO THE NEXT PAGE

Questions <u>71–74</u> refer to the following two-part experiment.

In Part 1, populations of two different species were grown separately under constant conditions, and each population was given the same amount of food each day. In Part 2, the two species were cultured together under constant conditions and given the same amount of food each day.

Figure 1 – Species A grown in isolation   **Figure 2** – Species B grown in isolation

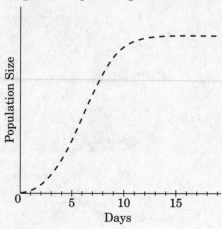

Figure 3 – Species A & B grown together

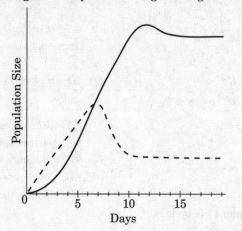

— Species A
- - Species B

GO ON TO THE NEXT PAGE

71. In Figure 1, the point on the curve at which the population growth levels off is called the

    (A) carrying capacity
    (B) niche
    (C) high point
    (D) displacement point
    (E) birth rate

72. When the two species were grown separately, which of the following factors most likely limited the growth of each population?

    (A) Predation
    (B) Parasitism
    (C) Disease
    (D) Competition among individuals of different species
    (E) Competition among individuals of the same species

73. Which of the following statements is supported by the data in Figure 3?

    (A) When the two species are grown together, Species A has the larger population size on Day 2.
    (B) When the two species are grown together, Species B outcompetes Species A.
    (C) When the two species are cultured separately, Species A and Species B both have similar growth patterns.
    (D) When the two species are grown together, Species B has the larger population size on Day 12.
    (E) When the two species are cultured separately, Species A and B both reach their maximum population size on Day 8.

74. Of the following, which might be hypothesized from the data recorded when Species A and Species B were cultured together?

    (A) Species B is a stronger competitor than Species A.
    (B) When resources were abundant, there was little need for competition between Species A and B.
    (C) Species A will soon eliminate all individuals in Species B.
    (D) Species A and B are mutualistic.
    (E) If the population of Species A were to suddenly die off, while the rest of the environment in the culture remained the same, the population of Species B would also diminish.

GO ON TO THE NEXT PAGE

Questions 75–77 refer to taxonomy and classification.

Phylum	Traits					
	Endoderm & Ectoderm	Gut With at Least 1 Opening	Gut with 2 Openings	Heart	Deuterostome Development	Notochord
A	Yes	Yes	Yes	Yes	Yes	Yes
B	Yes	Yes	No	No	No	No
C	No	No	No	No	No	No
D	Yes	Yes	Yes	No	No	No
E	Yes	Yes	Yes	Yes	No	No

75. Of the choices below, which two phyla are most closely related?

(A) A and C
(B) A and D
(C) C and E
(D) B and D
(E) A and B

76. Phylum A is which of the following?

(A) Porifera
(B) Chordata
(C) Arthropoda
(D) Nematoda
(E) Mollusca

77. According to the information in the table, which drawing shows the proper evolutionary tree of phyla A, B, C, D, and E?

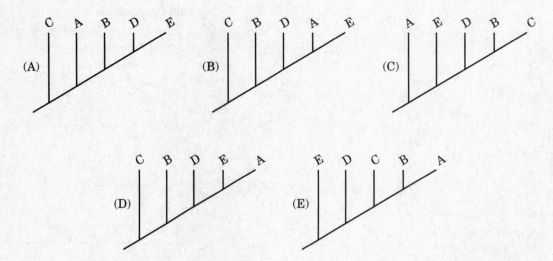

GO ON TO THE NEXT PAGE

10 Practice Exams for the SAT Subject Tests

<u>Questions 78–80</u> refer to the following experiment in which nutrients were added to six lakes.

Each year, nutrients were added to three of the lakes (lakes 1, 2, and 3), and the remaining three lakes were left unaltered. Each summer, scientists measured the biomass of photosynthetic phytoplankton in each lake. The researchers hypothesized that adding nutrients would more than double the biomass of the phytoplankton.

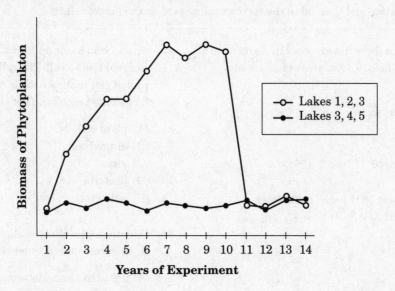

78. Biomass of phytoplankton was greatest in

    (A) lakes 1–3 during year 1
    (B) lakes 4–6 during year 1
    (C) lakes 1–3 during year 5
    (D) lakes 4–6 during year 5
    (E) lakes 1–3 during year 9

79. In what year do you think the experiment ended (i.e., nutrients were no longer added to lakes 1, 2, and 3)?

    (A) Year 3
    (B) Year 5
    (C) Year 8
    (D) Year 10
    (E) Year 14

80. Which of the following can be concluded based on the design of this experiment?

    I. Lakes 1, 2, and 3 served as the "controls" for the experiment.
    II. The dependent variable in this experiment is the biomass of phytoplankton.
    III. The results of the experiment support the researchers' hypothesis.

    (A) I only
    (B) II only
    (C) III only
    (D) I and III only
    (E) II and III only

S T O P

IF YOU FINISH BEFORE TIME IS CALLED, YOU MAY CHECK YOUR WORK ON THE ENTIRE BIOLOGY-E TEST ONLY. DO NOT TURN TO ANY OTHER TEST IN THIS BOOK.

BIOLOGY-M SECTION

If you are taking the Biology-M test, continue with questions 81–100.
Be sure to start this section of the test by filling in oval 81 on your answer sheet.

Directions: Each of the questions or incomplete statements below is followed by five suggested answers or completions. Some questions pertain to a set that refers to a laboratory or experimental situation. For each question, select the one choice that is the best answer to the question and then fill in the corresponding oval on the answer sheet.

81. If you wanted to look at a three-dimensional image of a sperm cell that is magnified 10,000x, you would use a(n)

    (A) light microscope
    (B) compound light microscope
    (C) electron microscope
    (D) magnifying glass
    (E) proton laser microscope

82. Which of the following was NOT found in the early atmosphere of the Earth?

    (A) Hydrogen
    (B) Water
    (C) Ammonia
    (D) Methane
    (E) Oxygen

83. A girl puts five drops of red food coloring into a test tube of water and then shakes the tube. The liquid in the tube becomes pink. The process by which the food coloring and water molecules mixed is called

    (A) diffusion
    (B) active transport
    (C) osmosis
    (D) hyperfusion
    (E) ion transport

84. Turner's Syndrome (XO) is a chromosomal disorder that can be diagnosed by

    (A) pedigree analysis
    (B) biochemical analysis
    (C) Punnett square analysis
    (D) karyotyping
    (E) blood type analysis

85. An asteroid lands on Earth, and a scientist studying the asteroid finds a cell. The cell has circular DNA and a cell wall; it can replicate itself, and it moves using a threadlike propeller. This alien cell most resembles a(n)

    (A) plant cell
    (B) animal cell
    (C) virus
    (D) bacteria
    (E) eukaryote

86. Scientists who study evolution consider cytochrome c to be an excellent molecular clock because

    (A) scientists have determined when cytochrome c was first evolved by an organism
    (B) changes or mutations in cytochrome c occur at regular intervals over time
    (C) cytochrome c has a known half-life that can be used to date the time when an organism lived
    (D) cytochrome c exists in far greater quantities on asteroids than on Earth; large deposits of cytochrome c in the fossil record indicate asteroid impact
    (E) cytochrome c is the molecule in bones that hardens and leaves fossils after death

87. A vineyard owner makes wine by fermenting yeast in grape juice. Which of the following best represents the fermentation reaction that is taking place?

    (A) Pyruvate + NADH $\rightarrow$ lactic acid + NAD^+
    (B) $6CO_2 + 6H_2O \rightarrow$ light $\rightarrow C_6H_{12}O_6 + 6O_2$
    (C) Pyruvate + NADH $\rightarrow$ ethanol + $NAD^+ + CO_2$
    (D) $6O_2 + C_6H_{12}O_6 \rightarrow 6CO_2 + 6H_2O$ + ATP energy
    (E) $6CO_2 + 6H_2O \rightarrow$ light $\rightarrow$ ethanol + $NAD^+ + CO_2$

GO ON TO THE NEXT PAGE

Questions 88–90 refer to the following data set.

Students are monitoring the water chemistry and biota of a stream near their school. They collect data on the pH of the water, the concentration of dissolved oxygen, and the insects present.

Month of Sampling	pH of Stream Water	Concentration of Dissolved Oxygen
November	7.0	8.5 mg/L
December	7.5	9.0 mg/L
January	8.0	9.0 mg/L
March	7.6	8.0 mg/L
May	7.7	7.5 mg/L

88. Rank the samples from highest to lowest hydrogen ion concentration.

   (A) January, December, November, March, May
   (B) January, May, March, December, November
   (C) November, December, March, May, January
   (D) May, March, November, December, January
   (E) March, May, November, December, January

89. A type of algae found in the stream thrives in a neutral environment but is extremely sensitive to minor changes in pH. From November to May, the population size of algae in the stream

   (A) began at a high point in November and fell over the next four months
   (B) rose in November and December to a high point in January, then fell in March and May
   (C) remained constant, since stream water moves quickly and will remove any excess hydrogen ions
   (D) spiked to its highest point in December, fell quickly in January and more slowly in March and May
   (E) reached high points in December and March and low points in November and January

90. Which of the following is the best prediction of what would happen if the dissolved oxygen concentration of the water were to drop to very low levels?

   (A) Fish populations would grow exponentially.
   (B) Heterotrophic vertebrates would not have enough oxygen for photosynthesis and would all die.
   (C) The water would be toxic to the animals that drink it.
   (D) The water would get colder.
   (E) Heterotrophic animals would not have enough oxygen for respiration, and their population sizes might decrease.

GO ON TO THE NEXT PAGE

Questions 91–93 refer to the early development of a human fetus.

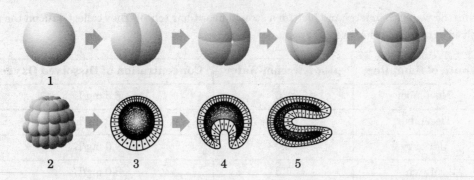

91. Structure 1 is

    (A) haploid
    (B) diploid
    (C) a gamete
    (D) a blastula
    (E) an unfertilized egg

92. Which structure is the morula?

    (A) 1
    (B) 2
    (C) 3
    (D) 4
    (E) 5

93. Which embryonic tissue layers does Structure 5 possess?

    (A) Endoderm only
    (B) Endoderm and mesoderm only
    (C) Endoderm and ectoderm only
    (D) Mesoderm and ectoderm only
    (E) Endoderm, mesoderm, and ectoderm

GO ON TO THE NEXT PAGE

<u>Questions 94–96</u> refer to the following laboratory exercise.

Students in a laboratory were given 5 unknown solutions and asked to correctly identify them. The solutions were: water, glucose syrup, a pure protein shake, salt water, and vegetable oil. Students ran 4 tests.

Silver Nitrate Test – A solution containing chloride will turn brown when silver nitrate is added.

Sudan Test – A solution containing fats will turn red when Sudan IV is added.

Biuret Test – A solution containing proteins will turn purple when NaOH and $CuSO_4$ are added.

Benedict's Test – A solution containing monosaccharides will turn greenish yellow when Benedict's solution is added.

Test	Solution A	Solution B	Solution C	Solution D	Solution E
Benedict's Test	+	–	–	–	–
Biuret Test	–	–	+	+	–
Silver Nitrate Test	–	+	–	–	–
Sudan Test	–	–	–	+	–

94. Solution B contains

    (A) lipids
    (B) nucleic acids
    (C) chloride ions
    (D) carbohydrates
    (E) amino acids

95. The correct identity of Solution A is

    (A) water
    (B) glucose syrup
    (C) protein shake
    (D) salt water
    (E) vegetable oil

96. A student added a test reagent to his solution, and the solution turned red. What reagent did he add?

    (A) Protein shake
    (B) Vegetable oil
    (C) Salt water
    (D) Water
    (E) Glucose syrup

GO ON TO THE NEXT PAGE

Questions 97–100 refer to the pedigree for albinism.

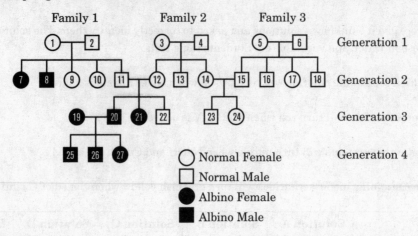

97. The inheritance pattern for this disorder is

    (A) simple recessive
    (B) simple dominant
    (C) sex-linked recessive
    (D) sex-linked dominant
    (E) simple sex-linked

98. Which of the following statements is false?

    (A) Both Individuals 1 and 2 must be carriers of the disorder.
    (B) Both Individuals 3 and 4 must be carriers of the disorder.
    (C) Individual 11 does not have albinism.
    (D) Neither Individual 5 nor Individual 6 could be a carrier of the disorder.
    (E) Individual 8 received a recessive allele from each parent.

99. If Individual 21 were to have a child with a person who is genotypically normal for this trait, what is the probability that their child would have albinism?

    (A) 0%
    (B) 25%
    (C) 50%
    (D) 75%
    (E) 100%

100. Which of the following individuals could be incorrectly matched with his or her genotype? ("A" is dominant; "a" recessive.)

    (A) 3 – Aa
    (B) 7 – aa
    (C) 12 – AA
    (D) 14 – Aa
    (E) 22 – AA

S T O P

IF YOU FINISH BEFORE TIME IS CALLED, YOU MAY CHECK YOUR WORK ON THE ENTIRE BIOLOGY-M TEST ONLY. DO NOT TURN TO ANY OTHER TEST IN THIS BOOK.

BIOLOGY PRACTICE TEST 2 ANSWERS

SAT BIOLOGY E/M PRACTICE TEST 2 EXPLANATIONS

BIOLOGY PRACTICE TEST 2 ANSWERS

Question Number	Answer	Right	Wrong	Question Number	Answer	Right	Wrong
1	D	___	___	51	A	___	___
2	B	___	___	52	D	___	___
3	E	___	___	53	C	___	___
4	D	___	___	54	B	___	___
5	C	___	___	55	D	___	___
6	B	___	___	56	B	___	___
7	E	___	___	57	B	___	___
8	E	___	___	58	D	___	___
9	A	___	___	59	C	___	___
10	C	___	___	60	B	___	___
11	E	___	___	61	C	___	___
12	C	___	___	62	D	___	___
13	B	___	___	63	D	___	___
14	A	___	___	64	E	___	___
15	C	___	___	65	A	___	___
16	E	___	___	66	E	___	___
17	A	___	___	67	C	___	___
18	B	___	___	68	C	___	___
19	D	___	___	69	A	___	___
20	B	___	___	70	A	___	___
21	D	___	___	71	A	___	___
22	E	___	___	72	E	___	___
23	B	___	___	73	C	___	___
24	A	___	___	74	B	___	___
25	E	___	___	75	D	___	___
26	C	___	___	76	B	___	___
27	D	___	___	77	D	___	___
28	E	___	___	78	E	___	___
29	B	___	___	79	D	___	___
30	C	___	___	80	E	___	___
31	B	___	___	81	C	___	___
32	E	___	___	82	E	___	___
33	B	___	___	83	A	___	___
34	E	___	___	84	D	___	___
35	A	___	___	85	D	___	___
36	D	___	___	86	B	___	___
37	C	___	___	87	C	___	___
38	C	___	___	88	C	___	___
39	B	___	___	89	A	___	___
40	D	___	___	90	E	___	___
41	B	___	___	91	B	___	___
42	C	___	___	92	B	___	___
43	B	___	___	93	E	___	___
44	E	___	___	94	C	___	___
45	D	___	___	95	B	___	___
46	A	___	___	96	B	___	___
47	E	___	___	97	A	___	___
48	B	___	___	98	D	___	___
49	D	___	___	99	A	___	___
50	C	___	___	100	C	___	___

CALCULATING YOUR SCORE

Your raw score for the SAT Biology E/M Test is calculated from the number of questions you answer correctly and incorrectly. Once you have determined your composite score, use the conversion table on page 26 of this book to calculate your scaled score. To calculate your raw score, count the number of questions you answered correctly:

_____
A

Count the number of questions you answered incorrectly, and multiply that number by $\frac{1}{4}$:

$$\frac{\rule{3cm}{0.4pt}}{B} \times \frac{1}{4} = \frac{\rule{3cm}{0.4pt}}{C}$$

Subtract the value in field C from the value in field A:

_____
D

Round the number in field D to the nearest whole number. This is your raw score:

_____
E

BIOLOGY E/M CLASSIFICATION QUESTIONS

1. D Organismal Biology
Hemoglobin is an iron-containing protein that can bind to oxygen. The question is a little tricky because red blood cells contain hemoglobin, and students are often taught that red blood cells carry oxygen. The key is that the question asks for a protein, and a red blood cell has many more types of organic molecules than just a single protein.

2. B Organismal Biology
Red blood cells have no nucleus or major organelles and, as a result, have a biconcave shape. Red blood cells are the most abundant cell type in blood, are packed with hemoglobin, and are produced by specialized cells in the bone marrow.

3. E Organismal Biology
Platelets are not really cells but rather are fragments of cytoplasm. Platelets circulate in the blood. When they encounter a wound in a blood vessel, they secrete a protein that causes red blood cells to clot and close the wound.

4. D Organic and Biochemistry
Carbohydrates are molecules that contain carbon, hydrogen, and oxygen in a ratio of about 1:2:1. Glucose is an example of a carbohydrate.

5.   **C**   Organic and Biochemistry

A nitrogenous base is a nitrogen-containing compound found in the nucleotides of DNA and RNA. In addition to a nitrogenous base, each nucleotide also has a sugar and a phosphate group. The nitrogenous bases are adenine, guanine, thymine, cytosine, and uracil. Adenine, guanine, and cytosine are found in both DNA and RNA. Thymine is found in DNA but not in RNA. Uracil is found in RNA but not in DNA.

6.   **B**   Organic and Biochemistry

Lipids are distinguished from other macromolecules because they contain hydrocarbon chains—strings of carbon with hydrogens attached to them. These hydrocarbon chains are nonpolar and make lipids hydrophobic.

7.   **E**   Organic and Biochemistry

Proteins are comprised of carbon, hydrogen, oxygen, and nitrogen.

8.   **E**   Organic and Biochemistry

Amylase is an enzyme—a type of protein—that acts as a biological catalyst. Hemoglobin is a protein compound found in red blood cells. Insulin is a hormone—a type of protein—that converts glucose to glycogen.

9.   **A**   Evolution and Diversity

Members of phylum Mollusca include snails, slugs, squid, octopuses, clams, and oysters. Members of this phylum typically have a muscular "foot" for movement, a rasping tongue for eating, and a mantle that secretes a hard shell for protection.

10.   **C**   Evolution and Diversity

Phylum Arthropoda contains the majority of the animal species on Earth—more than all of the other animal phyla combined. Within phylum Arthropoda, the largest class is Insecta.

11.   **E**   Evolution and Diversity

Phylum Echinodermata includes sea urchins, sea cucumbers, and sea stars. Members of this phylum may look primitive, but their embryonic development suggests that they are more closely related to the chordates than to the other animal phyla.

12.   **C**   Genetics

In a diploid organism, the two copies of each gene can have a different sequence and a gene can have several sequences in a population. These different versions of a gene are called alleles.

13.   **B**   Genetics

A gamete is a haploid sex cell. The male gamete is the sperm, and the female gamete is the egg. The gametes fuse during fertilization to make a diploid zygote that can develop into a diploid individual.

14. **A** Genetics

The phenotype is the physical expression of a certain trait. The genotype is the genetic makeup of the trait, as indicated by a set of alleles. For example, a person's phenotype for eye color might be "blue," while that person's genotype for eye color would be "bb."

15. **C** Genetics

An allele is an alternative gene form located at a specific position on a specific chromosome—in other words, it exists for a specific gene locus (location).

BIOLOGY E/M SOLITARY MULTIPLE CHOICE

16. **E** Cell Processes

Photosynthesis is the process by which plants use energy from the sun to synthesize glucose from CO_2 and water. The carbon comes from atmospheric CO_2. CO_2 diffuses into the plant through the stomata in the leaves. The chemical equation for photosynthesis is

$$6CO_2 + 6H_2O + light \rightarrow C_6H_{12}O_6 + 6O_2$$

17. **A** Evolution and Diversity

In small populations, a chance event such as a fire or flood can reduce a population to only a few survivors. Genetic drift refers to the random changes in the genetic makeup of the population that might result from such an event. If a particular allele were found in only a few individuals, a chance event that killed those individuals would eliminate that allele from the gene pool, resulting in a less diverse population.

18. **B** Organismal Biology

A blood vessel with thin walls and unidirectional valves is a vein, so statement I cannot be true. All veins return blood to the heart (statement II must be true), but while most veins carry deoxygenated blood, the pulmonary vein carries oxygen-rich blood. Therefore, statement III is not necessarily true. Arteries are thicker than blood vessels because the heart pumps blood out to the body with great force, and the arteries must be able to withstand that force. There is less pressure in the veins, so they do not need to be as thick as arteries. Muscles around the veins contract and move blood by squeezing the veins.

19. **D** Ecology

An exponential growth curve shows a population with a constant rate of growth and an exponential increase in size. The curve is J-shaped. A population grows exponentially if there are unlimited resources, no predation, and no disease. Exponential population growth rarely happens in nature.

20. **B** Genetics

There are four gametes that could be created by a person with the genotype XXYyZz. The gametes are XYZ, XYz, XyZ, and Xyz.

21. **D**   Organismal Biology

There are four kinds of tissues in the body: nervous tissue, epithelial tissue, muscle tissue, and connective tissue. Connective tissue provides support, insulation, and protection. Cartilage, bone, tendons, blood, and fat are all connective tissues. Skeletal muscle is muscle tissue.

22. **E**   The Cell

The phospholipid bilayer is made of two sheets of phospholipids. The heads of the phospholipids are polar and thus hydrophilic. They face the watery regions on the inside and outside of the cell. The long hydrocarbon chains (tails) of the phospholipids are nonpolar and hydrophobic. They are attracted to one another and repelled by the water on the inside and outside of the cell. The hydrocarbon chains are in the interior of the bilayer.

23. **B**   Ecology

Biogeochemistry is the study of the cycling of chemicals between living organisms and the non-living components of the earth (atmosphere, soil, water). The nitrogen, water, and carbon cycles are all biogeochemical cycles.

24. **A**   Organismal Biology

The correct pathway for the elimination of urine is: kidney, ureter, bladder, urethra.

25. **E**   Ecology

The elephant eats plants, which signifies that it is a primary consumer. The size of an animal is not necessarily related to its role in the food chain.

26. **C**   Evolution and Diversity

Not all chordates have a four-chambered heart. Only chordates that evolved after birds have a four-chambered heart. However, all members of phylum Chordata possess a dorsal, hollow nerve cord, a notochord, gill slits present at least during embryonic development, and a post-anal tail present at least during embryonic development.

27. **D**   Genetics

Let's say that the allele for brown eyes is "B," and the allele for blue eyes is "b." For a person to have brown eyes, they must have the genotype "BB" or "Bb." For a person to have blue eyes, they must have the genotype "bb." If the father and the mother both have blue eyes, their genotypes must both be "bb." It is not possible for any of their biological children to have brown eyes because they have no "B" allele to pass on to their offspring.

28. **E**   Organismal Biology

The larynx is a structure composed of cartilage that contains the vocal chords. The larynx is sometimes called the "voice box." If the larynx were sufficiently damaged, a person would lose the ability to speak.

29. **B**   Cell Processes

In prophase of mitosis, the double-chromatid chromosomes have formed and are visible under a microscope, the centrioles move to opposite poles of the cell, the mitotic spindle begins to form, and the nuclear membrane disintegrates.

30. **C**   Ecology

As an ecological community goes through ecological succession from pioneer organisms to climax community, the biomass of the community will increase, as will the biodiversity, size of organisms, and life span of organisms. The system will also become *more* adept at maintaining nutrients, the opposite of what is stated in **C**.

31. **B**   Organismal Biology

Members of the kingdom Fungi are heterotrophic and obtain their energy by breaking down non-living organic matter and absorbing the nutrients. Therefore, fungi are decomposers. The terms "decomposer" and "saprophyte" are often used synonymously.

32. **E**   Evolution and Diversity

Eagles and penguins live in very different environments, and eagles use their wings to fly while penguins use their flippers to help propel them through water. Nonetheless, the two organisms are both birds and both share a common ancestor. Their wings (and flippers) therefore are homologous—which means that they are similar in form but differ in their current function.

33. **B**   Organic and Biochemistry

The male reproductive parts of a flower are the anther and filament—collectively called the stamen. The female reproductive parts of a flower are the stigma, style, and ovary—collectively called the pistil.

34. **E**   Ecology

Only **E** describes a path that carbon might take through the carbon cycle. **A** is incorrect because carbon-fixing bacteria do not exist; **B** and **C** are incorrect because carbon dioxide is taken in by plants through photosynthesis, not respiration; **D** is wrong because plants take in carbon dioxide, not elemental carbon, during photosynthesis.

35. **A**   Cell Processes

Uracil is found in RNA but not in DNA. In DNA, cytosine pairs with guanine and adenine pairs with thymine. In RNA, thymine is replaced with uracil.

36. **D**   Ecology

The receding glacier is the only example in which bare rock is exposed and no residual plant life is present. Like the volcanic island, the receding glacier is an example of primary succession. The other examples are of secondary succession.

37. **C**   Evolution and Diversity

Movement first evolved in phylum Cnidaria, which includes jellyfish, hydras, sea anemones, and coral. The only animal phylum more primitive than phylum Cnidaria is phylum Porifera, which includes sponges. Sponges are not capable of movement.

38. **C**   Organic and Biochemistry

Stomach fluid is acidic, which means it has a high hydrogen ion concentration. The pH scale ranges from 1 to 14, 1 being the most acidic and 14 being the most basic. Solutions that are acidic have a high concentration of hydrogen ions. In fact, pH is defined as the negative log of the hydrogen ion concentration, $pH = -\log(H^+)$.

39. **B**   Ecology
As some chemicals travel through the trophic levels in a food chain, they become more and more concentrated. This process is called biomagnification.

40. **D**   Organismal Biology
A single strand of DNA contains the nitrogenous bases adenine, cytosine, guanine, and thymine, while a strand of mRNA contains adenine, cytosine, guanine, and uracil. When a strand of DNA pairs with a strand of mRNA, the two strands together must contain adenine, cytosine, guanine, thymine, *and* uracil. Therefore, **A** and **B** can be eliminated. Of the remaining answers, you may have been tempted to choose **C** because nitrogenous bases pair complementarily. However, this question is a little tricky because while the adenine in DNA pairs with uracil in the mRNA, the adesine in mRNA pairs with thymine in the DNA. Therefore, when mRNA bonds with DNA, there is twice as much adesine as uracil or thymine in the strand. Only **D** provides the proper proportions.

41. **B**   Ecology
When a rabbit eats a flower, it absorbs what carbon matter it can and gives off the rest as waste. The carbon that is absorbed and incorporated into the rabbit's body is returned to the environment when the rabbit dies and decomposes. It's true that rabbits give off carbon dioxide through respiration, but this carbon dioxide is not directly related to the carbon that the rabbit ingests from the flower.

42. **C**   Genetics
The genotype is the genetic composition of an organism. The genotype can be heterozygous or homozygous and determines the phenotype. If the alleles for eye color are B = brown and b = blue, then an individual's genotype for eye color could be BB, Bb, or bb. Their phenotype could either be brown or blue.

43. **B**   Organismal Biology
Angiosperms are divided into two groups—monocots and dicots. All angiosperms have vascular tissue, xylem and phloem, so that is not a characteristic that could be used to distinguish between monocots and dicots. Monocots and dicots can be distinguished on the basis of the number of cotyledons they have, the venation pattern of their leaves, the arrangement of the vascular bundles in their stems, the types of roots they have, and whether the flower parts are in groups of 3, 4, or 5. Monocots have one cotyledon (seed leaf) during embryonic development, while dicots have two cotyledons. Monocots have leaves with parallel veins, and dicots have leaves with a net-like venation. The vascular bundles of monocots are scattered throughout the stem, while the vascular bundles of dicots are arranged in rings. Monocots tend to have fibrous roots, and dicots can have a long taproot. Monocots have flower parts in multiples of three. Dicots have flower parts in multiples of four or five.

44. **E**   Organic and Biochemistry
Adding more enzymes to the solution would increase the rate of product formation. Lowering the temperature would slow the movement of the molecules and decrease the rate at which substrate molecules collide with the enzymes. Increasing the temperature to such an extreme would denature the three-dimensional shape of the enzyme (protein) and render it less effective. Adding more substrate would not increase the rate of the

reaction because the solution is already saturated with substrate. Adding an inhibitor would slow the rate of the reaction.

45. D   Ecology
Latitude increases from 0° at the equator to 90° at the North Pole. The proper ranking of biomes from lowest to highest latitudes is: rainforest, temperate deciduous forest, taiga, tundra.

46. A   Organismal Biology
All of the adaptations listed could be found in animals that are proficient at conserving water. A nocturnal lifestyle keeps the animal out of the heat; exceptionally long loops of Henle in the kidney help with the reabsorption of water; a waxy exoskeleton would limit evaporation; and an amniotic egg decreases water loss as offspring develop. However, the kangaroo rat is a mammal and would not have an exoskeleton or an amniotic egg. Mammals have an internal skeleton and give birth to live young.

BIOLOGY E/M GROUP MULTIPLE CHOICE

47. E   Evolution and Diversity
In the experiment depicted in Figure I, Group A is exposed to the lowest concentration of pesticide, Group B to a middle concentration, and Group C to the highest concentration. In the experiment, the most individual fleas died in Group C, with a moderate number dying in Group B and the fewest dying in Group A. This data indicates that as the pesticide increases in concentration, it becomes increasingly effective at killing fleas.

48. B   Evolution and Diversity
The first experiment exposed the various groups of fleas to different concentrations of pesticide. The low concentration killed few fleas, while the higher concentration killed many fleas. However, another way to look at it is that the high concentration of pesticides selected the hardiest fleas for survival, while the lower concentration let less hardy fleas sneak through. When the offspring of the fleas were then exposed to a moderate level of pesticide concentration, a greater percentage of the offspring in Group C (the offspring of the hardiest fleas) survived. This is natural selection in action.

49. D   Genetics
When recessive and dominant individuals have offspring, genetics states that the majority of offspring will be phenotypically dominant. The question states that resistance to pesticide in fleas is recessive, so if resistant fleas and non-resistant fleas produce offspring, the majority will *not* be resistant. **E** is tricky because it assumes that the breeding fleas are *always* living in the presence of pesticide, which is not stated in the problem. In the absence of pesticide, there is no competitive edge to being resistant to pesticide.

50. C   Evolution and Diversity
The scientific definition of species is "a discrete group of organisms that can only breed within its own confines." When the resistant fleas became unable to mate and produce viable offspring with the fleas from the original culture, the resistant fleas became a new species—a process known as speciation.

51. **A** Genetics

PKU is an autosomal recessive disease. You can infer that the disease is recessive because heterozygous individuals do not manifest the disease, even if they are carriers. The disease is not sex-linked because males and females are equally likely to have the disease.

52. **D** Genetics

Because the parents are carriers of the disease, they can pass the disease to their off-spring. Any carrier of the disease most likely received the recessive allele from a parent. The man and woman are genetic carriers of the disease, but they do not have the disease and therefore cannot die from it.

53. **C** Genetics

Each of the couple's children will have a 50% chance of being a heterozygous carrier of the disease, a 25% chance of being homozygous for the disease, and a 25% chance of being homozygous for the normal phenotype.

	P	p
P	PP	Pp
p	Pp	pp

54. **B** Genetics

Punnett squares are often misunderstood. Students may think that if the couple has four children, then three of them will be phenotypically normal, and one of them will have the disease. That is not true. Each child that is conceived will have a 25% chance of being homozygous for the disease, a 50% chance of being a heterozygous carrier of the disease, and a 25% chance of being genotypically normal / free of the disease.

55. **D** The Cell

The organelles are a mitochondrion and a chloroplast. Both of these organelles would be found in a eukaryotic cell, which is more complex and evolutionarily advanced than a prokaryotic cell. The only eukaryotic organism on the list is the plant. Bacteria are prokaryotes and are members of phylum Monera. Bacteria would not have either mito-chondria or chloroplasts. Viruses are not as complex as eukaryotes and do not possess these organelles. Animal cells are eukaryotic. Animal cells have mitochondria, but they cannot photosynthesize and would not have chloroplasts.

56. **B** The Cell

Structure 2 is a chloroplast. Photosynthesis occurs in chloroplasts.

57. **B** The Cell

Both chloroplasts and mitochondria are thought to have originated from endosymbiotic bacteria. The organelles are similar to bacteria because of their size and the fact that they contain their own circular DNA and ribosomes. Only chloroplasts contain chlorophyll. The chloroplast is not found in animal cells. Both mitochondria and chloroplasts have double membranes. Both contain circular DNA that is not housed in a nucleus.

58. **D**   Organismal Biology

Directly after a meal is eaten, the blood sugar levels rise, which prompts the release of insulin. The role of insulin is to lower blood sugar levels by promoting the accumulation of glycogen by the liver and by stimulating the uptake of glucose by muscles. Glucagon is a hormone that has the opposite effect of insulin. Glucagon prompts the liver to release sugar into the bloodstream.

59. **C**   Organismal Biology

At 3:00 p.m., the students who ate meal #4 had the highest blood glucose levels, and the students who ate meal #2 had the lowest blood glucose levels. Students who ate meals #1 and #3 had intermediate blood glucose levels.

60. **B**   Organismal Biology

Subjects who ate meal #2 had the earliest drop in blood sugar levels and the lowest blood sugar levels in the afternoon. This is the meal that probably has the highest simple sugar-to-protein ratio. Simple sugars are more quickly digested than proteins or complex carbohydrates. For this reason, eating simple sugars does not promote a steady and moderate blood sugar level.

BIOLOGY-E SOLITARY MULTIPLE CHOICE

61. **C**   Ecology

The components in the blood that control clotting are called platelets. Red blood cells carry the oxygen- and carbon dioxide–containing hemoglobin around the body. White blood cells are important in defense against pathogens. Plasma is the liquid matrix in which the blood cells are suspended.

62. **D**   Ecology

A temperate deciduous forest has trees that drop their leaves during a period of winter dormancy. This biome has distinct summer and winter seasons and supports animals such as deer, squirrels, raccoons, foxes, and owls.

63. **D**   Evolution and Diversity

A lizard is a reptile. Reptiles evolved after fish and amphibians but before birds and mammals.

64. **E**   Organismal Biology

Panting is not a mechanism used to deal with cold temperatures but rather a behavior that lowers body heat by evaporative cooling. Therefore, panting is something that animals do when they are hot, not cold.

65. **A**   Ecology

A population is a group of organisms of the same species that inhabit a specific area. Only **A** describes a group of organisms within a limited area.

66. **E** Evolution and Diversity

Radioactive isotopes are used to determine the age of fossils. Radioactive isotopes decay at a regular rate called a half-life. The half-life is the amount of time that the isotope takes to decay into another atom. 16,800 years is three half-lives of carbon-14, so the sample would contain one-eighth the original amount of carbon-14.

67. **C** Organismal Biology

Carbon monoxide is dangerous because it displaces oxygen molecules carried by hemoglobin. Without oxygen, the cells of the body must undergo anaerobic respiration, which does not produce enough ATP to keep the body's systems running.

68. **C** Organismal Biology

In the image of the life cycle of a plant, two gametes fuse to form a zygote. The name of the process in which this occurs is fertilization.

69. **A** Organismal Biology

The spores are haploid, not diploid. The spores are created when the diploid sporophyte undergoes meiosis.

70. **A** Organismal Biology

Alternation of generations is common in plants and is a life cycle in which a multicellular haploid generation alternates with a multicellular diploid generation. The cycle begins when the male and female gametes fuse to form a diploid zygote. The diploid zygote develops into a diploid sporophyte via mitosis. The sporophyte undergoes meiosis to create haploid spores. The haploid spores develop into the haploid gametophytes via mitosis. The gametes are formed from the gametophyte via mitosis.

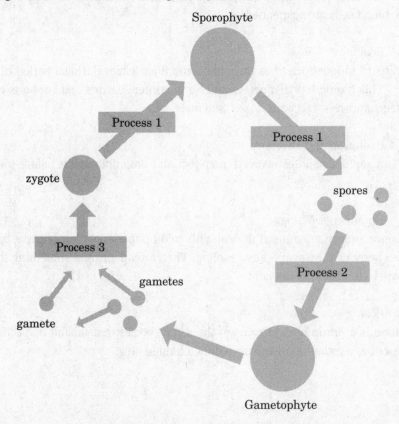

BIOLOGY-E GROUP MULTIPLE CHOICE

71. A   Ecology
In Figure 1, the point on the curve at which the population growth levels off is called the carrying capacity. The carrying capacity is the maximum number of individuals within a population that can be sustained in a given environment.

72. E   Ecology
Factors that can limit population growth include shortage of resources, predation, and disease. In the trials in which the species were grown separately and in isolated, constant conditions, there was no occurrence of predation or disease. The population growth was limited most likely because there was a finite amount of food. Because there was only one species being cultured, competition for the food was between individuals of the same species.

73. C   Ecology
When cultured separately, Species A and Species B both have similar growth patterns. When cultured together, the two species compete with one another and have different growth patterns. Species A is the better competitor, and the population of Species A grows to a larger size than does the population of Species B.

74. B   Ecology
The graph in Figure 3 shows that the populations of Species A and B both initially increased, but as the populations both grew, Population A continued to increase and level off, while Population B plummeted before leveling off. This data clearly indicates that Species A has outcompeted Species B and gives no evidence to support the idea that the two species are mutualistic. Since both populations leveled off, though, there is also no reason to believe that Species A will eventually eliminate all of the individuals in Species B. Since Species B thrived in the culture environment when it was alone, it is much more likely that if Species A were to suddenly die off, Species B would begin to thrive rather than decline. Of the answer choices, the only one that the data supports is **B**. Because both populations originally grew at fairly normal rates, it is easy to hypothesize that there was little competition between the two populations when resources were relatively abundant. Only as the populations grew in size and had to compete for food did it become clear that Species A was more dominant.

75. D   Evolution and Diversity
To determine which of the phyla are most closely related, you have to see which phyla share the most common traits. Checking over the chart, it becomes apparent that phyla B and D share all but one trait, making them the most closely related.

76. B   Evolution and Diversity
Of the phyla in the chart, phylum A is the only one that contains organisms with notochords. Similarly, Chordata is the only phylum among the answer choices to have notochords.

77. **D**   Evolution and Diversity

An evolutionary tree shows the relative evolutionary closeness between organisms, or, in the case of this question, phyla. The phylum with the fewest traits in the chart will be the least evolutionarily advanced, and therefore, the first to appear in the tree. In the chart, phylum C has none of the traits, so it should appear first on the tree. You can eliminate answers **C** and **E** as possibilities. Only phylum C has all of the traits listed on the chart, so it should appear last on the tree, giving you the correct answer, **D**.

78. **E**   Ecology

The greatest biomass of phytoplankton was observed in years 7 and 9 in lakes 1, 2, and 3.

79. **D**   Ecology

After year 10, the biomass of phytoplankton decreased to the levels observed prior to the addition of nutrients in the lakes. Year 10 was the last year of the experiment.

80. **E**   Ecology

Lakes 4, 5, and 6 served as the controls for this experiment. The dependent variable is the biomass of phytoplankton. The hypothesis of the researchers was that an increase in nutrients would more than double the biomass of phytoplankton. This hypothesis was supported by the data.

BIOLOGY-M SOLITARY MULTIPLE CHOICE

81. **C**   The Cell

There are two major types of microscopes used to look at cells—the light microscope and the electron microscope. Light microscopes magnify their subjects using light and lenses. The light microscopes typically found in high schools can magnify an object up to 430x. Electron microscopes use beams of electrons rather than light to magnify their subjects. An electron microscope can offer a much higher resolution than a light microscope and can magnify objects 10,000x or more.

82. **E**   Evolution and Diversity

Oxygen was not a component of the atmosphere of the early earth.

83. **A**   Cell Processes

Diffusion is the movement of molecules from an area of higher concentration to an area of lower concentration. Diffusion tends to distribute molecules uniformly. The red food coloring was concentrated in one area when it first was dropped into the water. Shaking the test tube allowed the food coloring and water to diffuse and mix uniformly. Diffusion resulted in a pink liquid rather than a liquid with a red phase and a clear phase.

84. **D**   Genetics

Karyotyping would detect Turner's syndrome, a genetic disorder that involves a missing X-chromosome. A karyotype in an enlarged photograph of an individual cell's chromosomes. Chromosomes are lined up in homologous pairs according to size. Missing, extra, or abnormal chromosomes can be identified by looking at a karyotype. None of the other types of analysis would detect a disorder in the chromosomes.

85. **D** The Cell

This cell most resembles a bacteria, or prokaryote. Prokaryotes have circular DNA and a cell wall, and they can self-replicate. Prokaryotes often also have whiplike flagella to propel themselves in liquid. Plant and animal cells are eukaryotes and are more advanced than bacteria. Viruses cannot self-replicate.

86. **B** Evolution and Diversity

Molecular clocks are genes or proteins that change at a constant rate over time. Scientists can use the rate of change in the gene or protein to calculate the point at which two species last shared a common ancestor.

87. **C** Cell Processes

Alcoholic fermentation is a type of anaerobic respiration. Glycolysis converts glucose to pyruvate. During fermentation, the pyruvate is reduced to ethanol, NAD^+ is regenerated and CO_2 is formed. The overall equation is: Pyruvate $+$ NADH $\rightarrow$ ethanol $+$ NAD^+ $+$ CO_2.

BIOLOGY-M GROUP MULTIPLE CHOICE

88. **C** Organic and Biochemistry

The pH is the negative log of the hydrogen ion concentration. A low pH indicates a high hydrogen ion concentration. A high pH indicates a low hydrogen ion concentration. The pH scale goes from 1 to 14, with one being the most acidic and 14 being the most basic. A pH of 7 is neutral. The ranking of the samples from highest to lowest hydrogen ion concentration, in terms of pH, would be: 7.0 > 7.5 > 7.6 > 7.7 > 8.0.

89. **A** Organic and Biochemistry

pH is neutral at 7. Therefore, the algae population would be at its peak in November, when the pH of the water was 7, and would fall in all of the following months, when the pH was non-neutral.

90. **E** Organic and Biochemistry

Heterotrophs are animals that cannot synthesize their own food. They eat other organisms to get glucose and other nutrients. Cellular respiration is the process by which cells break down glucose to generate energy. Heterotrophs (and autotrophs too) require oxygen for cellular respiration. Low dissolved oxygen concentrations in the water mean that organisms may not have enough oxygen for cellular respiration, and their populations would decline.

91. **B** Organismal Biology

Structure 1 is a fertilized egg, or zygote. It was formed when the haploid gametes (sperm and egg) fused to form a diploid zygote.

92. **B** Organismal Biology

Structure 2 is the morula. Within 24 hours of fertilization, the single-celled zygote begins to divide into more and more cells until a solid ball of cells known as the morula is formed.

93. **E**   Organismal Biology

Structure 5 is a late-stage gastrula. The late-stage gastrula has all three embryonic tissue layers, endoderm, mesoderm, and ectoderm. Structures 3 (blastula) and 4 (early stage gastrula) have only two embryonic tissue layers—ectoderm and endoderm.

94. **C**   Organic and Biochemistry

Solution B gave a positive result for the silver nitrate test. The explanation of the silver nitrate test tells you that silver nitrate is an indicator of the presence of chloride ions.

95. **B**   Organic and Biochemistry

Solution A gave a positive result for Benedict's Test. There must be monosaccharides in the solution. Of the solutions given, dilute glucose syrup stands out because glucose is a monosaccharide.

96. **B**   Organic and Biochemistry

If you look at the descriptions of each test, the only test that shows a positive result by turning red is the Sudan Test. The Sudan Test, as stated in the question, identifies the presence of fats. Of the five answer choices, only vegetable oil contains fats.

97. **A**   Genetics

The inheritance pattern for albinism is simple recessive. In simple recessive disorders, not everyone who manifests the disease has a parent who also manifests the disease. If two parents have the disease, all of their children will have the disease. The trait is not sex-linked because males and females have an equal chance of getting the disease.

98. **D**   Genetics

None of the offspring of Individuals 5 and 6 display albinism, and none of their offspring's offspring do, either. But, since albinism is a recessive disorder, it is necessary for both parents to carry and pass on the recessive gene in order for their offspring to be an albino. In other words, nothing in this pedigree proves that Individuals 5 and 6 are not carriers. It is quite possible that one of them is a carrier. In fact, it's possible that both are carriers but that they just did not both pass on the recessive gene to the same children.

99. **A**   Genetics

If an albino woman were to have children with a man who does not carry the allele for albinism, then none of their children would manifest the trait because none of them would be homozygous recessive for albinism.

	a	a
A	Aa	Aa
A	Aa	Aa

100. **C**   Genetics

Some of the offspring of Individual 12 are albino, which means that Individual 12 cannot possibly have the genotype AA. A person who only has two dominant alleles cannot pass the recessive albino allele on to his or her children.

THE SAT CHEMISTRY TEST

INTRODUCTION TO THE SAT CHEMISTRY TEST

THE BEST WAY TO DO WELL ON THE SAT CHEMISTRY TEST IS to be really good at chemistry. For that, there is no substitute. But the chemistry geek who spends the night before taking the test cramming all of the nuances of crystal-field theory and coordination compounds probably won't fare any better on the test than the average student who reviews this book carefully. Why? Because the SAT Chemistry Test doesn't cover crystal-field theory and coordination compounds.

Happy? Good. This chapter will tell you precisely what the SAT Chemistry Test *will* test you on, how the test breaks down, and what format the questions will take. Take this information to heart and base your study plan around it. There's no use spending hours on end studying topics you won't be tested on.

CONTENT OF THE SAT CHEMISTRY TEST

The SAT Chemistry Test is written to test your understanding of the topics of chemistry that are typically taught in a one-year college-preparatory–level high school chemistry course.

Well, math and chemistry go hand in hand, right? You might be surprised, then, to learn that you aren't allowed to use a calculator on the SAT Chemistry Test. The math you'll need to do on the test never goes beyond simple arithmetic and manipulation of equations, which is good news for you—you won't be a victim of careless errors made on your calculator.

That said, you should be able to solve problems using ratios, direct and inverse proportions, scientific notation, and some simpler exponential functions. Since the test is an hour long, this means you have an average of 42 seconds to answer each of the 85 questions. The people at ETS realize that isn't enough time to delve into problems involving simultaneous equations or complex algebra. They're more interested in testing your grasp of the basic concepts of chemistry. If you've grasped these concepts, your weakness in math problem solving isn't going to hurt you. You *will*, however, be provided with a simple periodic table. This periodic table will probably look more bare-boned than the one you might be accustomed to using: it will have only the symbols of the elements along with their atomic numbers and masses.

Now let's get into the nuts and bolts of what you'll see on the exam, which contains 85 questions altogether. ETS provides the following breakdown of the test, covering eight basic categories:

Topic	Approximate % of the Test	Approximate No. of Questions
Structure of Matter Includes atomic theory and structure, chemical bonding, and molecular structure; nuclear reactions	25	21
States of Matter Includes kinetic molecular theory of gases, gas laws, liquids, solids, and phase changes; solutions, concentration units, solubility, conductivity, and colligative properties	15	13
Reaction Types Includes acids and bases, oxidation-reduction, and precipitation	14	12
Stoichiometry Includes the mole concept, Avogadro's number, empirical and molecular formulas, percentage composition, stoichiometric calculations, and limiting reagents	12	10
Equilibrium and Reaction Rates Including gas equilibria, ionic equilibria, Le Chatelier's principle, equilibrium expressions; factors affecting rate of reaction	7	6
Thermodynamics Includes energy changes in chemical reactions and physical processes, Hess's law, and randomness	6	5
Descriptive Chemistry Includes physical and chemical properties of elements and their more familiar compounds, chemical reactivity and products of chemical reactions, simple examples from organic chemistry and environmental chemistry	13	11
Laboratory Includes equipment, measurement, procedures, observations, safety, calculations, and interpretation of results	8	7

Each question in the practice tests has been categorized according to these eight categories so you can precisely identify your weaknesses and then concentrate on the areas you need to study most.

FORMAT OF THE SAT CHEMISTRY TEST

Question Types

The SAT Chemistry Test is an hour-long test composed of 85 questions. There are three question types: Classification, Relationship Analysis, and Five-choice completion. Each of the 85 questions on the SAT Chemistry Test is designed to gauge one of three broad types of skill.

Classification Questions

Classification questions are basically reverse-multiple-choice questions. They consist of five answer choices followed by a string of three to five numbered statements. To make things more confusing, the answer choices may be used once, more than once, or not at all—so although a classification question often looks like simple matching, it isn't!

On the test, expect to see about 25 classification questions altogether—approximately 7 sets of 3–5 questions each. The level of difficulty in any one set of classification questions is generally pretty random: you can't count on the first question in a set being easier than the last. However, in the test as a whole, each set of classification questions is generally a bit harder than the one that came before.

Familiarize yourself with the following set of directions—if you read and understand them now, you won't waste precious time on test day.

> Directions: Each set of lettered choices below refers to the numbered questions or statements immediately following it. Select the one lettered choice that best answers each question or best fits each statement and then fill in the corresponding oval on the answer sheet. A choice may be used once, more than once, or not at all in each set.
>
> Questions 1–3
>
> (A) Zinc
> (B) Iron
> (C) Helium
> (D) Copper
> (E) Fluorine
>
> 1. A highly electronegative element
>
> 2. Forms colored solutions when dissolved in water
>
> 3. Normally exists as a diatomic molecule but can react to form a 2^- ion

You can usually answer classification questions a bit more quickly than the standard five-choice completion questions since you need to review only one set of answer choices to answer a series of questions. The answer to number 1 is **E**. Electronegativity is a measure of the ability of an atom in a chemical bond to attract electrons to itself. The answer to number 2 is **D**, copper. Copper often forms green/blue solutions. The answer to number 3 is **A**, zinc. Don't worry if you don't know the answers to these questions right now; after all, you bought this book in order to overcome your weakness—and improve your score. This example is meant mainly to show you how a classification question is formatted.

Relationship Analysis Questions

Relationship analysis questions consist of a specific statement, statement I, followed by another statement, statement II. To answer these questions, you must determine first whether statement I is true or false and then whether statement II is true or false. If both statements are true, next you must decide whether the statement II is the reason that statement I is true. These questions may appear intimidating to you since they're probably unfamiliar, but after taking the practice exams in this book, you should feel as comfortable with them as you do with the other question types.

One more thing about this question type: strangely enough, on the SAT Chemistry Test, the section containing relationship-analysis questions is always numbered starting with 101, although they usually appear early in the test rather than at the end. They also get their own special section on your answer sheet—also beginning with number 101. There are usually about 15 questions of this type on the SAT Chemistry exam. Again, take the time to familiarize yourself with these directions so you won't have to even look at them on test day. Here are the directions, along with two example questions—numbered as the first two questions of the section. Following the two questions is a sample answer grid.

> <u>Directions:</u> Each question below consists of two statements, statement I in the left-hand column and statement II in the right-hand column. For each question, determine whether statement I is true or false <u>and</u> whether statement II is true or false and fill in the corresponding T or F ovals on your answer sheet. <u>Fill in oval CE only if statement II is a correct explanation of statement I.</u>

	Statement I		Statement II
101.	A 1.0 M solution of HCl has a low pH	BECAUSE	HCl contains chlorine.
102.	An atom of chlorine is smaller than an atom of sulfur	BECAUSE	chlorine has a greater effective nuclear charge than sulfur.

	I	II	CE
101.	T F	T F	○
102.	T F	T F	○

Look at question 101. Statement I is true: HCl is an acid, which is a substance that's capable of donating H^+ ions in solution. Acids have a pH that's lower than 7, while bases have a pH above 7. Statement II is also true: HCl is made up of a hydrogen atom and a chlorine atom. Now do the final step—is the pH of HCl directly related to the concentration of the chlorine ions in solution? No, it is directly related to the number of H^+ ions given off by HCl in solution—you would not fill in the bubble marked **CE** (correct explanation).

Now the answer to question 102. Statement I is true. Statement II is also true. Atomic radius decreases from left to right across the periodic table because the more protons in the nucleus of the atom, the more tightly and more closely held are the atom's electrons. This is an example of another way you can use the periodic table while taking the test. If you understand periodic trends, you won't have to memorize the atomic radii of all of the elements. The **CE**, for "correct explanation," should be bubbled in.

Here's how the answer grid (bubble sheet) should be filled in to show correct answers to both questions:

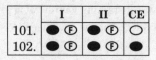

There's no partial credit for classification questions. For each one, you earn credit only if you fill in all the correct bubbles.

Five-Choice Completion Questions

These are the multiple-choice questions we all know and love, and which are the life-blood of any multiple-choice exam. You know the drill: they ask a question and give you five possible answer choices, and you pick the best one. Expect to encounter about 45 of these questions—all of them *after* the classification and relationship-analysis questions. In other words, this will be the third and final part of the exam.

Here are the directions you'll see on the exam, immediately preceding the first five-choice completion question:

> <u>Directions:</u> Each of the questions or incomplete statements below is followed by five suggested answers or completions. For each question, select the one choice that is the best answer to the question and then fill in the corresponding oval on the answer sheet.

Now look at a typical question of this type:

> 24. Which of the following molecules does not match its geometric shape?
>
> (A) BF_3 trigonal planar
>
> (B) $CHCl_3$ tetrahedral
>
> (C) H_2O V shape (bent)
>
> (D) CO_2 linear
>
> (E) PCl_3 trigonal planar

The answer is **E**—the shape of this compound is irregular tetrahedron (also known as trigonal pyramid). Now, the above question is a straightforward multiple choice, but there's another type of five-choice completion question on the test, and it looks like the next question:

25. Which of the following statements correctly describe the information necessary for finding the concentration of an unknown monoprotic acid by titration with KOH?

    I.   The concentration of the base
    II. The total starting volume of acid
    III. The volume of the base used to reach the equivalence point

    (A) I only
    (B) II only
    (C) I and II only
    (D) I and III only
    (E) I, II, and III

Let's analyze it. To find the concentration of the unknown acid, you'll need to know the molarity of the base used in the titration or, put in simpler language, the moles of base per liter of solution. So, statement I is necessary. We'll also need the information in statements II and III, as you'll learn in "Laboratory." The correct answer is **E**.

While knowing your chemistry inside and out is the best way to ensure that you'll do well on this test, it will also help you on test day if you've developed a strategy that enables you to answer all the questions that test you on chemistry you feel confident about and to guess intelligently on the questions on areas in which you feel less confident. We will talk about some strategies for how to deal with these harder questions in the next chapter.

SCORING THE SAT CHEMISTRY TEST

Scoring on the SAT Chemistry Test is the same as scoring for all other SAT Subject Tests. For every right answer, you earn one point. For every wrong answer, you lose $1/4$ of a point. For each question you leave blank, you earn zero points. These points combined equal your raw score. ETS converts your raw score to a scaled score using a curve tailored to the particular test you take. We've included a raw-to-scaled conversion chart on the next page so you can translate your raw score on a practice test into scaled scores.

This chart shows you that your score doesn't plummet with every question you can't answer confidently. You can do very well on this test without knowing or answering everything. In fact, you can attain a top score of 800 even if you get some questions wrong or leave a few blank, or both.

For example, on an 85-question test, you could score:

- 800 if you answered 80 right, 4 wrong, and left 1 blank
- 750 if you answered 74 right, 8 wrong, and left 3 blank
- 700 if you answered 67 right, 12 wrong, and left 5 blank
- 650 if you answered 60 right, 16 wrong, and left 8 blank
- 600 if you answered 54 right, 20 wrong, and left 11 blank

The key to doing well on the SAT Chemistry Test is to follow a strategy that ensures you will see and answer all the questions you can answer, while intelligently guessing on those slightly fuzzier questions. We'll talk more about these strategies in the next section.

Raw Score	Scaled Score	Raw Score	Scaled Score	Raw Score	Scaled Score
85	800	53	620	21	440
84	800	52	620	20	430
83	800	51	610	19	420
82	800	50	600	18	420
81	800	49	600	17	410
80	800	48	590	16	410
79	800	47	590	15	400
78	790	46	580	14	390
77	780	45	580	13	390
76	770	44	570	12	380
75	770	43	560	11	370
74	760	42	560	10	360
73	760	41	550	9	360
72	750	40	550	8	350
71	740	39	540	7	350
70	740	38	540	6	340
69	730	37	530	5	340
68	730	36	520	4	330
67	720	35	520	3	330
66	710	34	510	2	320
65	700	33	500	1	320
64	700	32	500	0	310
63	690	31	490	−1	310
62	680	30	490	−2	300
61	680	29	480	−3	300
60	670	28	480	−4	290
59	660	27	470	−5	280
58	660	26	470	−6	280
57	650	25	460	−7	270
56	640	24	450	−8	270
55	640	23	450	−9	260
54	630	22	440	−10	260

STRATEGIES FOR TAKING THE SAT CHEMISTRY TEST

Earlier we covered General SAT Subject Test Strategies, and now it's time to examine specific strategies. In this section, we'll tell you everything you need to know to kick butt on the SAT Chemistry Test.

All the strategies discussed earlier in this book can be applied equally to the SAT Chemistry Test and the SAT Modern Hebrew Test. That's why they're called "general strategies." However, as you may have noticed in the past, there are a number of dissimilarities between the study of chemistry and the study of modern Hebrew. And because chemistry is unlike modern Hebrew, and even unlike English and biology, a number of strategies apply uniquely to the SAT Chemistry exam. Some of these strategies will help you out in chemistry generally, while some are suited to the unique idiosyncrasies of the SAT format.

Strategy 1: Estimate.

This strategy goes hand in hand with General Strategy 5: Know What You're Being Asked. Don't dive blindly into the answer choices until you've already taken your best stab at coming up with the answer yourself. Obviously, estimation is only useful in questions involving calculation: you can't "estimate" which law of thermodynamics states that the world tends toward increasing disorder. In questions involving a calculation, though, it may save you from foolish errors if you, for example, have a sense of the order of magnitude you're looking at. If you're being asked to calculate the pH of a slightly acidic solution, you can be pretty confident that the answer won't be pH = 0.50, which would be too small, or pH = 14.00, which would be too big. You know that the correct answer must lie somewhere between 2 and 6. Estimating is a good way to eliminate some wrong answers when you're making an educated guess.

Strategy 2: Put It on Paper.

Don't be afraid to write and draw compulsively. The first thing you should do once you've made sure you understand the question is to make your own notes about what you're dealing with. Sketch molecules when dealing with a bonding question, electron configurations for periodic trend questions, or whatever else may be appropriate. Not only will a visual representation relieve some of the pressure on your beleaguered mind, it may also help the solution jump right off the page at you.

Don't forget to write down important information! Writing down all of the information may lead you to a correct answer even if you don't really understand the question. Suppose the question asks for the volume of a gas produced in a certain reaction. Write a balanced equation, plug in values, fiddle around a little, and see if you can come up with an answer that looks right. Chances are, it will be.

Strategy 3: Know Thy Formulae!

As you know, you aren't allowed to bring a calculator into the SAT Subject Test, nor are you allowed to bring in a sheet of paper with useful information on it. That means that if you haven't memorized formulas like Boyle's law and the ideal gas equation, you're going to lose points.

This doesn't mean you have to do a lot of rote memorization. In fact, it's more important to truly understand the principles of chemistry than it is for you to memorize equations. You'll find that as the principles of chemistry become second nature to you, the equations that express these principles will become increasingly intuitive. Knowing your chemistry will help guide you to the right conclusions.

A lot of people feel burdened coming into an exam with lots of formulas and equations in their head. It's like your mind is "full," and there's no room for the problem solving at hand. If you have trouble remembering formulas, you might want to look them over carefully in the minutes before the test and then, before you even look at the first question, write down the formulas you have a hard time remembering on the back of the question booklet. That way you can refer back to them without any painful effort of recollection.

Strategy 4: Answers Are Not Convoluted.

Remember, the SAT Chemistry Test doesn't let you use a calculator, and you're only given, on average, 42 seconds to answer each question. If you're working on a problem and you find yourself writing out lines and lines of conversions as you try to figure out the answer, you're probably not on the right track. These questions are designed in such a way that if you understand what you're being asked, you will need at most a couple of simple calculations to get the right answer.

Strategy 5: Eliminate Wrong Answers.

In General Strategy 6, Know How to Guess, we explained the virtues of eliminating answers you know to be wrong and taking a guess. For most questions, there will be at least one or two answer choices you can eliminate. There are also certain styles of questions that lend themselves to particular process-of-elimination methods.

Classification Questions

A unique feature of classification questions is that the same answer choices apply to several questions. Invariably, some of these answer choices will be tempting for some questions but not for others. Consider, for example, the following 3-question set:

Questions 1–3 relate to the following molecules:

    (A) Sugar
    (B) Ammonia
    (C) Hydrochloric acid
    (D) Carbon dioxide
    (E) Acetic acid

1.   An organic solid with a low melting point

2.   Acts as a weak base when bubbled into pure water

3.   Would be the best choice of the above to neutralize excess NaOH

If you're pretty sure that ammonia, hydrochloric acid, and acetic acid are not organic solids, just from your general knowledge of chemistry, then you can eliminate **B**, **C**, and **E**. This helps you narrow the answer choices down to two, and if you have to guess, you have a 50-50 chance of choosing the correct answer.

Another point that may help you guess in a pinch is that, for most sets of classification questions, you'll rarely find the same answer choice won't be correct for two different questions. True, the directions for classification questions explicitly state that an answer choice "may be used once, more than once, or not at all," but, on the whole, the ETS people shy away from the "more than once" possibility. This is by no means a sure bet, but if you're trying to eliminate answers, you might want to eliminate those choices that you've already used on other questions in the same set.

If you're wondering, the answers to the above questions are 1 **A**, 2 **B**, and 3 **C**.

"EXCEPT" Questions

"EXCEPT" questions are five-choice multiple-choice questions that contain a bunch of right answers and one wrong answer. The questions always contain an all-caps EXCEPT, LEAST, or some other similar word. Even if you aren't sure of the answer, you should be able to identify one or two of the answer choices as being true statements and eliminate them.

32. Most compounds containing primarily ionic bonds are characterized by all of the following EXCEPT

    (A) high melting points
    (B) exist mainly in the gaseous state of matter
    (C) an attraction between positive and negative ions
    (D) usually composed of a metal and nonmetal or polyatomic ion
    (E) most dissolve readily in water

Perhaps you're not sure which of the five answer choices is wrong. But you should be able to identify that choice **C** or **D** might be correct because of the word *ion* in the statement. See, you've already eliminated two possible answers and can make a pretty good guess from there.

If you're interested, the answer is **B**: ionic compounds usually exist as crystalline solids, not gases, at room temperature.

"I, II, and III" Questions

"I, II, and III" questions are multiple-choice questions that provide you with three possible answers, and the five answer choices list different combinations of those three. Here's an example:

11. A student performed an experiment to determine the heat of neutralization of a strong acid with a strong base. Which of the following statements are true of this type of experiment?

    I.   The reaction is exothermic.
    II. Energy for this reaction cannot be directly measured.
    III. The specific heat must be calculated for the acid.

    (A) I only
    (B) II only
    (C) I and II only
    (D) II and III only
    (E) I, II, and III

There's an upside and a downside to questions of this type. Suppose, for example, that you know that in experiments involving heat of neutralization for acids and bases, you need to know the specific heat—and you suspect that you need the specific heat for the acid. This means that you can eliminate **A**, **B**, and **C** and significantly increase your chance of guessing the right answer. As long as you're not afraid to guess—and remember that you should never be afraid to guess if you've eliminated an answer—these questions shouldn't be too daunting. By the way, the answer is **E**.

Now on to the practice sets!

SAT* CHEMISTRY PRACTICE TEST 1

SAT CHEMISTRY PRACTICE TEST 1 ANSWER SHEET

1. Ⓐ Ⓑ Ⓒ Ⓓ Ⓔ	25. Ⓐ Ⓑ Ⓒ Ⓓ Ⓔ	49. Ⓐ Ⓑ Ⓒ Ⓓ Ⓔ
2. Ⓐ Ⓑ Ⓒ Ⓓ Ⓔ	26. Ⓐ Ⓑ Ⓒ Ⓓ Ⓔ	50. Ⓐ Ⓑ Ⓒ Ⓓ Ⓔ
3. Ⓐ Ⓑ Ⓒ Ⓓ Ⓔ	27. Ⓐ Ⓑ Ⓒ Ⓓ Ⓔ	51. Ⓐ Ⓑ Ⓒ Ⓓ Ⓔ
4. Ⓐ Ⓑ Ⓒ Ⓓ Ⓔ	28. Ⓐ Ⓑ Ⓒ Ⓓ Ⓔ	52. Ⓐ Ⓑ Ⓒ Ⓓ Ⓔ
5. Ⓐ Ⓑ Ⓒ Ⓓ Ⓔ	29. Ⓐ Ⓑ Ⓒ Ⓓ Ⓔ	53. Ⓐ Ⓑ Ⓒ Ⓓ Ⓔ
6. Ⓐ Ⓑ Ⓒ Ⓓ Ⓔ	30. Ⓐ Ⓑ Ⓒ Ⓓ Ⓔ	54. Ⓐ Ⓑ Ⓒ Ⓓ Ⓔ
7. Ⓐ Ⓑ Ⓒ Ⓓ Ⓔ	31. Ⓐ Ⓑ Ⓒ Ⓓ Ⓔ	55. Ⓐ Ⓑ Ⓒ Ⓓ Ⓔ
8. Ⓐ Ⓑ Ⓒ Ⓓ Ⓔ	32. Ⓐ Ⓑ Ⓒ Ⓓ Ⓔ	56. Ⓐ Ⓑ Ⓒ Ⓓ Ⓔ
9. Ⓐ Ⓑ Ⓒ Ⓓ Ⓔ	33. Ⓐ Ⓑ Ⓒ Ⓓ Ⓔ	57. Ⓐ Ⓑ Ⓒ Ⓓ Ⓔ
10. Ⓐ Ⓑ Ⓒ Ⓓ Ⓔ	34. Ⓐ Ⓑ Ⓒ Ⓓ Ⓔ	58. Ⓐ Ⓑ Ⓒ Ⓓ Ⓔ
11. Ⓐ Ⓑ Ⓒ Ⓓ Ⓔ	35. Ⓐ Ⓑ Ⓒ Ⓓ Ⓔ	59. Ⓐ Ⓑ Ⓒ Ⓓ Ⓔ
12. Ⓐ Ⓑ Ⓒ Ⓓ Ⓔ	36. Ⓐ Ⓑ Ⓒ Ⓓ Ⓔ	60. Ⓐ Ⓑ Ⓒ Ⓓ Ⓔ
13. Ⓐ Ⓑ Ⓒ Ⓓ Ⓔ	37. Ⓐ Ⓑ Ⓒ Ⓓ Ⓔ	61. Ⓐ Ⓑ Ⓒ Ⓓ Ⓔ
14. Ⓐ Ⓑ Ⓒ Ⓓ Ⓔ	38. Ⓐ Ⓑ Ⓒ Ⓓ Ⓔ	62. Ⓐ Ⓑ Ⓒ Ⓓ Ⓔ
15. Ⓐ Ⓑ Ⓒ Ⓓ Ⓔ	39. Ⓐ Ⓑ Ⓒ Ⓓ Ⓔ	63. Ⓐ Ⓑ Ⓒ Ⓓ Ⓔ
16. Ⓐ Ⓑ Ⓒ Ⓓ Ⓔ	40. Ⓐ Ⓑ Ⓒ Ⓓ Ⓔ	64. Ⓐ Ⓑ Ⓒ Ⓓ Ⓔ
17. Ⓐ Ⓑ Ⓒ Ⓓ Ⓔ	41. Ⓐ Ⓑ Ⓒ Ⓓ Ⓔ	65. Ⓐ Ⓑ Ⓒ Ⓓ Ⓔ
18. Ⓐ Ⓑ Ⓒ Ⓓ Ⓔ	42. Ⓐ Ⓑ Ⓒ Ⓓ Ⓔ	66. Ⓐ Ⓑ Ⓒ Ⓓ Ⓔ
19. Ⓐ Ⓑ Ⓒ Ⓓ Ⓔ	43. Ⓐ Ⓑ Ⓒ Ⓓ Ⓔ	67. Ⓐ Ⓑ Ⓒ Ⓓ Ⓔ
20. Ⓐ Ⓑ Ⓒ Ⓓ Ⓔ	44. Ⓐ Ⓑ Ⓒ Ⓓ Ⓔ	68. Ⓐ Ⓑ Ⓒ Ⓓ Ⓔ
21. Ⓐ Ⓑ Ⓒ Ⓓ Ⓔ	45. Ⓐ Ⓑ Ⓒ Ⓓ Ⓔ	69. Ⓐ Ⓑ Ⓒ Ⓓ Ⓔ
22. Ⓐ Ⓑ Ⓒ Ⓓ Ⓔ	46. Ⓐ Ⓑ Ⓒ Ⓓ Ⓔ	70. Ⓐ Ⓑ Ⓒ Ⓓ Ⓔ
23. Ⓐ Ⓑ Ⓒ Ⓓ Ⓔ	47. Ⓐ Ⓑ Ⓒ Ⓓ Ⓔ	
24. Ⓐ Ⓑ Ⓒ Ⓓ Ⓔ	48. Ⓐ Ⓑ Ⓒ Ⓓ Ⓔ	

Chemistry

	I	II	CE
101.	Ⓣ Ⓕ	Ⓣ Ⓕ	◯
102.	Ⓣ Ⓕ	Ⓣ Ⓕ	◯
103.	Ⓣ Ⓕ	Ⓣ Ⓕ	◯
104.	Ⓣ Ⓕ	Ⓣ Ⓕ	◯
105.	Ⓣ Ⓕ	Ⓣ Ⓕ	◯
106.	Ⓣ Ⓕ	Ⓣ Ⓕ	◯
107.	Ⓣ Ⓕ	Ⓣ Ⓕ	◯
108.	Ⓣ Ⓕ	Ⓣ Ⓕ	◯
109.	Ⓣ Ⓕ	Ⓣ Ⓕ	◯
110.	Ⓣ Ⓕ	Ⓣ Ⓕ	◯
111.	Ⓣ Ⓕ	Ⓣ Ⓕ	◯
112.	Ⓣ Ⓕ	Ⓣ Ⓕ	◯
113.	Ⓣ Ⓕ	Ⓣ Ⓕ	◯
114.	Ⓣ Ⓕ	Ⓣ Ⓕ	◯
115.	Ⓣ Ⓕ	Ⓣ Ⓕ	◯

THE PERIODIC TABLE OF ELEMENTS

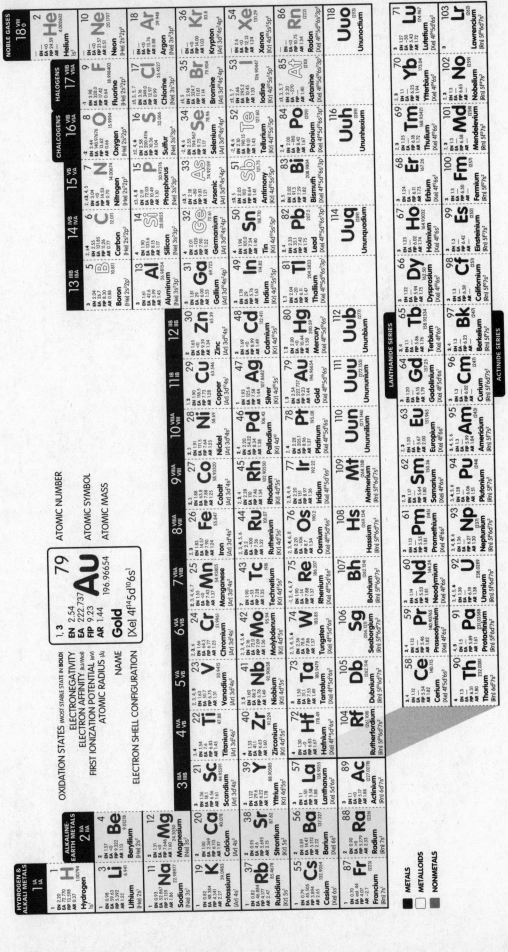

SAT CHEMISTRY PRACTICE TEST 1

Time—1 hour

<u>Note:</u> For all questions involving solutions and/or chemical equations, assume that the system is in pure water unless otherwise stated.

Part A

<u>Directions:</u> Each set of lettered choices below refers to the numbered questions or statements immediately following it. Select the one lettered choice that best answers each question or best fits each statement, and then fill in the corresponding oval on the answer sheet. <u>A choice may be used once, more than once, or not at all in each set.</u>

Questions 1–4

(A) AB
(B) AB_2
(C) A_2B
(D) AB_3
(E) A_2B_3

Which of the above represents the formula for the most common compound of A and B, where A and B represent given pairs of elements or polyatomic ions as indicated below?

	A	B
1.	Be	F
2.	NH_4^+	Cl
3.	H	S
4.	Al	O

Questions 5–7

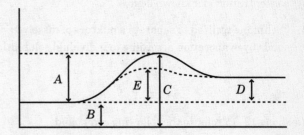

(A) A
(B) B
(C) C
(D) D
(E) E

5. Which letter corresponds to the activation energy in this reaction without the addition of a catalyst?

6. Which letter corresponds to the total change in energy for the overall reaction?

7. Which letter corresponds to the activation energy of the reaction after the addition of a catalyst?

GO ON TO THE NEXT PAGE

<u>Questions 8–11</u> refer to the following laboratory procedures:

    (A) Distillation
    (B) Chromatography
    (C) Fractional crystallization
    (D) Filtration
    (E) Titration

8. Technique utilized to separate a precipitate from a filtrate using a porous substance

9. Technique utilized to separate a mixture of liquids based on differences in their boiling points

10. Technique utilized to determine the unknown concentration of a known acid

11. Technique utilized to separate a mixture of dissolved solids by evaporation according to individual solubilities

<u>Questions 12–15</u> refer to the following compounds:

    (A) C_2H_6
    (B) C_2H_4
    (C) C_2H_2
    (D) C_2H_5OH
    (E) C_3H_8

12. Exists as a liquid at room temperature

13. Contains carbons that are sp^2 hybridized

14. Is a linear molecule

15. Dissolves in water

<u>Questions 16–20</u>

    (A) $1s^2 2s^2\, 2p^6 3s^2 3p^2$
    (B) $1s^2 2s^2\, 2p^6 3s^2 3p^4$
    (C) $1s^2 2s^2\, 2p^6 3s^2 3p^5$
    (D) $1s^2 2s^2\, 2p^6 3s^2 3p^6$
    (E) $1s^2 2s^2\, 2p^6 3s^2 3p^6 4s^1$

16. Is the electron configuration for an element that reacts exothermically with water to produce an alkaline solution and hydrogen gas

17. Is isoelectronic with Ca^{2+}

18. Forms diatomic molecules

19. Has the largest atomic radius

20. Has the greatest first ionization energy

<u>Questions 21–25</u>

    (A) SO_2
    (B) $Ba(OH)_2$
    (C) KCl
    (D) $Fe(NO_3)_3$
    (E) $LiC_2H_3O_2$

21. Is known to produce acid rain

22. Is a salt that forms acidic aqueous solutions

23. Is a salt that forms basic aqueous solutions

24. Is a salt that forms neutral aqueous solutions

25. Is a strong base

GO ON TO THE NEXT PAGE

PLEASE GO TO THE SPECIAL SECTION OF YOUR ANSWER SHEET LABELED CHEMISTRY AND ANSWER QUESTIONS 101–115 ACCORDING TO THE FOLLOWING DIRECTIONS.

Part B

Directions: Each question below consists of two statements, statement I in the left-hand column and statement II in the right-hand column. For each question, determine whether statement I is true or false <u>and</u> whether statement II is true or false and fill in the corresponding T or F ovals on your answer sheet. <u>Fill in oval **CE** only if statement II is a correct explanation of statement I.</u>

EXAMPLES:

	I		II
EX 1.	H_2SO_4 is a strong acid	BECAUSE	H_2SO_4 contains sulfur.
EX 2.	An atom of oxygen is electrically neutral	BECAUSE	an oxygen atom contains an equal number of protos and electrons.

SAMPLE ANSWERS

	I	II	CE
EX 1	● Ⓕ	● Ⓕ	○
EX 2	● Ⓕ	● Ⓕ	●

	I		II
101.	Increasing the pressure on a confined sample of a gas will decrease its volume	BECAUSE	gas molecules move more slowly as their kinetic energy decreases.
102.	Water droplets form on the outside of a beaker containing an ice bath	BECAUSE	water vapor molecules in the air lose energy when they collide with the cold glass surface and condense.
103.	Alpha particles are the most penetrating radio-active particle	BECAUSE	alpha particles are the smallest of the radioactive particles.
104.	Atomic radius generally increases as you move across the periodic table from left to right	BECAUSE	the atomic number is increasing from left to right as you move across the periodic table.
105.	The ionization energy generally increases as you move from left to right across the periodic table	BECAUSE	shielding increases as you move from left to right across the periodic table.
106.	Water has a higher boiling point than molecules of a similar mass	BECAUSE	each molecule forms a hydrogen bond with an adjacent molecule.
107.	Evaporation is an endothermic process	BECAUSE	heat is absorbed as a substance cools.

GO ON TO THE NEXT PAGE

	I		II
108.	Nonmetallic oxides are usually basic anhydrides	BECAUSE	nonmetal oxides form acids when placed in water.
109.	Nitrogen gas effuses faster than oxygen gas	BECAUSE	nitrogen gas has a molecular mass of 14 g/mol while oxygen gas has a molecular mass of 16 g/mol.
110.	The fluoride ion has a larger radius than the fluorine atom	BECAUSE	the fluoride ion has 8 electrons and 9 protons.
111.	The Al^{3+} ion needs to be reduced to form aluminum metal	BECAUSE	reduction is a gain of electrons.
112.	Metals are good conductors of electricity	BECAUSE	metals exist as positive ions with delocalized electrons.
113.	The transmutation decay of carbon-14 can be shown as $^{14}_{6}C \rightarrow\ ^{0}_{7}\beta +\ ^{14}_{7}N$	BECAUSE	The decay of carbon-14 is accompanied by the release of a beta particle.
114.	$^{14}_{6}C$ and $^{12}_{6}C$ are isomers of the element carbon	BECAUSE	isomers contain the same number of protons but a different number of neutrons.
115.	A sample of gas is heated at constant pressure from 200K to 400K and its volume doubles	BECAUSE	each molecule expands to twice its original volume.

GO ON TO THE NEXT PAGE

10 Practice Exams for the SAT Subject Tests

Part C

Directions: Each of the questions or incomplete statements below is followed by five suggested answers or completions. Select the one choice that is best in each case and then fill in the corresponding oval on the answer sheet.

---

26. A measured mass of an unreactive metal was dropped into a small graduated cylinder half filled with water. The following measurements were made:

Mass of metal	25 g
Volume of water before addition of metal	12.5 mL
Volume of water after addition of metal	15.0 mL

The density of the metal should be reported as

(A) 0.92 g/mL
(B) 1.68 g/mL
(C) 2.02 g/mL
(D) 8.40 g/mL
(E) 10.0 g/mL

Questions 27–28

Consider the following equilibrium:

$$X_{2(g)} + 2H_{2(g)} \Leftrightarrow 2H_2X_{(g)} + \text{energy}$$

27. Addition of X_2 to a system described by the above equilibrium will

(A) increase the equilibrium concentration of $[H_2]$
(B) increase the equilibrium concentration of $[H_2X]$
(C) decrease the equilibrium concentration of $[H_2X]$
(D) have no effect on the equilibrium concentrations
(E) decrease the amount of heat energy given off by the system

28. Addition of argon to the above equilibrium will

(A) increase the equilibrium concentration of $[H_2]$
(B) increase the equilibrium concentration of $[H_2X]$
(C) decrease the equilibrium concentration of $[H_2X]$
(D) have no effect on the equilibrium concentrations
(E) decrease the amount of heat energy given off by the system

GO ON TO THE NEXT PAGE

29. Which compound contains the highest percent by mass of hydrogen?

    (A) HCl
    (B) H_2O
    (C) H_2SO_4
    (D) H_2S
    (E) HF

Questions 30–31:

Consider the following equilibrium system:

$$3H_{2(g)} + N_{2(g)} \iff 2NH_{3(g)}$$

30. What is the mass action expression (equilibrium constant expression) for the equilibrium system above?

    (A) $K = \dfrac{1}{[H_2]}$

    (B) $K = \dfrac{1}{[H_2][N_2]}$

    (C) $K = [H_2][N_2][NH_3]$

    (D) $K = \dfrac{[NH_3]^2}{[H_2]^3[N_2]}$

    (E) $K = \dfrac{[H_2]^3[N_2]}{[NH_3]^2}$

31. If the total pressure of the system is increased when the reaction represented above is at equilibrium, which of the following occurs?

    (A) The concentration of H_2 increases.
    (B) The concentration of N_2 increases.
    (C) The reaction will shift to the right.
    (D) The reaction will shift to the left.
    (E) The H_2 gas condenses.

32. When the equation for the reaction represented below is balanced and all coefficients are reduced to lowest whole-number terms, the coefficient for $Al_{(s)}$ is

    $$\ldots Al_{(s)} + \ldots O_{2(g)} \rightarrow \ldots Al_2O_{3(s)}$$

    (A) 1
    (B) 2
    (C) 3
    (D) 4
    (E) 6

33. Nitric acid contains approximately what percent hydrogen by mass?

    (A) 2%
    (B) 5%
    (C) 7%
    (D) 10%
    (E) 20%

34. If the equilibrium constant for the reaction represented by equation I below is 5.0, what is the value of the equilibrium constant for the reaction represented by equation II?

    I. $X + Y \rightarrow 2Z$
    II. $4Z \rightarrow 2X + 2Y$

    (A) $\dfrac{1}{25.00}$

    (B) $\dfrac{1}{5.00}$

    (C) 5.00

    (D) 10.0

    (E) 25.0

35. The mass of 3.01×10^{23} molecules of a gas is 32.0 grams. Approximately what volume does 8.00 grams of the gas occupy at STP?

    (A) 2.80 L
    (B) 8.00 L
    (C) 11.2 L
    (D) 22.4 L
    (E) 64.0 L

GO ON TO THE NEXT PAGE

36. When the equation for the reaction represented below is balanced and the coefficients are reduced to the lowest whole-number terms, the coefficient for H_2O is

$$\ldots KOH_{(aq)} + \ldots H_3PO_{4(aq)} \rightarrow \ldots K_3PO_{4(aq)} + \ldots H_2O$$

(A) 1
(B) 2
(C) 3
(D) 4
(E) 5

37. An atom of silicon has a mass number of 29. How many neutrons does it have?

(A) 14
(B) 15
(C) 16
(D) 28
(E) 29

38. What is the empirical formula of a compound that contains 0.05 mole of magnesium, 0.05 mole of sulfur, and 0.20 mole of oxygen?

(A) $MgSO$
(B) $MgSO_2$
(C) $MgSO_3$
(D) $MgSO_4$
(E) MgS_2O_2

39. The rate at which a solid dissolves in water is increased by which of the following?

   I.   Crushing the solid into smaller pieces
   II. Agitating the mixture
   III. Placing the mixture in an ice bath

(A) I only
(B) II only
(C) I and II only
(D) I and III only
(E) I, II, and III

40. When the equation for the reaction represented below is balanced and the coefficients are reduced to the lowest whole-number terms, the coefficient for H_2O is

$$\ldots C_6H_{14(l)} + \ldots O_{2(g)} \rightarrow \ldots CO_{2(g)} + \ldots H_2O_{(l)}$$

(A) 1
(B) 2
(C) 6
(D) 13
(E) 14

41. How many milliliters of 0.400 M potassium hydroxide must be added to a 200 mL solution of 0.100 M hydrochloric acid to obtain a solution with a pH of 7.00?

(A) 10.0 mL
(B) 25.0 mL
(C) 50.0 mL
(D) 100.0 mL
(E) 200.0 mL

42. Given the equation $3X + Y \rightarrow Z$, you react 2 moles of X with 1 mole of Y. Which of the following is true?

(A) X is the limiting reactant because of its higher molar mass.
(B) X is the limiting reactant because you need 3 moles of X and have 2.
(C) Y is the limiting reactant because you have fewer moles of Y than X.
(D) Y is the limiting reactant because $3X$ molecules react with 1 Y molecule.
(E) Neither reactant is limiting.

GO ON TO THE NEXT PAGE

43. Which of the following statements is true about a balloon filled with 1.00 mol of CO_2 at STP?

    I.   The contents of the balloon have a mass of 44.0 g.
    II. The balloon has a volume of 22.4 L.
    III. The balloon contains 6.02×10^{23} molecules.

    (A) I only
    (B) III only
    (C) I and II only
    (D) II and III only
    (E) I, II, and III

44. A 1.0 L sample of 0.05 M $Al_3(PO_4)_2$ contains a total of

    (A) 0.05 M Al^{3+}
    (B) 0.10 M Al^{3+}
    (C) 0.25 M Al^{3+}
    (D) 0.05 M PO_4^{3+}
    (E) 0.10 M PO_4^{3+}

Use the following to answer questions 45–46:

Consider three 1-L flasks at STP. Flask A contains CH_4 gas, flask B contains NO_2 gas, and flask C contains O_2 gas.

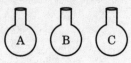

45. Which flask contains the largest number of molecules?

    (A) Flask A
    (B) Flask B
    (C) Flask C
    (D) All flasks contain the same number of molecules since they are at the same temperature.
    (E) All flasks contain the same number of molecules since they are at the same temperature and pressure.

46. In which flask do the molecules have the highest average velocity?

    (A) Flask A
    (B) Flask B
    (C) Flask C
    (D) The molecules in all of the flasks have the same velocity since they are at the same temperature.
    (E) The molecules in all of the flasks have the same velocity since they are at the same temperature and pressure.

GO ON TO THE NEXT PAGE

47. Which of the following is the best qualitative graph of T versus V for a sample of gas at constant pressure and number of molecules?

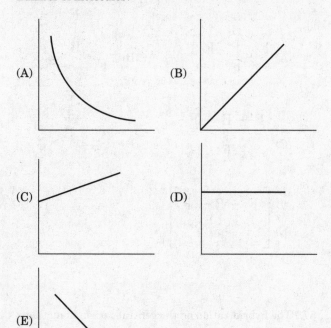

(A)

(B)

(C)

(D)

(E)

48. Which of the following conditions is/are closely associated with the behavior of ideal gases?

   I.   High pressure
   II. High temperature
   III. High numbers of moles of gas in the sample

   (A) I only
   (B) II only
   (C) I and II only
   (D) II and III only
   (E) I and III only

49. A student adds $AgNO_{3(aq)}$ to $HCl_{(aq)}$. Which of the following should the student easily observe?

   I.   A precipitate is formed.
   II. The solution turns yellow.
   III. Bubbles are produced as a gas is evolved.

   (A) I only
   (B) II only
   (C) III only
   (D) I and II only
   (E) I, II, and III

50. What volume of $H_2O_{(g)}$ measured at STP is produced by the combustion of 8.00 g of methane gas, CH_4, according to the following equation?

$$CH_{4(g)} + 2O_{2(g)} \rightarrow CO_{2(g)} + 2H_2O_{(g)}$$

   (A) 5.60 L
   (B) 11.2 L
   (C) 22.4 L
   (D) 33.6 L
   (E) 44.8 L

51. Which of the following electron configurations corresponds to a transition element?

   (A) $1s^2 2s^2 2p^6 3s^2 3p^6$
   (B) $1s^2 2s^2 2p^6 3s^2 3p^6 4s^2$
   (C) $1s^2 2s^2 2p^6 3s^2 3p^6 3d^2 4s^2$
   (D) $1s^2 2s^2 2p^6 3s^2 3p^6 3d^{10} 4s^2 4p^1$
   (E) $1s^2 2s^2 2p^6 3s^2 3p^6 3d^2 4s^2 4p^6 4f^1$

52. When the equation for the reaction represented below is balanced and the coefficients are reduced to the lowest whole-number terms, the coefficient for SO_2 is

$$\ldots ZnS_{(s)} + \ldots O_{2(g)} \rightarrow \ldots ZnO_{(s)} + \ldots SO_{2(g)}$$

   (A) 1
   (B) 2
   (C) 3
   (D) 4
   (E) 5

53. Which of the following will result when the temperature is increased as the chemical reaction proceeds?

    I.   Increased molecular collision frequency
    II. Increased numbers of molecules possessing energy greater than the activation energy
    III. Decreased randomness of the system

    (A) I only
    (B) II only
    (C) I and II only
    (D) I and III only
    (E) I, II, and III

54. Which of the following has the highest second ionization energy?

    (A) Cl
    (B) S
    (C) Na
    (D) Mg
    (E) Al

55. Which of the following forms the largest of the −1 ions?

    (A) F
    (B) Cl
    (C) Br
    (D) I
    (E) H

56. Which of the following indicates the electron dot structure for BF_3?

 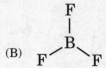

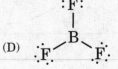

(A)   (B)   (C)   (D)   (E)

57. The hybridization on the central carbon in methane, CH_4, is

    (A) sp
    (B) sp^2
    (C) sp^3
    (D) $sp3d$
    (E) $sp3d^2$

GO ON TO THE NEXT PAGE

Questions 58–60

58. Which of the following elements is the best oxidizing agent?

 (A) Ca
 (B) Au
 (C) H
 (D) Fe
 (E) Cu

59. Of the following, the element that reacts most readily with hydrochloric acid to produce hydrogen gas is

 (A) Cu
 (B) Hg
 (C) Ag
 (D) Zn
 (E) Au

60. In the electrochemical cell shown below, which of the following half-reactions occurs at the cathode?

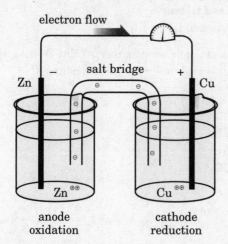

electron flow

salt bridge

Zn −   + Cu

Zn $^{\oplus\oplus}$ Cu $^{\oplus\oplus}$

anode   cathode
oxidation   reduction

 (A) $Cu^{2+} + e^- \rightarrow Cu^+$
 (B) $Zn_{(s)} \rightarrow Zn^{2+} + 2e^-$
 (C) $Zn^{2+} + 2e^- \rightarrow Zn_{(s)}$
 (D) $Cu_{(s)} \rightarrow Cu^{2+} + 2e^-$
 (E) $Cu^{2+} + 2e^- \rightarrow Cu_{(s)}$

61. When HCO_3^- acts as a Brønsted base, which of the following is formed?

 (A) CO_2
 (B) CO_3
 (C) CO_3^{2-}
 (D) H_2CO_3
 (E) $H_3CO_3^+$

62. $\quad \ldots MgCl_{2(aq)} + \ldots NH_{3(aq)} + \ldots H_2O \rightarrow$

 Which of the following is one of the products obtained from the reaction above?

 (A) Mg_3N_2
 (B) MgH_2
 (C) Mg
 (D) $Mg(NO_3)_2$
 (E) $Mg(OH)_2$

63. Petroleum is an important source for all of the following EXCEPT

 (A) Plastics
 (B) Rubber
 (C) Kerosene
 (D) Gasoline
 (E) Propane

64. The method by which we separate a mixture of pure liquids based on the differences in their boiling points is known as

 (A) Condensation
 (B) Distillation
 (C) Fractional crystallization
 (D) Hydration
 (E) Chromatography

GO ON TO THE NEXT PAGE

65. Which pair of ions listed below will form a precipitate when mixed together in aqueous solution?

    (A) Na^+ and $C_2O_4^{2-}$
    (B) Ag^+ and NO_3^-
    (C) Pb^{2+} and Cl^-
    (D) $Mg+$ and $C_2H_3O_2^-$
    (E) NH_4^+ and CO_3^{2-}

66. A certain mass of sulfur required 16 grams of oxygen to be converted into sulfur dioxide, SO_2. If this same mass of sulfur were to be converted into sulfur trioxide, SO_3, the mass of oxygen required would be

    (A) 4.0 g
    (B) 8.0 g
    (C) 12 g
    (D) 24 g
    (E) 32 g

67. The balanced net ionic reaction for the neutralization reaction between solutions of sodium hydroxide and hydrochloric acid is

    (A) $Na^+_{(aq)} + OH^-_{(aq)} + H^+_{(aq)} + Cl^-_{(aq)} \rightarrow H_2O_{(l)} + NaCl_{(aq)}$
    (B) $Na^+_{(aq)} + Cl^-_{(aq)} \rightarrow NaCl_{(aq)}$
    (C) $OH^-_{(aq)} + H^+_{(aq)} \rightarrow H_2O_{(l)}$
    (D) $NaOH_{(aq)} + NaCl_{(aq)} \rightarrow H_2O_{(l)} + NaCl_{(aq)}$
    (E) $Na^+_{(aq)} + OH^-_{(aq)} + H^+_{(aq)} + Cl^-_{(aq)} \rightarrow H_2O_{(l)} + Na^+_{(aq)} + Cl^-_{(aq)}$

68. Which of the following must be true for a system whose equilibrium constant is less than 1?

    (A) It will take a short time to reach equilibrium.
    (B) It will take a long time to reach equilibrium.
    (C) The equilibrium lies to the left.
    (D) The equilibrium lies to the right.
    (E) It requires a higher concentration of reactants to reach equilibrium.

69. An ammonium nitrate product dissolves easily in water at room temperature, and the process causes the solution to become quite cold. Which of the following is/are true about the dissolution of ammonium nitrate?

    I. The process is endothermic.
    II. The solubility will be greater in warmer water.
    III. S^o for the reaction is negative.

    (A) I only
    (B) II only
    (C) I and II only
    (D) I and III only
    (E) I, II, and III

70. Which of the following gases is LEAST dense when all are measured under the same conditions?

    (A) N_2
    (B) $Cl2$
    (C) CH_4
    (D) NO_2
    (E) CO_2

S T O P

IF YOU FINISH BEFORE TIME IS CALLED, YOU MAY CHECK YOUR WORK ON THIS TEST ONLY.
DO NOT TURN TO ANY OTHER TEST IN THIS BOOK.

CHEMISTRY PRACTICE TEST 1 ANSWERS

SAT CHEMISTRY PRACTICE TEST 1 EXPLANATIONS

CHEMISTRY PRACTICE TEST 1 ANSWERS

Question Number	Answer	Right	Wrong	Question Number	Answer	Right	Wrong
Part A				**Part C**			
1	B	—	—	26	E	—	—
2	A	—	—	27	B	—	—
3	C	—	—	28	D	—	—
4	E	—	—	29	B	—	—
5	A	—	—	30	D	—	—
6	D	—	—	31	C	—	—
7	E	—	—	32	D	—	—
8	D	—	—	33	A	—	—
9	A	—	—	34	A	—	—
10	E	—	—	35	A	—	—
11	C	—	—	36	C	—	—
12	D	—	—	37	B	—	—
13	B	—	—	38	D	—	—
14	C	—	—	39	C	—	—
15	D	—	—	40	E	—	—
16	E	—	—	41	C	—	—
17	D	—	—	42	B	—	—
18	C	—	—	43	E	—	—
19	E	—	—	44	E	—	—
20	D	—	—	45	E	—	—
21	A	—	—	46	A	—	—
22	D	—	—	47	B	—	—
23	E	—	—	48	B	—	—
24	C	—	—	49	A	—	—
25	B	—	—	50	C	—	—
Part B				51	C	—	—
101	T T	—	—	52	B	—	—
102	T T CE	—	—	53	C	—	—
103	F F	—	—	54	C	—	—
104	F T	—	—	55	D	—	—
105	T F	—	—	56	D	—	—
106	T T CE	—	—	57	C	—	—
107	T F	—	—	58	B	—	—
108	F T	—	—	59	D	—	—
109	T F	—	—	60	E	—	—
110	T F	—	—	61	D	—	—
111	T T	—	—	62	E	—	—
112	T T CE	—	—	63	B	—	—
113	T T	—	—	64	B	—	—
114	F F	—	—	65	C	—	—
115	T F	—	—	66	D	—	—
				67	C	—	—
				68	C	—	—
				69	C	—	—
				70	C	—	—

CALCULATING YOUR SCORE

Your raw score for the SAT Chemistry Test is calculated from the number of questions you answer correctly and incorrectly. Once you have determined your composite score, use the conversion table on page 123 of this book to calculate your scaled score. To calculate your raw score, count the number of questions you answered correctly:

_____
A

Count the number of questions you answered incorrectly, and multiply that number by $\frac{1}{4}$:

$$\underline{}_{B} \times \frac{1}{4} = \underline{}_{C}$$

Subtract the value in field C from the value in field A:

_____
D

Round the number in field D to the nearest whole number. This is your raw score:

_____
E

PART A

The first 25 questions on this exam are classification set questions. These should be some of the easier points to obtain on the exam. You need to read only one set of answer choices to complete several questions. Approach these questions by reading all of the choices, read each statement that follows, answer, and then match your answer with the best answer choice.

1. **B**   Atomic Structure, Formula Writing
The correct formula is BeF_2 since Be is in group 2A and has a charge of $+2$, while F is in group 7A and has a charge of -1. This means that the compound has the formula AB_2.

2. **A**   Atomic Structure, Formula Writing
The correct formula is NH_4Cl. Ammonium has a charge of $+1$; this is a polyatomic ion, and its charge was provided. Cl is in group 7A and has a charge of -1. This means that the compound has the formula AB.

3. **C**   Atomic Structure, Formula Writing
The correct formula is H_2S. Hydrogen is considered to be in group 1A and has a $+1$ charge in its cationic form. Sulfur is in group 6A and most commonly has a -2 charge. This means that the compound has the formula A_2B.

4. E   Atomic Structure, Formula Writing

The correct formula is Al_2O_3. Al is in group 3A and has a charge of $+3$ while O is in group 6A with a charge of -2. The lowest common multiple of 2 and 3 is 6. Each element must then have a subscript to achieve a total of 6. This means that the compound has the formula A_2B_3.

5. A   Thermodynamics and Equilibrium, Energy Diagram

To be successful on this series of questions, you could label the diagram with the reactants, products, activation energy, and ΔH before beginning. Remember that the activation energy is the energy required to get the reaction going: it's the distance from the reactants' energy level to the peak of the activated complex. Letter A represents this distance.

6. D   Thermodynamics and Equilibrium, Enthalpy

The overall energy change in the reaction would be represented by the energy difference between the products and the reactants. If you labeled the diagram, as we suggested, this problem isn't difficult. This diagram represents an endothermic process—the products have more energy than the reactants, so energy was absorbed during the reaction.

7. E   Reaction Rates, Factors that Affect Reaction Rates

A catalyst lowers the activation energy of a reaction. The dashed line represents a lower activation energy barrier, and **E** shows the new, lowered activation energy.

8. D   Laboratory, Equipment

Filtration is the technique used to separate a precipitate from a filtrate (the liquid part of the mixture). Porous filter paper is used to filter the solution.

9. A   Laboratory, Lab Techniques

Distillation is the technique used to separate a mixture of liquids based on differences in their boiling points. In distillation, a device called a condenser is used. A condenser is a glass tube within a tube: the outer tube has cold water circulating throughout it, while the inner tube contains the vapor of one of the liquids in the mixture. The liquid with the lowest boiling point vaporizes first. Its vapor is less dense, so it rises and travels through the inner tube of the condenser. Next it is cooled, re-condenses, and then drips out the other end of the condenser into a collection flask.

10. E   Laboratory, Lab Techniques

A titration is the technique used to determine the unknown concentration of a known acid. Usually an indicator is used that has been carefully selected so that its color change coincides with the equivalence point in the reaction, where moles of acid equal moles of base. From this relationship and from the very carefully measured quantities of both the acid and the base, you can calculate the unknown molarity.

11. C   Laboratory, Lab Techniques

Fractional crystallization is the technique used to separate a mixture of dissolved solids by evaporation. This technique relies on differences in the individual solubilities at different temperatures.

12. **D**   Descriptive Chemistry, Organic Chemistry

The best way to begin this question set would be to draw the structures for each of the choices. An OH group is the functional group of an alcohol; this hydroxyl group gives a compound the ability to hydrogen bond and thus be in the liquid state. Each of the other answer choices is nonpolar and these molecules are held by weak London forces. Remember the general rule of thumb that only hydrocarbon chains that contain five to ten carbons will be present in the liquid state.

A
$$\begin{array}{c} \text{H} \quad \text{H} \\ | \quad\quad | \\ \text{H} - \text{C} - \text{C} - \text{H} \\ | \quad\quad | \\ \text{H} \quad \text{H} \end{array}$$

B
$$\begin{array}{c} \text{H} \quad\quad\quad \text{H} \\ \diagdown \quad\quad \diagup \\ \text{C} = \text{C} \\ \diagup \quad\quad \diagdown \\ \text{H} \quad\quad\quad \text{H} \end{array}$$

C
$$\text{H} - \text{C} \equiv \text{C} - \text{H}$$

D
$$\begin{array}{c} \text{H} \quad \text{H} \\ | \quad\quad | \\ \text{H} - \text{C} - \text{C} - \ddot{\text{O}}: \\ | \quad\quad | \\ \text{H} \quad \text{H} \end{array}$$

E
$$\begin{array}{c} \text{H} \quad \text{H} \quad \text{H} \\ | \quad\quad | \quad\quad | \\ \text{H} - \text{C} - \text{C} - \text{C} - \text{H} \\ | \quad\quad | \quad\quad | \\ \text{H} \quad \text{H} \quad \text{H} \end{array}$$

13. **B**   Atomic Structure, Valence Bond Theory

Once you've drawn each molecule, this question should be fairly easy. sp^2 hybridization occurs when there are three areas of electrons around the carbon center. Since ethene, C_2H_4, contains one double bond between its carbons, it has a trigonal planar arrangement and thus sp^2 hybridization.

14. **C**   Atomic Structure, Chemical Bonding

Acetylene, C_2H_2, which is also known as ethyne, contains a triple bond. The two hydrogen atoms will orient themselves for maximum repulsion; therefore the molecule is linear.

15. **D**   States of Matter, Intermolecular Forces

Water is a polar molecule, and ethanol, C_2H_5OH, is also a polar molecule. Polar molecules have a dipole moment. The other four choices list molecules that are nonpolar and would not be expected to mix well with water.

16.   Atomic Structure, Periodic Trends

In a set such as this, first check and make sure that all of the electron configurations are plausible ones. All of these choices represent elements. Add the total number of electrons and write the symbol of the element next to each one—this will save time when answering the next questions in this series. The ending configuration of $4s^1$ represents an alkali metal—in particular, potassium. Alkali metals are known to react violently with water. Metals also produce basic solutions in water as well as hydrogen gas. See the equation below:

$$2K_{(s)} + 2H_2O_{(l)} \rightarrow 2KOH_{(aq)} + H_{2(g)}$$

17. **D**   Atomic Structure, Electron Configuration

Two elements that have the same electron configuration are said to be isoelectronic. The calcium ion must have lost two electrons to have a +2 charge since calcium metal has

20 electrons – 2 electrons = the calcium ion (Ca^{2+} ion), which has 18 electrons. **D** represents argon, which also has 18 electrons, so this answer choice is isoelectronic.

18.   **C**   Structure of Matter, Electron Configuration and Periodic Properties

Once the elements are identified, this is just a matter of choosing chlorine; you should have memorized the diatomic molecules, and none of the other elements exist as diatomic molecules. The seven diatomic molecules are N, O, F, Cl, Br, I, H.

19.   **E**   Structure of Matter, Electron Configuration and Periodic Trends

The more principal energy levels in an atom, the larger the atom. **E** is the only choice that has electrons in the fourth principal energy level.

20.   **D**   Structure of Matter, Electron Configuration and Periodic Trends

The ionization energy of an atom is the energy that must be expended to remove an electron. Which elements in the periodic table do not want to lose their electrons? Right—the noble gases—group 8A. Argon, with 18 electrons, has a filled energy level and so is in a very stable energy state and will require much more energy to remove an electron than any of the others; thus it has the highest first ionization energy.

21.   **A**   Descriptive Chemistry, Environmental Chemistry

An acid is produced from a nonmetal oxide dissolved in water. Remember that some of the gases in the air that act as pollutants are the SO_x and NO_x gases. SO_2 is the only choice listed that fits this category.

22.   **D**   Reaction Types, Acid-Base Reactions

$Fe(NO_3)_3$ is an acidic salt. In order to be *neutral*, the salt must have been formed from a strong acid and a strong base (or from a weak acid-base that have the same K_a/K_b values). Since you know that nitric acid is a strong acid and $Fe(OH)_3$ is not a very soluble hydroxide (it is a weak base), the resulting salt must be acidic.

23.   **E**   Reaction Types, Acid-Base Reactions

$LiC_2H_3O_2$ is a salt that forms basic solutions. Using the same reasoning as in the previous question, you will know that acetic acid is a weak acid and LiOH must be a strong base since it is in group 1A.

24.   **C**   Reaction Types, Acid-Base Reactions

KCl is a neutral salt. KOH is a strong base, and HCl is a strong acid. Therefore, the salt that they form, KCl, will be neutral.

25.   **B**   Reaction Types, Chemistry of Acids and Bases

Many strong bases have a hydroxide group with a metal cation, as **B** does. The strong bases are those in group 1A and the larger atoms in group 2A with hydroxide. Barium hydroxide is the only strong base in this list.

PART B

By now you are well versed in how these questions work. Remember that to be successful on this type of question, you should read each statement individually and decide whether it is true or false. Then if both statements are true, read the second statement again and see if it is the *reason* the first statement is true.

101. T T   States of Matter, Boyle's Law
Statement I is true. Boyle's law states that increasing the pressure on a fixed amount of gas will decrease the volume when the number of particles and temperature remain constant. Statement II is also true. When kinetic energy is decreased, particles will slow down. However, slowing down gas particles is not the reason for the pressure-volume relationship in statement I. Therefore you should not have filled in the **CE** oval.

102. T T CE   States of Matter, Phase Changes
Statement I is true. You have probably noticed that water droplets form on the outside of a glass of ice water. Statement II is also true. When particles of water vapor in the air hit the cold glass, they will slow down. If they slow enough, intermolecular forces of attraction will take over. As a substance moves from a less-ordered state (gas) to a more-ordered state (liquid), energy will be released. Statement II explains why water droplets form on the outside of the glass beaker, so the **CE** oval should also be filled in for this question.

103. F F   Structure of Matter, Nuclear Reactions
Statement I is false. Alpha particles are the least penetrating form of radiation: these particles can be stopped by paper, skin, and clothing. Statement II is also false. Alpha particles are the largest of the main types of radiation. An alpha particle is a helium nucleus—^4_2He. Since both statements are false, the **CE** oval should not be filled in.

104. F T   Atomic Structure, Periodic Trends
Statement I is false. As you move across the periodic table within a period, the atoms become smaller. The effective nuclear charge increases, the shielding stays constant, and with the same number of energy levels, the nucleus pulls more tightly and thus the atoms become smaller. Statement II is a true statement. Atomic number does increase as you move across a period on the periodic table. Since statement I was false, however, this second true statement cannot be a correct explanation for it. **CE** should not be filled in.

105. T F   Atomic Structure, Periodic Trends
Statement I is true. Ionization energy is the energy needed to remove an electron from an atom. Group 8A, and specifically He, would be the most unwilling to give up an electron; therefore it has the greatest ionization energy. Statement II is a false statement. As you move across a period on the periodic table, the atoms do not have an increased number of principal energy levels; therefore shielding stays constant. Since statement II is false, the **CE** oval should not be filled in.

106. T T CE States of Matter, Periodic Trends and Chemical Bonding

Statement I is true. Other molecules that have a mass near the mass of water are all gases at room temperature. Statement II is also true. Since water is a polar molecule and contains the highly electronegative oxygen atom, hydrogen bonding (a strong intermolecular force) will attract water molecules to each other. Since both statements are true, check to see if statement II is the reason for statement I. In this case, fill in the **CE** oval because hydrogen bonding is the reason for water's high boiling point.

107. T F Thermodynamics, Enthalpy and Spontaneous Reactions

Statement I is true. When a substance evaporates, it must change from a relatively condensed state (liquid) to a very random state (gas), and this change requires the input of energy. Since energy must be put into the system to make this change happen, the reaction is endothermic. Statement II is false. This statement is in direct disagreement with statement I. When a substance cools, molecules slow down and must release energy. Do not fill in the **CE** oval.

108. F T Reaction Types, Acid-Base Reactions

Statement I is false. An example of a nonmetallic oxide would be CO_2. When carbon dioxide dissolves in water, it forms carbonic acid. Therefore, it is known as an acidic anhydride. This explanation shows that statement II is true.

109. T F States of Matter, Graham's Law

Statement I is true. Graham's law states that the rate of effusion is inversely proportional to the square root of the masses of the two gases. Statement II is false, but this is hard to catch. The masses given are for single elements—both of these gases are diatomic, so the masses should be doubled.

110. T F Atomic Structure, The Periodic Table and Properties

Statement I is true. As an atom gains one electron, its size will increase. Statement II is false. The fluoride ion has ten electrons and nine protons. The fluoride ion tends to gain one electron to form an ion; it bears a negative charge.

111. T T Reaction Types, Redox and Electrochemistry

Statement I is a true statement. In order for Al^{3+} to form Al^0, three electrons must be gained; it must be reduced. Statement II is also true, but it does not constitute an explanation for how an aluminum ion forms aluminum metal.

112. T T CE Atomic Structure, Chemical Bonding

Statement I is true: metals are good conductors of electricity. Statement II is also true: it gives a description of metallic bonding. Statement II gives the reason that metals are such good conductors—because of their sea of electrons—so fill in the **CE** oval.

113. T T Atomic Structure, Nuclear Reactions and Beta Decay

Statement I is true. The nuclear reaction shown is properly balanced and does represent the decay of carbon-14. Statement II is also true. A beta particle is shown as a product with nitrogen-14. However, the reason that carbon-14 releases a beta particle has to do with the stability (or lack thereof) of the nucleus. You should not fill in the **CE** oval.

114. **F F**   Atomic Structure, Isotopes

Statement I and statement II are both false. By changing the word *isomer* to *isotope* each of the statements would be true. Isomers are compounds that have the same molecular formula but different structures. These are encountered frequently in organic chemistry.

115. **T F**   States of Matter, Charles's Law

Statement I is true. Charles's law states that as temperature increases, the volume increases when pressure and number of particles are held constant. Gas laws are worked using the Kelvin scale; if the temperature in Kelvin doubles, the volume should also double. Statement II is false. This statement implies that the gas molecule itself changes size—gases are mostly empty space. The space that they must occupy to keep the same pressure must double at the given temperature, but the molecules themselves do not change in size.

PART C

The remaining questions on the test are the traditional multiple choice that you know and love. Eliminate any choices that you can initially, then see which answer choice is most similar to your answer.

26. **E**   Laboratory, Common Lab Techniques

Density is mass per unit of volume. The mass given is 25.200 g. The volume must be calculated. 15.0 mL – 12.5 mL = 2.5 mL. Find the density using the equation $\frac{25.200 \text{ g}}{2.5 \text{ mL}}$ is equal to about 10 g/mL.

27. **B**   Equilibrium, Le Chatelier's Principle

Since X_2 is a reactant, adding more of it will cause a shift in equilibrium toward the products. The only product listed among the answer choices is H_2X, so this is the correct answer.

28. **D**   Equilibrium, Le Chatelier's Principle

Adding an inert gas will not effect equilibrium concentrations since it is not involved in the reaction.

29. **B**   Stoichiometry, Percent Composition

You can solve this problem by putting the total mass of hydrogen in each compound over the total mass of the compound. There is no need to calculate—it should be obvious which fraction is closest to $\frac{1}{1}$.

$$\text{HCl} = \frac{1}{36} \quad \text{H}_2\text{O} = \frac{2}{18} \quad \text{H}_2\text{SO}_4 = \frac{2}{98} \quad \text{H}_2\text{S} = \frac{2}{32} \quad \text{HF} = \frac{1}{20}$$

As you can see, the compound H_2O (water) contains the highest percent by mass of hydrogen among the five compounds listed.

30. D   Equilibrium, Equilibrium Expression

The equilibrium expression is the ratio of products to the reactants, each raised to the power of their coefficients. All substances are in the gaseous state, so all should appear in this expression; knowing this means that you can eliminate **A** and **B**. Only **D** shows NH_3 in the numerator of the expression.

31. C   Equilibrium and Reaction Rates, Equilibrium

When the pressure of a gaseous system is increased, the volume is decreased. The increase in pressure places a stress on the side of the reaction that has the most moles of gas and will shift to the side with the lesser number of moles in order to decrease the stress in the system. The reactant side contains 4 moles of gas and the product side contains 2 moles of gas. Therefore, the shift will be to the products—NH_3.

32. D   Reaction Types, Balancing Equations

The balanced equation should be as follows:

$$4Al_{(s)} + 3O_{2\ (g)} \rightarrow 2Al_2O_{3(s)}$$

Since oxygen had 2 on the reactant side and 3 on the product side, the common denominator of 6 had to be obtained by multiplying by 3 and 2, respectively. This made 4 aluminums on the product side, so place a coefficient of 4 on the reactant side.

33. A   Stoichiometry, Percent Composition

The formula for nitric acid is HNO_3. The relative amount of hydrogen in this molecule is about $\frac{1}{63}$. Make the math easy since you will not have a calculator—round the fraction to $\frac{1}{60}$, which is a bit less than $\frac{1}{50}$, or 2%. Of the five choices, **A** provides the nearest value.

34. A   Equilibrium and Reaction Rates, Equilibrium Constants

Compare equation I and equation II to each other. Equation II is the reverse of equation I and has been doubled. Reversing the equation will give you the value of $\frac{1}{K}$. Doubling the equation raises the expression to 2 exponentially, so the expression should be squared. Since the value of K is 5.0 for equation I, the reverse reaction would give a K of $\frac{1}{5}$; this should then be squared: $\frac{1}{5} \times \frac{1}{5}$; $\frac{1}{25.00}$ is the answer.

35. A   States of Matter, Gas Laws

At STP, 1 mole of any gas occupies 22.4 L of gas. 1 mole of gas = 6.02×10^{23}. The problem states that 3.01×10^{23} molecules of this gas has a mass of 32.00 g, so 0.50 mole of the gas has a mass of 32.00 g. Therefore, we would expect this gas to occupy a volume of 11.2 L at STP. 8.00 g is $\frac{1}{4}$ of this mass, so we would expect that it should occupy $\frac{1}{4}$ of 11.2 L. $\frac{1}{4}$ of 10 would be 2.5—you are looking for an answer that's in this range. **A** is the closest answer, so it is correct.

36. **C**   Reaction Types, Balancing Equations
The balanced equation should be as follows:

$$3KOH_{(aq)} + H_3PO_{4(aq)} \rightarrow K_3PO_{4(aq)} + 3H_2O$$

Counting the hydrogens here is a bit tricky. By placing a 3 in front of KOH, you are left with 6 total H's on the reactant side (3 from KOH and 3 from H_3PO_4). Since H's are found only in water on the product side, you need to give water a coefficient of 3, resulting in 6 hydrogens.

37. **B**   Structure of Matter, Atomic Structure
The mass number of silicon is 29; the mass number represents the number of protons plus the number of neutrons. The atomic number for silicon is 14. (You can look this up in the periodic table.) The atomic number of an element is equal to its number of protons. To obtain the number of neutrons, you would subtract the atomic number from the mass number: $29 - 14 = 15$.

38. **D**   Stoichiometry, Percent Composition
To find the empirical formula for a compound, you must set up the mole ratio for each element. Divide each of the moles given by the smallest number of moles and this should give the subscripts.

$$\frac{0.05 \; mole \; Mg}{0.05} = 1 \qquad \frac{0.05 \; mole \; S}{0.05} = 1 \qquad \frac{0.20 \; mole \; O}{0.05} = 4$$

These are your subscripts: $MgSO_4$.

39. **C**   States of Matter, Solution Formation
Statement I is true. By crushing the solid into smaller pieces, you increase the surface area, and the solvent is able to come in contact with solute at a faster rate; thus it dissolves more quickly. Statement II is a true statement. By stirring the mixture, you bring solute and solvent in contact with each other more often, and the solid will dissolve more quickly. Statement III is false. When the temperature of the system is lowered, the molecules move more slowly, which prevents the solute and solvent from making contact as often. Since only statements I and II are true, the correct answer is **C**.

40. **E**   Reaction Types, Balancing Equations
The balanced equation should be as follows:

$$2C_6H_{14} + 19O_2 \rightarrow 12CO_2 + 14H_2O$$

In this equation, begin by balancing the carbons so you have six on each side, but then you'll end up with an odd number of oxygens. When this happens, the trick is to double the hydrocarbon number and start over. When you're done, make sure you can't reduce them all by a common number.

41. **C**   Reactions Type, Conjugate Acid-Base Pairs
First write the reaction and determine what you're starting with:

KOH	+	HCl	$\rightarrow$	KCl	+	H_2O
0.400 M		0.100 M				
?		200 mL				

This represents a reaction between a strong acid and a strong base. When the moles of acid equal the moles of base, the reaction will have a pH of 7.00. In this case, the KOH is 4 times more concentrated than the HCl, so it should take only $\frac{1}{4}$ the volume to obtain an equal number of moles: $\frac{200}{4}$ = 50 mL.

42. **B**   Stoichiometry, Limiting Reagents

Refer to the equation $3X + Y \rightarrow Z$. The mole:mole ratio is 3:1:1. The question says you react 2 moles of X with 1 mole of Y. What if you use all of Y? You'd need 3 moles of X due to the mole:mole ratio. You only have 2 moles of X, so X is the limiting reactant, and the answer is **B**.

43. **E**   Stoichiometry, The Mole

A balloon filled with 1.00 mol of CO_2 at STP contains a molar mass of gas in grams (44.0 g/mol), occupying a volume of 22.4 L. This balloon contains Avogadro's number of molecules.

44. **E**   Stoichiometry, The Mole

The easiest way to solve this problem is to figure out concentrations and then match them to the answer.

$$Al_3(PO_4)_2 \quad\quad \rightarrow \quad\quad 3Al^{3+} \quad\quad + \quad\quad 2PO_4{}^{3-}$$

$$0.5 \text{ M} \quad\quad\quad\quad\quad 3(0.05) = 0.15 \quad\quad\quad 2(0.05) = 0.10$$

The only answer that agrees is **E**—0.10 M phosphate ions.

45. **E**   States of Matter, Avogadro's Law

All flasks contain gases that have the same volume, the same temperature, and the same pressure; therefore Avogadro's law indicates that the number of molecules should be equal. **D** and **E** give almost the same answer, but **E** is the best answer.

46. **A**   States of Matter, Graham's Law

Since all of the molecules are at the same temperature and pressure, their average kinetic energy should be the same. Graham's law states that smaller molecules should move faster because they will have fewer collisions. CH_4 is by far the smaller of the molecules, so you would expect that the methane molecules would have the higher average velocity.

47. **B**   States of Matter, Gas Laws

For gases, temperature in Kelvins and volume are directly proportional. The only graph that shows this direct relationship is **B**. **A** would be a good Boyle's law graph (inverse relationship). **E** is a good graph of kinetics data.

48. **B**   States of Matter, The Ideal Gas Law

An ideal gas has no intermolecular attractive or repulsive forces and occupies little or no volume. Statement I is false. The higher the pressure, the more molecules are colliding with each other. Statement II is true. The higher the temperature, the faster the particles are moving. This means that intermolecular forces will have a harder time keeping the particles together. Statement III is false. The more molecules that are in a given area, the more collisions there will be, and the greater the chance for intermolecular forces to take effect. This would not lead to ideal conditions.

49. A   Laboratory, Common Experiments
Write a reaction to see what's produced:

$$AgNO_3 + HCl \rightarrow AgCl + HNO_3$$

$$\text{Net ionic: } Ag^+ + Cl^- \rightarrow AgCl$$

Silver chloride is not soluble. It is a white precipitate. Statement I is true, but statement II is false. (Silver iodide, AgI, is a yellow precipitate.) Statement III is false. No gas is produced in this reaction.

50. C   Stoichiometry, Complex Stoichiometric Calculations
To solve this problem, set up the following table:

Molar mass	16	32	44	18
Balanced equation	CH_4 +	$2O_2 \rightarrow$	CO_2 +	$2H_2O$
Number of moles	0.50 mole	1	0.5	1
Amount	8 g			22.4 L

51. C   Atomic Structure, Electron Configuration
The electron configurations are not written in filling order. Transition elements fill in the d orbital. **A** and **B** are easy to eliminate since they have no d levels in their configuration. **C** is the correct answer. The last level to be filled here would actually be the $3d$. **D** has the $3d$ level completely filled. **E** is written incorrectly—the last orbital should be $4d$ instead of $4f$.

52. B   Reaction Types, Balancing Equations
The balanced equation should be as follows:

$$2ZnS_{(s)} + 3O_{2(g)} \rightarrow 2ZnO_{(s)} + 2SO_{2(g)}$$

Begin by placing a coefficient of 2 in front of ZnO to give you an even number of oxygens on the product side. From here, place 2 in front of ZnS, then 2 in front of SO_2, and finally balance the oxygens.

53. C   Reaction rates, Factors Affecting Reaction Rates
Statement I is true. When temperature is increased, molecules will collide more often. Statement II is true. The faster the molecules are traveling, the greater the force of their collisions and the greater the number of them that can overcome the activation energy barrier needed to become products. Statement III is false. An increase in temperature will make particles become more chaotic, which represents an increase in entropy. **C** contains the true statements.

54. **C** Atomic Structures, Periodic Trends

The second ionization energy is the energy needed to remove the second-most loosely held electron. Use the periodic table to write a simplified electron configuration for each element:

$$Cl \ [Ne] \ 3s^23p^5$$

$$S \ [Ne] \ 3s^23p^4$$

$$Na \ [Ne] \ 3s^1$$

$$Mg \ [Ne] \ 3s^2$$

$$Al \ [Ne] \ 3s^23p^1$$

After writing the configurations, it should be easy to tell that the second electron removed from sodium would come from an inner energy level. The closer the electrons are to the nucleus, the harder they are to remove.

55. **D** Atomic Structure, Periodic Trends

All of the elements listed are in the same family with the exception of hydrogen. Moving down a family in the table, the number of energy levels increases—and so does atomic size. Ions follow the same periodic trends. The largest would be I, which has five principal energy levels.

56. **D** Atomic Structure, Chemical Bonding

BF_3 would have B (3 valence e^-) + F (3(7) valence e^-) = 24 electrons. By placing boron in the middle and the three F's around it, six electrons are used for bonding. This leaves 18 electrons. Place 6 on each F to complete their octet. Boron is an exception to the octet rule and ends up with only six electrons. This structure will be trigonal planar in shape.

57. **C** Atomic Structure, Valence Bond Theory

Methane has four shared pairs of electrons, a tetrahedral arrangement. The hybridization will be sp^3. **A**, sp, reflects a linear arrangement. **B**, sp^2, is characteristic of a trigonal planar arrangement. **D**, sp^3d, is characteristic of trigonal bipyramid. **E**, sp^3d^2, is the hybridization for an octahedral arrangement.

58. **B** Reaction Types, Redox

The best oxidizing agent will be the element that is most easily reduced. Since the elements are listed in order of decreasing reactivity, Au will be the least reactive, so it should be the most easily reduced. **A**, Ca, is the most active and will be the most easily oxidized. **C**, **D**, and **E** are all scattered in the activity series and can therefore be easily eliminated.

59. **D** Reaction Types, Redox

The most reactive metal is Ca. Zn is the closest element to Ca among the choices that are given, so it will react most readily.

60. **E**   Reaction Types, Electrochemistry

The cathode half-cell is clearly labeled in the diagram given. **B** and **C** can be eliminated immediately since Zn is the anode half-cell. Reduction, the gain of electrons, takes place at the cathode. This allows the elimination of **C** since this reaction is written as an oxidation. Of the two choices left, the best choice will be **E**. Copper (II) ions will be fully reduced to copper metal if this reaction takes place at standard conditions.

61. **D**   Reaction Types, Chemistry of Acids-Bases

A Brønsted base is a proton acceptor. Write the equation to see what would be produced with this definition. There's only one choice after seeing it!

$$HCO_3^- \quad + \quad H_2O \quad \rightarrow \quad H_2CO_3 \quad + \quad OH^-$$

base   acid   conj. acid   conj. base

62. **E**   Reaction Types, Types of Chemical Reactions

You're given the reaction $MgCl_{2(aq)} + \ldots NH_{3(aq)} + \ldots H_2O \rightarrow$? Treat ammonia and water like NH_4OH and perform a double replacement reaction. One of your products will be $Mg(OH)_2$ when the formula is balanced.

63. **B**   Descriptive Chemistry, Organic Chemistry

A, **C**, **D**, and **E** are all known products of petroleum, but rubber has traditionally been produced from the rubber plant.

64. **B**   Laboratory, Common Lab Techniques

A, condensation, is the change from gas to liquid. **B**, distillation, is the process of vaporizing a substance and recondensing it to produce pure fractions. This process does separate substances according to their differing boiling points. **C**, fractional crystallization, involves the change of liquid to solid. **D**, hydration, is the dissolving of a substance into water. **E**, chromatography, is the separation of substances based on their polarities to a solvent.

65. **C**   States of Matter, Solutions

Group 1A and NH_4^+ compounds are all soluble. **A** and **E** can be eliminated if you know this rule. **B**, silver nitrate, would be soluble because all nitrates are soluble. **C**, $PbCl_2$, would form a precipitate. Pb, Hg, and Ag are the heavy metals that will precipitate the halogens. **D**, magnesium acetate, will be soluble because acetates are very soluble.

66. **D**   Stoichiometry, Complex Stoichiometric Calculations

This problem requires that you write two balanced equations. The first equation is the formation of SO_2:

$$S + O_2 \rightarrow SO_2$$
$$16 \text{ g}$$

Since sulfur and oxygen, O_2, have the same molecular masses, this reaction should require 16 grams of sulfur. This same amount of sulfur was used in the following reaction:

$$2S + 3O_2 \rightarrow 2S_2$$
$$16 \text{ g}$$

The question here is the amount of oxygen needed. The ratio is not 1:1, so try to simplify.

Molar mass	32	32	80
Balanced equation	2S +	$3O_2 \rightarrow$	$2SO_3$
Number of moles	0.5 moles	1.5	0.5
Amount	16 g	24 g	

67. **C** Reaction types, Net Ionic Reactions

You must apply the solubility rules and realize that both the acid and base are strong, so they completely ionize. Next you must realize that the salt formed is soluble, so the ions forming the salt are both spectator ions. Here's the reaction: $OH^-_{(aq)} + H^+_{(aq)} \rightarrow H_2O_{(l)}$.

68. **C** Equilibrium

If the value of K is small, meaning less than 1, then the concentration of reactants is greater at equilibrium; thus the equilibrium lies to the left. K has nothing to do with the time that a reaction takes to reach equilibrium.

69. **C** Thermodynamics, Enthalpy

When a solution becomes cold over the course of a reaction, the reaction is endothermic, so statement I is true. Statement II is also true: energy is a reactant in an endothermic reaction, so increasing the temperature would result in more products. Statement III is false. Because $\Delta S°$ is entropy, the two driving forces of a chemical reaction are enthalpy and entropy. Exothermic reactions are favored—since this reaction is endothermic, entropy must be the driving force, and thus disorder must be increasing. Increasing entropy would have a positive value. The answer is **C**.

70. **C** States of Matter, Density of Gases

Density is a measure of mass per unit volume. When you are dealing with gases, the units of density are usually grams per liter. Since all gases are measured under the same conditions, the only difference would be the mass. The masses are 28, 71, 16, 46, and 44, respectively. Therefore, methane, CH_4, would be the least dense of the choices since it has the least mass.

SAT* CHEMISTRY PRACTICE TEST 2

SAT CHEMISTRY PRACTICE TEST 2 ANSWER SHEET

1. Ⓐ Ⓑ Ⓒ Ⓓ Ⓔ	25. Ⓐ Ⓑ Ⓒ Ⓓ Ⓔ	49. Ⓐ Ⓑ Ⓒ Ⓓ Ⓔ
2. Ⓐ Ⓑ Ⓒ Ⓓ Ⓔ	26. Ⓐ Ⓑ Ⓒ Ⓓ Ⓔ	50. Ⓐ Ⓑ Ⓒ Ⓓ Ⓔ
3. Ⓐ Ⓑ Ⓒ Ⓓ Ⓔ	27. Ⓐ Ⓑ Ⓒ Ⓓ Ⓔ	51. Ⓐ Ⓑ Ⓒ Ⓓ Ⓔ
4. Ⓐ Ⓑ Ⓒ Ⓓ Ⓔ	28. Ⓐ Ⓑ Ⓒ Ⓓ Ⓔ	52. Ⓐ Ⓑ Ⓒ Ⓓ Ⓔ
5. Ⓐ Ⓑ Ⓒ Ⓓ Ⓔ	29. Ⓐ Ⓑ Ⓒ Ⓓ Ⓔ	53. Ⓐ Ⓑ Ⓒ Ⓓ Ⓔ
6. Ⓐ Ⓑ Ⓒ Ⓓ Ⓔ	30. Ⓐ Ⓑ Ⓒ Ⓓ Ⓔ	54. Ⓐ Ⓑ Ⓒ Ⓓ Ⓔ
7. Ⓐ Ⓑ Ⓒ Ⓓ Ⓔ	31. Ⓐ Ⓑ Ⓒ Ⓓ Ⓔ	55. Ⓐ Ⓑ Ⓒ Ⓓ Ⓔ
8. Ⓐ Ⓑ Ⓒ Ⓓ Ⓔ	32. Ⓐ Ⓑ Ⓒ Ⓓ Ⓔ	56. Ⓐ Ⓑ Ⓒ Ⓓ Ⓔ
9. Ⓐ Ⓑ Ⓒ Ⓓ Ⓔ	33. Ⓐ Ⓑ Ⓒ Ⓓ Ⓔ	57. Ⓐ Ⓑ Ⓒ Ⓓ Ⓔ
10. Ⓐ Ⓑ Ⓒ Ⓓ Ⓔ	34. Ⓐ Ⓑ Ⓒ Ⓓ Ⓔ	58. Ⓐ Ⓑ Ⓒ Ⓓ Ⓔ
11. Ⓐ Ⓑ Ⓒ Ⓓ Ⓔ	35. Ⓐ Ⓑ Ⓒ Ⓓ Ⓔ	59. Ⓐ Ⓑ Ⓒ Ⓓ Ⓔ
12. Ⓐ Ⓑ Ⓒ Ⓓ Ⓔ	36. Ⓐ Ⓑ Ⓒ Ⓓ Ⓔ	60. Ⓐ Ⓑ Ⓒ Ⓓ Ⓔ
13. Ⓐ Ⓑ Ⓒ Ⓓ Ⓔ	37. Ⓐ Ⓑ Ⓒ Ⓓ Ⓔ	61. Ⓐ Ⓑ Ⓒ Ⓓ Ⓔ
14. Ⓐ Ⓑ Ⓒ Ⓓ Ⓔ	38. Ⓐ Ⓑ Ⓒ Ⓓ Ⓔ	62. Ⓐ Ⓑ Ⓒ Ⓓ Ⓔ
15. Ⓐ Ⓑ Ⓒ Ⓓ Ⓔ	39. Ⓐ Ⓑ Ⓒ Ⓓ Ⓔ	63. Ⓐ Ⓑ Ⓒ Ⓓ Ⓔ
16. Ⓐ Ⓑ Ⓒ Ⓓ Ⓔ	40. Ⓐ Ⓑ Ⓒ Ⓓ Ⓔ	64. Ⓐ Ⓑ Ⓒ Ⓓ Ⓔ
17. Ⓐ Ⓑ Ⓒ Ⓓ Ⓔ	41. Ⓐ Ⓑ Ⓒ Ⓓ Ⓔ	65. Ⓐ Ⓑ Ⓒ Ⓓ Ⓔ
18. Ⓐ Ⓑ Ⓒ Ⓓ Ⓔ	42. Ⓐ Ⓑ Ⓒ Ⓓ Ⓔ	66. Ⓐ Ⓑ Ⓒ Ⓓ Ⓔ
19. Ⓐ Ⓑ Ⓒ Ⓓ Ⓔ	43. Ⓐ Ⓑ Ⓒ Ⓓ Ⓔ	67. Ⓐ Ⓑ Ⓒ Ⓓ Ⓔ
20. Ⓐ Ⓑ Ⓒ Ⓓ Ⓔ	44. Ⓐ Ⓑ Ⓒ Ⓓ Ⓔ	68. Ⓐ Ⓑ Ⓒ Ⓓ Ⓔ
21. Ⓐ Ⓑ Ⓒ Ⓓ Ⓔ	45. Ⓐ Ⓑ Ⓒ Ⓓ Ⓔ	69. Ⓐ Ⓑ Ⓒ Ⓓ Ⓔ
22. Ⓐ Ⓑ Ⓒ Ⓓ Ⓔ	46. Ⓐ Ⓑ Ⓒ Ⓓ Ⓔ	70. Ⓐ Ⓑ Ⓒ Ⓓ Ⓔ
23. Ⓐ Ⓑ Ⓒ Ⓓ Ⓔ	47. Ⓐ Ⓑ Ⓒ Ⓓ Ⓔ	
24. Ⓐ Ⓑ Ⓒ Ⓓ Ⓔ	48. Ⓐ Ⓑ Ⓒ Ⓓ Ⓔ	

Chemistry

	I	II	CE
101.	Ⓣ Ⓕ	Ⓣ Ⓕ	◯
102.	Ⓣ Ⓕ	Ⓣ Ⓕ	◯
103.	Ⓣ Ⓕ	Ⓣ Ⓕ	◯
104.	Ⓣ Ⓕ	Ⓣ Ⓕ	◯
105.	Ⓣ Ⓕ	Ⓣ Ⓕ	◯
106.	Ⓣ Ⓕ	Ⓣ Ⓕ	◯
107.	Ⓣ Ⓕ	Ⓣ Ⓕ	◯
108.	Ⓣ Ⓕ	Ⓣ Ⓕ	◯
109.	Ⓣ Ⓕ	Ⓣ Ⓕ	◯
110.	Ⓣ Ⓕ	Ⓣ Ⓕ	◯
111.	Ⓣ Ⓕ	Ⓣ Ⓕ	◯
112.	Ⓣ Ⓕ	Ⓣ Ⓕ	◯
113.	Ⓣ Ⓕ	Ⓣ Ⓕ	◯
114.	Ⓣ Ⓕ	Ⓣ Ⓕ	◯
115.	Ⓣ Ⓕ	Ⓣ Ⓕ	◯

THE PERIODIC TABLE OF ELEMENTS

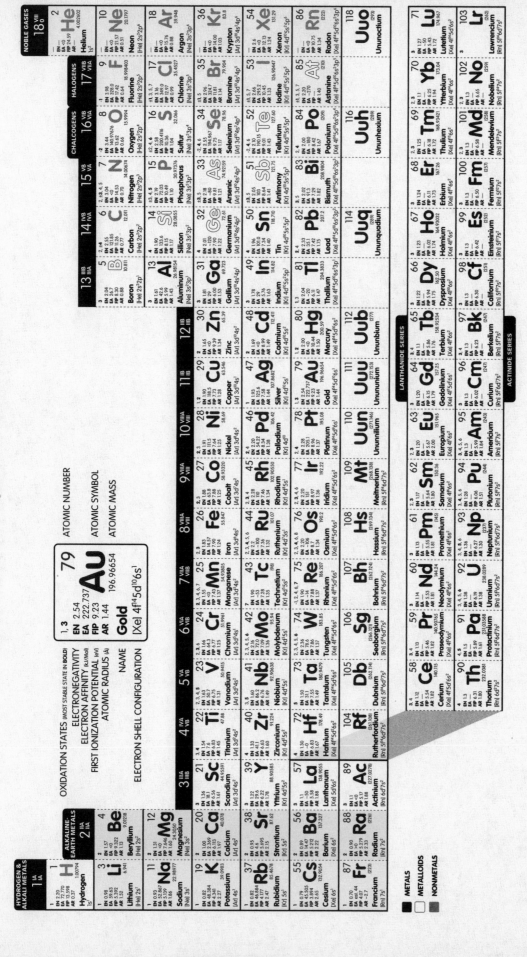

SAT CHEMISTRY PRACTICE TEST 2

Time—1 hour

<u>Note:</u> For all questions involving solutions and/or chemical equations, assume that the system is in pure water unless otherwise stated.

Part A

<u>Directions:</u> Each set of lettered choices below refers to the numbered questions or statements immediately following it. Select the one lettered choice that best answers each question or best fits each statement, and then fill in the corresponding oval on the answer sheet. <u>A choice may be used once, more than once, or not at all in each set.</u>

<u>Questions 1–5</u>

(A) K
(B) Ca
(C) Br
(D) Kr
(E) Zn

1. Which element has the smallest atomic radii?

2. Which element has the highest electronegativity?

3. Which element has the largest electron affinity?

4. Which element has the largest first ionization energy?

5. Which element reacts most explosively in water?

<u>Questions 6–10</u>

(A) Nonpolar covalent substance
(B) Polar covalent substance
(C) Ionic substance
(D) Metallic substance
(E) Noble gas

6. Solid magnesium carbonate

7. Ammonia gas

8. Tungsten filament

9. Exists as cations with delocalized electrons

10. Emits energy in the form of bright red light when an electric current is passed through a confined gaseous sample

<u>Questions 11–15</u> refer to the following segments on the heating curve for water:

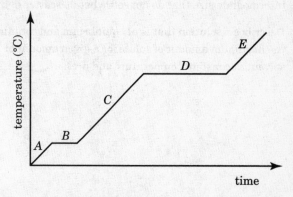

11. Corresponds to 0°C when the pressure of the system is held constant at 1.0 atm

12. The part of the curve that represents only the vapor phase when the pressure of the system is held constant at 1.0 atm

13. The part of the curve where the energy changes can be calculated using the formula $q = mc_{steam}T$

14. The part of the curve that represents the following chemical equation:

$$H_2O_{(g)} \rightarrow H_2O_{(l)}$$

15. The part of the curve that corresponds to the greatest change in the average kinetic energy of the molecules

GO ON TO THE NEXT PAGE

Questions 16–19

    (A) Miscible
    (B) Suspension
    (C) Colloid
    (D) Saturated
    (E) Supersaturated

16. Describes a solution that contains more solute than it should theoretically be able to hold at a given temperature

17. A mixture from which some of the solute particles will settle on standing

18. Describes a solution containing solute particles of intermediate size that do not settle but do scatter light

19. Describes a solution that is at equilibrium and contains the maximum amount of solute for a given amount of solvent at constant temperature and pressure

Questions 20–25 refer to the five types of chemical reactions listed below:

    (A) Decomposition
    (B) Synthesis
    (C) Combustion
    (D) Single replacement
    (E) Double replacement

20. Octane burns in air.

21. Two aqueous solutions are mixed and a precipitate is formed.

22. A solid piece of silver metal reacts with oxygen in the air and tarnishes.

23. An electric current is sent through a sample of water.

24. An iron nail, solid iron metal, rusts.

25. A solid piece of sodium reacts violently with water.

GO ON TO THE NEXT PAGE

SAT CHEMISTRY PRACTICE TEST 2—*Continued*

PLEASE GO TO THE SPECIAL SECTION OF YOUR ANSWER SHEET LABELED CHEMISTRY AND ANSWER QUESTIONS 101–115 ACCORDING TO THE FOLLOWING DIRECTIONS.

Part B

<u>Directions:</u> Each question below consists of two statements, statement I in the left-hand column and statement II in the right-hand column. For each question, determine whether statement I is true or false <u>and</u> whether statement II is true or false and fill in the corresponding T or F ovals on your answer sheet. <u>Fill in oval **CE** only if statement II is a correct explanation of statement I.</u>

EXAMPLES:

	I		II
EX 1.	H_2SO_4 is a strong acid	BECAUSE	H_2SO_4 contains sulfur.
EX 2.	An atom of oxygen is electrically neutral	BECAUSE	an oxygen atom contains an equal number of protos and electrons.

SAMPLE ANSWERS

	I	II	CE
EX 1	● Ⓕ	● Ⓕ	○
EX 2	● Ⓕ	● Ⓕ	●

	I		II
101.	After a period of time in a closed container, the rate of evaporation of a liquid will equal the rate of condensation	BECAUSE	an equilibrium will be established between a liquid and its vapor in a closed container held at constant temperature.
102.	Water boils below 100°C at high altitudes	BECAUSE	atmospheric pressure is inversely related to altitude.
103.	The temperature of a substance always increases as heat energy is added to the system	BECAUSE	the average kinetic energy of the particles in the system increases with an increase in temperature.
104.	Gases are more easily compressed than liquids	BECAUSE	gases expand to fill their container.
105.	$MgCl_2$ is the correct formula for magnesium chloride	BECAUSE	chlorine is always diatomic.
106.	In general, within a family, boiling point increases with increasing molecular mass	BECAUSE	the larger a molecule, the more likely its electron cloud is to polarize and establish dispersion intermolecular forces.

GO ON TO THE NEXT PAGE ➡

	I		II
107.	A spontaneous reaction is always exothermic	BECAUSE	exothermic reactions release energy from the system.
108.	The rate of a chemical reaction is affected by temperature	BECAUSE	an increase in temperature causes more effective collisions to occur between the particles reacting.
109.	Zinc metal is the reducing agent in the following reaction: $Cu^{2+}_{(aq)} + Zn_{(s)} \rightarrow Cu_{(s)} + Zn^{2+}_{(aq)}$	BECAUSE	the reducing agent causes reduction but is itself oxidized in an oxidation-reduction reaction.
110.	A large value for the equilibrium constant indicates that products are favored at equilibrium	BECAUSE	the ratio of products to reactants at equilibrium is always greater than one.
111.	The freezing of water is an exothermic process	BECAUSE	energy is lost when covalent bonds are formed.
112.	Ionic compounds only dissolve in water	BECAUSE	hydration is the process of dissolving an ionic solid in water.
113.	O_2 contains a double bond	BECAUSE	O_2 is diatomic.
114.	The electronic geometry of the ammonia molecule is tetrahedral	BECAUSE	ammonia obeys the octet rule.
115.	The molecular geometry of a CO_2 molecule is linear	BECAUSE	all molecules having only three atoms form bond angles of 180°.

GO ON TO THE NEXT PAGE

Part C

> Directions: Each of the questions or incomplete statements below is followed by five suggested answers or completions. Select the one choice that is best in each case and then fill in the corresponding oval on the answer sheet.

26. Which of the following is a correct electron configuration for a molecule known to form a diatomic gas?

(A) $1s^2 2s^2 2p^6 3s^2 3p^2$
(B) $1s^2 2s^2 2p^6 3s^3 3p^4$
(C) $1s^2 2s^2 2p^6 3s^5 3p^2$
(D) $1s^2 2s^2 2p^6 3s^2 3p^5$
(E) $1s^2 2s^2 2p^6 3s^6 3p^1$

27. Which of the following is the density of nitrogen at STP?

(A) 0.33 g/L
(B) 0.65 g/L
(C) 0.80 g/L
(D) 1.25 g/L
(E) 1.60 g/L

28. The hydrogen sulfate or bisulfate ion, HSO_4^-, can act as either an acid or a base in water solution. In which of the following equations does HSO_4^- act as an acid?

(A) $HSO_4^- + H_2O \rightarrow H_2SO_4 + OH^-$
(B) $HSO_4^- + H_3O^+ \rightarrow SO_3 + 2H_2O$
(C) $HSO_4^- + OH^- \rightarrow H_2SO_4 + O^{2-}$
(D) $HSO_4^- + H_2O \rightarrow SO_4^{2-} + H_3O^+$
(E) None of these

29. Which nuclide is formed as a result of this fission reaction?

$$^{235}_{92}U + {}^1_0n \rightarrow 3{}^1_0n + {}^{139}_{56}Ba + \underline{\qquad}$$

(A) $^{96}_{35}Br$

(B) $^{96}_{36}Kr$

(C) $^{94}_{37}Rb$

(C) $^{94}_{36}Kr$

(E) $^{90}_{38}Sr$

30. A substance contains 35.0 g nitrogen, 5.05 g hydrogen, and 60.0 g oxygen. How many grams of oxygen are there in a 200 g sample of the substance?

(A) 10.1 g
(B) 60.0 g
(C) 70.0 g
(D) 120 g
(E) 140 g

31. The ground state electron configuration of the cobalt atom is characterized by which of the following?

    I.   Partially filled $3d$ orbitals
    II. The presence of unpaired electrons
    III. All electrons paired

(A) I only
(B) II only
(C) I and II only
(D) I and III only
(E) I, II, and III

32. What would happen to the equilibrium system shown here if oxygen were added?

$$4NH_{3(g)} + 5O_{2(g)} \leftrightarrow 4NO_{(g)} + 6H_2O_{(g)}$$

(A) More ammonia would be produced.
(B) More oxygen would be produced.
(C) The equilibrium would shift to the right.
(D) The equilibrium would shift to the left.
(E) Nothing would happen since the temperature is constant.

GO ON TO THE NEXT PAGE

33. You have two samples of the same gas in a 1.0 L container at 1.0 atm pressure. The temperature of the gas in the first container has a Kelvin temperature four times that of the gas in the other container. The ratio of the number of moles of gas in the first container to that in the second container is

    (A) 1:1
    (B) 1:2
    (C) 1:4
    (D) 2:1
    (E) 4:1

34. Which of the following statements about catalysts is INCORRECT?

    (A) They have no effect on the value of the equilibrium constant.
    (B) They increase the amount of product present at equilibrium.
    (C) They provide an alternate pathway for effective collisions.
    (D) They lower the activation energy.
    (E) They are reusable since they are regenerated at the end of the reaction.

Questions 35–36:

Consider the chemical system

$$CO + Cl_2 \leftrightarrow COCl_2$$
$$K = 4.6 \times 10^9 \text{ L/mol}$$

35. What does the value of K indicate about the system once it has achieved equilibrium?

    (A) A great quantity of reactants remain and little product is formed.
    (B) Few reactants remain and a great deal of product is formed.
    (C) At equilibrium, the concentration of the products equals the concentration of the reactants.
    (D) The reaction is endothermic.
    (E) The reaction is exothermic.

36. If the concentration of the reactants were to double while temperature remained unchanged, how would the value of the equilibrium constant, K, be affected?

    (A) K would double.
    (B) K would become half its current value.
    (C) K would quadruple.
    (D) K would remain unchanged.
    (E) K would depend on the initial conditions of the reactants.

37. Argon has a density of 1.78 g/L at STP. Which of the following gases, each considered individually, has a density at STP greater than that of argon?

    I. F_2
    II. H_2S
    III. NH_3
    IV. CO_2

    (A) I only
    (B) II only
    (C) IV only
    (D) I and III only
    (E) II and IV only

38. Which of the following combinations represents a 2⁺ ion having a mass number of 40?

	Protons	Electrons	Neutrons
(A)	18	17	22
(B)	18	17	23
(C)	19	20	21
(D)	20	18	20
(E)	20	20	20

39. Which factor listed below is most important in determining the strength of an oxyacid?

    (A) The size of the molecule
    (B) The molecular mass of the molecule
    (C) The identity of the central atom in the molecule
    (D) The number of oxygen atoms present in the molecule
    (E) The ability of the molecule to vaporize

40. In the Lewis dot formula for NH_3, how many unshared pairs of electrons are in the outer shell of the central nitrogen atom?

    (A) 0
    (B) 1
    (C) 2
    (D) 4
    (E) 6

41. Which of the following would give the highest pH when dissolved in water to form a 0.10 M solution?

    (A) A strong acid
    (B) A weak acid
    (C) The sodium salt of a strong acid
    (D) The ammonium salt of a strong acid
    (E) The sodium salt of a weak acid

42. Which of the species below, when dissolved in H_2O, will NOT produce a basic solution?

    (A) MgO
    (B) NH_3
    (C) K_2O
    (D) $Ba(OH)_2$
    (E) CH_3OH

GO ON TO THE NEXT PAGE

43. Consider the following orderings and decide which of them give(s) a correct trend in ionization energy:

    I. $Al < Si < P < Cl$
    II. $Be < Mg < Ca < Sr$
    III. $I < Br < Cl < F$
    IV. $Na^+ < Mg^{2+} < Al^{3+} < Si^{4+}$

    (A) I only
    (B) III only
    (C) I and II only
    (D) I and IV only
    (E) I, III, and IV only

44. Of the following elements, which is most likely to form a negative ion with a charge of 1?

    (A) Ba
    (B) Ca
    (C) Si
    (D) P
    (E) Cl

45. The hybridization associated with the central atom of a molecule in which all the bond angles are 120° is

    (A) sp
    (B) sp^2
    (C) sp^3
    (D) sp^3d
    (E) sp^3d^2

46. The hydrogen halides HF, HCl, HBr, and HI are all polar molecules. The strength of the acid each forms in water is based on which of the following?

    I.   The polarity of the molecule
    II. The size of the molecule
    III. The strength of the bond

    (A) I only
    (B) II only
    (C) III only
    (D) I and III only
    (E) II and III only

47. A sample of ammonia has a mass of 51.1 g. How many molecules are in this sample?

    (A) 1.8×10^{23}
    (B) 3.6×10^{23}
    (C) 9.1×10^{23}
    (D) 1.8×10^{24}
    (E) 3.6×10^{24}

48. Which of these statements best describes a galvanic cell?

    (A) Reduction occurs at the anode.
    (B) Oxidation occurs at the anode.
    (C) Energy is required from an external source.
    (D) The cathode is negative.
    (E) $E°_{cell}$ is negative.

GO ON TO THE NEXT PAGE

49. What is the molar mass of ammonium carbonate, $(NH_4)_2CO_3$?

    (A) 48.06 g/mol
    (B) 96.11 g/mol
    (C) 82.09 g/mol
    (D) 78.05 g/mol
    (E) 192.2 g/mol

50. If the Kelvin temperature of a gas is tripled and the volume is doubled, the new pressure will be

    (A) $\frac{1}{6}$ of the original pressure

    (B) $\frac{1}{3}$ of the original pressure

    (C) $\frac{2}{3}$ of the original pressure

    (D) $\frac{3}{2}$ of the original pressure

    (E) 3 times the original pressure

51. How many grams are in a 7.0 mol sample of sodium hydroxide?

    (A) 40.0
    (B) 140.0
    (C) 280.0
    (D) 340.0
    (E) 420.0

52. Hydrofluoric acid contains what percent hydrogen by mass?

    (A) 1.0%
    (B) 5.0%
    (C) 10%
    (D) 15%
    (E) 20%

53. Determine the coefficient for O_2 when the following equation is balanced in standard form (smallest whole number integers):

$$\ldots C_4H_{10(g)} + \ldots O_{2(g)} \rightarrow \ldots CO_{2(g)} + \ldots H_2O_{(g)}$$

    (A) 4
    (B) 8
    (C) 10
    (D) 13
    (E) 26

54. Which of these types of chemical reactions is NOT a redox reaction?

    (A) Decomposition into elements
    (B) Single replacement
    (C) Double replacement
    (D) Combustion
    (E) Synthesis of two elements

55. Which of the following is paired incorrectly?

    (A) HCl—strong acid
    (B) HNO_3—weak acid
    (C) $Ba(OH)_2$—strong base
    (D) HI—strong acid
    (E) NH_3—weak base

GO ON TO THE NEXT PAGE

Questions 56–59 refer to the experiment shown below in which the molar volume of a gas was determined in order to calculate the ideal gas constant. Throughout the experiment, the temperature was held constant at 25°C, and the atmospheric pressure remained at 760 mmHg.

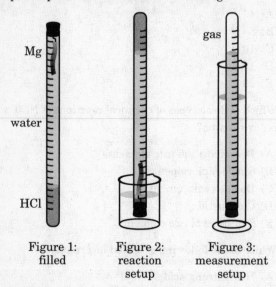

Figure 1:
filled

Figure 2:
reaction
setup

Figure 3:
measurement
setup

56. Which of the following gases is produced as a result of inverting the tube in Figure 1?

$$\text{Hydrochloric acid} \rightarrow$$

(A) H_2
(B) O_2
(C) N_2
(D) CO_2
(E) $H_2O_{(g)}$

57. What is the purpose of the procedure illustrated in Figure 3?

(A) Raising the tube out of the water so that the numbers can be read more easily
(B) Equalizing the pressure of the gas within the tube to atmospheric pressure
(C) Providing more space in the graduated cylinder so that the water displaced by the gas does not cause overflow of water from the graduated cylinder
(D) Checking to see that all of the magnesium ribbon has reacted
(E) Raising the tube so that it is separated from any unreacted acid

58. What is the total pressure of the dry gas collected if the vapor pressure due to water at 25°C is 24 mmHg?

(A) 24 mmHg
(B) 240 mmHg
(C) 736 mmHg
(D) 760 mmHg
(E) 784 mmHg

59. Which of the following, each considered individually, is a possible source of error in the results of this experiment?

I. Failure to correct for humidity
II. The presence of unreacted magnesium
III. Failure to convert the temperature of the gas to Kelvins

(A) I only
(B) II only
(C) III only
(D) I and II only
(E) II and III only

GO ON TO THE NEXT PAGE

60. Balanced chemical equations imply which of the following?

    I.   The number of molecules are conserved in chemical change.

    II. The number of atoms are conserved in chemical change.

    III. Mass is conserved in chemical change.

(A) I only

(B) II only

(C) I and III only

(D) II and III only

(E) I, II, and III

61. The balanced net ionic equation for the reaction of calcium chloride and sodium phosphate contains which of the following terms?

(A) $Ca^{2+}_{(aq)}$

(B) $PO^{3-}_{4(aq)}$

(C) $2Ca_3(PO_4)_{2(s)}$

(D) $6NaCl_{(aq)}$

(E) $3Ca^{2+}_{(aq)}$

62. Assume equilibrium has been reached in the following reaction:

$$A_{(g)} + B_{(g)} \leftrightarrow C_{(g)} + D_{(g)}$$

Upon an increase in the pressure, the system will

(A) shift to the products

(B) shift to the reactants

(C) not change because pressure never affects equilibrium positions

(D) not change as long as the temperature is constant

(E) not change because there are equal number of moles of gas in reactant and product

Questions 63–64

$$C_{(s)} + O_{2(g)} \rightarrow CO_{2(g)} + 394 \text{ kJ}$$

63. Carbon dioxide is produced from carbon and oxygen by the exothermic reaction represented above. When 2 moles of carbon dioxide are produced by the reaction, which of the following occurs?

(A) 197 kilojoules are absorbed.

(B) 394 kilojoules are absorbed.

(C) 788 kilojoules are absorbed.

(D) 197 kilojoules are released.

(E) 788 kilojoules are released.

64. According to the reaction above, what mass of oxygen gas is required to produce 88 g of carbon dioxide?

(A) 12 g

(B) 16 g

(C) 24 g

(D) 32 g

(E) 64 g

GO ON TO THE NEXT PAGE

Questions 65–67 refer to the experiment shown below in which a sample of solid potassium chlorate ($KClO_3$) was heated in a test tube and decomposed by the following reaction:

$$2KClO_{3(s)} \rightarrow 2KCl_{(s)} + 3O_{2(g)}$$

The oxygen produced was collected by displacement of water at 22°C and a pressure of 750 mmHg. The volume of the gas collected was 2.24 L. (The vapor pressure of water at 22°C is 20.0 mmHg.)

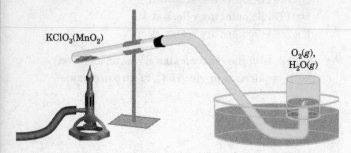

KClO₃(MnO₂)

$O_2(g)$, $H_2O(g)$

65. The partial pressure of O_2 in the gas collected is

(A) 790 mmHg
(B) 770 mmHg
(C) 750 mmHg
(D) 730 mmHg
(E) 710 mmHg

66. If 61.0 g of solid $KClO_3$ (molar mass = 122 g/mol) were to be completely decomposed by this method, what mass of $KCl_{(s)}$ would you expect to remain in the test tube?

(A) 111 g
(B) 74 g
(C) 56 g
(D) 37 g
(E) 19 g

67. Which of the following is NOT a possible source of error in this experiment?

(A) Inaccurate weighing of the KCl
(B) Leakage around the rubber stopper
(C) Failure to correct for the water vapor present
(D) Insufficient amount of the catalyst added
(E) Misreading of the thermometer

68. How many grams of H_2O will be formed when 16.0 g of H_2 is mixed with 16.0 g of O_2 and allowed to react to form water?

(A) 9.0
(B) 18.0
(C) 32.0
(D) 36.0
(E) 72.0

69. Consider the following reaction:

$$2X + Y \rightarrow 3Z$$

3.0 mol X and 2.0 mol Y react to form 4.0 mol Z. What is the percent yield of this reaction?

(A) 50%
(B) 67%
(C) 75%
(D) 89%
(E) 100%

70. When potassium chloride and lead (II) nitrate react in an aqueous solution, which of the following terms will be present in the balanced molecular equation?

(A) $PbCl_{(s)}$
(B) $Pb_2Cl_{(s)}$
(C) $KNO_{3(aq)}$
(D) $2KNO_{3(aq)}$
(E) $2KCl_{2(s)}$

S T O P

IF YOU FINISH BEFORE TIME IS CALLED, YOU MAY CHECK YOUR WORK ON THIS TEST ONLY.
DO NOT TURN TO ANY OTHER TEST IN THIS BOOK.

CHEMISTRY PRACTICE TEST 2 ANSWERS

SAT CHEMISTRY PRACTICE TEST 2 EXPLANATIONS

CHEMISTRY PRACTICE TEST 2 ANSWERS

Question Number	Answer	Right	Wrong	Question Number	Answer	Right	Wrong
Part A				**Part C**			
1	D	___	___	26	D	___	___
2	C	___	___	27	D	___	___
3	C	___	___	28	D	___	___
4	D	___	___	29	D	___	___
5	A	___	___	30	D	___	___
6	C	___	___	31	C	___	___
7	B	___	___	32	C	___	___
8	D	___	___	33	C	___	___
9	D	___	___	34	B	___	___
10	E	___	___	35	B	___	___
11	B	___	___	36	D	___	___
12	E	___	___	37	C	___	___
13	E	___	___	38	D	___	___
14	D	___	___	39	D	___	___
15	C	___	___	40	B	___	___
16	E	___	___	41	E	___	___
17	B	___	___	42	E	___	___
18	C	___	___	43	D	___	___
19	D	___	___	44	E	___	___
20	C	___	___	45	B	___	___
21	E	___	___	46	E	___	___
22	B	___	___	47	D	___	___
23	A	___	___	48	B	___	___
24	B	___	___	49	B	___	___
25	D	___	___	50	D	___	___
Part B				51	C	___	___
101	T T CE	___	___	52	B	___	___
102	T T CE	___	___	53	D	___	___
103	F T	___	___	54	C	___	___
104	T T	___	___	55	B	___	___
105	T T	___	___	56	A	___	___
106	T T CE	___	___	57	B	___	___
107	F T	___	___	58	C	___	___
108	T T CE	___	___	59	B	___	___
109	T T CE	___	___	60	D	___	___
110	T F	___	___	61	E	___	___
111	T T	___	___	62	E	___	___
112	F T	___	___	63	E	___	___
113	T T	___	___	64	E	___	___
114	T T	___	___	65	D	___	___
115	T F	___	___	66	D	___	___
				67	D	___	___
				68	B	___	___
				69	D	___	___
				70	D	___	___

CALCULATING YOUR SCORE

Your raw score for the SAT Chemistry Test is calculated from the number of questions you answer correctly and incorrectly. Once you have determined your composite score, use the conversion table on page 123 of this book to calculate your scaled score. To calculate your raw score, count the number of questions you answered correctly:

_____
A

Count the number of questions you answered incorrectly, and multiply that number by $\frac{1}{4}$:

$$\frac{\quad\quad\quad}{B} \times \frac{1}{4} = \frac{\quad\quad\quad}{C}$$

Subtract the value in field C from the value in field A:

_____
D

Round the number in field D to the nearest whole number. This is your raw score:

_____
E

PART A

The first 25 questions on this exam are classification set questions. These should be some of the easier points to obtain on the exam. You need to read only one set of answer choices to complete several questions. Approach these questions by reading all of the choices, read each statement that follows, answer, and then match your answer with the best answer choice.

1. **D** Structure of Matter, Periodic Trends
All of the elements listed are in period 4. As you move left to right across a period, atomic size decreases as effective nuclear charge increases. Kr, **D**, is the element that lies farthest to the right on the table, so it is the smallest.

2. **C** Structure of Matter, Periodic Trends
Electronegativity is the ability of an atom to attract a shared pair of electrons when a chemical bond is formed. Nonmetals attract electrons. **C**, Br, and **D**, Kr, are the only non-metals listed. Krypton is a noble gas and has a low attraction for electrons. Bromine, **C**, needs one more electron to minimize electron repulsion and have a filled valence shell, so it has the highest electronegativity.

3. **C** Structure of Matter, Periodic Trends
Electron affinity is the attraction that an atom has for electrons, and for the same reasons listed in question 2, bromine is the answer.

4.   **D**   Structure of Matter, Periodic Trends

The first ionization energy is the energy needed to remove the first electron from an atom. Metals tend to lose electrons readily, so traditionally they have lower first ionization energies than do nonmetals. The choice is again narrowed down to Br, **C**, and Kr, **D**. Krypton wins this time. It will take great amounts of energy to remove an electron from a completely filled energy level, and so the answer is **D**.

5.   **A**   Structure of Matter, Periodic Trends

The most reactive metal family in the periodic table is group 1A. The most reactive non-metal family is group 7A. Knowing these two facts, you can narrow the choice to **A** or **C**. Halogens are not known for their reactivity in water. However, **A**, potassium, is very reactive in water. All of group 1A metals are so reactive that they must be stored under oil.

6.   **C**   Structure of Matter, Chemical Bonding

Solid magnesium carbonate, $MgCO_3$, contains a polyatomic ion. This is a dead giveaway that it will bond ionically—the answer is **C**.

7.   **B**   Structure of Matter, Chemical Bonding

Ammonia gas, NH_3, is composed of two nonmetals. It contains covalent bonds. To figure out if the answer is **A** or **B**, you should draw the molecule. The one unshared pair of electrons on the nitrogen atom will make this substance polar.

8.   **D**   Structure of Matter, Chemical Bonding

Tungsten filament is just a fancy way of saying tungsten, which has the chemical symbol W. This metal is found in many lightbulbs and is composed of only one type of metal atom, so it is metallically bonded.

9.   **D**   Structure of Matter, Chemical Bonding

Metallic bonds are characterized by delocalized electrons. The delocalized electrons are what allow metals to be such good conductors.

10.   **E**   Structure of Matter, Atomic Structure

Noble gases are often used for lighting. As the gases are heated, electrons are excited and move away from the ground state position into an excited state. As the electrons fall back into the ground state, energy is emitted, often in the form of light. Neon light has a reddish glow.

11.   **B**   Equilibrium, Energy Diagram

This is the energy diagram for water. Water freezes at 0°C and begins to boil at 100°C. The two plateaus represent these two phase change transitions. Line *B* would represent the freezing point. The line labeled *A* would represent ice at temperatures below 0°C.

12.   **E**   Equilibrium, Energy Diagram

The highest point of the graph would represent the vapor phase. This question is a bit tricky. Read closely: the question asks for only vapor present, so line *E* would be the appropriate choice.

13. **E**   Equilibrium, Energy Diagram

The formula $q = mc_{steam} T$ is specific for steam. Water is in a vapor state (as steam) at line segment E on the graph. Along line D, both steam and liquid water are present.

14. **D**   Equilibrium, Energy Diagram

As mentioned above, line D represents the phase change between liquid and vapor.

15. **C**   Equilibrium, Energy Diagram

Average kinetic energy can be related to temperature change. According to this graph, the greatest temperature change occurs between ice, 0°C, and liquid water at the point of vaporization, 100°C. This segment of the curve has the greatest slope. No temperature change takes place at line segments B or D. Line A and E are not as long as line C.

16. **E**   States of Matter, Solutions

A supersaturated solution is defined as one that is holding more solute than is theoretically possible. This type of solution is created by heating the solution and adding solute at a high temperature. Supersaturated solutions are usually unstable and often crystallize when disturbed.

17. **B**   States of Matter, Solutions

A solution in which particles will settle on standing is known as a suspension. In a suspension, the particles may stay suspended for a period of time but will eventually settle to the bottom of the container.

18. **C**   States of Matter, Solutions

Solutions that contain particles that stay suspended and have the ability to scatter light are known as colloids. The scattering of light is known as the Tyndall effect. Particles in a colloid usually range from 100 to 1000 nm in size.

19. **D**   States of Matter, Solutions

A solution that holds the maximum amount of solvent that it can theoretically hold at a given temperature and pressure is called a saturated solution. In a solution, solute and solvent particles are in a state of dynamic equilibrium.

20. **C**   Reaction Types, Types of Chemical Reactions

Write at least a sketch of the equation described to determine the type of reaction. There's no need to waste time balancing equations in this group of questions since you are just placing the reactions into categories.

$$C_8H_{18} + O_2 \rightarrow CO_2 + H_2O$$

This is a hydrocarbon combustion reaction. Octane is a hydrocarbon—it contains hydrogen and carbon only, and it combusts in the presence of enough oxygen, producing carbon dioxide and water.

21. **E**   Reaction Types, Types of Chemical Reactions

Since a precipitate is formed when two aqueous solutions are mixed, this must be a double replacement reaction. This type of reaction might look something like the following:

$$AgNO_3 + NaCl \rightarrow NaNO_3 + AgCl_{(s)}$$

22. **B**   Reaction Types, Types of Chemical Reactions
Write the sketch of the reaction:

$$Ag + O_2 \rightarrow Ag_2O$$

Tarnishing is the reaction of a substance with the oxygen in the air. Since silver is reacting with oxygen here, this must be a synthesis reaction.

23. **A**   Reaction Types, Types of Chemical Reactions
Write the sketch of the reaction:

$$H_2O \rightarrow H_2 + O_2$$

The electric current passing through water serves to break water apart into its two diatomic elements, hydrogen and oxygen. A reaction in which one reactant produces two or more products is a decomposition reaction.

24. **B**   Reaction Types, Types of Chemical Reactions
Write the sketch of a possible reaction:

$$Fe + O_2 \rightarrow Fe_2O_3$$

In rusting, iron would react with oxygen in the air to produce, among other compounds, Fe_2O_3. When two elements combine, a synthesis reaction has taken place.

25. **D**   Reaction Types, Types of Chemical Reactions
Write the sketch of the reaction:

$$Na + H_2O \rightarrow NaOH + H_2$$

When one element reacts with one compound to produce a different element and a different compound, this is known as a single replacement reaction.

PART B

By now you are well versed in how these questions work. Remember that to be successful on this type of question, you should read each statement individually and decide whether it is true or false. Then if both statements are true, read the second statement again and see if it is the *reason* the first statement is true.

101. **T T CE** Equilibrium and Reaction Rates, Equilibrium
The first statement is true. In a closed container liquid particles will gain enough energy to overcome the intermolecular attractive forces that hold them and escape into the gaseous phase. Once the gas phase is filled with particles, these particles will collide and lose energy and drop back down. This is the premise behind a terrarium. Statement II is true. At a constant temperature the particles will escape and return at a constant rate—this is called a state of dynamic equilibrium. Since statement II is the reason for statement I, fill in the **CE** oval.

102. **T T CE** States of Matter, Phase Change

Statement I is true. At higher altitudes, the boiling point of water will be lower than it is at sea level pressure. Statement II is also true. As altitude increases, the atmospheric pressure drops. Boiling point is the point at which the vapor pressure of the liquid is equal to the atmospheric pressure, so statement II is the explanation for statement I. Fill in the **CE** oval.

103. **F T** States of Matter, Phase Change

Statement I is false. During a phase change, the temperature of a substance remains constant even with added energy. The energy being added is all used to break intermolecular forces so that particles can move between phases, so the temperature does not change. Statement II is true. Particles will have a higher average kinetic energy with an increase in temperature. Since statement I is false, you should not fill in the **CE** oval.

104. **T T** States of Matter, Gas Laws

Statement I is true. Gas particles are mostly empty space and are therefore easily compressible. Liquid particles are very close together; pressure has no effect on a liquid. Statement II is true. Gases do expand to fill their container. With two true statements you must decide if statement II is a reason for statement I. In this case, you just have two separate facts about gases. You should not fill in the **CE** oval.

105. **T T** States of Matter, Formula Writing

Statement I is true. Magnesium has a charge of + 2 and Cl has a charge of –1, so this formula is correct as written. Statement II is also true. Chlorine is one of the seven diatomic molecules on the periodic table. But the fact that chlorine is diatomic has nothing to do with the formula for magnesium chloride. You would not fill in the **CE** oval.

106. **T T CE** Structure of Matter, Periodic Trends

Statement I is true: larger molecules usually have a higher boiling point. Statement II is also true: the change from liquid to gas requires the breaking of attractive intermolecular forces. Larger molecules have more electrons that can polarize; thus they have a greater chance for more attractive forces. Statement II does a good job of explaining the observable trend of the periodic table, so fill in the **CE** oval.

107. **F T** Thermodynamics, Spontaneous Reactions and Enthalpy

Statement I is false. Spontaneity is a measure of free energy, while the state of being exothermic is a measure of enthalpy. Many reactions are exothermic but not all. Remember that the spontaneity of a reaction depends on enthalpy *and* entropy. Statement II is true. Energy is released during the course of an exothermic reaction.

108. **T T CE** Reaction Rates, Factors that Affect Reaction Rates

Statement I is true: temperature does affect the rate of a reaction. When temperature is increased, reactions generally will occur more quickly, and when the temperature is decreased, the reactions will occur more slowly. This is why we store food in a refrigerator. Statement II is true. When the temperature is increased, particles will collide more often and with more force; therefore more particles will have the necessary energy to overcome the energy of activation. This statement does give an explanation for statement I, so fill in the **CE** oval.

109. T T CE Reaction Types, Redox

Statement I is true since the half-reaction involving zinc, $Zn_{(s)} \rightarrow Zn^{2+}_{(aq)}$, is an oxidation, which means zinc metal is the reducing agent (it accepts electrons). Whichever reactant is oxidized causes the other reactant to be reduced. Statement II is thus true and a correct explanation.

110. T F Equilibrium and Reaction Rates, Equilibrium

Statement I is true. The larger the K value, the more products are present at equilibrium compared to the amount of reactants. Statement II is false. The value of K at equilibrium is often a small number, a number less than 1.

111. T T Thermodynamics, Enthalpy

Statement I is true: as molecules come close together and position themselves in fixed, ordered positions, they will lose energy, and this represents an exothermic reaction. Statement II is also true. When two or more elements come together and form a bond, they release energy. The reason bonds form is to minimize energy and become more stable. Statement II does not explain the first statement, however, so you would not fill in the **CE** oval.

112. F T States of Matter, Solutions

Statement I is false. Ionic compounds may dissolve in any polar or ionic substance, according to the "like dissolves like" rule. Statement II is true. When an ionic solid dissolves in water, this is called a hydration reaction. Water molecules actually surround the ions of the ionic compound, pull them apart, and hold them in place within the solution.

113. T T Structure of Matter, Chemical Bonding

Statement I is true. Each oxygen contributes 6 electrons ($2(6e^-) = 12\ e^-$ total). If only a single bond were formed, each oxygen wouldn't be able to have a stable octet, but with the creation of a double bond, the octet rule is fulfilled. Statement II is true. Oxygen is a diatomic molecule. However, the fact that it is diatomic does not explain *why* it is diatomic.

114. T T Structure of Matter, Molecular Structure

Statement I is true. The electronic geometry of a molecule refers to the number of areas of electrons around its central atom. Nitrogen does have four areas of electrons in the ammonia molecule; therefore it is tetrahedral with respect to electrons. Statement II is true. With eight electrons around nitrogen, ammonia does obey the octet rule. However, the fact that it obeys the octet rule is not the reason for its geometry. Do not fill in the **CE** oval.

115. T F Structure of Matter, Molecular Shape

Statement I is true. In carbon dioxide, carbon is the central atom, and the two oxygen atoms on either side are each connected to the oxygen with a double bond. There are no unshared pairs of electrons left on carbon after the two double bonds are created, so oxygen atoms spread as far apart as possible, which gives rise to linear shape. Statement II is false. Carbon dioxide does have three atoms, and it does have a bond angle of 180°. However, there are many other three-atom molecules that have unshared pairs on the central atom that would have different bond angles. One example of this is water, H_2O. It has a bent shape and a bond angle of 104.5°.

PART C

The remaining questions on the test are the traditional multiple choice that you know and love. Eliminate any choices that you can initially, then see which answer choice is most similar to your answer.

26. D   Structure of Matter, Electron Configurations
The only correctly written electron configurations are **A** and **D**. However, **A** is incorrect because Si (silicon) does not form a diatomic molecule. **B**, **C**, and **E** are incorrect because s orbitals can only hold 2 electrons. So, the only correctly written configuration that forms a diatomic molecule is **D** (chlorine, Cl).

27. D   States of Matter, Density of Gases
The density of a gas is measured in g/L. To answer this question, you would first find the mass for nitrogen, N_2, from the periodic table: 2×14.00 g/mol = 28.00 g/mol for diatomic nitrogen. At STP, molar volume for a gas is 22.4 L/mol. Density = $\frac{28}{22.4}$, or just a bit greater than mol. The only possible choices would be **D** or **E**. Of these two choices, **D** clearly provides the value nearest to the value of this fraction.

28. D   Reaction Types, Conjugate Acid/Base Pairs
HSO_4^- can act as an acid and donate a proton to form SO_4^{2-}, so you're looking for the equation that has the sulfate ion as a product, and this is answer **D**. Just to clarify, HSO_4^- can also act as a base in water solution by accepting a proton to become H_2SO_4. Chemical species that do this are called amphiprotic or amphoteric species.

29. D   Structure of Matter, Nuclear Reactions
In a transmutation reaction, the superscripts on each side should be equal, as should the subscripts.

$$^{235}_{92}U + ^{1}_{0}n \rightarrow 3\,^{1}_{0}n + ^{139}_{56}Ba + \underline{\hspace{2cm}}$$

The total for the superscripts on the reactant side is 236. The total on the product side is 142. (This is a bit tricky—the coefficient in front of the neutron multiplies through, so the neutron contributes 3.) This means that the mass number of the missing element is $236 - 142 = 94$. The total for the subscripts on the reactant side is 92, while on the product side the total is 56. Therefore, the atomic number will be $92 - 56 = 36$. This is the atomic number for krypton, so **D** is correct.

30. D   Stoichiometry, Percent Composition
This question looks scary, but the math is not very hard. The mass of the sample is $35 + 5 + 60 = 100$ g, a nice, round number. If it's a 200 g sample, it will contain twice as much oxygen, or $2(60.0 \text{ g}) = 120$ g.

31. **C**   Structure of Matter, Electron Configuration

The ground state electron configuration represents the electrons at minimum energy levels. First write the electron configuration for cobalt. The cobalt atom has 27 electrons, and its electron configuration is $1s^2 2s^2 2p^6 3s^2 3p^6 4s^2 3d^7$. Statement I is true. The $3d$ sublevel is not filled: it could hold a maximum of 10 electrons, but it holds only 7. Statement II is also true. The d sublevel has five orbitals. Hund's rule says that each electron will occupy an orbital and then pairing will occur when necessary. Two of the five orbitals will have paired electrons and three orbitals will have a single electron. Statement III must be false since it opposes statement II. The answer choice that contains I and II is **C**.

32. **C**   Equilibrium, Le Chatelier's Principle

Oxygen is a reactant in this reaction, so if more oxygen is added, the reaction will shift toward the products to relieve the stress put on the system. This means that **A**, ammonia, which is also a reactant in the reaction, would decrease and not increase. The only answer choice that indicates a shift toward products is **C**.

33. **C**   States of Matter, Gas Laws

The Kelvin temperature is directly related to the number of moles of gas present. If the volume and pressure are the same for the two gas samples but the temperature is four times greater in the first container, then the second container must have four times as many molecules as the first to maintain the same pressure. The ratio will be 1:4 (1 molecule in container 1 to every 4 molecules in container 2).

34. **B**   Reaction Rates, Factors that Affect Reaction Rates

You are in search of the one false statement. **A** is a true statement. A catalyst speeds up the rate of the forward reaction and the reverse reaction, and the equilibrium constant of the reaction is unaffected. **B** must then be a false statement since equilibrium concentrations are not affected. **C** and **D** are both true statements. A catalyst gives a reaction an alternate pathway by decreasing the energy of activation. **E** is a true statement. A catalyst is not consumed during the reaction.

35. **B**   Equilibrium and Reaction Rates, Equilibrium

Since the value given to K exceeds a billion, the reaction lies very significantly on the side of the product that is formed once equilibrium is achieved. Recall that the value of K is equal to the following ratio: [product]/[reactant].

36. **D**   Equilibrium and Reaction Rates, Equilibrium

K is independent of either reactant or product concentration alone. It is dependent on temperature, and since the temperature is unchanged in this question, the equilibrium constant, K, will remain unchanged.

37. **C**   States of Matter, Gas Density

To answer this question, you'll need to calculate the masses of the gases given as choices and compare them to the mass of argon. The mass of argon is 40.0 g/mol, and F_2 = 38 g/mol, H_2S = 34 g/mol, NH_3 = 17 g/mol, and CO_2 = 44 g/mol. Carbon dioxide, IV, is the only gas that has a greater mass than argon; therefore it is the only gas with a greater density at STP. **C** is the answer.

38.   D   Structure of Matter, Atomic Structure

The key to solving this problem is to figure out what the answer is before looking at the choices. To have a $+2$ charge, the ion must have two more protons than electrons. The other criterion is that the mass equal 40, and the mass number is equal to the number of protons plus the number of neutrons. There is only one answer choice with two more protons than electrons: it's **D**, so there's no need to calculate the mass.

39.   D   Reaction Types, Chemistry of Acid and Bases

An oxyacid is a polyatomic ion containing oxygen. Oxygen is very electronegative. The more oxygens found in the acid, the harder they will pull the electrons and the easier it will be for the hydrogen to be extracted from the acid. Therefore, **D** is the correct answer. The concentration of hydrogen ions in solution determines the strength of the acid.

40.   B   Structure of Matter, Chemical Bonding

Nitrogen has one unshared pair of electrons after it has bonded with three hydrogen atoms, as it has in ammonia. Here's the Lewis dot diagram:

$$H:\overset{\displaystyle ..}{\underset{\displaystyle H}{N}}:H$$

41.   E   Reaction Types, Acid-Base Reactions

Solutions with a high pH are basic, so this question essentially asks which solution would be most basic. That means that the substance you're looking for should be either a strong base or a salt that was formed from the reaction of a strong base with a weak acid. **A**, **B**, and **D** can be quickly eliminated. Remember that strong bases are oxides and hydroxides of 1A and 2A metals. Since a strong base is not present among the answers, we must look for the salt of a 1A or 2A metal. The sodium salt of a weak acid is our best choice, and the answer is **E**.

42.   E   Reaction Types, Chemistry of Acids and Bases

Keep in mind that alcohols are not bases in spite of their OH⁻ group. Ammonia is the classic weak base, while the other answers are oxides and hydroxides of 1A and 2A metals, which form strong bases in aqueous solution.

43.   D   Structure of Matter, Periodic Trends

Statement I lists elements from the same period, avoiding the p^4 anomaly, so it indeed represents a correct general trend: increasing Z_{eff} corresponds with increasing ionization energy. Statement II is backward since IE decreases as you move down a family, and III is backward for the same reason. The ions listed in statement IV all have helium's electron configuration, so their IE depends solely on the Z_{eff}; the order is correct since the Z_{eff} increases in the series.

44.   E   Reaction Types, Redox

Halogens are most likely to form –1 oxidation states. Number your periodic table as soon as you open your test so that the 1A column is $+1$ and the 2A column is $+2$ until you reach the carbon family, which is ± 4. Then halogens, 7A, are –1, the oxygen family is –2, and the nitrogen family is –3. This will make formula writing and oxidation state questions much easier since these numbers remind you of the most probable oxidation state for that family of elements.

45. **B**   Structure of Matter, Valence Bond Theory

When a molecule has bond angles of 120°, it is trigonal planar. That means it has three sites of electron density: it requires one s and two p orbitals, so it is sp^2 hybridized.

46. **E**   Reaction Types, Chemistry of Acids and Bases

The strength of the acid formed when each of these hydrogen halides is dissolved in water is dependent on the size of the molecule and the strength of the bond in the molecule. For example, the small size of F contributes to the strength of the bond that forms between it and H. F is so strongly attracted to H that the H cannot be easily removed by hydration, so HF remains primarily undissociated in aqueous solutions and is classified as a weak acid. (Statement I is incorrect because halide molecules are not polar.)

47. **D**   Stoichiometry, The Mole

You must know that the molecular formula of ammonia is NH_3, so you can easily calculate its molar mass: round the molar mass of N to 14 and the mass of H to 1, and the molar mass of ammonia is 17. Also estimate 51.1 as 51, and your calculation is 51 g divided by 17 g/mole = 3 moles. 3 moles (6.02×10^{23}) = roughly 18×10^{23}, which is 1.8×10^{24} molecules. The answer is **D**.

48. **B**   Reaction Types, Electrochemistry

Galvanic cells, voltaic cells, and batteries all have a $+E^\circ_{cell}$ and convert chemical energy into useful electrical energy. Rely on the mnemonic devices. <u>Red cat</u>—reduction occurs at the cathode. <u>An ox</u>—oxidation occurs at the anode. The cathode is the positive electrode; to help you remember that you might think of the t in the word *cathode* as a plus sign in the middle of the word. By default the anode must be negative. The only correct statement given is **B**.

49. **B**   Stoichiometry, The Mole

This molecule has 14 atoms; apply the distributive property to find the molar mass of $(NH_4)_2CO_3$. The molar mass is $2(14) + 8(1) + 12 + 3(16) = 28 + 8 + 12 + 48 = 48 + 48 =$ slightly more than 96 g/mol.

50. **D**   States of Matter, Gas Laws

You must combine all of your gas law knowledge here. The combination of P, V, and T into one formula results in the combined gas law.

$$\frac{P_1 V_1}{T_1} = \frac{P_2 V_2}{T_2}$$

To solve the formula quickly, plug in easy numbers. Let all of the first set be values of 1.

For the second set, manipulate the values as the problem tells you to:

$$\frac{(1)(1)}{(1)} = \frac{(P_2)(2)}{(3)}$$

So you get $1 = \frac{2P_2}{3}$, and to solve for P_2, multiply both sides of the equation by $\frac{3}{2}$; your answer is $\frac{3}{2}$.

51.   C   Stoichiometry, The Mole
The formula for sodium hydroxide is NaOH, so its molar mass is $23 + 16 + 1 = 40$ g/mol, and 7 moles $\times$ 40 g/mol = 280 g.

52.   B   Stoichiometry, Percent Composition
Hydrofluoric acid is HF. Hydrogen weighs 1 and fluorine weighs 19, so the percent hydrogen is $\dfrac{1}{\text{molar mass}}$ of HF, or $\dfrac{1}{20} \times 100\%$, which is 5%.

53.   D   Reaction Types, Balancing Chemical Equations
This one is a bit tricky. If you begin with the rather scary-looking C_4H_{10}, then you soon find out that you end up with an odd number of oxygen molecules. That is your signal to double the C_4H_{10} and start again.

   The balanced equation is $2C_4H_{10(g)} + 13O_{2(g)} \rightarrow 8CO_{2(g)} + 10H_2O_{(g)}$, so the coefficient for oxygen is 13.

54.   C   Reaction Types, Redox
All redox reactions involve a change in oxidation state. Let's break it down. Compounds usually undergo decomposition into elements—the oxidation numbers of the elements in a compound are not usually zero. However, the products of a "decomposition into elements" reaction—meaning the elements—have oxidation numbers of zero. This represents a clear change in oxidation state. Next, in a single replacement reaction, an element with an oxidation number of zero is "bumping" out a member of a compound to take its place. The element now has an oxidation state that is *not* zero; again, a clear change in oxidation state. In a combustion reaction, the element oxygen has an oxidation state of zero as a reactant but −2 as a member of either water or carbon dioxide. Synthesis of two elements with oxidation states of zero forms compounds with oxidation states that are rarely zero. The only choice that shows a type of reaction in which there is usually not a change in oxidation state is the double replacement reaction.

55.   B   Reaction Types, Conjugate Acid/Base Pairs
HCl, HBr, HI, HNO_3, H_2SO_4, and $HClO_4$ are the six strong acids. The strong bases are oxides and hydroxides of 1A and 2A metals. HNO_3 is a strong acid, not a weak one, so it is paired incorrectly.

56.   A   Laboratory, Common Experiments
The reaction is between magnesium ribbon and hydrochloric acid. This single replacement reaction is written $Mg + 2HCl \rightarrow MgCl_2 + H_2$. **A**, hydrogen, must be the answer.

57.   B   Laboratory, Common Lab Techniques
Figure 3 shows the adjustment of the tube so that the gas level matches the water level. The purpose of this is to equalize the pressure. Air pressure and water pressure are not the same. Boyle's law is in action in this experiment. The gas that is trapped in the tube will change volume as the tube is moved in and out of the water.

58.   C   Laboratory and States of Matter, Dalton's Law
Recall Dalton's law of partial pressure. The total pressure is given in the paragraph above the diagram, so you'll need to look back to that paragraph—the total pressure is given as

760 mmHg. The pressure of the water vapor at 25°C is given as 24 mmHg. To find the pressure of the hydrogen gas, subtract:

$$P_{total} = P_{H_2} - P_{H_2O} = 760 - 24 = 736 \text{ mmHg}$$

59. **B**   Laboratory, Common Lab Techniques

Statements I and III will result in incorrect final answers for this laboratory exercise, but they are not true sources of error from the lab. However, if there were leftover magnesium ribbon that did not react, this would cause the amount of hydrogen produced to be too low, so **B** is the best answer.

60. **D**   Reaction Types, Balancing Equations

Both the number of atoms, II, and the total mass, III, are conserved in a chemical change. This is exactly why we balance chemical equations, and this is what allows us to perform stoichiometric calculations. Statement I is false. The number of molecules is not necessarily conserved in a chemical reaction.

61. **E**   Reaction Types, Net Ionic Equations

You must know your solubility rules to solve this problem. Calcium chloride and sodium phosphate are both soluble. This is a double replacement reaction, and sodium chloride is soluble, but calcium phosphate is not. The balanced molecular equation is

$$3CaCl_2 + 2Na_3PO_4 \rightarrow 6NaCl + Ca_3(PO_4)_2$$

The balanced net ionic equation is

$$3Ca^{2+}_{(aq)} + 2PO_4^{3-}_{(aq)} \rightarrow Ca_3(PO_4)_{2(s)}$$

62. **E**   Equilibrium and Reaction Rates, Equilibrium

When the pressure of the system is increased, the volume is decreased, and equilibrium tends to shift in the direction that produces the fewer moles. However, in this case there are two moles of gaseous reactant and two moles of gaseous product. Therefore, no shift will occur, and the answer is **E**.

63. **E**   Thermodynamics, Enthalpy

The reaction is written with energy as a product: 394 kJ of energy are produced along with every 1 mole of CO_2. You would expect two moles of CO_2 to be double this number—788 kJ. Be careful: there are two answer choices with this number, so read closely. Since energy is a product, energy is released, and the correct answer is **E**.

64. **E**   Stoichiometry, Complex Stoichiometric Calculations

Setting up a table is helpful in answering this question:

Molar mass	12	32	44
Balanced equation	C^+	$O_2 \rightarrow$	CO_2
Number of moles	2	2	2
Amount		64 g	88 g

194

65. **D** Laboratory and States of Matter, Dalton's Law

Dalton's law of partial pressure states $P_{total} = P_{H2O} + P_{O2}$. The pressure of oxygen will be the total pressure, 750 mmHg – 20 mmHg, the vapor pressure of water at this temperature; 730 mmHg is the pressure due to oxygen.

66. **D** Stoichiometry, Complex Stoichiometric Calculations

To solve this problem, set up a table.

Molar mass	122	74	32
Balanced equation	$KClO_3 \rightarrow$	KCl^+	O_2
Number of moles	0.50	0.50	1.5
Amount	61 g	37 g	

67. **D** Laboratory, Common Lab Techniques

A is a true statement though vague—inaccurate measurements would cause error. Choice **B** is a true statement. This is probably the largest contributor to experimental error in this experiment. **C** would cause an error in the final mathematical answer. **D** would not affect the answer in any way. The reaction would still proceed with or without a catalyst—just at a different rate. **E** would ultimately affect the water vapor that gets subtracted, if it is misread.

68. **B** Stoichiometry, Limiting Reactant

You know this is a limiting reagent problem since you were given two starting amounts, so write a balanced equation and determine the moles of each substance, hydrogen and oxygen. Start by looking at hydrogen: we have 8 moles. Since H:O is 2:1, we need 4 moles of oxygen to use up all of our hydrogen. We do not have 4 moles of oxygen, we only have $\frac{1}{2}$ of a mole, so oxygen is clearly the limiting reagent here. If we use the $\frac{1}{2}$ mole of oxygen, we will need twice as much hydrogen, or 1.0 mole. This produces 1.0 mole of water as a product. 1 mole = a molar mass in grams = 18 g.

Molar mass	2	32	18
Balanced equation	$2H_2 +$	$O_2 \rightarrow$	$2H_2O$
Number of moles	8 moles	0.5 mole	1.0 mole produced
Amount	16 g	16 g	18 g

69. **D** Stoichiometry, Chemical Yield

Percent yield is calculated by this formula:

$$\frac{\text{actual yield}}{\text{theoretical yield}} \times 100\% = \text{percent yield}$$

The amount you calculate using stoichiometry constitutes the theoretical yield of the reaction. The moles of product should *not* go into the table, only the numbers of reactant moles. We'd need 1.5 moles of Y, and we have 2.0 moles, so X is the limiting reactant. With 1.5 moles of Y, the theoretical yield of Z is 4.5 moles.

Molar mass			
Balanced equation	$2X$ +	Y →	$3Z$
Mole:mole	2	1	3
Number of moles	3 moles used	1.5 moles used 2 moles	4.5 moles theoretically produced

Now we can calculate the percent yield. We were told that only 4 moles of Z were produced, so the % yield = $\frac{4}{4.5} \times 100\%$ = about 90%.

70. **D**   Reaction Types, Balancing Chemical Equations

To solve this problem, you must first translate words into chemical formulas, then recognize the reaction as a double displacement reaction, and then predict the products. The balanced molecular equation is

$$2KCl + Pb(NO_3)_2 \rightarrow Pb_2Cl_{(s)} + 2KNO_{3(aq)}$$

The answer is **D**.

THE SAT
MATH
LEVEL 1 TEST

INTRODUCTION TO THE SAT MATH LEVEL 1 TEST

THE KEY TO SUCCESS ON ANY TEST IS PROBABLY CLEAR TO you by now: know your subject. But just knowing the material isn't enough to guarantee a good score on the SAT Math Level 1—if you walked into an exam completely blind, with no preparation besides having read a textbook, and no knowledge of how you'd even be tested, you might spend so much energy trying to figure out *how* to take the test that you'd only get halfway through it.

That's where this chapter comes in handy. First we help you decide which math test to take. We've also broken down the Math Level 1 Test by content and format, giving you a behind-the-scenes look at how your exam is written, organized, and scored. You'll know what to expect before you even enter the testing room.

DECIDING WHICH MATH TEST TO TAKE

Few students take both Math SAT Tests. Instead, you should choose which test to take based on several factors.

Test Content

The two tests cover similar topics, but the Math Level 2 Test covers more material than the Math Level 1 Test does. Level 1 covers three years of college-preparatory math: two years of algebra and one year of geometry. Level 2 assumes that in addition to those three years, you have also taken a year of trigonometry and/or precalculus.

Math Level 1

- Algebra
- Plane geometry (lines and angles, triangles, polygons, circles)
- Solid geometry (cubes, cylinders, cones, spheres, etc.)
- Coordinate geometry (in two dimensions)
- Basic trigonometry (properties and graphs of sine, cosine, and tangent functions, identities)
- Algebraic functions

- Statistics and sets (distributions, probability, permutations and combinations, groups and sets, data interpretation)
- Miscellaneous topics (number theory and operations, logic, series, limits, complex and imaginary numbers, vectors, matrices)

Math Level 2

- Algebra
- Geometry (emphasis on 3-dimensional geometry and transformations)
- Algebraic functions (including logarithmic, inverse, exponential, parametric, and piecewise functions)
- Coordinate geometry (in two and three dimensions, vectors, polar coordinates, parametric equations)
- Trigonometry (including cosecant, secant, cotangent functions, inverse functions, non-right triangles, the laws of sines and cosines, graphs of trigonometric functions)
- Statistics and sets (including standard deviation and regression)
- Miscellaneous topics

College Choice

As you choose between the two tests, keep in mind the specific colleges you're applying to. Colleges with a strong focus on math, such as MIT and Cal Tech, require the Math Level 2 Test. Most other colleges have no such requirement, but some may prefer that you take the Level 2 Test.

If you have the skills to take the Level 2 Test, you should go for it. Some students decide on Math Level 1 because it's easier, even though they have taken a precalculus course. We don't recommend this. Colleges will be more impressed by a student who does fairly well on SAT Math Level 2 than one who does very well on SAT Math Level 1. Also, the friendly curve of the Math Level 2 Test means that if you know enough math to take Level 2, you might very well get a better score than you would on Level 1.

Battle of the Test Curves

The Math Level 2 Test is scored on a much more liberal curve: you can miss six or seven questions and still achieve a score of 800. On the Math Level 1 Test, however, you would probably need to answer all the questions correctly to get a perfect score. If you wanted to score a 600 on either test, you would need around 20 correct answers on the Level 2 Test and 33 on the Level 1 Test. Some students with strong math backgrounds think that they can get a marvelous score on the less difficult Math Level 1 Test while their score on the Level 2 Test will only be average. But if you get tripped up by just one or two questions on the Math Level 1 Test, your score will not be as impressive as you might expect.

If after all this you still can't decide which of the two Math SATs to take, try taking a practice test for each.

CONTENT OF THE SAT MATH LEVEL 1 TEST

The Math Level 1 Test consists of 50 multiple-choice questions covering a variety of topics. Below is a broad breakdown of coverage.

This breakdown is accurate, but it is too broad to help you direct your studying in any meaningful way. That's why we created this more detailed breakdown of the test:

Topic	Approximate % of the Test	Approximate No. of Questions
Algebra Includes inequalities; equation solving; binomials, polynomials, quadratics	30	14
Plane Geometry Includes lines and angles; triangles, polygons, circles	20	9
Solid Geometry Includes solids (cubes, cylinders, cones, etc.); inscribed solids (prisms), solids by rotation	6	3
Coordinate Geometry Includes lines and distance; graphing and symmetry; conic sections (parabolas, circles)	12	6
Trigonometry Includes basic functions (sine, cosine, tangent); trigonometric identities	8	4
Functions Includes basic and compound functions; domain and range of functions	12	6
Statistics and Sets Includes mean, median, mode; probability; permutations and combinations; graphs and plots	2	5
Miscellaneous Includes arithmetic and geometric series; logic; number theory	6	4

Each question in the practice tests is grouped by categories like the ones listed above so that you can very precisely identify your weaknesses and address them.

FORMAT OF THE SAT MATH LEVEL 1 TEST

The SAT Math Level 1 Test is a one-hour test composed of 50 multiple-choice questions. The instructions for the test are very simple; you should memorize them so you don't waste time reading them on the day of the test.

> For each of the following problems, decide which is the BEST of the choices given. If the exact numerical value is not one of the choices, select the choice that best approximates this value. Then fill in the corresponding oval on the answer sheet.

Have you read the directions? Have you memorized them? Good. Now here's some specific information about the test's format:

- The 50 questions progress in order of difficulty for most students: the easiest questions come first, the moderately difficult questions are in the middle, and the hardest questions are last.
- You can skip around while taking the test. The ability to skip the occasional question is helpful, as we explain in the next chapter.
- All questions are worth the same number of points, no matter their difficulty.

THE CALCULATOR

Unlike the SAT, in which a calculator is permitted but not essential to the test, the Math Level 1 Test demands the use of a calculator; some questions on the test are specifically designed to test your calculator-using skills.

It is therefore wise to learn all the essentials about calculators before taking SAT Math Level 1. First, make sure you have the right type of calculator. Virtually any calculator may be used during the test, including programmable and graphing calculators. Laptops, minicomputers, or any machine that prints, makes noise, or needs to be plugged in are prohibited.

Whatever calculator you use for the test should have all the following functions:

- Exponential powers
- Base-10 logarithms
- Sine, cosine, tangent

Make sure you practice each of these functions on your calculator before taking the test. We tell you more about how to use calculators for the test in the next chapter.

SCORING THE SAT MATH LEVEL 1 TEST

Scoring on the SAT Math Level 1 Test is the same as the scoring for all other SAT Subject Tests. For every right answer, you earn one point. For every wrong answer, you lose $1/4$ of a point. For every answer left blank, you earn zero points. These points combined equal your raw score. ETS converts your raw score to a scaled score according to a special curve tailored to the particular test you take. We have included a generalized version of that curve in a table. Use the table on the next page to convert your raw scores on practice tests into an approximate scaled score.

As you can see, this curve is not very forgiving. Getting just one question wrong will lower your scaled score by 20 points. Reiterating what we said earlier, you can miss a bunch of questions on the Math Level 2 Test and still get the same score you would receive on the Math Level 1 Test if you missed just one. For example, a raw score of 41 on the Math Level 2 Test receives an equivalent scaled score as a raw score of 49 on the Math Level 1 Test.

But all is not hopeless on the SAT Math Level 1 Test. On a 50-question test, you could score:

- 780 if you answered 49 right, 0 wrong, and left 1 blank
- 740 if you answered 46 right, 0 wrong, and left 4 blank
- 700 if you answered 43 right, 4 wrong, and left 3 blank
- 650 if you answered 39 right, 8 wrong, and left 3 blank
- 600 if you answered 36 right, 12 wrong, and left 2 blank

These sample scores suggest that when taking the test, you shouldn't imagine your score plummeting with every question you can't confidently answer. Don't get unnecessarily wound up if you run into a difficult question; the key to doing well on SAT Math Level 1 is to follow a strategy that ensures you will see and answer all the questions you can, while intelligently guessing on those slightly fuzzier questions. We discuss these strategies in the next section.

Raw Score	Scaled Score	Raw Score	Scaled Score
50	800	18–19	480
49	780	17	470
48	770	16	460
47	760	15	450
46	740	14	440
45	730	13	430
44	720	12	430
43	710	11	420
42	700	10	410
41	690	9	400
40	680	8	390
39	670	7	380
38	660	6	370
37	650	5	370
36	640	4	360
35	630	3	350
34	610	2	340
33	600	1	330
32	590	0	330
31	580	−1	320
30	570	−2	310
29	560	−3	300
28	550	−4	300
27	550	−5	290
26	540	−6	280
25	530	−7	270
24	520	−8	260
23	510	−9	260
22	510	−10	250
21	500	−11	240
20	490	−12	230

STRATEGIES FOR TAKING THE SAT MATH LEVEL 1 TEST

The best strategy for doing well on the SAT Math Level 1 Test is to . . . know the strategies. Learn the general strategies, then learn the specific strategies covered in this chapter.

Strategy 1: Know What's in the Reference Area.

At the beginning of SAT Math Level 1, there is a reference area that provides you with basic geometry formulas and information. Here's essentially what you'll see:

> THE FOLLOWING INFORMATION IS FOR YOUR REFERENCE IN ANSWERING SOME OF THE QUESTIONS IN THIS TEST.
>
> Volume of a right circular cone with radius r and height h: $V = \frac{1}{3}\pi r^2 h$
>
> Lateral area of a right circular cone with circumference of the base c and slant height l: $S = \frac{1}{2}cl$
>
> Volume of a sphere with radius r: $V = \frac{4}{3}\pi r^3$
>
> Surface area of a sphere with radius r: $S = 4\pi r^2$
>
> Volume of a pyramid with base area B and height h: $V = \frac{1}{3}Bh$

You should know all these formulas without needing the reference area; don't neglect to memorize and understand the formulas because you have the reference area as a crutch. Instead, see the reference area as a hint to you about what formulas are likely to be needed on the test. If you know those formulas without having to flip back to the reference area, you'll save time, which puts you one step ahead.

Strategy 2: Remember the Order of Difficulty.

Imagine that you are taking a test that consists of two questions. After your teacher hands out the test, and before you set to work, a helpful little gnome whispers to you, "The first problem is very simple, the second is much harder." Would the gnome's statement affect the way you approach the two problems? Yes. For a "very simple" question, it seems likely that you should be able to answer it quickly and with little or no agonized second-guessing. You will probably have to spend much more time on a "much harder" question, both to come up with an answer and to check your work to make sure you didn't make an error somewhere along the way.

What about all the other students who didn't hear the gnome? They might labor over the first, easy question, exhaustively checking their work and wasting time that they'll need for the tricky second problem. Then, when those other students do get to the second problem, they might not check their work or be wary of traps, since they have no idea that the problem is so difficult.

The moral here is you should spend less time on the simpler questions that appear early in the test, and devote more time to the harder questions appearing later. Because Math Level 1 questions are ordered by difficulty, it's as if you have that helpful little gnome sitting next to you for the entire test.

Knowing When to Be Wary

Most students answer the easy Math Level 1 questions correctly. Only some students get moderate questions right. Very few students get difficult questions right. What does this mean to you? It means that when you are going through the test, you can often trust your first instincts on an easy question. With difficult questions, however, you should be more cautious. There is a reason most people get these questions wrong: not only are they more difficult, containing more sophisticated vocabulary or mathematical concepts, they are also often tricky, full of enticing wrong answers that seem as if they must be correct. But because the SAT orders its questions by difficulty, the test tips you off about when to take a few extra seconds to make sure you haven't been fooled by an answer that only *seems* right.

The tricky answers seem right because they are actually the answers you would get if you were to make a mathematical or logical mistake while working on the problem. For example, let's say you're flying through the test and have to multiply 6 × 8 × 3. So you quickly multiply 6 and 8 to get 42 and then multiply 42 by 3 to get 126. You look down at the answers, and there's 126! You mark it down as your answer and you get the question wrong. 6 × 8 equals 48, *not* 42, making the correct answer 144.

From this example, you should learn that just because the answer you arrived at is among the answers does not mean you definitely have it right. The SAT is designed to punish those who make careless errors. Don't be one of them. After you get an answer, quickly check your work again.

Strategy 3: Watch the Clock.

There are often several ways to answer a Math Level 1 question. You can use trial and error, you can set up and solve an equation, and, for some questions, you might be able to answer the question quickly, intuitively, and elegantly, if you can just spot how to do it. These different approaches to answering questions vary in the amount of time they take. Trial and error generally takes the longest, while the elegant method of relying on an intuitive understanding of conceptual knowledge takes the least amount of time.

Take, for example, the following problem:

> Which has a greater area, a square with sides measuring 4 cm or a circle with a radius of the same length?

The most obvious way to solve this problem is simply to plug 4 into the formula for the area of a square and area of a circle. Let's do it: Area of a square = s^2, so the area of this square = 4^2 = 16. Area of a circle = πr^2, and the area of this circle must therefore be $\pi 4^2$ = 16π. 16π is obviously bigger than 16, so the circle must be bigger. That worked nicely. But a faster approach would have been to draw a quick to-scale diagram with the square and circle superimposed.

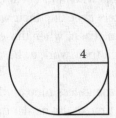

An even quicker way would have been to understand the equations for the area of a square and a circle so well that it was obvious that the circle was bigger, since the equation for the circle will square the 4 and multiply it by π, whereas the equation for the square will only square the 4.

While you may be a math whiz and just *know* the answer, you can learn to look for a quicker route, such as choosing to draw a diagram instead of working out the equation. And, as with the example above, a quicker route is not necessarily a less accurate one. Making such choices comes down to practice, having an awareness that those other routes are out there, and basic mathematical ability.

The value of time-saving strategies is obvious: less time spent on some questions allows you to devote more time to difficult problems. It is this issue of time that separates the students who do terrifically on the math section and those who merely do well. Whether or not the ability to find accurate shortcuts is an actual measure of mathematical prowess is not for us to say (though we can think of arguments on either side), but the ability to find those shortcuts absolutely matters on this test.

Shortcuts Are Really Math Intuition

We've told you all about shortcuts, but now we're going to give you some advice that might seem strange: you shouldn't go into every question searching for a shortcut. If you have to search and search for a shortcut, it might end up taking longer than the typical route. But at the same time, if you're so frantic about calculating out the right answer, you might miss the possibility that a shortcut exists. If you go into each question knowing there might be a shortcut and keep your mind open, you have a chance to find the shortcuts you need.

To some extent, you can teach yourself to recognize when a question might contain a shortcut. From the problem above, you know that there will probably be a shortcut for all those questions that give you the dimensions of two shapes and ask you to compare them. A frantic test-taker might compulsively work out the equations every time. But if you are a little calmer, you can see that drawing a diagram is the best, and quickest, solution.

The fact that we advocate using shortcuts doesn't mean you shouldn't focus on learning how to work out problems. We can guarantee that you won't find a shortcut for a problem *unless* you know how to work it out the long way. After all, a shortcut requires using your existing knowledge to spot a faster way to answer the question. When we use the term *math shortcut*, we're really referring to your *math intuition*.

Strategy 4: Make Your Calculator Work for You.

As we've already mentioned, the calculator is a very important part of the Math Level 1 Test. You need to have the right kind of calculator, be familiar with its operations, and, above all, know how to use it intelligently.

There are four types of questions on the test: those that are calculator-friendly, calculator-neutral, calculator-unfriendly, and calculator-useless. According to ETS, about 60 percent of the test falls under the calculator-neutral and -friendly categories. That is, calculators are useful or necessary on 30 of the 50 questions on SAT Math Level 1. The other 20 questions are calculator-unfriendly and -useless. The trick is to be able to identify the different types of questions when presented with them on the test. Here's a breakdown of each of the four types, with examples.

Calculator-Friendly Questions

A calculator is extremely helpful and often necessary to solve calculator-friendly questions. Problems demanding exact values for exponents, logarithms, or trigonometric functions will most likely need a calculator. Computations that you can't do easily in your head are prime candidates. Here's an example:

If $f(x) = \sqrt{x} - 2x^2 + 5$, then what is $f(3.4)$?

(A) -18.73
(B) -16.55
(C) -16.28
(D) -13.32
(E) -8.42

This is a simple function question in which you are asked to evaluate $f(x)$ at the value 3.4. All you have to do to solve this problem is plug in 3.4 for the variable x and carry out the operations in the function. But unless you know the square root and square of 3.4 off the top of your head (which most test-takers wouldn't), this problem is extremely difficult to answer without a calculator.

But with a calculator, all you need to do is take the square root of 3.4, subtract twice the square of 3.4, and then add 5. You get answer choice **C**, -16.28.

Calculator-Neutral Questions

You have two choices when faced with a calculator-neutral question. A calculator is useful for these types of problems, but it's probably just as quick and easy to work the problem out by hand.

If $8^x = 4^3 \times 2^3$, what is the value of x?

(A) 2
(B) 3
(C) 5
(D) 7
(E) 8

When you see the variable x as a power, you should think of logarithms. A logarithm is the power to which you must raise a given number to equal another number, so in this case, we need to find the exponent x, such that $8^x = 4^3 \times 2^3$. From the definition of logarithms, we know that if given an equation of the form $a^x = b$, then $\log_a b = x$. So you could type in $\log_8 (4^3 \times 2^3)$ on your trusty calculator and find that $x = 3$.

Or, you could recognize that 2 and 4 are both factors of 8, and, thinking a step further, that $2^3 = 8$ and $4^3 = 64 = 8^2$. Put together, $4^3 \times 2^3 = 8^2 \times 8 = 8^3$. We come to the same answer that $x = 3$ and that **B** is the right answer.

These two processes take about the same amount of time, so choosing one over the other is more a matter of personal preference than one of strategy. If you feel quite comfortable with your calculator, then you might not want to risk the possibility of making a mental math mistake and should choose the first method. But if you're more prone to error when working with a calculator, then you should choose the second method.

Calculator-Unfriendly Questions

While it's possible to answer calculator-unfriendly questions using a calculator, it isn't a good idea. These types of problems often have built-in shortcuts—if you know and understand the principle being tested, you can bypass potentially tedious computations with a few simple calculations. Here's a problem that you could solve much more quickly and effectively without the use of a calculator:

$$\frac{\left[\cos^2(3 \times 63°) + \sin^2(3 \times 63°)\right]^4}{2} =$$

(A) .3261
(B) .5
(C) .6467
(D) .7598
(E) .9238

If you didn't take a moment to think about this problem, you might just rush into it wielding your calculator, calculating the cosine and sine functions, squaring them each and then adding them together, etc.

But take a closer look: $\cos^2(3 \times 63°) + \sin^2(3 \times 63°)$ is a trigonometric identity. More specifically, it's a Pythagorean identity: $\sin^2 q + \cos^2 q = 1$ for any angle q. So, the expression given in the question simplifies to

$$\frac{1^4}{2} = \frac{1}{2} = .5$$

B is correct.

Calculator-Useless Questions

Even if you wanted to, you wouldn't be able to use your calculator on calculator-useless problems. For the most part, problems involving algebraic manipulation or problems lacking actual numerical values would fall under this category. You should be able to easily identify problems that can't be solved with a calculator. Quite often, the answers for these questions will be variables rather than numbers. Take a look at the following example:

$(x + y - 1)(x + y + 1) =$

(A) $(x + y)^2$
(B) $(x + y)^2 - 1$
(C) $x^2 - y^2$
(D) $x^2 + x - y + y^2 + 1$
(E) $x^2 + y^2 + 1$

This question tests you on an algebraic topic—that is, it asks you how to find the product of two polynomials—and requires knowledge of algebraic principles rather than calculator acumen. You're asked to manipulate variables, not produce a specific value. A calculator would be of no use here.

To solve this problem, you need to notice that the two polynomials are in the format of what's called the difference of two squares: $(a + b)(a - b) = a^2 - b^2$. In our case, $a = x + y$ and $b = 1$. As a result, $(x + y - 1)(x + y + 1) = (x + y)^2 - 1$. **B** is correct.

Don't Immediately Use Your Calculator

The fact that the test contains all four of these question types means that you shouldn't get trigger-happy with your calculator. Just because you've got an awesome shiny hammer doesn't mean you should try to use it to pound in thumbtacks. Using your calculator to try to answer every question on the test would be just as unhelpful.

Instead of reaching instinctively for your calculator, first take a brief look at each question and understand exactly what it's asking you to do. That short pause will save you a great deal of time later on. For example, what if you came upon the question:

If $(3, y)$ is a point on the graph of $f(x) = \dfrac{x^2 - 5x + 4}{11x - 44}$, then what is y?

(A) −3

(B) −1.45

(C) 0

(D) .182

(E) 4.87

A trigger-happy calculator user might immediately plug in 3 for x. But the student who takes a moment to think about the problem will probably see that the calculation would be much simpler if the function were simplified first. To start, factor 11 out of the denominator:

$$f(x) = \frac{x^2 - 5x + 4}{11x - 44} = \frac{x^2 - 5x + 4}{11(x - 4)}$$

Then, factor the numerator to its simplest form:

$$f(x) = \frac{x^2 - 5x + 4}{11(x - 4)} = \frac{(x - 4)(x - 1)}{11(x - 4)}$$

The $(x - 4)$ cancels out, and the function becomes $f(x) = (x - 1) \div 11$. At this point you could shift to the calculator and calculate $f(x) = (3 - 1) \div 11 = {}^2/_{11} = .182$, which is **D**. If you were very comfortable with math, however, you would see that you don't even have to work out this final calculation. ${}^2/_{11}$ can't work out to any answer other than **D**, since you know that ${}^2/_{11}$ isn't a negative number (like **A** and **B**), won't be equal to zero (**C**), and also won't be greater than 1 (**E**).

Strategy 5: Master Your Approach.

Regardless of the type of question you're up against, there is a standard procedure that you should use to approach any question on the Math Level 1 Test:

1. Read the question without looking at the answers. Determine what the question is asking and come to some conclusion about how to solve it. Do not look at the answers unless you decide that using one of the two methods discussed on the next two pages is a better way to go.

2. If you think you can solve the problem, go ahead. Once you've derived an answer, only then see if your answer matches one of the choices.

3. Once you've decided on an answer, test it quickly to make sure it's correct, then move on.

Working Backward from the Answer Choices

If you run into difficulty, you might want to try out each answer choice to see which one works. For every question, the answer is right in front of you, among five answer choices. So if you can't solve the problem directly, you might be able to plug each answer into the question to see which one works.

Not only can this process help you when you can't figure out a question, there are times when it can actually be faster than setting up an equation, especially if you work strategically. Take the following example:

> A classroom contains 31 chairs, some of which have arms and some of which do not. If the room contains 5 more armchairs than chairs without arms, how many armchairs does it contain?
>
> (A) 10
> (B) 13
> (C) 16
> (D) 18
> (E) 21

Given this question, you could build the following two equations:

$$\text{total chairs } (31) = \text{armchairs } (x) + \text{normal chairs } (y)$$
$$\text{normal chairs } (y) = \text{armchairs } (x) - 5$$

Then, since $y = x - 5$ you can write the following equation and solve for x:

$$31 = x + (x - 5)$$
$$31 = 2x - 5$$
$$36 = 2x$$
$$x = 18$$

There are 18 armchairs in the classroom.

This approach of building and working out the equations will produce the right answer, but it takes a long time! What if you strategically plugged in the answers instead? Since the numbers ascend in value, let's choose the one in the middle: 16 (**C**). This is a smart strategic move because if we plug in 16 and discover that it is too small a number to satisfy the equation, we can eliminate **A** and **B** along with **C**. Alternatively, if 16 is too big, we can eliminate **D** and **E** along with **C**.

So our strategy is in place. Now let's work it out. If we have 16 armchairs, then we would have 11 normal chairs and the room would contain 27 total chairs. We needed the total number of chairs to equal 31, so clearly **C** is not the right answer. But because the total number of chairs is too few, we can also eliminate **A** and **B**, the answer choices with smaller numbers of armchairs. If we then plug in **D**, 18, we have 13 normal chairs and 31 total chairs. There's our answer. In this instance, plugging in the answers takes less time, and just seems easier in general.

Now, working backward and plugging in is not always the best method. For some questions it won't be possible to work backward at all. For the test, you will need to build up a sense of when working backward can most help you. Here's a good rule of thumb:

Work backward when the question describes an equation of some sort and the answer choices are all simple numbers.

If the answer choices contain variables, working backward will often be more difficult than actually working out the problem. If the answer choices are complicated, with hard fractions or radicals, plugging in might prove so complex that it's a waste of time.

Substituting Numbers

Substituting numbers is a lot like working backward, except the numbers you plug into the equation *aren't* in the answer choices. Instead, you have to strategically decide on numbers to substitute into the question to take the place of variables.

For example, take the question:

> If p and q are odd integers, then which of the following must be odd?
>
> (A) $p + q$
> (B) $p - q$
> (C) $p^2 + q^2$
> (D) $p^2 \times q^2$
> (E) $p + q^2$

It might be hard to conceptualize how the two variables in this problem interact. But what if you chose two odd numbers, let's say 5 and 3, to represent the two variables? You get:

> (A) $p + q = 5 + 3 = 8$
> (B) $p - q = 5 - 3 = 2$
> (C) $p^2 + q^2 = 25 + 9 = 34$
> (D) $p^2 \times q^2 = 25 \times 9 = 225$
> (E) $p + q^2 = 5 + 9 = 14$

As you can see, the correct answer must be **D**, because $p^2 \times q^2$ is the only expression among the five choices that equals an odd number. (By the way, you could have answered this question without any multiplication work at all, as two odd numbers, when multiplied, *always* result in an odd number.)

Substituting numbers can help you transform problems from the abstract to the concrete. However, you have to remember to keep the substitution consistent. If you're using a 5 to represent p, don't suddenly start using 3. Also, when picking numbers to use as substitutes, pick wisely. Choose numbers that are easy to work with and that fit the definitions provided by the question.

Strategy 6: Guess.

Should you guess on SAT Math Level 1? We'll answer this question by posing a question of our own:

> G. O. Metry is holding five cards, numbered 1–5. Without telling you, he has selected one of the numbers as the "correct" card. If you pick a single card, what is the probability that you will choose the correct card?

One out of 5, or $\frac{1}{5}$, of course! And that's precisely the situation you're in when you blindly guess the answer on any SAT Math Level 1 question: you have a 1 in 5 chance of getting the question right. If you were to guess on 10 questions, probability says you'll get two questions right and eight questions wrong.

- 2 right answers earn you 2 raw points.
- 8 wrong answers get you –2 raw points (8 × –$\frac{1}{4}$ points).

Those ten answers, therefore, net you a total of 0 points. And that's exactly what ETS wants. They designed the test to make blind guessing pointless.

Educated Guessing

But what if your guessing isn't blind? Consider the following question:

If $x + 2x = 6$, what is the value of x ?

(A) –2
(B) 1
(C) 0
(D) 2
(E) 3

Let's say you have no idea how to solve this problem or you're running out of time during the test. But you look at the answer choices, and realize that 0 multiplied by any number equals 0. If you plug that into the equation, $0 + 2 \times 0$ *cannot* add up to 6. You can eliminate "0" as a possible answer, and now have four choices from which to choose. Now is it worth it to guess? Yes. Probability states that if you are guessing between four choices you will get one question right for every three you get wrong. For that one correct answer, you'll get one point, and for the three incorrect answers, you'll lose a total of $\frac{3}{4}$ of a point: $1 – \frac{3}{4} = \frac{1}{4}$. If you can eliminate even one answer, the odds of guessing turn in your favor: you become more likely to gain points than to lose points.

The rule for guessing on the Math Level 1 Test is simple: *if you can eliminate even one answer choice on a question, you should definitely guess.*

Now on to the practice tests!

SAT* MATH LEVEL 1 PRACTICE TEST 1

SAT MATH LEVEL 1 PRACTICE TEST 1 ANSWER SHEET

1.	Ⓐ	Ⓑ	Ⓒ	Ⓓ	Ⓔ	18.	Ⓐ	Ⓑ	Ⓒ	Ⓓ	Ⓔ	35.	Ⓐ	Ⓑ	Ⓒ	Ⓓ	Ⓔ
2.	Ⓐ	Ⓑ	Ⓒ	Ⓓ	Ⓔ	19.	Ⓐ	Ⓑ	Ⓒ	Ⓓ	Ⓔ	36.	Ⓐ	Ⓑ	Ⓒ	Ⓓ	Ⓔ
3.	Ⓐ	Ⓑ	Ⓒ	Ⓓ	Ⓔ	20.	Ⓐ	Ⓑ	Ⓒ	Ⓓ	Ⓔ	37.	Ⓐ	Ⓑ	Ⓒ	Ⓓ	Ⓔ
4.	Ⓐ	Ⓑ	Ⓒ	Ⓓ	Ⓔ	21.	Ⓐ	Ⓑ	Ⓒ	Ⓓ	Ⓔ	38.	Ⓐ	Ⓑ	Ⓒ	Ⓓ	Ⓔ
5.	Ⓐ	Ⓑ	Ⓒ	Ⓓ	Ⓔ	22.	Ⓐ	Ⓑ	Ⓒ	Ⓓ	Ⓔ	39.	Ⓐ	Ⓑ	Ⓒ	Ⓓ	Ⓔ
6.	Ⓐ	Ⓑ	Ⓒ	Ⓓ	Ⓔ	23.	Ⓐ	Ⓑ	Ⓒ	Ⓓ	Ⓔ	40.	Ⓐ	Ⓑ	Ⓒ	Ⓓ	Ⓔ
7.	Ⓐ	Ⓑ	Ⓒ	Ⓓ	Ⓔ	24.	Ⓐ	Ⓑ	Ⓒ	Ⓓ	Ⓔ	41.	Ⓐ	Ⓑ	Ⓒ	Ⓓ	Ⓔ
8.	Ⓐ	Ⓑ	Ⓒ	Ⓓ	Ⓔ	25.	Ⓐ	Ⓑ	Ⓒ	Ⓓ	Ⓔ	42.	Ⓐ	Ⓑ	Ⓒ	Ⓓ	Ⓔ
9.	Ⓐ	Ⓑ	Ⓒ	Ⓓ	Ⓔ	26.	Ⓐ	Ⓑ	Ⓒ	Ⓓ	Ⓔ	43.	Ⓐ	Ⓑ	Ⓒ	Ⓓ	Ⓔ
10.	Ⓐ	Ⓑ	Ⓒ	Ⓓ	Ⓔ	27.	Ⓐ	Ⓑ	Ⓒ	Ⓓ	Ⓔ	44.	Ⓐ	Ⓑ	Ⓒ	Ⓓ	Ⓔ
11.	Ⓐ	Ⓑ	Ⓒ	Ⓓ	Ⓔ	28.	Ⓐ	Ⓑ	Ⓒ	Ⓓ	Ⓔ	45.	Ⓐ	Ⓑ	Ⓒ	Ⓓ	Ⓔ
12.	Ⓐ	Ⓑ	Ⓒ	Ⓓ	Ⓔ	29.	Ⓐ	Ⓑ	Ⓒ	Ⓓ	Ⓔ	46.	Ⓐ	Ⓑ	Ⓒ	Ⓓ	Ⓔ
13.	Ⓐ	Ⓑ	Ⓒ	Ⓓ	Ⓔ	30.	Ⓐ	Ⓑ	Ⓒ	Ⓓ	Ⓔ	47.	Ⓐ	Ⓑ	Ⓒ	Ⓓ	Ⓔ
14.	Ⓐ	Ⓑ	Ⓒ	Ⓓ	Ⓔ	31.	Ⓐ	Ⓑ	Ⓒ	Ⓓ	Ⓔ	48.	Ⓐ	Ⓑ	Ⓒ	Ⓓ	Ⓔ
15.	Ⓐ	Ⓑ	Ⓒ	Ⓓ	Ⓔ	32.	Ⓐ	Ⓑ	Ⓒ	Ⓓ	Ⓔ	49.	Ⓐ	Ⓑ	Ⓒ	Ⓓ	Ⓔ
16.	Ⓐ	Ⓑ	Ⓒ	Ⓓ	Ⓔ	33.	Ⓐ	Ⓑ	Ⓒ	Ⓓ	Ⓔ	50.	Ⓐ	Ⓑ	Ⓒ	Ⓓ	Ⓔ
17.	Ⓐ	Ⓑ	Ⓒ	Ⓓ	Ⓔ	34.	Ⓐ	Ⓑ	Ⓒ	Ⓓ	Ⓔ						

SAT MATH LEVEL 1 PRACTICE TEST 1

Time—1 hour

For each of the following problems, decide which is the BEST of the choices given. If the exact numerical value is not one of the choices, select the choice that best approximates this value. Then fill in the corresponding oval on the answer sheet.

<u>Notes:</u>   (1) A calculator will be necessary for answering some (but not all) of the questions in this test. For each question you will have to decide whether or not you should use a calculator. The calculator you use must be at least a scientific calculator; programmable calculators and calculators that can display graphs are permitted.

(2) For some questions in this test you may need to decide whether your calculator should be in radian or degree mode.

(3) Figures that accompany problems in this test are intended to provide information useful in solving the problems. They are drawn as accurately as possible EXCEPT when it is stated in a specific problem that its figure is not drawn to scale. All figures lie in a plane unless otherwise indicated.

(4) Unless otherwise specified, the domain of any function f is assumed to be the set of all real numbers x for which $f(x)$ is a real number.

REFERENCE INFORMATION

THE FOLLOWING INFORMATION IS FOR YOUR REFERENCE IN ANSWERING SOME OF THE QUESTIONS IN THIS TEST:

Volume of a right circular cone with radius r and height h: $V = \frac{1}{3}\pi r^2 h$

Lateral area of a right circular cone with circumference of the base c and slant height l: $S = \frac{1}{2}cl$

Volume of a sphere with radius r: $V = \frac{4}{3}\pi r^3$

Surface area of a sphere with radius r: $S = 4\pi r^2$

Volume of a pyramid with base area B and height h: $V = \frac{1}{3}Bh$

USE THIS SPACE FOR SCRATCHWORK.

1.   If $\dfrac{3}{5-x} = \dfrac{1}{x-2}$, then $x =$

(A) $\dfrac{11}{4}$

(B) $\dfrac{5}{2}$

(C) 2

(D) $\dfrac{3}{2}$

(E) 1

GO ON TO THE NEXT PAGE

USE THIS SPACE FOR SCRATCHWORK.

2. The stem-and-leaf plot in Figure 1 indicates the speed, in miles per hour (mph), of cars observed at the same spot along a road. What is the median observed speed of the cars?

   (A) 47 mph
   (B) 49 mph
   (C) 51 mph
   (D) 54 mph
   (E) 55 mph

```
3 | 3  5  6  7
4 | 0  4  5  8  9
5 | 1  2  6
6 | 2  3  4  5  7  8  9

6 | 7 = 67 mph
```

Figure 1

3. In Figure 2, if $\triangle ABC$ is an isosceles right triangle, what is the value of k ?

   (A) –9
   (B) –7
   (C) 7
   (D) 9
   (E) 10

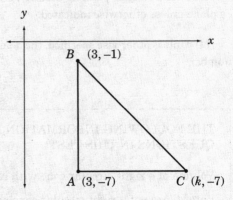

Figure 2

4. If $f(x) = \dfrac{x+1}{x-2}$, what is the value of $f(3)$?

   (A) 5
   (B) 4
   (C) 2
   (D) 1
   (E) –1

5. If $z = x^2$ and $x = 4j$, what is the value of z when $j = 3$?

   (A) $\dfrac{9}{16}$

   (B) 25

   (C) 81

   (D) 144

   (E) 169

GO ON TO THE NEXT PAGE

10 Practice Exams for the SAT Subject Tests

USE THIS SPACE FOR SCRATCHWORK.

6. There are 20 students in a room. 14 of the students have brown eyes, and 12 have blond hair. What is the minimum fraction of students in the room that have brown eyes and blond hair?

   (A) $\frac{1}{5}$

   (B) $\frac{3}{10}$

   (C) $\frac{2}{5}$

   (D) $\frac{7}{20}$

   (E) $\frac{3}{5}$

7. The graph in Figure 3 could be a reasonable interpretation of which of the following situations?

   (A) The volume of a balloon as a function of the radius
   (B) The weight of a steel rod as a function of the radius
   (C) The height of a tree as a function of time
   (D) The temperature of a bowl of ice cream left on a table as a function of time
   (E) The temperature of a bowl of hot soup left on a table as a function of time

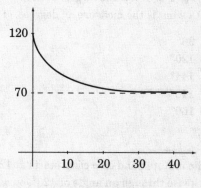

Figure 3

8. At what point does the line $y = \frac{3}{4}x - 6$ intersect the x-axis?

   (A) $x = 8$
   (B) $x = 0$
   (C) $x = 6$
   (D) $x = -2$
   (E) $y = 6$

9. A number n is decreased by 1. If the square root of that result equals $\frac{5}{4}$, what is the value of n?

   (A) $\frac{41}{16}$

   (B) $\frac{40}{16}$

   (C) $\frac{25}{16}$

   (D) $\frac{39}{27}$

   (E) $\frac{3}{5}$

GO ON TO THE NEXT PAGE

10. If $2x - 3y = 7$ and $3x - 2y = 5$, then $x =$

   (A) $\dfrac{35}{2}$

   (B) 5

   (C) $\dfrac{1}{2}$

   (D) $\dfrac{1}{5}$

   (E) 0

11. The measures of the 4 interior angles of a quadrilateral are in a ratio of $1 : 2 : 3 : 4$. If the largest such angle measures less than $180°$, what is the measure, in degrees, of the largest angle?

   (A) $36°$
   (B) $120°$
   (C) $144°$
   (D) $148°$
   (E) $160°$

12. If the minute hand on a clock starts at 12:00 and rotates clockwise through an angle of $120°$, on which number does the minute hand stop?

   (A) 4
   (B) 5
   (C) 6
   (D) 8
   (E) 9

13. If $f(x) = 3x^3 + 7x^2 + 2x + 1$, what is the value of $f(6.1)$?

   (A) 161.8
   (B) 221.7
   (C) 430.8
   (D) 433.7
   (E) 631.9

GO ON TO THE NEXT PAGE

14. If $x + y = 12$ and $x - y = 16$, then $\frac{x}{y} =$

   (A) -7

   (B) -6

   (C) 0

   (D) $\frac{1}{7}$

   (E) 7

15. A circular wheel of radius 6 rolls without slipping for a distance of 700π feet. How many complete revolutions does the wheel make?

   (A) 63
   (B) 62
   (C) 61
   (D) 59
   (E) 58

16. Which of the following is the solution to $|x - 3| \leq 3$?

   (A) $-3 \leq x \leq 3$
   (B) $0 < x < 6$
   (C) $0 \leq x \leq 6$
   (D) $-3 < x < 3$
   (E) $0 \leq x \leq 3$

17. In Figure 4, if chord $\overline{AB}$ = chord $\overline{CD}$, then which of the following must be true?

   I.   Arc $\widehat{AC}$ = Arc $\widehat{BD}$

   II. Arc $\widehat{CB}$ = $\frac{1}{2}$ Arc $\widehat{APD}$

   III. $\angle BAD \cong \angle CDA$

   (A) I only
   (B) II only
   (C) I and II only
   (D) I and III only
   (E) I, II, and III

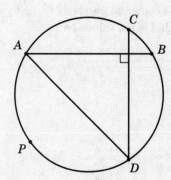

Note: Figure not drawn to scale.
Figure 4

GO ON TO THE NEXT PAGE

18. If $24^n = 2^4 \cdot 6^2$, then $n =$

    (A) 6
    (B) 5
    (C) 4
    (D) 3
    (E) 2

19. Sequential arrangements of dots are formed according to a pattern. Each arrangement after the first is formed by adding another layer to the bottom of the pentagon, as shown in Figure 5. If this pattern continues, which of the following is the number of dots in the 4th arrangement?

    (A) 36
    (B) 35
    (C) 34
    (D) 33
    (E) 32

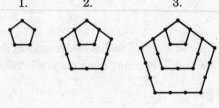

Figure 5

20. In Figure 6, line l is parallel to line m. What is the value of z in terms of x and y?

    (A) $180 - x - y$
    (B) $x + y$
    (C) $180 + x + y$
    (D) $x + y - 180$
    (E) $180 - 2(x + y)$

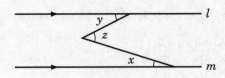

Figure 6

21. If a and b are real numbers, $i^2 = -1$, and $(2a - b) + 3i = 4 + ai$, then what is the value of b?

    (A) 4
    (B) 3
    (C) 2
    (D) $2 + i$
    (E) $2 - i$

GO ON TO THE NEXT PAGE

22. John has 5 different history books in his library. If he puts 3 of them next to one another on a shelf, how many different arrangements are possible?

    (A) 122
    (B) 120
    (C) 90
    (D) 80
    (E) 60

23. Referring to Figure 7, what is the value of $\cos \angle ABC$?

    (A) $\frac{5}{12}$
    (B) $\frac{5}{13}$
    (C) $\frac{7}{8}$
    (D) $\frac{12}{13}$
    (E) $\frac{15}{12}$

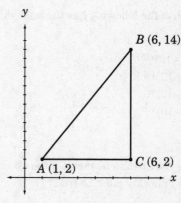

Figure 7

24. The perimeter of a rectangle is 36, and its area is 72. What is the length of the rectangle's longer side?

    (A) 6
    (B) 8
    (C) 11
    (D) 12
    (E) 14

25. In Figure 8, what is the area of the shaded region?

    (A) 1.5
    (B) 1.67
    (C) 1.89
    (D) 2
    (E) 2.01

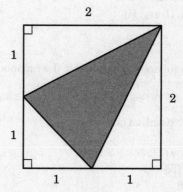

Figure 8

GO ON TO THE NEXT PAGE

26. What is the distance between the points $(-6, -9)$ and $(12, 15)$ on the xy-plane?

   (A) 28.75
   (B) 29
   (C) 30
   (D) 30.18
   (E) 31.18

27. Which of the following has the least value?

   (A) 10^{-100}
   (B) $(-10)^{-100}$
   (C) $(-10)^{100}$
   (D) $(-10)^{101}$
   (E) $(-10)^{102}$

28. If A is the arithmetic mean of the real numbers $x, y,$ and z, which of the following must be true?

   I. $A = \dfrac{x + y + z}{3}$

   II. $(A - x) + (A - y) + (A - z) = 0$

   III. $A + 3 = \dfrac{x + y + z + 3}{3}$

   (A) I only
   (B) II only
   (C) I and III only
   (D) I and II only
   (E) I, II, and III

29. A useful approximation for the exponential function e^x is given by the polynomial $1 + x + \dfrac{x^2}{2} + \dfrac{x^3}{6}$. Using this polynomial, find an approximation of e^1.

   (A) $\dfrac{271}{100}$

   (B) $\dfrac{8}{3}$

   (C) $\dfrac{9}{4}$

   (D) $\dfrac{11}{5}$

   (E) 2

GO ON TO THE NEXT PAGE

USE THIS SPACE FOR SCRATCHWORK.

30. A rectangle has sides of length 7 and 8, as shown in Figure 9. What is the value of $\angle CAD$?

    (A) 37.8°
    (B) 38.7°
    (C) 40.9°
    (D) 41.0°
    (E) 41.2°

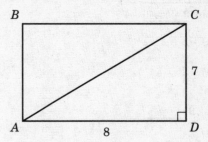

Note: Figure not drawn to scale.
Figure 9

31. If P and Q are two points on a cube with sides of length 10, then the maximum straight line distance between P and Q is

    (A) 17.3
    (B) 16.9
    (C) 16.8
    (D) 15.1
    (E) 12.7

32. If $f(x) = 6x - 7$ for all real x, then the slope of the line given by $y = f(3 - x)$ is

    (A) 6
    (B) 0
    (C) −1
    (D) −6
    (E) −7

33. In Figure 10, what is the value of x?

    (A) 3.2
    (B) 3.6
    (C) 3.8
    (D) 4.0
    (E) 4.4

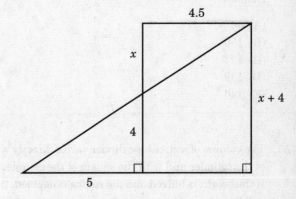

Note: Figure not drawn to scale.
Figure 10

GO ON TO THE NEXT PAGE

34. $\left(\dfrac{2}{\sin^2\theta + \cos^2\theta - 4}\right)^2 =$

    (A) -1

    (B) $-\dfrac{4}{9}$

    (C) $\dfrac{4}{9}$

    (D) $\dfrac{1}{2}$

    (E) 3

35. Given $6x^2 - 18x + 7 = 0$, if the sum of the roots is S and the product of the roots is P, then $S - P =$

    (A) $-\dfrac{29}{6}$

    (B) $-\dfrac{25}{6}$

    (C) -4

    (D) 0

    (E) $\dfrac{11}{6}$

36. If the measure of one angle in a rhombus is $72°$, and if the sides in the rhombus have a length of 12, then what is the area of the rhombus?

    (A) 44
    (B) 136
    (C) 137
    (D) 139
    (E) 140

37. The volume of a circular cylinder varies directly with the height of the cylinder and with the square of the cylinder's radius. If the height is halved and the radius is doubled, then the volume will be

    (A) unchanged
    (B) quadrupled
    (C) tripled
    (D) doubled
    (E) halved

GO ON TO THE NEXT PAGE

38. Let $x \lozenge y$ be defined for pairs of positive integers as $x \lozenge y = \dfrac{x-y}{xy}$.

    If $x \lozenge y \geq 0$, then x and y could satisfy which of the following?

    I. $x = y$
    II. $x < y$
    III. $x > y$

    (A) I only
    (B) II only
    (C) III only
    (D) I and III only
    (E) I, II, and III

39. In quadrilateral $ABCD$, $AB = 2$, $BC = 4$, and $CD = 5$. Which of the following represents all possible values for AD ?

    (A) $0 < AD < 11$
    (B) $0 \leq AD \leq 11$
    (C) $1 \leq AD < 11$
    (D) $1 < AD \leq 7$
    (E) $0 < AD < 7$

40. How are the graphs of $y_1 = x + 2$ and $y_2 = \dfrac{x^2 - 4}{x - 2}$ related?

    (A) They are different except when $x = 2$.
    (B) They are totally different.
    (C) They are exactly the same.
    (D) They are the same except at $x = 2$.
    (E) They are the same except at $x = -2$.

41. Rectangle $ABCD$ is inscribed in a circle as shown in Figure 11. If the length of side AB is 18 and the length of side BC is 24, what is the area of the shaded region?

    (A) 289.9
    (B) 288.0
    (C) 280.2
    (D) 275.1
    (E) 274.9

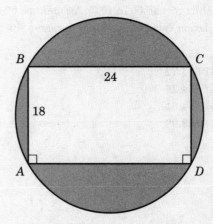

Note: Figure not drawn to scale.
Figure 11

GO ON TO THE NEXT PAGE

42. If $f(x) = 3 - x^3$ and if f^{-1} is the inverse function of f, then what is $f^{-1}(7)$?

    (A) -1.59
    (B) -1.21
    (C) -0.19
    (D) 1.59
    (E) 2.13

43. If $f(x) = x + 3$ and $g(x) = \sqrt{x}$, which of the following is the range of $y = f(g(x))$?

    (A) $0 \leq y$
    (B) $y \leq 3$
    (C) $3 \leq y$
    (D) $y \leq 0$
    (E) $0 < y < 3$

44. If $\log_b a = x$, which of the following must be true?

    (A) $b^x = a$
    (B) $a^x = b$
    (C) $a^b = x$
    (D) $x^b = a$
    (E) $x^a = b$

45. A shirt cost $8.00 in 1975. Assuming a 6% annual rate of inflation, how much should the same shirt cost in 2008?

    (A) $55.61
    (B) $54.72
    (C) $54.26
    (D) $54.01
    (E) $53.98

GO ON TO THE NEXT PAGE

46. For which of the following graphs does $f(-x) = -f(x)$?

(A)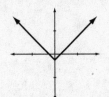

(B)

(C)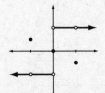

(D)

(E)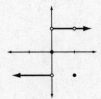

47. A laundry bag contains 160 black socks and 300 red socks. How many black socks must be added so that the probability of choosing a black sock is $\frac{7}{8}$?

(A) 425
(B) 820
(C) 1,300
(D) 1,939
(E) 1,940

GO ON TO THE NEXT PAGE

48. If $R + S = \begin{bmatrix} 5 & -3 \\ -3 & 5 \end{bmatrix}$, then R and S could be:

(A) $\begin{bmatrix} 1 & -1 \\ -5 & 2 \end{bmatrix}$ and $\begin{bmatrix} 4 & -2 \\ 2 & 3 \end{bmatrix}$

(B) $\begin{bmatrix} 5 & -1 \\ -3 & -1 \end{bmatrix}$ and $\begin{bmatrix} 1 & 3 \\ 1 & -5 \end{bmatrix}$

(C) $\begin{bmatrix} 2 & -2 \\ -4 & 1 \end{bmatrix}$ and $\begin{bmatrix} 3 & 1 \\ 1 & 4 \end{bmatrix}$

(D) $\begin{bmatrix} 0 & 5 \\ -1 & 6 \end{bmatrix}$ and $\begin{bmatrix} 5 & -8 \\ 3 & -1 \end{bmatrix}$

(E) $\begin{bmatrix} 4 & 2 \\ -6 & -1 \end{bmatrix}$ and $\begin{bmatrix} 1 & -4 \\ 3 & 4 \end{bmatrix}$

49. The faces of the front, side, and bottom of a rectangular solid have areas of 15 square feet, 7 square feet, and 4.2 square feet, respectively. What is the volume of this solid?

(A) 21
(B) 22
(C) 441
(D) 607
(E) Not enough information to tell

50. If the lateral surface area S of the right circular cone in Figure 12 is twice the area of the cone's base, what is the cone's height h in terms of the radius r ?

(A) $\sqrt{2}r$
(B) $\sqrt{3}r$
(C) πr
(D) $\sqrt{5}r$
(E) $\sqrt{7}r$

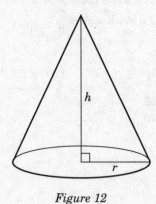

Figure 12

S T O P

IF YOU FINISH BEFORE TIME IS CALLED, YOU MAY CHECK YOUR WORK ON THIS TEST ONLY.
DO NOT TURN TO ANY OTHER TEST IN THIS BOOK.

SAT MATH LEVEL 1 PRACTICE TEST 1 EXPLANATIONS

MATH LEVEL 1 PRACTICE TEST 1 ANSWERS

Question Number	Answer	Right	Wrong	Question Number	Answer	Right	Wrong
1	A	___	___	26	C	___	___
2	C	___	___	27	D	___	___
3	D	___	___	28	D	___	___
4	B	___	___	29	B	___	___
5	D	___	___	30	E	___	___
6	B	___	___	31	A	___	___
7	E	___	___	32	D	___	___
8	A	___	___	33	B	___	___
9	A	___	___	34	C	___	___
10	D	___	___	35	E	___	___
11	C	___	___	36	C	___	___
12	A	___	___	37	D	___	___
13	D	___	___	38	D	___	___
14	A	___	___	39	A	___	___
15	E	___	___	40	D	___	___
16	C	___	___	41	E	___	___
17	D	___	___	42	A	___	___
18	E	___	___	43	C	___	___
19	B	___	___	44	A	___	___
20	B	___	___	45	B	___	___
21	C	___	___	46	C	___	___
22	E	___	___	47	E	___	___
23	D	___	___	48	A	___	___
24	D	___	___	49	A	___	___
25	A	___	___	50	B	___	___

CALCULATING YOUR SCORE

Your raw score for the SAT Math Level 1 Test is calculated from the number of questions you answer correctly and incorrectly. Once you have determined your composite score, use the conversion table on page 204 of this book to calculate your scaled score. To calculate your raw score, count the number of questions you answered correctly:

_____
A

Count the number of questions you answered incorrectly, and multiply that number by $\frac{1}{4}$:

$$\underline{\hspace{2cm}} \times \frac{1}{4} = \underline{\hspace{2cm}}$$
B   C

Subtract the value in field C from the value in field A:

_____
D

Round the number in field D to the nearest whole number. This is your raw score:

_____
E

MATH LEVEL 1 TEST 1 EXPLANATIONS

1. **A** Algebra: Equation Solving

Because x is in the denominators of the two fractions, you should cross multiply to simplify this equation.

$$\frac{3}{5-x} = \frac{1}{x-2}$$
$$3x - 6 = 5 - x$$
$$4x = 11$$
$$x = \frac{11}{4}$$

2. **C** Statistics: Data Interpretation

The plot shows speeds for a total of 19 different cars. (For example, the first row indicates four speeds of at least 30 mph but less than 40 mph: 33, 35, 36, and 37 mph.) The median speed is the middle value among the 19 speeds—in other words, 9 of the numbers are less than the median, while 9 are greater than the median. As you can see, the 10th number in value is 51 (counting from the least value: 33, 35, 36, 37, 40, 44, 45, 48, 49, 51).

3. **D** Coordinate Geometry: Coordinate Plane; Plane Geometry: Triangles

The question tells you that $\triangle ABC$ is a right isosceles triangle, which means that the legs of the triangle, AB and AC, are equal in length. You can find the length of the legs by using the coordinates of points A, B, and C. The length of AB is equal to the difference in the y-coordinates of A and B: $(-1) - (-7) = 6$. The length of AC is equal to the difference in the x-coordinates of A and C: $k - 3$. Since $AB = AC$, you know that $k - 3 = 6$ and $k = 9$.

4. **B** Functions: Evaluating Functions

Plug in 3 for x in $f(x)$:

$$f(3) = \frac{3+1}{3-2}$$
$$= \frac{4}{1}$$
$$= 4$$

5. **D** Functions: Evaluating Functions

You can solve this problem through substitution. If $j = 3$, then $x = 4 \times 3 = 12$. If $x = 12$, then $z = 12^2 = 144$.

6. **B** Statistics: Probability

The total number of students with either brown eyes or blond hair is 26 (14 + 12). However, the question states that there are only 20 students altogether in the room. Therefore, at least 6 of the students must have both of these traits. In other words, at least $\frac{6}{20}$, or $\frac{3}{10}$, of the students should have brown eyes *and* blond hair.

7.   **E**   Functions: Graphs of Functions

You need to interpret the graph and apply your interpretation to the answer choices. The graph shows a y value that starts at 120 and decreases to 70, where it remains constant as the x value increases. Of the answer choices, this graph best represents **E**, since a bowl of hot soup left out on a table would cool to room temperature over time, and it would stay at room temperature as time passed.

8.   **A**   Coordinate Geometry: Lines; Algebra: Equation Solving

When a line intersects the x-axis, the value of y is zero. So you can find the x-intercept of the line by plugging in $y = 0$.

$$y = \frac{3}{4}x - 6$$

$$0 = \frac{3}{4}x - 6$$

$$\frac{3}{4}x = 6$$

$$x = 8$$

9.   **A**   Algebra: Writing Equations

Translate the problem into an algebraic expression. "A number n is decreased by 1" means the same thing as $(n - 1)$. You can write "the square root of that result equals $\frac{5}{4}$" as $\sqrt{n-1} = \frac{5}{4}$. Now solve for n. Start by squaring both sides of the equation.

$$\sqrt{n-1} = \frac{5}{4}$$

$$n - 1 = \frac{25}{16}$$

$$n = \frac{25}{16} + 1$$

$$n = \frac{41}{16}$$

10.   **D**   Algebra: Systems of Equations

You have two unknown variables and two equations. In order to solve for x, you need x to be the only variable in an equation. One way to isolate x is to use substitution: solve for y in terms of x in one equation, and then plug that value for y into the second equation to find x.

$$3x - 2y = 5$$

$$2y = 3x - 5$$

$$y = \frac{3x - 5}{2}$$

Now plug this value for y into the other equation and solve for x:

$$2x - 3y = 7$$
$$2x - 3\left(\frac{3x-5}{2}\right) = 7$$
$$2x - \frac{9x-15}{2} = 7$$
$$4x - 9x + 15 = 14$$
$$-5x = -1$$
$$x = \frac{1}{5}$$

11. C Algebra: Writing Equations; Plane Geometry: Polygons

The sum of the interior angles in a quadrilateral is $360°$ (assuming all such angles measure less than $180°$). If you make x the measure of the smallest angle in the quadrilateral, you can set up an equation for the angles by using the ratio given in the question.

$$360° = x + 2x + 3x + 4x$$
$$= 10x$$
$$x = 36°$$

The largest angle in the quadrilateral is equal to $4x$, or $4 \cdot 36° = 144°$.

12. A Coordinate Geometry: Circles, Word Problems

If the minute hand starts at 12:00 and rotates $120°$, it has traveled $\frac{120°}{360°} = \frac{1}{3}$ of the way around the full circle (since there are $360°$ in a circle). Since there are 12 hours (at even intervals) on a clock, $\frac{1}{3}$ of the circle represents $\left(\frac{1}{3} \cdot 12\right)$ hours, or 4 hours. Since the hand starts at 12:00, it ends up pointing at 4:00.

13. D Functions: Evaluating Functions

Plug 6.1 into $f(x)$, and figure out the answer on your calculator.

$$f(6.1) = 3(6.1)^3 - 7(6.1)^2 + 2(6.1) + 1$$
$$= 3 \cdot 226.981 - 7 \cdot 37.21 + 12.2 + 1$$
$$= 680.943 - 260.47 + 13.2$$
$$\approx 433.7$$

14. A Algebra: Systems of Equations

The fastest way to answer this problem is to add together the equations $x + y = 12$ and $x - y = 16$. Once you add the equations, the y terms cancel out, and you end up with $2x = 28$. Now you can find that $x = 14$. If you plug $x = 14$ into one of the original equations, such as $x + y = 12$, you'll find that $y = -2$. To answer the problem, divide x by y:

$$\frac{x}{y} = \frac{14}{-2} = -7$$

15. **E**   Plane Geometry: Circles

The distance a wheel rolls in one complete revolution is equal to the wheel's circumference. If the radius of a wheel is 6, then the circumference of the wheel is 12π, since $C = 2\pi r$. You can find the number of revolutions the wheel makes by dividing the total distance by the circumference:

$$\text{number of revolutions} = \frac{\text{total distance}}{\text{circumference}}$$

$$= \frac{700\pi}{12\pi}$$

$$= 58\frac{1}{3}$$

Since the question asks you for the number of revolutions completed by the wheel, the correct answer is 58.

16. **C**   Algebra: Inequalities, Absolute Value

When you see an inequality with an absolute value on one side, you're actually dealing with two inequalities. $|x - 3| \leq 3$ can be rewritten as $x - 3 \leq 3$ and $x - 3 \geq -3$. First, solve these inequalities separately:

$$x - 3 \leq 3$$
$$x \leq 6$$

And:

$$x - 3 \geq -3$$
$$x \geq 0$$

You can rewrite these two inequalities as $0 \leq x \leq 6$.

17. **D**   Plane Geometry: Circles

In a circle, chords of equal length intercept arcs of equal length, so $\overarc{AB} = \overarc{CD}$. You can also see from the figure that $\overarc{AC} + \overarc{CB} = \overarc{AB}$ and $\overarc{BD} + \overarc{CB} = \overarc{CD}$. Now you can write:

$$\overarc{AC} + \overarc{CB} = \overarc{BD} + \overarc{CB}$$
$$\overarc{AC} = \overarc{BD}$$

So Option I must be true.

Option III must also be true. If $\overarc{AB} = \overarc{CD}$, then $\angle BAD \cong \angle CDA$ because the angles intersect arcs of equal length.

Option II is not necessarily true, though. For instance, if both *AB* and *CD* were diameters of the circle, then points *A*, *B*, *C*, and *D* would divide the circle into four equal arcs:

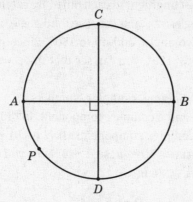

As you can see in the figure above, $\overset{\frown}{CB} = \overset{\frown}{APD}$, so option II, which says $\overset{\frown}{CB} = \frac{1}{2}\overset{\frown}{APD}$, cannot be true.

18. E   Fundamentals: Exponents
To answer this question you need to know the following laws of exponents: $A^x \cdot B^x = (AB)^x$ and $(A^x)^y = A^{xy}$. You should apply these laws to the problem given in the question: $24^n = 2^4 \cdot 6^2$. Rewrite 2^4 as $(2^2)^2$, which you can simplify to 4^2. Now you have:

$$24^n = 4^2 \cdot 6^2$$
$$= (4 \cdot 6)^2$$
$$24^n = 24^2$$
$$n = 2$$

19. B   Miscellaneous Math: Patterns
The best way to solve this problem is to draw the fourth arrangement, continuing the pattern shown in the question:

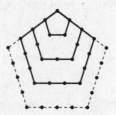

The fourth arrangement adds 13 new dots to the 22 dots in the third arrangement. The total number of dots in the fourth arrangement is 35.

20. B   Plane Geometry: Lines and Angles
Try redrawing the figure like this:

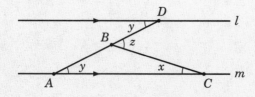

By extending the line *BD* to point *A*, you can see that *BD* is part of a transversal intersecting two parallel lines. When two parallel lines are cut by a transversal, the alternate interior angles $\angle y$ and $\angle CAB$ are congruent to each other. By extending *BD*, you also create a triangle $\triangle ABC$, with two angles: $\angle y$ and $\angle x$. The third angle, $\angle ABC$, is supplementary to $\angle z$. In other words, the two angles add up to $180°$. Since $m\angle z + m\angle ABC = 180°$ and $m\angle x + m\angle y + m\angle ABC = 180°$, you can see that $m\angle z = m\angle x + m\angle y$.

21. **C**   Algebra: Equation Solving, Complex Numbers

This equation has both a real and a complex component. In order to solve the equation, you first need to equate the complex components. If $(2a - b) + 3i = 4 + ai$, then the complex part of the equation states $3i = ai$, so $a = 3$. Now you can equate the real components: if $2a - b = 4$ and $a = 3$, then:

$$2a - b = 4$$
$$6 - b = 4$$
$$b = 2$$

22. **E**   Statistics: Permutations and Combinations

When John picks the first book to put on the shelf, he has a total of 5 choices (since there are 5 books). When he picks the second book, he has 4 choices, since he's already removed one of the books. Finally, when he makes his third pick, he has 3 books to choose from. You can calculate the number of possible arrangements by multiplying $5 \cdot 4 \cdot 3 = 60$ possible arrangements.

23. **D**   Trigonometry: Basic Functions; Coordinate Geometry: Coordinate Plane

You can use the coordinates of points *A*, *B*, and *C* to find the lengths of the sides of $\triangle ABC$. The length of *AC* is equal to the difference between the *x*-coordinates of points *A* and *C*: $6 - 1 = 5$. The length of *BC* is equal to the difference between the *y*-coordinates of *B* and *C*: $14 - 2 = 12$. Now that you know the lengths of the two legs of the triangle, you can find the length of its hypotenuse. A right triangle with two legs of lengths 5 and 12 must have a hypotenuse of 13 (it's a special right triangle). If you don't remember this special triangle, you can use the Pythagorean theorem to find *AB*:

$$(AB)^2 = 5^2 + 12^2$$
$$= 169$$
$$AB = 13$$

Now you can solve for $\cos \angle ABC$, since *BC* is the adjacent side to the angle and *AB* is the hypotenuse of the triangle:

$$\cos \angle ABC = \frac{BC}{AB}$$
$$= \frac{12}{13}$$

24. D   Plane Geometry: Polygons

Draw a picture of the rectangle, labeling the long sides y and the short sides x.

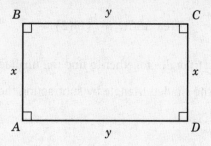

The perimeter of $\square ABCD$ is 36. You know that the perimeter of a polygon is the sum of its sides, so you can write $2x + 2y = 36$, or $x + y = 18$. Since you have two unknown variables, you need to write a second equation. The area of $\square ABCD$ is 72. You calculate the area of a rectangle by multiplying its short side by its long side, so you have $xy = 72$. Rewrite the first equation as $y = 18 - x$ and substitute this value for y into the second equation:

$$x \cdot y = 72$$
$$x(18 - x) = 72$$
$$18x - x^2 = 72$$
$$x^2 - 18x + 72 = 0$$
$$(x - 6)(x - 12) = 0$$
$$x = 6 \text{ or } x = 12$$

Since 12 is greater than 6, 12 is the length of the rectangle's long side.

25. A   Plane Geometry: Polygons, Triangles

You'll waste a lot of time trying to calculate the area of the triangle by figuring out the length of the base and the height. The fastest way to answer this problem is to subtract the unshaded area from the area of the whole figure. The area of the whole figure is the area of the square $\square ABCD$. You can calculate the square's area by multiplying its sides together: Area $\square ABCD = 2 \cdot 2 = 4$. The unshaded area consists of three right triangles:

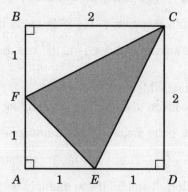

The figure in the question gives you the bases and heights of these three triangles, so you can calculate their areas:

$$\text{Area } \triangle AFE = \frac{1}{2}(1)(1) = \frac{1}{2}$$

$$\text{Area } \Delta FBC = \frac{1}{2}(1)(2) = 1$$

$$\text{Area } \Delta ECD = \frac{1}{2}(1)(2) = 1$$

Add the areas of the three triangles together to find the unshaded area: $\frac{1}{2} + 1 + 1 = 2\frac{1}{2}$.

You can find the area of the shaded triangle by subtracting the unshaded area from the

total area:

$$4 - 2\frac{1}{2} = 1\frac{1}{2} = 1.5$$

26. **C**   Coordinate Geometry: Lines and Distance

You should definitely memorize the formula for finding the distance between two points in a plane. If you have two points (x_1, y_1) and (x_2, y_2), then the distance formula is: $d = \sqrt{(x_2 - x_1)^2 + (y_2 - y_1)^2}$. Plug the points $(-6, -9)$ and $(12, 15)$ into this formula:

$$
\begin{aligned}
d &= \sqrt{(12 - (-6))^2 + (15 - (-9))^2} \\
&= \sqrt{18^2 + 24^2} \\
&= \sqrt{900} \\
&= 30
\end{aligned}
$$

27. **D**   Fundamentals: Exponents

The answer choices are probably too large for your calculator to compute, so you should compare their values on your own. $10^{-100} = \frac{1}{10^{100}}$, which is an extremely small positive number; $(-10)^{-100}$ is equal to 10^{-100}, since the exponent is an even number. (If you don't understand why this is true, try replacing 10 and 100 with smaller numbers: $(-2)^{-2} = 0.25$ and $2^{-2} = 0.25$.) $(-10)^{100}$ is a very large positive number—in fact, it's equal to 10^{100}. $(-10)^{101}$ is a very large negative number; if you raise a negative number to an odd number, the result is negative. $(-10)^{102}$ is a very large positive number, since the exponent is even. Of the answer choices, $(-10)^{101}$ has the least value.

28. **D**   Statistics: Arithmetic Mean

You calculate the arithmetic mean of a numbers by dividing the sum of the numbers by a. The question says that A is the mean of three numbers—x, y, and z—so you should realize that option I, $A = \frac{x + y + z}{3}$, must be true. Try to manipulate this equation to see whether you can derive options II and III. If you multiply both sides of $A = \frac{x + y + z}{3}$ by 3, you get $3A = x + y + z$.

$$
\begin{aligned}
3A - x - y - z &= 0 \\
A + A + A - x - y - z &= 0 \\
(A - x) + (A - y) + (A - z) &= 0
\end{aligned}
$$

242

Option II must also be true, since it's a rewriting of the equation in option I. Option III says:

$$A + 3 = \frac{x + y + z + 3}{3}$$

$$= \frac{x + y + z}{3} + \frac{3}{3}$$

$$= A + 1$$

$$A + 3 \neq A + 1$$

Because you can't derive option III from option I, you know that option III is not necessarily true.

29. **B** Functions: Evaluating Functions

The phrasing of this question is the trickiest thing about it. The question says that $1 + x + \frac{x^2}{2} + \frac{x^3}{6}$ is an approximation of e^x. All this means is that the result of plugging x into $1 + x + \frac{x^2}{2} + \frac{x^3}{6}$ is close to the value of e^x. So to find e^1, simply plug $x = 1$ into $1 + x + \frac{x^2}{2} + \frac{x^3}{6}$:

$$e^1 \approx 1 + (1) + \frac{1^2}{2} + \frac{1^3}{6}$$

$$\approx 1 + 1 + \frac{1}{2} + \frac{1}{6}$$

$$\approx \frac{8}{3}$$

30. **E** Trigonometry: Basic Functions

If you look at the figure, you'll see that you have a right triangle $\triangle ACD$ with legs of lengths 7 and 8. You can use right triangle trigonometry to find the measure of angle $\angle CAD$. Since you're given the two legs of the triangle, you should use tangent to solve for the angle. Since 7 is opposite the angle and 8 is adjacent to it, you can write:

$$\tan \angle CAD = \frac{7}{8}$$

$$\angle CAD = \tan^{-1}\left(\frac{7}{8}\right)$$

$$\angle CAD \approx 41.2$$

31. **A** Solid Geometry: Prisms

The maximum distance between any two points in a cube is the long diagonal of the cube:

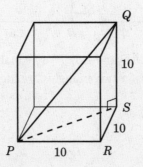

To find *PQ*, you first need to find *PS*. Since you know the sides of the cube are equal to 10, you can use the Pythagorean Theorem to find *PS*, which is the hypotenuse of the right triangle Δ*PSR*:

$$(PS)^2 = 10^2 + 10^2$$
$$(PS)^2 = 200$$

You don't need to take the square root of 200 because you're now going to plug $(PS)^2$ into the Pythagorean Theorem to find *PQ*. In this case, *PS* and *QS* (a side of the cube) are the legs of a right triangle and *PQ* is its hypotenuse:

$$(PQ)^2 = 10^2 + (PS)^2$$
$$= 100 + 200$$
$$= 300$$
$$PQ = \sqrt{300}$$
$$\approx 17.3$$

32. **D** Functions: Evaluating Functions; Coordinate Geometry: Lines and Slope
Your first step should be to plug $(3 - x)$ into $f(x)$:

$$f(3 - x) = 6(3 - x) - 7$$
$$= 18 - 6x - 7$$
$$= -6x + 11$$

Now you have the line of an equation, $y = -6x + 11$. Since *m* is the slope of a line $y = mx + b$, the slope of the line in this question is –6.

33. **B** Plane Geometry: Lines and Angles, Triangles
Lines *FB* and *AC* must be parallel, since *FB* and *DC* are opposite sides of a rectangle. *AB* is a transversal line cutting the two parallel lines. When a transversal cuts parallel lines, the alternate interior angles created by these intersections are equal; in this case, $\angle EBF = \angle EAD$. You also know that $\angle EFB = \angle EDA = 90°$, since *FD* must be perpendicular to both *FB* and *AD*.

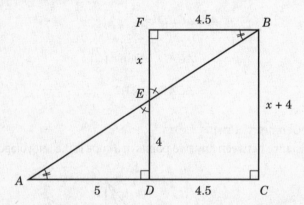

If two of the three angles in Δ*AED* and Δ*BEF* are equal, then their third angles must be equal as well. When the angles in two triangles are identical, the triangles are similar:

$\triangle AED \sim \triangle BEF$. In other words, the proportions of the sides in the triangles are the same. You can set up a proportion to find the length of x:

$$\frac{EF}{FB} = \frac{ED}{DA}$$

$$\frac{x}{4.5} = \frac{4}{5}$$

$$x = \frac{18}{5}$$

$$x = 3.6$$

34. **C** Trigonometry: Pythagorean Identities

One of the most useful trigonometric identities is: $\sin^2\theta + \cos^2\theta = 1$. Substitute this identity into the expression:

$$\left(\frac{2}{\sin^2\theta + \cos^2\theta - 4}\right)^2 = \left(\frac{2}{1-4}\right)^2$$

$$= \left(\frac{2}{-3}\right)^2$$

$$= \frac{4}{9}$$

35. **E** Algebra: Polynomials

For a quadratic equation $ax^2 + bx + c = 0$, the sum of the roots is equal to $-\frac{b}{a}$ and the product of the roots is equal to $\frac{c}{a}$. In $6x^2 - 18x + 7 = 0$, you have $a = 6$, $b = -18$, and $c = 7$. So the sum S of the roots is:

$$S = -\frac{b}{a}$$

$$= -\frac{(-18)}{6}$$

$$= 3$$

And the product P of the roots is:

$$P = \frac{c}{a}$$

$$= \frac{7}{6}$$

Now find the answer: $S - P = 3 - \frac{7}{6} = \frac{11}{6}$.

36. C   Plane Geometry: Polygons

A rhombus is a parallelogram with sides of equal length. Draw a picture of the rhombus described in the question:

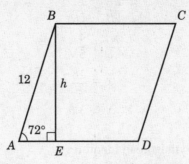

The area of a rhombus is its base multiplied by its height. You know that the base of the rhombus is 12, since all the sides have length 12, but you need to calculate the height. If you draw a perpendicular line down from point B, you'll create the right triangle, $\triangle ABE$, which has a hypotenuse 12. You can apply trigonometry to find the height:

$$\sin 72° = \frac{h}{12}$$
$$h = 12 \sin 72°$$

Now you can find the area of the rhombus:

$$A = bh$$
$$= 12 \cdot 12 \sin 72°$$
$$\approx 137$$

There's a faster way to answer this question. If you know that the area of a parallelogram is the product of the lengths of the sides multiplied by the sine of the included angle (the angle between the sides), you can jump straight away to:

$$A = 12 \cdot 12 \cdot \sin 72°$$
$$\approx 137$$

37. D   Solid Geometry: Prisms; Algebra: Writing Equations

The question asks you what happens to the volume of a cylinder when its height is halved and its radius doubled. First you need to know that the formula for the volume of a cylinder is $V = \pi r^2 h$; this equation gives you the volume of a cylinder with height h and radius r. To find out what happens when you halve the height and double the radius, plug in $\frac{h}{2}$ for the new height and $2r$ for the new radius. The volume of the altered cylinder is:

$$V' = \pi(2r)^2 \cdot \frac{h}{2}$$
$$= \pi(4r^2) \cdot \frac{h}{2}$$
$$= 2\pi r^2 h$$

The original cylinder's volume was $V = \pi r^2 h$. If $V' = 2\pi r^2 h$, then $V' = 2V$. In other words, the new volume, V', is double the old volume, V.

38. **D** Functions: Evaluating Functions

Since $x \Diamond y = \frac{x-y}{xy}$, solving $x \Diamond y \geq 0$ is the same as solving $\frac{x-y}{xy} \geq 0$. Split $\frac{x-y}{xy}$ into 2

fractions: $\frac{x}{xy} - \frac{y}{xy}$, which simplifies as $\frac{1}{y} - \frac{1}{x}$. Now set up the inequality:

$$\frac{1}{y} - \frac{1}{x} \geq 0$$

$$\frac{1}{y} \geq \frac{1}{x}$$

Now cross multiply (you don't need to worry about the direction of the inequality sign, since the question says x and y are both positive integers):

$$x \geq y$$

Since this inequality says that x is greater than or equal to y, both options I and III could be true.

39. **A** Plane Geometry: Polygons

You're looking for the smallest and largest possible values of AD that will allow $ABCD$ to remain a quadrilateral:

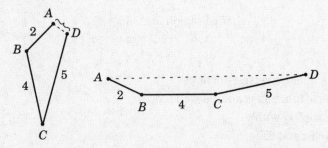

From the figure on the left, you can see that AD must be greater than zero in order for $ABCD$ to be a quadrilateral. If AD is equal to zero, A and D will be the same point and you'll have a triangle. From the figure on the right, you can see that AD must be less than the length of $AB + BC + CD$. If AD were equal to the sum of the three other lengths, you would have a line. You can put together the inequality:

$$0 < AD < (AB + BC + CD)$$
$$0 < AD < (2 + 4 + 5)$$
$$0 < AD < 11$$

40. **D** Functions: Evaluating Functions

You don't need to graph these equations in order to answer the problem. Factoring an equation will almost always simplify a problem on the Math Level 1 If you factor the numerator of $y_2 = \frac{x^2 - 4}{x - 2}$, you get

$$y_2 = \frac{(x+2)(x-2)}{x-2}$$
$$= (x+2), \text{ as long as } x \neq 2$$

You need to remember that x can't be equal to 2 here. If $x = 2$, y_2 is undefined because the denominator of the function is equal to zero. Since $y_1 = x + 2$, you know that $y_1 = y_2$, except when $x = 2$, where y_2 is undefined.

41. **E**   Plane Geometry: Polygons, Circles

To find the area of the shaded region, you should subtract the area of the rectangle from the area of the circle. You can find the area of the rectangle by multiplying together its sides: $18 \cdot 24 = 432$. You need to find the radius of the circle in order to find its area. When you inscribe a rectangle in a circle, the diagonal of the rectangle is equal to the diameter of the circle, so the radius of the circle is equal to half the length of the rectangle's diagonal. Find the diagonal using the Pythagorean Theorem, where AC is the hypotenuse of a right triangle, and AB and BC are the triangle's sides:

$$(AC)^2 = 18^2 + 24^2$$
$$(AC)^2 = 900$$
$$AC = 30$$

The radius of the circle is $30 \div 2 = 15$. Plug 15 into the formula for the area of a circle: $A = \pi r^2 = 225\pi$. Now find the area of the shaded region by the rectangle's area from the circle's:

$$\text{shaded region} = 225\pi - 432$$
$$\approx 274.9$$

42. **A**   Functions: Inverse Functions

Solving an inverse function is a three-step process:

   Step 1: Replace $f(x)$ with y.
   Step 2: Switch x and y.
   Step 3: Solve for y.

   The expression you get for y is equal to $f^{-1}(x)$. Use these steps to find the inverse function of $f(x) = 3 - x^3$:

$$y = 3 - x^3$$
$$x = 3 - y^3$$
$$y^3 = 3 - x$$
$$y = \sqrt[3]{3 - x}$$
$$f^{-1}(x) = \sqrt[3]{3 - x}$$

The question asks you to evaluate $f^{-1}(x)$ at $x = 7$:

$$f^{-1}(7) = \sqrt[3]{3 - 7}$$
$$= \sqrt[3]{-4}$$
$$\approx -1.59$$

43. **C**   Functions: Compound Functions, Domain, and Range

First find the compound function $f(g(x))$ by plugging $g(x) = \sqrt{x}$ into $f(x) = x + 3$:

$$f(g(x)) = f(\sqrt{x})$$
$$= \sqrt{x} + 3$$

The range of this compound function is all the real values of $y = f(g(x))$. To find the range, you can use your calculator to graph the function. Alternatively, you can simply realize that $\sqrt{x}$ is always greater than or equal to zero (in order for it to be a real number); thus $\sqrt{x} + 3$ must always be greater than or equal to 3.

44. **A** Fundamentals: Logarithms

This problem asks you for the definition of a logarithm, which you should definitely memorize for the Math Level 1 Test. $\log_b a = x$ is equivalent to $b^x = a$.

45. **B** Algebra: Equation Solving, Exponential Growth and Decay

Questions on exponential growth often show up on the Math Level 1 Test, so you should make sure to memorize this formula: $A(t) = A_o(1 + r)^t$, where $A(t)$ is a value after time t; A_o is the initial value (when $t = 0$; r is the rate of inflation, written as a decimal; and t is time). In this case, $A_o = \$8.00$, $r = 0.06$, $t = 2008 - 1975 = 33$. Plug these values into the formula:

$$A(33) = 8(1 + 0.06)^{33}$$
$$= 8(1.06)^{33}$$
$$\approx 54.72$$

46. **C** Functions: Transformations and Symmetry

If $f(-x) = -f(x)$, the graph of $y = f(x)$ is said "symmetric with respect to the origin." (A good example of a function that's symmetric with respect to the origin is $f(x) = x^3$.) Of the graphs in the answer choices, only the one in **C** is symmetric with respect to the origin. **A** and **D** are symmetric with respect to the y-axis, and **B** and **E** aren't symmetric at all.

47. **E** Algebra: Writing Equations; Statistics: Probability

You want the probability of choosing a black sock to be $\frac{7}{8}$, which means that 7 out of 8 socks in the bag are black. Make B equal to the number of black socks initially in the bag and T equal to the initial total of socks. The question tells you that B is equal to 160, and you can figure out that T is equal to 460, by adding 160 black sock and 300 red socks. Now have x equal the number of black socks you need to add to make the probability $\frac{7}{8}$. Remember that for every black sock you add, you increase not only the number of black socks but the total number of socks in the bag.

$$\frac{B + x}{T + x} = \frac{7}{8}$$
$$\frac{160 + x}{460 + x} = \frac{7}{8}$$

Cross multiply to get:

$$1,280 + 8x = 3,220 + 7x$$
$$x = 1,940$$

48. **A** Numbers and Operations: Matrices

To determine each entry in $R + S$, add together corresponding entries in R and S. Considering **A**, adding together the first entry in row 1 of R (1) and the first entry in row 1 of S (4) gives you the first entry in row 1 of $R + S$ (5). The other entries in **A** add up correctly as well.

49. **A** Solid Geometry: Prisms

Draw a picture of a rectangular solid:

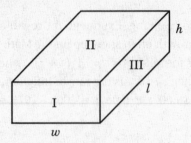

The question asks you for the volume of the rectangular solid. You know the following about the solid: the area of face I is equal to $w \cdot h$; the area of face II is equal to $w \cdot l$; the area of face III is equal to $l \cdot h$. The trick to getting this question is multiplying:

$$(\text{face I}) \cdot (\text{face II}) \cdot (\text{face III}) = (w \cdot h)(w \cdot l)(l \cdot h)$$
$$= w^2 l^2 h^2$$
$$= (w \cdot l \cdot h)^2$$

Since the volume equals $w \cdot l \cdot h$, the volume squared equals $(w \cdot l \cdot h)^2$. To find the volume of this rectangular solid, multiply together the areas of the three faces and take the square root of this number.

$$\text{Volume} = \sqrt{(15) \cdot (7) \cdot (4.2)}$$
$$= 21$$

50. **B** Solid Geometry: Solids that Aren't Prisms

The formula for the lateral surface area of a cone is given to you on the formula page at the beginning of the test. The formula is $S = \frac{1}{2}cl$, where c is the circumference of the base and l is the slant height. Draw a picture of the cone:

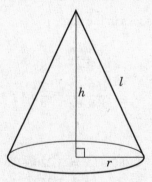

The radius r, the height h, and the slant height l of the cone form a right triangle, so you know $l^2 = r^2 + h^2$ and $l = \sqrt{r^2 + h^2}$. The circumference of the base is equal to $2\pi r$.

Plug these two values into the lateral area formula, and you get $S = \frac{1}{2}(2\pi r)(\sqrt{r^2 + h^2})$, which reduces to $S = \pi r\sqrt{r^2 + h^2}$. The question also tells you that the lateral area of the cone is equal to twice the area of the base, which is πr^2, so you have $S = 2\pi r^2$. Set these two equations for the lateral area equal to each other:

$$\pi r\sqrt{r^2 + h^2} = 2\pi r^2$$
$$\sqrt{r^2 + h^2} = 2r$$

Square both sides of the equation:

$$r^2 + h^2 = 4r^2$$
$$h^2 = 3r^2$$
$$h = r\sqrt{3}$$

SAT* MATH LEVEL 1 PRACTICE TEST 2

SAT MATH LEVEL 1 PRACTICE TEST 2 ANSWER SHEET

1.	Ⓐ	Ⓑ	Ⓒ	Ⓓ	Ⓔ	18.	Ⓐ	Ⓑ	Ⓒ	Ⓓ	Ⓔ	35.	Ⓐ	Ⓑ	Ⓒ	Ⓓ	Ⓔ
2.	Ⓐ	Ⓑ	Ⓒ	Ⓓ	Ⓔ	19.	Ⓐ	Ⓑ	Ⓒ	Ⓓ	Ⓔ	36.	Ⓐ	Ⓑ	Ⓒ	Ⓓ	Ⓔ
3.	Ⓐ	Ⓑ	Ⓒ	Ⓓ	Ⓔ	20.	Ⓐ	Ⓑ	Ⓒ	Ⓓ	Ⓔ	37.	Ⓐ	Ⓑ	Ⓒ	Ⓓ	Ⓔ
4.	Ⓐ	Ⓑ	Ⓒ	Ⓓ	Ⓔ	21.	Ⓐ	Ⓑ	Ⓒ	Ⓓ	Ⓔ	38.	Ⓐ	Ⓑ	Ⓒ	Ⓓ	Ⓔ
5.	Ⓐ	Ⓑ	Ⓒ	Ⓓ	Ⓔ	22.	Ⓐ	Ⓑ	Ⓒ	Ⓓ	Ⓔ	39.	Ⓐ	Ⓑ	Ⓒ	Ⓓ	Ⓔ
6.	Ⓐ	Ⓑ	Ⓒ	Ⓓ	Ⓔ	23.	Ⓐ	Ⓑ	Ⓒ	Ⓓ	Ⓔ	40.	Ⓐ	Ⓑ	Ⓒ	Ⓓ	Ⓔ
7.	Ⓐ	Ⓑ	Ⓒ	Ⓓ	Ⓔ	24.	Ⓐ	Ⓑ	Ⓒ	Ⓓ	Ⓔ	41.	Ⓐ	Ⓑ	Ⓒ	Ⓓ	Ⓔ
8.	Ⓐ	Ⓑ	Ⓒ	Ⓓ	Ⓔ	25.	Ⓐ	Ⓑ	Ⓒ	Ⓓ	Ⓔ	42.	Ⓐ	Ⓑ	Ⓒ	Ⓓ	Ⓔ
9.	Ⓐ	Ⓑ	Ⓒ	Ⓓ	Ⓔ	26.	Ⓐ	Ⓑ	Ⓒ	Ⓓ	Ⓔ	43.	Ⓐ	Ⓑ	Ⓒ	Ⓓ	Ⓔ
10.	Ⓐ	Ⓑ	Ⓒ	Ⓓ	Ⓔ	27.	Ⓐ	Ⓑ	Ⓒ	Ⓓ	Ⓔ	44.	Ⓐ	Ⓑ	Ⓒ	Ⓓ	Ⓔ
11.	Ⓐ	Ⓑ	Ⓒ	Ⓓ	Ⓔ	28.	Ⓐ	Ⓑ	Ⓒ	Ⓓ	Ⓔ	45.	Ⓐ	Ⓑ	Ⓒ	Ⓓ	Ⓔ
12.	Ⓐ	Ⓑ	Ⓒ	Ⓓ	Ⓔ	29.	Ⓐ	Ⓑ	Ⓒ	Ⓓ	Ⓔ	46.	Ⓐ	Ⓑ	Ⓒ	Ⓓ	Ⓔ
13.	Ⓐ	Ⓑ	Ⓒ	Ⓓ	Ⓔ	30.	Ⓐ	Ⓑ	Ⓒ	Ⓓ	Ⓔ	47.	Ⓐ	Ⓑ	Ⓒ	Ⓓ	Ⓔ
14.	Ⓐ	Ⓑ	Ⓒ	Ⓓ	Ⓔ	31.	Ⓐ	Ⓑ	Ⓒ	Ⓓ	Ⓔ	48.	Ⓐ	Ⓑ	Ⓒ	Ⓓ	Ⓔ
15.	Ⓐ	Ⓑ	Ⓒ	Ⓓ	Ⓔ	32.	Ⓐ	Ⓑ	Ⓒ	Ⓓ	Ⓔ	49.	Ⓐ	Ⓑ	Ⓒ	Ⓓ	Ⓔ
16.	Ⓐ	Ⓑ	Ⓒ	Ⓓ	Ⓔ	33.	Ⓐ	Ⓑ	Ⓒ	Ⓓ	Ⓔ	50.	Ⓐ	Ⓑ	Ⓒ	Ⓓ	Ⓔ
17.	Ⓐ	Ⓑ	Ⓒ	Ⓓ	Ⓔ	34.	Ⓐ	Ⓑ	Ⓒ	Ⓓ	Ⓔ						

SAT MATH LEVEL 1 PRACTICE TEST 2

Time—1 hour

For each of the following problems, decide which is the BEST of the choices given. If the exact numerical value is not one of the choices, select the choice that best approximates this value. Then fill in the corresponding oval on the answer sheet.

<u>Notes:</u> (1) A calculator will be necessary for answering some (but not all) of the questions in this test. For each question you will have to decide whether or not you should use a calculator. The calculator you use must be at least a scientific calculator; programmable calculators and calculators that can display graphs are permitted.

(2) For some questions in this test you may need to decide whether your calculator should be in radian or degree mode.

(3) Figures that accompany problems in this test are intended to provide information useful in solving the problems. They are drawn as accurately as possible EXCEPT when it is stated in a specific problem that its figure is not drawn to scale. All figures lie in a plane unless otherwise indicated.

(4) Unless otherwise specified, the domain of any function f is assumed to be the set of all real numbers x for which $f(x)$ is a real number.

REFERENCE INFORMATION

THE FOLLOWING INFORMATION IS FOR YOUR REFERENCE IN ANSWERING SOME OF THE QUESTIONS IN THIS TEST:

Volume of a right circular cone with radius r and height h: $V = \frac{1}{3}\pi r^2 h$

Lateral area of a right circular cone with circumference of the base c and slant height l: $S = \frac{1}{2}cl$

Volume of a sphere with radius r: $V = \frac{4}{3}\pi r^3$

Surface area of a sphere with radius r: $S = 4\pi r^2$

Volume of a pyramid with base area B and height h: $V = \frac{1}{3}Bh$

USE THIS SPACE FOR SCRATCHWORK.

1. If $x + 7(2 - x) = 6(2 - x) + 3(x - 2)$, then $x =$

(A) $\frac{8}{3}$

(B) 0

(C) −3

(D) $-\frac{7}{3}$

(E) −4

GO ON TO THE NEXT PAGE

USE THIS SPACE FOR SCRATCHWORK.

2. Which of the following integers is NOT divisible by 2, 3, and 7 ?

   (A) 84
   (B) 168
   (C) 294
   (D) 398
   (E) 420

3. At what value of x do the lines $y = x + 1$ and $y = 1 - x$ intersect?

   (A) −1
   (B) 0
   (C) 1
   (D) 2
   (E) 3.5

4. $\dfrac{2^2 - 1}{2 - 1} + \dfrac{3^2 - 1}{3 - 1} + \dfrac{4^2 - 1}{4 - 1} + \dfrac{5^2 - 1}{5 - 1} =$

   (A) 18
   (B) 20
   (C) 22
   (D) 24
   (E) 26

5. In Figure 1, if $AC = x + 2$ and $BD = 12 - x$ and $BC = 3$, then what is the length of AD ?

   (A) 19
   (B) 15
   (C) 11
   (D) $2x - 5$
   (E) $2x + 13$

   ```
   |------+------+------+------|
   A      B      C           D
   ```

   Note: Figure not drawn to scale
   Figure 1

6. If $x = y^2$ and $y = \dfrac{z}{3}$, what is the value of x when $z = 9$?

   (A) 1
   (B) 3
   (C) 8
   (D) 9
   (E) 36

GO ON TO THE NEXT PAGE

USE THIS SPACE FOR SCRATCHWORK.

7. Line l intersects plane P perpendicularly at point p. Line m intersects line l perpendicularly at point q. If p and q are distinct, then which of the following must be true?

   (A) Line m is parallel to line l.
   (B) Line m intersects plane P at one point.
   (C) Line m is contained in plane P.
   (D) Line m is parallel to plane P.
   (E) Line m is perpendicular to plane P.

8. If $x \neq -3$, $\dfrac{x^2 + x - 6}{x + 3} =$

   (A) $x - 3$
   (B) $x + 2$
   (C) $x - 2$
   (D) 1
   (E) 2

9. If a recipe for two servings calls for x cups of flour, then how many quarts of flour will be required for 7 servings (1 quart = 4 cups)?

   (A) $\dfrac{8x}{7}$
   (B) $\dfrac{7x}{8}$
   (C) $\dfrac{7x}{4}$
   (D) $\dfrac{7x}{2}$
   (E) $3x$

10. The cube in Figure 2 consists of 64 small cubes. If the outside of the larger cube is painted red, then what percentage of the smaller cubes will NOT have paint on any of their faces?

    (A) 12.5%
    (B) 14.7%
    (C) 35%
    (D) 50%
    (E) 87.5%

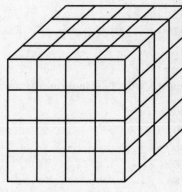

Figure 2

GO ON TO THE NEXT PAGE

USE THIS SPACE FOR SCRATCHWORK.

11. What is the perimeter of triangle *ABC* in Figure 3?

   (A) 45
   (B) 47
   (C) 48
   (D) 50
   (E) 58

12. Referring to Figure 4, what is the cosine of ∠*DAB* ?

   (A) 0.50
   (B) 0.57
   (C) 0.61
   (D) 0.66
   (E) 0.83

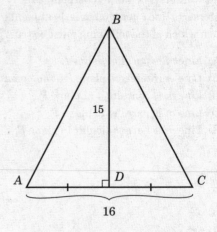

Note: Figure not drawn to scale.
Figure 3

13. If $3n + 7m = 27$ and n and m are both positive integers, then which of the following could be $n + m$?

   (A) 2
   (B) 3
   (C) 4
   (D) 5
   (E) 6

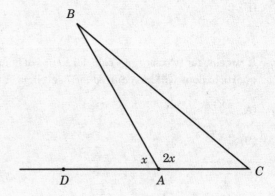

Figure 4

14. If $\dfrac{1}{t} + \dfrac{2}{3t} = \dfrac{1}{3}$, then $t =$

   (A) 6
   (B) 5
   (C) 4.5
   (D) 3.5
   (E) 2.5

15. In Figure 5, what is θ in terms of x and y ?

   (A) $90 - x - y$
   (B) $90 - x + y$
   (C) $90 + x - y$
   (D) $180 - x - y$
   (E) $180 - x + y$

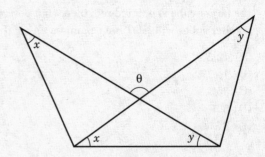

Figure 5

GO ON TO THE NEXT PAGE

10 Practice Exams for the SAT Subject Tests

16. John can paint a house in d days. If John works for x days and then stops, then what fraction of the house remains unpainted in terms of x and d ? (Assume $d > x$.)

    (A) $\dfrac{d-x}{d}$

    (B) $1 - \dfrac{d}{x}$

    (C) $\dfrac{x-d}{x}$

    (D) x

    (E) $d - x$

17. A line passes through the points $(k, k+1)$ and $(2k, 2-k)$. If the slope of the line is $\dfrac{1}{3}$, then what is the value of k ?

    (A) $\dfrac{1}{7}$

    (B) $\dfrac{1}{3}$

    (C) $\dfrac{3}{7}$

    (D) $\dfrac{9}{4}$

    (E) $\dfrac{7}{3}$

18. If a two-digit positive integer is selected at random and then divided by 5, what is the probability that the remainder is either zero or an even integer?

    (A) $\dfrac{1}{5}$

    (B) $\dfrac{2}{5}$

    (C) $\dfrac{3}{5}$

    (D) $\dfrac{4}{5}$

    (E) $\dfrac{5}{6}$

GO ON TO THE NEXT PAGE

19. Which of the following is the solution set to $|x - 1| + 3 \le 0$?

    (A) $-2 < x < 4$
    (B) $-2 \le x \le 4$
    (C) $x \le -2$ or $x \ge 4$
    (D) $0 \le x \le 4$
    (E) The inequality has no solutions.

20. Let $x \otimes y$ be defined on all positive real numbers as

    $x \otimes y = \dfrac{x - y}{x + y}$. If $3 \otimes k = 3.5$ then $k =$

    (A) $-\dfrac{15}{7}$

    (B) $-\dfrac{5}{3}$

    (C) $-\dfrac{3}{2}$

    (D) -1

    (E) $-\dfrac{15}{13}$

21. If $20^{k-1} = 4^3 \cdot 5^3$, then $k =$

    (A) 4
    (B) 3
    (C) 2.5
    (D) 2
    (E) 1.8

22. If the area of a triangle is $18x^2$, and if its base and height are equal, what is the length of the base of the triangle?

    (A) 9
    (B) 3
    (C) x
    (D) $3x$
    (E) $6x$

GO ON TO THE NEXT PAGE

USE THIS SPACE FOR SCRATCHWORK.

23. The circle in Figure 6 has center O and radius r. According to the figure, which of the following equations must a, b, and r satisfy?

(A) $a + b = 2r$
(B) $a^2 + b^2 = r^2$
(C) $a^2 + b^2 = 2r^2$
(D) $a^2 + b^2 = 4r^2$
(E) $a^2 + b^2 = 8r^2$

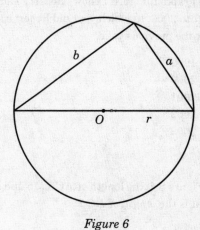

Figure 6

24. If a third of a circle's area is 6, then the circle's radius must be equal to

(A) 2.39
(B) 3.02
(C) 3.14
(D) 3.26
(E) 4.07

25. If $f(x) = x^2 + 1$, $g(x) = 3x - 2$, and $h(x) = \frac{1}{2}x$, then $f(g(h(8))) =$

(A) 55.5
(B) 67
(C) 93.2
(D) 100
(E) 101

26. Which of the following is the graph of the solution set to $2 \le |x| \le 3$?

(A)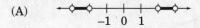

(B)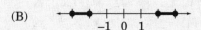

(C)

(D)

(E)

GO ON TO THE NEXT PAGE

27. The graph in Figure 7 shows Robert's salary over the period from 1997 to 2003. In which year did Robert's salary increase by 60% over the previous year?

   (A) 1999
   (B) 2000
   (C) 2001
   (D) 2002
   (E) 2003

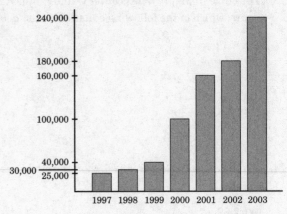

Figure 7

28. In Figure 8, if the length of AC is 15 and if m$\angle CAB = 69°$, then what is the length of BC ?

   (A) 33.2
   (B) 39.1
   (C) 41.7
   (D) 44.0
   (E) 44.8

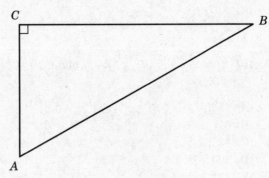

Figure 8

29. The geometric mean of two positive integers, a and b, is defined by $G_{ab} = \sqrt{a \cdot b}$. How many ordered pairs of positive integers (a, b) satisfy $G_{ab} = 3$?

   (A) One
   (B) Two
   (C) Three
   (D) Four
   (E) Infinitely many

30. In Figure 9, if $\triangle PQR$ is first reflected across the x-axis and then reflected across the y-axis, which of the following will be the coordinates of the point Q ?

   (A) $(1, -3)$
   (B) $(2, -3)$
   (C) $(1, 3)$
   (D) $(-1, 3)$
   (E) $(-1, -3)$

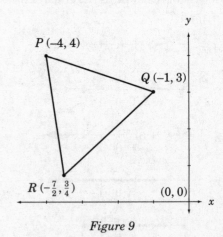

Figure 9

GO ON TO THE NEXT PAGE

31. The formula for the total surface area of a right circular cone with equal radius and height is given by $SA(r) = \pi r(r + \sqrt{2r^2})$, where r is the radius of the cone. If a cone has a radius and height equal to 7, which of the following is the best approximation of the surface area?

    (A) 249
    (B) 254
    (C) 298
    (D) 370
    (E) 372

32. The average grade on a history test was 80. If 2 students had each scored 10 points higher than they actually did, then the average would have been 82. How many students are in the class?

    (A) 7
    (B) 8
    (C) 9
    (D) 10
    (E) 12

33. If $f(x) = \dfrac{1}{\sqrt{5 - 4x}}$, which of the following is in the domain of f?

    (A) $-\dfrac{5}{4}$

    (B) $\dfrac{5}{4}$

    (C) $\dfrac{3}{2}$

    (D) 2

    (E) $\dfrac{7}{3}$

34. If the area of $\triangle ABC$ (shown in Figure 10) is an integer, then which of the following must be true of a ?

    (A) a is a factor of c
    (B) a is a prime number
    (C) a is a positive multiple of 4
    (D) a is a positive even integer
    (E) a is a positive odd integer

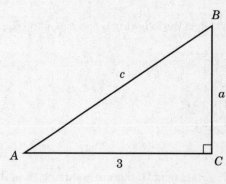

Figure 10

GO ON TO THE NEXT PAGE

35. A fair coin is flipped 4 times. What is the probability of obtaining at least 3 heads?

    (A) 0.125
    (B) 0.25
    (C) 0.3125
    (D) 0.375
    (E) 0.5

36. A line segment connects the origin to the point (a, a^2). What is the slope of a line perpendicular to this line segment?

    (A) $-a$

    (B) $-\dfrac{1}{a}$

    (C) $2a$

    (D) $\dfrac{a^2 - 1}{a}$

    (E) $\dfrac{a}{a^2 + 1}$

37. If the origin is the midpoint of the line segment between the points $(-1, 4)$ and (x, y), then $(x, y) =$

    (A) $(-4, 1)$
    (B) $(-4, -1)$
    (C) $(1, 4)$
    (D) $(1, -4)$
    (E) $(-1, -4)$

38. Which of the following is one root of the equation $x^2 + 13 = 4x$?

    (A) $4 + i$
    (B) $3 - 2i$
    (C) $4 + 3i$
    (D) $2 - 6i$
    (E) $2 + 3i$

39. The statement "If the sun is shining, then the grass is dry" is logically equivalent to which of the following?

    (A) If the sun is not shining, then the grass is not dry.
    (B) If the grass is not dry, then the sun is shining.
    (C) If the sun is shining, then the grass is not dry.
    (D) If the grass is not dry, then the sun is not shining.
    (E) If the grass is dry, then the sun is shining.

GO ON TO THE NEXT PAGE

USE THIS SPACE FOR SCRATCHWORK.

40. If $\log_{16}8 = x$, then $x =$

(A) $\dfrac{3}{4}$

(B) $\dfrac{4}{3}$

(C) $\dfrac{3}{2}$

(D) 2

(E) $\dfrac{5}{2}$

41. In Figure 11, the radius of circle O is 5. If the length of chord AB is 5, then the area of the shaded region is approximately

(A) 5.10
(B) 4.35
(C) 3.10
(D) 2.25
(E) 1.85

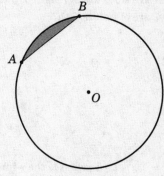

Figure 11

42. If the point $(6, -3)$ is on the graph of $y = f(x)$, and if $f(x)$ is defined for all real numbers, then which of the following points must be on the graph of $y = f(-x) - 1$?

(A) $(-6, -4)$
(B) $(-6, -3)$
(C) $(-6, -2)$
(D) $(6, -4)$
(E) $(6, 4)$

43. If $0 < \theta < 90°$, then $\cot\theta\sin\theta\sec\theta =$

(A) $\dfrac{1}{\cos\theta}$

(B) $\sin\theta$

(C) $\cot\theta$

(D) -1

(E) 1

GO ON TO THE NEXT PAGE

44. The nth term in the sequence of numbers {2, 5, 10, 17, ...} can be determined by which of the following?

    (A) $5n - 3$
    (B) $2 + 3(n - 1)$
    (C) $3n - 1$
    (D) $n^2 + 1$
    (E) $n^2 - 1$

45. The volume V of a regular polyhedron varies directly with the cube of the length of its sides. If the volume V is 100 when the polyhedron's sides are of length 3, then what is the volume when the sides are of unit length?

    (A) 2.7
    (B) 2.9
    (C) 3.3
    (D) 3.7
    (E) 4.0

46. If $f(x) = \sqrt[3]{x - 1} - 1$, what is the y-intercept of the graph of $f^{-1}(x)$?

    (A) 0
    (B) 1
    (C) 2
    (D) 3
    (E) 3.3

47. In Figure 12, a regular hexagon is inscribed in a rectangle with sides of length 1 and $\frac{\sqrt{3}}{2}$. What is the length of the sides of the hexagon?

    (A) $\frac{1}{4}$

    (B) $\frac{1}{3}$

    (C) $\frac{1}{2}$

    (D) $\frac{2}{3}$

    (E) $\frac{3}{4}$

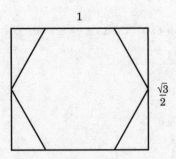

Figure 12

GO ON TO THE NEXT PAGE

USE THIS SPACE FOR SCRATCHWORK.

48. In Figure 13, if the area of parallelogram *ABCD* is 49, which of the following could be the degree measure of θ ?

   (A) 61°
   (B) 66°
   (C) 72°
   (D) 79°
   (E) 81°

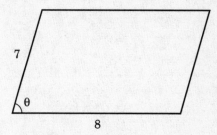

7

θ

8

Note: Figure not drawn to scale.
Figure 13

49. Figure 14 shows a cube with a volume of 64. If the cube is divided into two pieces along the plane through points *A*, *B*, *C*, and *D*, then what is the total surface area of the resulting solids?

   (A) $96 + 32\sqrt{2}$
   (B) $96 + 32\sqrt{3}$
   (C) $96 + 64\sqrt{2}$
   (D) $96 + 96\sqrt{2}$
   (E) 192

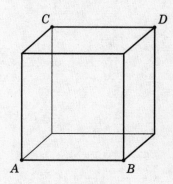

Figure 14

50. If the third term in a geometric sequence is 4 and the seventh term is 64, then what is the twentieth term in the sequence?

   (A) 65,536
   (B) 131,072
   (C) 262,144
   (D) 524,288
   (E) 1,048,576

S T O P

IF YOU FINISH BEFORE TIME IS CALLED, YOU MAY CHECK YOUR WORK ON THIS TEST ONLY.
DO NOT TURN TO ANY OTHER TEST IN THIS BOOK.

SAT MATH LEVEL 1 PRACTICE TEST 2 EXPLANATIONS

MATH LEVEL 1 PRACTICE TEST 2 ANSWERS

Question Number	Answer	Right	Wrong	Question Number	Answer	Right	Wrong
1	A	___	___	26	B	___	___
2	D	___	___	27	C	___	___
3	B	___	___	28	B	___	___
4	A	___	___	29	C	___	___
5	C	___	___	30	A	___	___
6	D	___	___	31	E	___	___
7	D	___	___	32	D	___	___
8	C	___	___	33	A	___	___
9	B	___	___	34	D	___	___
10	A	___	___	35	C	___	___
11	D	___	___	36	B	___	___
12	A	___	___	37	D	___	___
13	D	___	___	38	E	___	___
14	B	___	___	39	D	___	___
15	D	___	___	40	A	___	___
16	A	___	___	41	D	___	___
17	C	___	___	42	A	___	___
18	C	___	___	43	E	___	___
19	E	___	___	44	D	___	___
20	B	___	___	45	D	___	___
21	A	___	___	46	C	___	___
22	E	___	___	47	C	___	___
23	D	___	___	48	A	___	___
24	A	___	___	49	A	___	___
25	E	___	___	50	D	___	___

CALCULATING YOUR SCORE

Your raw score for the SAT Math Level 1 Test is calculated from the number of questions you answer correctly and incorrectly. Once you have determined your composite score, use the conversion table on page 204 of this book to calculate your scaled score. To calculate your raw score, count the number of questions you answered correctly:

_____
A

Count the number of questions you answered incorrectly, and multiply that number by $\frac{1}{4}$:

_____ $\times \frac{1}{4} =$ _____
B   C

Subtract the value in field C from the value in field A:

_____
D

Round the number in field D to the nearest whole number. This is your raw score:

_____
E

MATH LEVEL 1 TEST 2 EXPLANATIONS

1. A Algebra: Equation Solving

Distribute the terms in this equation to solve for x:

$$x + 7(2 - x) = 6(2 - x) + 3(x - 2)$$
$$x + 14 - 7x = 12 - 6x + 3x - 6$$
$$14 - 6x = 6 - 3x$$
$$8 = 3x$$
$$\frac{8}{3} = x$$

2. D Fundamentals: Integers

You need to know the basic properties of the integers for the Math Level 1 Test. If a number is divisible by 2, 3, and 7, then it must also be divisible by the product of these numbers: $2 \times 3 \times 7 = 42$. Divide each of the answer choices by 42. Only **D** is not evenly divisible by 42, so it's the correct answer.

3. B Algebra: Equation Solving

The two lines intersect at the point when their x values are equal and their y values are equal. You can find the point of intersection by setting $y = x + 1$ and $y = 1 - x$ equal to each other:

$$1 - x = x + 1$$
$$0 = 2x$$
$$0 = x$$

4. A Algebra: Writing Equations, Exponents

You could use a calculator to work out the answer to this question, but it is easier to solve by hand, especially if you can spot its pattern.

$$\frac{2^2 - 1}{2 - 1} = 3$$

$$\frac{3^2 - 1}{3 - 1} = 4$$

In general, the following rule works:

$$\frac{n^2 - 1}{n - 1} = \frac{(n - 1)(n + 1)}{n - 1}$$
$$= n + 1$$

Applying this rule, you can reduce the problem to $3 + 4 + 5 + 6 = 18$.

5. C Algebra: Equation Solving

The length of AD is equal to $AC + BD - BC$. Since AC and BD overlap on the segment BC, you need to subtract BC from the sum of AC and BD so you don't double count it.

$$AD = AC + BD - BC$$
$$= x + 2 + 12 - x - 3$$
$$= 14 - 3$$
$$= 11$$

6. **D**   Algebra: Equation Solving

In order to find the value of x, you first need to find the value of y, since $x = y^2$. Start by plugging $z = 9$ into $y = \frac{z}{3}$:

$$y = \frac{9}{3}$$
$$= 3$$

Now plug this value of y into $x = y^2$:

$$x = 3^2$$
$$= 9$$

7. **D**   Plane Geometry: Lines and Planes

Try drawing a picture of the situation described in the question:

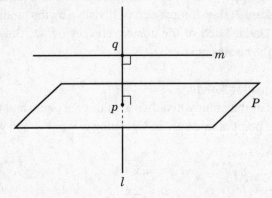

You should be able to see from this picture that the line m must run parallel to the plane P.

8. **C**   Algebra: Polynomials

When you have a polynomial in unfactored form, you should try factoring it since factoring often reveals a solution to the problem. In this case, factor the polynomial in the numerator:

$$\frac{x^2 + x - 6}{x + 3} = \frac{(x + 3)(x - 2)}{(x + 3)}$$
$$= x - 2$$

9. **B**   Algebra: Writing Equations, Word Problems

The question tells you that you need x cups of flour for every 2 servings of food, and you can express this relationship as $\frac{x}{2}$ cups per serving. You need to figure out how many cups of flour you need in order to make 7 servings of food. Since the proportion of flour in the recipe should be the same whether you make 2 or 7 servings, you can set up the equation: $\frac{x}{2} = \frac{y}{7}$, where y is the number of cups of flour you need for 7 servings. Now solve for y:

$$\frac{7x}{2} = y$$

Finally, you need to convert this amount from cups per serving to quarts per serving:

$$\frac{7x}{2}\frac{\text{cups}}{\text{serving}} \times \frac{1 \text{ quart}}{4 \text{ cups}} = \frac{7x}{8}\frac{\text{quarts}}{\text{serving}}$$

10. **A**   Solid Geometry: Prisms

The larger cube consists of 64 smaller cubes, and you can see from the figure that each side of the larger cube is 4 small cubes in length. When the outside of the larger cube is painted, every small cube that has at least one side facing out will be painted. To find the number of cubes without any paint, you simply strip off this outer layer of small painted cubes, as in the figure below:

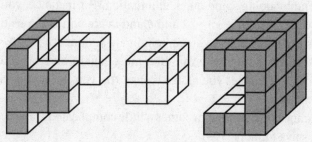

You can see that there are 8 smaller cubes untouched by paint. The percentage of the unpainted smaller cubes is $\frac{8}{64} = 0.125$, or 12.5%.

11. **D**   Plane Geometry: Triangles

The triangle in the figure can be broken down into two right triangles, $\triangle ABD$ and $\triangle CBD$:

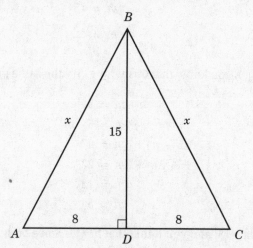

In order to find the perimeter of the large triangle, you first need to figure out the hypotenuse of one of the small right triangles. Each of the two small right triangles has legs of lengths 8 and 15. You might recognize that the three sides conform to the special Pythagorean ratio 8:15:17, where 17 is the hypotenuse (x in this case). If not, use the Pythagorean Theorem to solve for the hypotenuse x:

$$\begin{aligned} x^2 &= 15^2 + 8^2 \\ &= 255 + 64 \\ &= 289 \\ x &= 17 \end{aligned}$$

Now add up the sides of the large triangle to find the perimeter: $17 + 17 + 16 = 50$.

12.　**A**　Plane Geometry: Lines and Angles; Trigonometry: Basic Functions

Angles x and $2x$ are supplementary angles, which means that they add up to 180°. You can solve for x using the equation $x + 2x = 180$.

$$3x = 180$$
$$x = 60$$

Now take the cosine of x, since $\angle DAB = x$: $\cos 60° = \dfrac{1}{2}$.

13.　**D**　Algebra: Equation Solving

This problem isn't particularly difficult, but it is time consuming. You can cut down on the time you spend by doing some quick elimination. For instance, you know that in **A** both n and m equal 1, since $n + m = 2$ and n and m are non-zero positive integers. But $3(1) + 7(1)$ does not equal 27, so you can eliminate **A**. Similarly, for **B**, which says that $n + m = 3$, you know that one of the variables must equal 1 and the other must equal 2. No matter which of these values you assign to n and m, you can't produce $3n + 7m = 27$, so you can eliminate **B**.

Now your fiddling with n and m becomes a little complicated. Take **C**, which says that $n + m = 4$, and solve for n:

$$n = 4 - m$$

Plug this value for n into $3n + 7m = 27$:

$$3(4 - m) + 7m = 27$$
$$12 - 3m + 7m = 27$$
$$4m = 15$$
$$m = \frac{15}{4}$$

Since m is not an integer, you know that **C** is wrong. Try the same procedure on **D**:

$$n + m = 5$$
$$n = 5 - m$$
$$3(5 - m) + 7m = 27$$
$$15 - 3m + 7m = 27$$
$$4m = 12$$
$$m = 3$$

Plug $m = 3$ into $n + m = 5$, and you'll find that $n = 2$. Since both n and m are integers, you know that **D** is correct.

14.　**B**　Algebra: Equation Solving

There are a number of ways you can solve this problem. One easy method is to create a common denominator, $3t$, on the left side of the equation:

$$\frac{1}{t} + \frac{2}{3t} = \frac{1}{3}$$
$$\frac{3}{3t} + \frac{2}{3t} = \frac{1}{3}$$
$$\frac{5}{3t} = \frac{1}{3}$$

Now cross multiply to get rid of the denominators:

$$15 = 3t$$
$$5 = t$$

15. **D** Plane Geometry: Lines and Angles, Triangles

To solve this problem, you need to know about the angles created by intersecting lines and the angles in a triangle. When you have two intersecting lines, the angles opposite each other are congruent, or equal in measure:

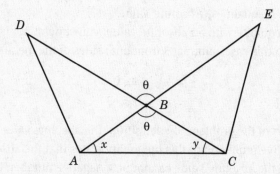

In the figure, $\angle DBE$ is equal to $\angle ABC$ because they are created by intersecting lines. $\angle ABC$ is the third angle in a triangle with angles x and y. Since the three angles in a triangle add up to $180°$, you can write the equation $x + y + \theta = 180$, or $\theta = 180 - x - y$.

16. **A** Algebra: Writing Equations, Word Problems

If John can paint a house in d days, then his rate of work is $\frac{1}{d}$ houses per day. Since work equals rate multiplied by time, in x days John paints $\frac{1}{d} \cdot x = \frac{x}{d}$. The amount of the house left unpainted is $1 - \frac{x}{d}$, since 1, or $\frac{d}{d}$, represents the completion of the house. Now turn $1 - \frac{x}{d}$ into a single fraction:

$$1 - \frac{x}{d} = \frac{d}{d} - \frac{x}{d}$$
$$= \frac{d - x}{d}$$

17. **C** Coordinate Geometry: Lines and Slope

The slope of a line is equal to the change in y-value divided by the change in x-value, or $\frac{y_1 - y_2}{x_1 - x_2}$. Plug the x and y values of $(k, k + 1)$ and $(2k, 2 - k)$ into the slope formula:

$$\frac{\Delta y}{\Delta x} = \frac{(2 - k) - (k + 1)}{2k - k}$$
$$= \frac{1 - 2k}{k}$$

Set this expression equal to $\frac{1}{3}$, and solve for k:

$$\frac{1}{3} = \frac{1 - 2k}{k}$$
$$k = 3 - 6k$$
$$7k = 3$$
$$k = \frac{3}{7}$$

18. C Fundamentals: Integers; Statistics: Probability

This problem is easier than it seems because you don't need to do any division. If a two-digit positive integer is divided by 5, then the set of all possible remainders is $\{0, 1, 2, 3, 4\}$. (If the remainder is greater than or equal to 5, then 5 can go into the number at least one more time.) Of the possible remainders, only $\{0, 2, 4\}$ are even integers. So the probability that you'll get either a zero or an even integer is 3 in 5, or $\frac{3}{5}$.

19. E Algebra: Inequalities, Absolute Value

When solving an inequality with an absolute value, you should first isolate the absolute value on one side. In this case, subtract 3 from both sides of the inequality:

$$|x - 1| + 3 \le 0$$
$$|x - 1| \le -3$$

Here's the tricky part of the problem. By definition, the absolute value of any number or expression is a positive number, but this inequality states that the absolute value of $(x - 1)$ is negative. Since the absolute value cannot be a negative number, this inequality has no solution set.

20. B Functions: Evaluating Functions

This problem may seem intimidating because the function $x \otimes y$ is unfamiliar, but finding the solution is merely a matter of plugging values into the definition you're given. The question tells you that $x \otimes y = \frac{x - y}{x + y}$ and asks you to find $3 \otimes k$. Simply plug $x = 3$ and $y = k$ into $\frac{x - y}{x + y}$:

$$3 \otimes k = \frac{3 - k}{3 + k}$$

Now set this expression equal to 3.5 to find k:

$$\frac{3 - k}{3 + k} = 3.5$$
$$3 - k = 3.5(3 + k)$$
$$3 - k = 10.5 + 3.5k$$
$$-7.5 = 4.5k$$
$$k = -\frac{7.5}{4.5}$$
$$= -\frac{5}{3}$$

21. A Algebra: Equation Solving, Exponents

The fastest way to answer this question is to use the law of exponents that says $A^x \cdot B^x = (AB)^x$:

$$20^{k-1} = 4^3 \cdot 5^3$$
$$= (20)^3$$
$$20^{k-1} = 20^3$$

Since the bases of these two terms are equal, you know that their exponents must be equal:

$$k - 1 = 3$$
$$k = 4$$

22. E   Plane Geometry: Triangles; Algebra: Equation Solving

The formula for the area of a triangle is $\frac{1}{2}bh$, where b is the triangle's base and h is its height. According to the question, the base and height of this triangle are equal, so you can write the area as $\frac{1}{2}b^2$. Set this expression equal to $18x^2$:

$$18x^2 = \frac{1}{2}b^2$$
$$36x^2 = b^2$$
$$6x = b$$

23. D   Plane Geometry: Circles, Triangles

If a triangle is inscribed within a circle such that one of the triangle's sides passes through the circle's origin, then the triangle must be a right triangle. In these cases, the triangle's hypotenuse is the circle's diameter. Since the diameter of the circle is twice the length of the radius r, you know that the hypotenuse is equal to $2r$. The question asks you to find an equation that must always be true of the triangle's sides, a, b, and r. Since the Pythagorean Theorem applies to all right triangles, you know the triangle's sides must conform to the following equation:

$$a^2 + b^2 = (2r)^2$$
$$a^2 + b^2 = 4r^2$$

24. A   Plane Geometry: Circles

The area of a circle with radius r is given by the formula $A = \pi r^2$. Since a third of the circle's area is equal to 6, you can set up the following equation:

$$\frac{1}{3}A = 6$$
$$\frac{1}{3}\pi r^2 = 6$$
$$r^2 = \frac{18}{\pi}$$
$$r = \sqrt{\frac{18}{\pi}}$$
$$\approx 2.39$$

25. E   Functions: Compound Functions

When solving compound functions like $f(g(h(8)))$, you need to work from the inside out. First evaluate $h(8)$ by plugging $x = 8$ into $h(x)$:

$$h(x) = \frac{1}{2}x$$
$$h(8) = \frac{8}{2}$$
$$= 4$$

Now plug 4 into $g(x)$:

$$g(x) = 3x - 2$$
$$g(4) = 3(4) - 2$$
$$= 10$$

Finally, plug 10 into $f(x)$:

$$f(x) = x^2 + 1$$
$$f(10) = 10^2 + 1$$
$$= 101$$

26. B Algebra: Inequalities

An inequality that involves an absolute value has two solutions. One solution of $2 \leq |x| \leq 3$ is $2 \leq x \leq 3$. To find the second solution, multiply $2 \leq x \leq 3$ by -1, and remember that multiplying inequalities by negative numbers flips the inequality signs. The second solution is $-2 \geq x \geq -3$. On a number line graph, $2 \leq x \leq 3$ and $-2 \geq x \geq -3$ look like this:

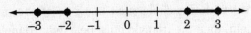

27. C Fundamentals: Percents

You need to find the year when Robert's salary increased by 60%—in other words, the year when it was 1.6 times larger than his salary the year before. According to the chart, his salary in 2001 was $160,000 and his salary in 2000 was $100,000. $1.6 \times 100,000 = 160,000$, so **C**, 2001, is correct.

28. B Trigonometry: Basic Functions

This question tests your understanding of the basic trigonometric functions. Add the information stated in the question to the figure:

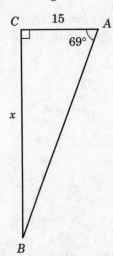

In the right triangle above, you know the size of $\angle CAB$ and the length of the side adjacent to $\angle CAB$. You're asked to find x, the length of the side opposite the given angle. The function that combines these elements is $\tan\theta = \dfrac{\text{opposite}}{\text{adjacent}}$. Plug the values you have into this function, and then solve for x:

$$\tan 69° = \frac{x}{15}$$
$$15\tan 69° = x$$
$$x = 39.1$$

29. C Algebra: Equation Solving; Fundamentals: Integers
This question doesn't really involve the geometric mean. All you need to do is set the equations $G_{ab} = \sqrt{a \cdot b}$ and $G_{ab} = 3$ equal to each other:

$$3 = \sqrt{a \cdot b}$$

Now square both sides of the equation to get:

$$9 = a \cdot b$$

a and b are positive integers, and they must also be factors of 9. Since the positive integer factors of 9 are 1, 3, and 9, the possible pairs of a and b are $(1, 9)$, $(3, 3)$, and $(9, 1)$.

30. A Functions: Transformations and Symmetry
Since you are interested only in the point $Q(-1, 3)$, you can ignore the rest of the triangle. If a point (a, b) is reflected across the x-axis, it becomes $(a, -b)$. If a point (a, b) is reflected across the y-axis it becomes $(-a, b)$. When you reflect point $Q(-1, 3)$ across the x-axis, then your new point is $Q(-1, -3)$. When you reflect this new point across the y-axis, it will become $Q(1, -3)$.

31. E Functions: Evaluating Functions
Solving this problem doesn't involve any solid geometry. All you need to do to get the answer is evaluate the surface area function at $r = 7$. Plug $r = 7$ into $SA(r)$, and then round your answer to the nearest integer:

$$SA(7) = \pi \cdot 7(7 + \sqrt{2 \cdot 7^2})$$
$$= \pi \cdot 7(7 + 7\sqrt{2})$$
$$\approx 372$$

32. D Algebra: Writing Equations, Arithmetic Mean
The average test score is equal to the sum of all the scores divided by the number of students who took the test. If T is the sum of all the scores and s is the number of students who took the test, then the average test score is $\dfrac{T}{s} = 80$, or $T = 80s$. Since you know neither T nor s, you need to write another equation to determine how many students are in the class. If two of the students had scored 10 points higher than they did, the average

test score would have been 82 and the sum of all scores would have been 20 points higher than it was, or 80s + 20. You can set up an equation for this new average:

$$\frac{80s + 20}{s} = 82$$

$$80s + 20 = 82s$$

$$2s = 20$$

$$s = 10$$

There are 10 students in the class.

33. A   Functions: Domain and Range

The domain of a function $f(x)$ is all the values of x that produce real values of $f(x)$. Try plugging each of the answer choices into the function, and remember that the function is undefined when the denominator is zero or when the number under the square root sign is negative. When you plug in **A**, you'll see that the function is defined for $x = -\frac{5}{4}$, so **A** is the correct answer.

$$f\left(-\frac{5}{4}\right) = \frac{1}{\sqrt{5 - 4\left(-\frac{5}{4}\right)}}$$

$$= \frac{1}{\sqrt{5 + 5}}$$

$$= \frac{1}{\sqrt{10}}$$

34. D   Fundamentals: Integers; Plane Geometry: Triangles

The area of $\triangle ABC$ is equal to $\frac{1}{2}bh$, where b is the base and h is the height of the triangle. As you can see from the figure, the triangle's base is 3, and its height is a, so the area is $\frac{1}{2}(3)a$. The question says that the area is a positive integer, so you know that a needs to be a positive multiple of 2 (in other words, an even integer) in order to cancel the denominator out of $\frac{1}{2}(3)a$.

35. C   Statistics: Probability

When a probability question asks you for *at least* 3 heads, you need to remember that *at least 3* means 3 or more—in this question, that translates to 3 or 4, since there are 4 tosses of the coin. You need to determine the number of sets in which either 3 or 4 heads are tossed; if you divide this number by the total number of possible sets, then you'll find the probability of tossing at least 3 heads. Remembering that the order of the tosses matters, you can find 5 possible sets that produce at least 3 heads: HHHT, HHTH, HTHH, THHH, or HHHH, where H is a head and T is a tail. In order to find the total number, first determine the number of possible outcomes on each toss: 2, since you can toss either a head or a tail. If you have two possible outcomes on each of the four tosses, then the total number of sets is $2 \cdot 2 \cdot 2 \cdot 2 = 16$ sets. Of these 16 sets, 5 achieve at least 3 heads, so the probability of tossing at least 3 heads is $\frac{5}{16} = 0.3125$.

36. B Coordinate Geometry: Lines

The slopes of perpendicular lines are negative reciprocals of each other. If one line has a slope of m, then the other line has a slope of $-\frac{1}{m}$. To solve this problem, first find the slope of the line segment that connects the origin, $(0, 0)$, to the point (a, a^2). The slope of a line is defined as the change in y over the change in x. In this case, the slope is $\frac{\Delta y}{\Delta x} = \frac{a^2 - 0}{a - 0} = \frac{a^2}{a} = a$. The negative reciprocal of a is the slope of the perpendicular line: $m_\perp = -\frac{1}{a}$.

37. D Coordinate Geometry: Lines and Distance

You should solve this problem by using the midpoint formula, which states that the midpoint of a line segment has coordinates equal to the average of the coordinates of the endpoints. You can write the formula as $(x_m, y_m) = \left(\frac{x_1 + x_2}{2}, \frac{y_1 + y_2}{2} \right)$. The question gives you the coordinates of the midpoint and one of the endpoints of the line segment; you can plug these coordinates into the formula to find the other endpoint:

$$(0, 0) = \left(\frac{-1 + x_2}{2}, \frac{4 + y_2}{2} \right)$$

Break this formula into parts to solve separately for the x and y coordinates of the endpoint:

$$\frac{x_2 - 1}{2} = 0$$
$$x_2 - 1 = 0$$
$$x_2 = 1$$

And:

$$\frac{4 + y_2}{2} = 0$$
$$4 + y_2 = 0$$
$$y_2 = -4$$

The other endpoint of this line is $(1, -4)$.

38. **E**   Algebra: Polynomials, Complex Numbers

First, rewrite the equation in the quadratic form: $x^2 - 4x + 13 = 0$ [$a = 1, b = -4, c = 13$]. Then, apply the quadratic formula:

$$x = \frac{-(-4) \pm \sqrt{(-4)^2 - 4(1)(13)}}{2(1)} = \frac{4 \pm \sqrt{16 - 52}}{2} = \frac{4 \pm \sqrt{-36}}{2} = \frac{4 \pm 6i}{2} = 2 \pm 3i$$

The two roots are $2 + 3i$ (**E**) and $2 - 3i$.

39. **D**   Miscellaneous Math: Logic

There is one rule of logic that you need to know for the Math Level 1: "if p, then q" is logically equivalent to its contrapositive "if *not q*, then *not p*." To find the contrapositive of a statement, reverse the order of the phrases and then put a "not" in front of each of them. In this case, "if the sun is shining, then the grass is dry" is equivalent to "if the grass is not dry, then the sun is not shining."

40. **A**   Algebra: Equation Solving, Logarithms

All you need to know to solve this problem is the definition of a logarithm: $\log_b a = x$ is equivalent to $b^x = a$. Rearrange the logarithm according to this definition and solve for x:

$$\log_{16} 8 = x$$

$$16^x = 8$$

Since 16 and 8 share the base 2, you can rewrite them as $16 = 2^4$ and $8 = 2^3$:

$$(2^4)^x = 2^3$$

$$2^{4x} = 2^3$$

Set the exponents equal to one another since the bases of both terms are equal:

$$4x = 3$$

$$x = \frac{3}{4}$$

41. **D**   Plane Geometry: Circles

The area of the shaded region is the difference between the area of the sector AOB and the area of $\triangle ABO$, as shown below.

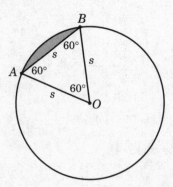

By drawing the radii AO and BO, you can see that $\triangle ABO$ is an equilateral triangle since each side has a length of 5. The fastest way to calculate the triangle's area is to use the formula Area $= \frac{\sqrt{3}}{4}s^2$, where s is the length of a side. You can also use the familiar formula Area $= \frac{1}{2} \cdot$ base $\cdot$ height. If you divide the triangle in half, you'll have a 30-60-90 triangle, where the adjacent side to the 60° angle has a length of $\frac{5}{2}$, and the hypotenuse has a length of 5. The opposite side to the 60° angle must have a length of $\frac{5\sqrt{3}}{2}$. The formula for the area of a sector is Area $= \frac{\theta}{360} \cdot \pi \cdot r^2$, where r is the radius and θ is the interior (or intercepted) angle. Since $\triangle ABO$ is equilateral, you know $\theta = 60°$. Subtract the area of the triangle from the area of the sector:

$$\left(\left(\frac{60}{360} \cdot \pi \cdot 5^2 \right) - \left(\frac{\sqrt{3}}{4} \cdot 5^2 \right) \right) = \left(\frac{25\pi}{6} - \frac{25\sqrt{3}}{4} \right)$$

The area of the shaded region is approximately 2.26.

42. A Functions: Transformations and Symmetry

You need to now how to transform graphs both vertically and horizontally. If you have the graph $y = f(x)$, then $y = f(-x)$ flips $y = f(x)$ across the y-axis. According to this rule, if (a, b) is on $y = f(x)$, then $(-a, b)$ must be on $y = f(-x)$. Also, if (a, b) is on $y = f(x)$, then $(a, b - 1)$ must be on $y = f(x) - 1$ since $f(x) - 1$ shifts the graph down by one unit. Now you can apply these rules to the function in the question. If $(6, -3)$ is on $y = f(x)$, then $(-6, -3)$ is on $y = f(-x)$. If $(-6, -3)$ is on $y = f(-x)$, then $(-6, -3 - 1)$, or $(-6, -4)$, is on $y = f(-x) - 1$.

43. E Trigonometry: Basic Functions

When you have a complicated trigonometric expression, you should try to rewrite it in terms of sine and cosine. Use the trigonometric definitions $\cot \theta = \frac{\cos \theta}{\sin \theta}$ and $\sec \theta = \frac{1}{\cos \theta}$ to simplify this problem:

$$\cot \theta \sin \theta \sec \theta = \frac{\cos \theta}{\sin \theta} \cdot \sin \theta \cdot \frac{1}{\cos \theta}$$
$$= \frac{\cos \theta}{\cos \theta} \cdot \frac{\sin \theta}{\sin \theta}$$
$$= 1$$

44. D Miscellaneous Math: Sequences

The question asks you for the nth term in the shown sequence, which is the same as asking for a general algebraic expression to represent the sequence. In the sequence given by the question, $n = 1$ indicates the first term of a sequence (in this case, 2), and $n = 2$ indicates the second (5).

The simplest way to find the correct algebraic expression for the sequence is to plug a value for n into each answer choice and then see which answer choice generates the number given in the sequence. Choose a value for n for which you know the outcome; for example, you know that when $n = 3$, you should end up with 10 when you plug 3 into the correct expression. Try to choose a value greater than $n = 2$. If you set n equal to 1 or 2 in this question, more than one expression will appear to work, and you'll eventually have to set $n = 3$. If you use $n = 3$, you'll see that only **D** generates 10.

45. D   Algebra: Writing Equations, Variation

This question looks really hard because it involves some complicated solid geometry, but you actually don't need to use solid geometry to solve this problem. Instead, set up a direct variation equation. If the volume of the polyhedron varies directly with the cube of the length of its sides, then $V = k \cdot s^3$, where V is the polyhedron's volume, s is the length of the polyhedron's sides, and k is a constant. You can find k by plugging in $V = 100$ and $s = 3$:

$$100 = k \cdot 3^3$$
$$k = \frac{100}{27}$$

The question asks for the value of V when the polyhedron's sides are of unit length, or $s = 1$. Plug s and k into the variation equation to find V:

$$P = \frac{100}{27} \cdot (1)^3$$
$$= \frac{100}{27}$$
$$= 3.7$$

46. C   Functions: Inverse Functions

The best way to solve this problem is to find $f^{-1}(x)$ and then plug in $x = 0$ to find its y-intercept. Finding the inverse function of $f(x)$ involves three steps. First, replace $f(x)$ with y:

$$f(x) = \sqrt[3]{x-1} - 1$$
$$y = \sqrt[3]{x-1} - 1$$

Second, switch x and y:

$$x = \sqrt[3]{y-1} - 1$$

Last, solve for y:

$$x = \sqrt[3]{y-1} - 1$$
$$x + 1 = \sqrt[3]{y-1}$$
$$(x+1)^3 = y - 1$$
$$(x+1)^3 + 1 = y$$

This equation for y is the inverse function of $f(x)$. Plug $x = 0$ into the inverse function to find its y-intercept: $f^{-1}(0) = (0 + 1)^3 + 1 = 2$.

286

47. C   Plane Geometry: Polygons

Redraw the figure, labeling the sides of the hexagon:

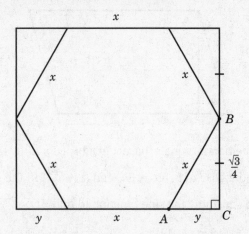

As you can see in the figure, the side of the hexagon is the hypotenuse of the right triangle ABC. In order to find the length of the side, you should figure out the length of the triangle's legs: BC and y. Since all of the hexagon's sides are equal, you know that B bisects the rectangle's side of length $\dfrac{3}{\sqrt{2}}$. Also, since B bisects the side, BC must be equal to half the side's length, or $BC = \dfrac{\sqrt{3}}{4}$. As you can also see from the figure, the rectangle's side of length 1 is equal to $y + x + y$, so you can set up the equation $2y + x = 1$, or $y = \dfrac{1-x}{2}$. Plug the legs of the right triangle into the Pythagorean Theorem to find the hypotenuse, x:

$$x^2 = \left(\frac{\sqrt{3}}{4}\right)^2 + \left(\frac{1-x}{2}\right)^2$$

$$x^2 = \frac{3}{16} + \frac{1}{4}(1 - 2x + x^2)$$

$$x^2 = \frac{3}{16} + \frac{1}{4} - \frac{1}{2}x + \frac{1}{4}x^2$$

$$\frac{3}{4}x^2 + \frac{1}{2}x - \frac{7}{16} = 0$$

Multiply through the equation by 16 to cancel out the denominator:

$$12x^2 + 8x - 7 = 0$$

$$(2x - 1)(6x + 7) = 0$$

$$x = -\frac{7}{6} \text{ or } x = \frac{1}{2}$$

Since it wouldn't make sense for the hexagon's sides to have a negative value, you know that the hexagon's sides must equal $\dfrac{1}{2}$.

48. **A** Trigonometry: Plane Geometry, Polygons

Draw an altitude line perpendicular to the base of the parallelogram (h in the next figure):

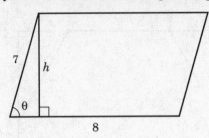

The area of any parallelogram equals base × height ($8 \times h$ in the preceding figure). Given an area of 49 and a base of 8, $49 = 8h$, and $h = \dfrac{49}{8}$. In the right triangle, leg h is opposite θ, and so you can apply the sine function to find θ:

$$\sin\theta = \frac{\frac{49}{8}}{7} = \frac{49}{8} \cdot \frac{1}{7} = \frac{7}{8} = .875$$

$$\theta = \sin^{-1}.875$$

$$\theta = 61°$$

49. **A** Solid Geometry: Prisms

A cube's volume is equal to the cube of its sides, or s^3 when a cube has a side length of s. If the cube's volume is 64, then you can find the length of its sides using this volume formula:

$$s^3 = 64$$

$$s = 4$$

Draw a cube with sides of length 4 and include the plane that passes through points A, B, C, and D:

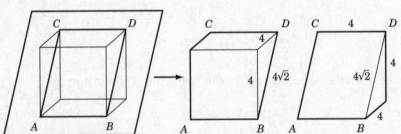

The plane divides the cube into two equal shapes. To calculate the total surface area of these solids, all you need to do is find the surface area of one solid and multiply it by two. Each solid has five sides. Two of the sides are squares of side 4. Calculate the surface area of these two squares: $2(4 \times 4) = 32$. Two of the sides are right triangles with base 4 and height 4. Calculate the surface area of these two triangles: $2\left(\dfrac{1}{2} \times 4 \times 4\right) = 16$. The

288

fifth side is the quadrilateral *ABCD*. You know that one of its sides, *CD*, is equal to 4, and you can find the other side using the Pythagorean Theorem:

$$(AC)^2 = 4^2 + 4^2$$
$$(AC)^2 = 32$$
$$AC = 4\sqrt{2}$$

To find the area of the polygon, multiply the sides together:

$$\text{Area}_{ABCD} = 4 \cdot 4\sqrt{2} = 16\sqrt{2}$$

Find the total surface area by adding all these areas together and multiplying by 2:

$2(32 + 16 + 16\sqrt{2}) = 96 + 32\sqrt{2}$.

50. **D**   Miscellaneous Math: Sequences

Sequence problems rarely occur on the Math Level 1 Test, but you should be prepared for when they do. The nth term in a geometric sequence is given by $a_n = a_1 \cdot r^{n-1}$, where a_n is the nth term, a_1 is the first term, and r is the constant ratio between terms. You're asked to find the 20th term in the sequence, but you know neither the value of the first term nor the ratio between terms. Since the question gives you the third term in the sequence ($a_3 = 4$), you can plug this value into the formula above to find a_1 in terms of the ratio r:

$$4 = a_1 \cdot r^{3-1}$$
$$4 = a_1 \cdot r^2$$
$$a_1 = \frac{4}{r^2}$$

The question also tells you the seventh term in the sequence: $a_7 = 64$. Plug a_7 into the formula to find another expression for a_1:

$$64 = a_1 \cdot r^{7-1}$$
$$64 = a_1 \cdot r^6$$
$$a_1 = \frac{64}{r^6}$$

Since both of these expressions equal a_1, you can set them equal to each other and find r:

$$\frac{4}{r^2} = \frac{64}{r^6}$$
$$\frac{r^6}{r^2} = \frac{64}{4}$$
$$r^4 = 16$$
$$r = 2$$

Now find a_1 by plugging r back into one of the equations:

$$a_1 = \frac{4}{r^2}$$
$$= \frac{4}{4}$$
$$= 1$$

Now that you have a_1 and r, you can find the 20th term in the sequence:

$$a_{20} = 1 \cdot 2^{20-1}$$
$$= 1 \cdot 2^{19}$$
$$= 524{,}288$$

THE SAT
MATH
LEVEL 2 TEST

INTRODUCTION TO THE SAT MATH LEVEL 2 TEST

TWO PEOPLE ARE TREKKING THROUGH A JUNGLE TOWARD A magical and therapeutic waterfall. Now, who will reach the soothing waters first, the native to the area, who never stumbles because she knows the placement of every tree and all the twists and turns, or the tourist who keeps falling down and losing his way because he doesn't pay any attention to the terrain? The answer is obvious. Even if the tourist is a little faster, the native will still win, because she knows how to navigate the terrain and turn it to her advantage.

There are no waterfalls or gorgeous jungle scenery on the SAT Subject Tests, but this example illustrates an important point. The structure of the SAT Math Level 2 Test is the jungle; taking the test is the challenging trek. Your score is the waterfall.

In this chapter we're going to describe the "terrain" of the Math Level 2 Test. We're also going to help you decide which math test to take. In the next chapter, on strategy, we will show you how to navigate and use the terrain to get the best score possible.

DECIDING WHICH MATH TEST TO TAKE

Some students take both Math SAT Subject Tests, but there really isn't a good reason for it. Instead, you should choose to take one test over the other. You should make this choice based on several factors.

Test Content

The two tests cover similar topics, but the Math Level 2 Test covers more material than the Math Level 1 Test does. Level 1 covers three years of college-preparatory math: two years of algebra and one year of geometry. Level 2 assumes that in addition to those three years, you have also taken a year of trigonometry and/or precalculus.

Math Level 1

- Algebra
- Plane geometry (lines and angles, triangles, polygons, circles)
- Solid geometry (cubes, cylinders, cones, spheres, etc.)

- Coordinate geometry (in two dimensions)
- Basic trigonometry (properties and graphs of sine, cosine, and tangent functions, identities)
- Algebraic functions
- Statistics and sets (distributions, probability, permutations and combinations, groups and sets, data interpretation)
- Miscellaneous topics (number theory and operations, logic, series, limits, complex and imaginary numbers, vectors, matrices)

Math Level 2

- Algebra
- Geometry (emphasis on 3-dimensional geometry and transformations)
- Algebraic functions (including logarithmic, inverse, exponential, parametric, and piecewise functions)
- Coordinate geometry (in two and three dimensions, vectors, polar coordinates, parametric equations)
- Trigonometry (including cosecant, secant, cotangent functions, inverse functions, non-right triangles, the laws of sines and cosines, graphs of trigonometric functions)
- Statistics and sets (including standard deviation and regression)
- Miscellaneous topics

College Choice

As you choose between the two tests, keep in mind the specific colleges you're applying to. Colleges with a strong focus on math, such as MIT and Cal Tech, require the Math Level 2 Test. Most other colleges have no such requirement, but some may prefer that you take the Level 2 Test.

All in all, if you have the math background to take the Level 2 Test, you should go for it. Some students decide to take the Math Level 1 Test because it's easier, even though they have taken a precalculus course. We don't recommend this plan. Colleges will be more impressed by a student who does fairly well on SAT Math Level 2 than one who does very well on SAT Math Level 1. Also, the friendly curve of the Math Level 2 Test means that students who know enough math to take the Level 2 Test might very well get a better score on the Level 2 Test than they would on the Level 1 Test.

Battle of the Test Curves

The two tests are scored by very different curves. The Level 2 Test is scored on a much more liberal curve: you can miss six or seven questions and still achieve a score of 800. On the Level 1 Test, however, you would probably need to answer all the questions correctly to get a perfect score. In another example, if you wanted to get a 600 on either test, you would need around 20 correct answers on the Level 2 Test and 33 on the Level 1 Test. Some students who have a math background that suggests they should take the Math Level 2 see that the Level 1 is a less difficult test and think that they can get a marvelous score on the Level 1 Test while their scores on the Level 2 Test will only be average. But if you get tripped up by just one or two questions on the Math Level 1 Test, your score will not be the impressive showstopper that you might expect.

If you still can't decide which of the two Math SAT Subject Tests to take, try a practice test of each.

CONTENT OF THE SAT MATH LEVEL 2 TEST

Math Level 2 consists of 50 multiple-choice questions covering a variety of mathematical topics. We've created the following detailed breakdown based on careful examination of the test (the precise breakdown varies slightly from test to test):

Topic	Approximate % of the Test	Approximate No. of Questions
Algebra Includes arithmetic; equation solving; binomials, polynomials, quadratics	18	9
Solid Geometry Includes solids (cubes, cylinders, cones, etc.); inscribed solids, solids by rotation	8	4
Coordinate Geometry Includes lines and distance; conic sections (parabolas, circles); coordinate space; graphing; vectors	12	6
Trigonometry Includes basic functions and right triangle trigonometry; laws of sines and cosines; trigonometric equations and identities; inverse trigonometric functions; trigonometry in non-right triangles; graphing trigonometric functions	20	10
Functions Includes basic functions; compound, inverse, logarithmic, and parametric functions; graphing functions; domain and range of functions	24	12
Statistics and Sets Includes mean, median, mode, standard deviation; probability; permutations and combinations	6	3
Miscellaneous Includes arithmetic and geometric series; logic; limits; imaginary numbers; matrices	12	6

Each question in the practice tests has been categorized according to these and other topics so that when you study your practice tests, you can very precisely identify your weaknesses and then use this book to address them.

FORMAT OF THE SAT MATH LEVEL 2 TEST

The SAT Math Level 2 Test is a one-hour long test made up of 50 multiple-choice questions. The instructions for the test are straightforward. You should memorize them so you don't waste time reading them on the day of the test.

> For each of the following problems, decide which is the BEST of the choices given. If the exact numerical value is not one of the choices, select the choice that best approximates this value. Then fill in the corresponding oval on the answer sheet.

Simple, right? Unfortunately, the instructions don't cover many important aspects about the format and rules of the test:

- The 50 questions progress in order of difficulty for most students, from the easiest to the hardest.
- You can skip to different questions during the test. While you don't want to skip around randomly, the ability to skip the occasional question is helpful, as we will explain in the next chapter.
- All questions are worth the same number of points, regardless of the level of difficulty.

These facts can greatly affect your approach to taking the test, as we will show in the next chapter, on strategy.

THE CALCULATOR

Unlike the SAT, in which a calculator is permitted but not essential to the test, the Math Level 2 Test demands the use of a calculator; some questions are specifically designed to test your calculator skills.

It is therefore wise to learn certain calculator essentials before taking SAT Math Level 2. First off, make sure you have the right type of calculator. Virtually every type of calculator is allowed on the test, including the programmable and graphing kinds. However, QWERTY or typewriter calculators are not permitted. Laptops, minicomputers, or any machine that prints, makes noise, or needs to be plugged in are not allowed.

Whatever calculator you use should have all the following functions:

- Exponential powers
- Base-10 logarithms
- Sine, cosine, tangent

Make sure you practice performing these functions well before the day of the test. More about how to use calculators on the test follows in the next chapter.

SCORING THE SAT MATH LEVEL 2 TEST

Scoring on the SAT Math Level 2 Test is very similar to the scoring for all other SAT Subject Tests. For every right answer, you earn 1 point. For every wrong answer, you lose $1/4$ of a point. For every question you leave blank, you earn 0 points. Add these points up, and you get your raw score. ETS then converts your raw score to a scaled score according to a special curve. We have included a generalized version of that curve in the table on the next page. Note that the curve changes slightly for each edition of the test, so the table shown will be close to, but not exactly the same as, the table used by ETS for the particular test you take. You should use this chart to convert your raw scores on practice tests into a scaled score.

In addition to its function as a conversion table, this chart contains crucial information: it tells you that you can do very well on the SAT Math Level 2 Test without answering every question correctly. In fact, you could skip some questions and get some other questions wrong and still earn a "perfect" score of 800.

For example, in a test of 50 questions, you could score:

- 800 if you answered 44 right, 4 wrong, and left 2 blank
- 750 if you answered 40 right, 8 wrong, and left 2 blank
- 700 if you answered 35 right, 8 wrong, and left 7 blank
- 650 if you answered 30 right, 12 wrong, and left 8 blank
- 600 if you answered 25 right, 16 wrong, and left 9 blank

This chart should prove to you that when you're taking the test, you should not imagine your score plummeting with every question you can't confidently answer. You can do very well on this test without knowing or answering everything. So don't get unnecessarily wound up if you run into a difficult question. The key to doing well on the SAT Math Level 2 Test is to take the whole test well, and to follow a strategy that ensures you will answer all the questions you can, while intelligently guessing on the questions you feel less certain about. We will talk about such strategies in the next chapter.

Raw Score	Scaled Score	Raw Score	Scaled Score
50	800	18	570
49	800	17	560
48	800	16	550
47	800	15	540
46	800	14	530
45	800	13	520
44	800	12	510
43	800	11	500
42	790	10	490
41	780	9	480
40	770	8	470
39	760	7	450
38	750	6	440
37	740	5	430
36	730	4	420
35	720	3	410
34	710	2	400
33	700	1	390
32	690	0	380
31	680	−1	370
30	680	−2	360
29	670	−3	350
28	660	−4	340
27	650	−5	330
26	640	−6	320
25	630	−7	310
24	630	−8	300
23	620	−9	300
22	610	−10	290
21	600	−11	290
20	590	−12	280
19	580	−13	280

STRATEGIES FOR TAKING THE SAT MATH LEVEL 2 TEST

If you want to score the score, then you've got to talk the talk and strategize the strategies. OK, so that little mantra might not make too much sense. The point is, though, that doing well on the SAT Math Level 2 Test requires you to master two sets of strategies, the general strategies we discuss earlier in this book and the test-specific strategies we cover in this chapter.

Strategy 1: Know What's in the Reference Area.

At the beginning of the SAT Math Level 2 Test there is a reference area that provides you with basic geometry formulas and information.

> THE FOLLOWING INFORMATION IS FOR YOUR REFERENCE IN ANSWERING SOME OF THE QUESTIONS IN THIS TEST.
>
> Volume of a right circular cone with radius r and height h: $V = \frac{1}{3}\pi r^2 h$
>
> Lateral area of a right circular cone with circumference of the base c and slant height l: $S = \frac{1}{2}cl$
>
> Volume of a sphere with radius r: $V = \frac{4}{3}\pi r^3$
>
> Surface area of a sphere with radius r: $S = 4\pi r^2$
>
> Volume of a pyramid with base area B and height h: $V = \frac{1}{3}Bh$

You should know all of these formulas without the reference; don't neglect to memorize and understand the formulas just because you have the reference area as a crutch. Instead, view the reference area as a guide to the formulas that will likely be on the test. If you know those formulas without having to flip back to the reference area, you'll save time, which puts you one step ahead.

Strategy 2: Remember the Order of Difficulty.

Imagine that you are taking a test that consists of two questions. After your teacher hands out the test and before you set to work, a helpful little gnome whispers, "The first problem is very simple; the second is much harder." Would the gnome's statement affect the way you approach the two problems? The answer, of course, is yes. For a "very simple" question, it seems likely that you should be able to answer it quickly and without much, or any, agonized second-guessing. On a "much harder" question, you will probably have to spend much more time, both to come up with an answer and to check your work to make sure you didn't make an error somewhere along the way.

What about all the other students who didn't hear the gnome? They might labor over the first, easy question, exhaustively checking their work and wasting time that they'll need for the tricky second problem. Then, when those other students do get to the second problem, they might not check their work or be wary of traps, since they have no idea that the problem is so difficult.

Because Math Level 2 questions are ordered by difficulty, it's as if you have that helpful little gnome sitting next to you for the entire test.

Knowing When to Be Wary

Most students answer the easy Math Level 2 questions correctly. Only some students get moderate questions right. Very few students get difficult questions right. What does this mean to you? It means that when you are going through the test, you can often trust your first instincts on an easy question. With difficult questions, however, you should be more cautious. There is a reason most people get these questions wrong: not only are they more difficult, containing more sophisticated vocabulary or mathematical concepts, they are also often tricky, full of enticing wrong answers that seem correct. But because the SAT orders its questions by difficulty, the test tells when to take a few extra seconds to make sure you haven't been fooled by an answer that only *seems* right.

The tricky answers seem right because they are actually the answers you would get if you were to make a mathematical or logical mistake while working on the problem. Let's say you're flying through the test, and in order to find the correct answer to a certain question you need to multiply 6 by 7 and then subtract 13 from the product. In your hurry, however, you *add* 13 to the product, which gives you 55 (instead of 29, which is the correct answer). You look at your test booklet, and 55 is indeed listed among the five answer choices! You mark that choice as the correct answer to the question, which of course is wrong. Ouch!

From this example you should learn that just because the answer you got is among the answers listed *does not* mean you definitely have it right. The SAT is designed to punish those who make careless errors. Don't be one of them. After you get an answer, quickly check your work again.

Strategy 3: Watch the Clock.

There are often several ways to answer a Math Level 2 question. You can use trial and error, you can set up and solve an equation, and, for some questions, you might be able to answer the question quickly, intuitively, and elegantly, if you can just spot how. These different approaches to answering questions vary in the amount of time they take. Trial and error generally takes the longest, while the elegant method of relying on an intuitive understanding of conceptual knowledge takes the least amount of time.

Take, for example, the following problem:

> Which has a greater area, a square with sides measuring 4 cm, or a circle with a radius of the same length?

The most obvious way to solve this problem is simply to plug 4 into the formula for the area of a square and area of a circle. Let's do it: Area of a square = s^2, so the area of this square = 4^2 = 16. Area of a circle = πr^2, so the area of this circle must therefore be $\pi 4^2$ = 16π. 16π is obviously bigger than 16, so the circle must be bigger. That worked nicely. But a different approach would have been to draw a quick to-scale diagram with the square and circle superimposed.

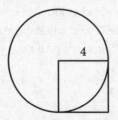

An even faster way would have been to understand the equations of area for a square and circle so well that it was just *obvious* that the circle was bigger, since the equation for the circle will square the 4 and multiply it by π whereas the equation for the square will only square the 4.

While you may not be able to become a math whiz and just *know* the answer, you can learn to look for a quicker route, such as choosing to draw a diagram instead of working out the equation. And, as with the example above, a quicker route is not necessarily a less accurate one. Making such choices comes down to practice, being aware that those other routes are out there, and basic mathematical ability.

The value of time-saving strategies is obvious: less time spent on some questions allows you to devote more time to difficult problems. It is this issue of time that separates the students who do terrifically on the test and those who merely do well. Whether or not the ability to find accurate shortcuts is an actual measure of mathematical prowess is not for us to say, but the ability to find those shortcuts absolutely matters on this test.

Shortcuts Are Really Math Intuition

Now that you know all about shortcuts, you should use them wisely. Don't go into every question searching for a shortcut; it might end up taking longer than the normal route. Instead of seeking out math shortcuts, you should simply be mindful of the possibility that one might exist. If you go into each question knowing there could be a shortcut and keep your mind open as you think about the question, you will find the shortcuts you need.

To some extent, with practice you can teach yourself to recognize when a question might contain a shortcut. For example, simply from the problem above, you know that there will probably be a shortcut for questions that give you the dimensions of two shapes and ask you to compare them: you can just draw a diagram. A frantic test-taker might see the information given and then seize on the simplest route and work out the equations. But with some calm and perspective you can see that drawing a diagram is the best idea.

The fact that we advocate using shortcuts doesn't mean you shouldn't focus on learning how to work out problems. In fact, we can guarantee that you're not going to find a shortcut for a problem *unless* you know how to work it out the long way. After all, a shortcut just uses your knowledge to find a faster way to answer the question. When we use the term *math shortcut*, we are really referring to your math intuition.

Strategy 4: Make Your Calculator Work for You.

As we've already mentioned, the calculator is a very important part of the Math Level 2 Test. You need to have the right kind of calculator, be familiar with its operations, and above all, know how to use it intelligently.

There are four types of questions on the test: calculator-friendly, calculator-neutral, calculator-unfriendly, and calculator-useless. According to the ETS, about 60 percent of the test falls under the calculator-neutral and -friendly categories. That is, calculators are useful or necessary on 30 out of the 50 questions on the SAT Math Level 2. The other 20 questions are calculator-unfriendly and -useless. The trick is to be able to identify the different types of questions on the test. Here's a breakdown of each of the four types, with examples.

Calculator-Friendly Questions

A calculator is extremely helpful and often necessary to solve calculator-friendly questions. Problems demanding exact values for exponents, logarithms, or trigonometric functions will most likely need a calculator. Computations that you wouldn't be able to do easily in your head are prime suspects for a calculator. Here's an example:

If $f(x) = \sqrt{x} - 2x^2 + 5$, then what is $f(3.4)$?

(A) -18.73
(B) -16.55
(C) -16.28
(D) -13.32
(E) -8.42

This is a simple function question in which you are asked to evaluate $f(x)$ at the value 3.4. All you have to do to solve this problem is plug in 3.4 for the variable x and carry out the operations in the function. But unless you know the square root and square of 3.4 off the top of your head, which most test-takers probably wouldn't (and shouldn't), then this problem is extremely difficult to answer without a calculator.

But with a calculator, all you need to do is take the square root of 3.4, subtract twice the square of 3.4, and then add 5. You get answer choice **C**, -16.28.

Calculator-Neutral Questions

You have two different choices when faced with a calculator-neutral question. A calculator is useful for these types of problems, but it's probably just as quick and easy to work the problem out by hand. Here's an example:

If $8^x = 4^3 \times 2^3$, what is the value of x?

(A) 2
(B) 3
(C) 5
(D) 8
(E) 16

When you see the variable x as a power, you should think logarithms. A logarithm is the power to which you must raise a given number to equal another number, so in this case, we need to find the exponent x, such that $8^x = 4^3 \times 2^3$. From the definition of logarithms, we know that given an equation of the form $a^x = b$, $\log_a b = x$. So you could type in $\log_8 (4^3 \times 2^3)$ on your trusty calculator and find that $x = 3$.

Or you could recognize that 2 and 4 are both factors of 8 and, thinking a step further, that $2^3 = 8$ and $4^3 = 64 = 8^2$. Put together, $4^3 \times 2^3 = 8^2 \times 8 = 8^3$. We come to the same answer that $x = 3$, and that **B** is the right answer.

These two processes take about the same amount of time, so choosing one over the other is more a matter of personal preference than one of strategy. If you feel quite comfortable with your calculator, then you might not want to risk the possibility of making a mental math mistake and should choose the first method. But if you're more prone to error when working with a calculator, then you should choose the second method.

Calculator-Unfriendly Questions

It is possible to answer calculator-unfriendly questions by using a calculator. But while it's possible, it isn't a good idea. These types of problems often have built-in shortcuts—if you know and understand the principle being tested, you can bypass potentially tedious computations with a few simple calculations. Here's a problem that you could solve much more quickly and effectively without the use of a calculator:

$$\frac{[\cos^2(3 \times 63°) + \sin^2(3 \times 63°)]^4}{2} =$$

(A) .3261
(B) .5
(C) .6467
(D) .7598
(E) .9238

If you didn't take a moment to think about this problem, you might just rush into it wielding your calculator, calculating the cosine and sine functions, squaring them each and then adding them together, etc. But if you take a closer look, you'll see that $\cos^2(3 \times 63°) + \sin^2(3 \times 63°)$ is a trigonometric identity. More specifically, it is a Pythagorean identity: $\sin^2 q + \cos^2 q = 1$ for any angle q. So, the expression given in the question simplifies to

$$\frac{1^4}{2} = \frac{1}{2} = .5$$

B is correct.

Calculator-Useless Questions

Even if you wanted to, you wouldn't be able to use your calculator on calculator-useless problems. For the most part, problems involving algebraic manipulation or problems lacking actual numerical values would fall under this category. You should easily be able to identify problems that can't be solved with a calculator. Quite often, the answers for these questions will be variables rather than numbers. Take a look at the following example:

$(x + y - 1)(x + y + 1) =$

(A) $(x + y)^2$
(B) $(x + y)^2 - 1$
(C) $x^2 - y^2$
(D) $x^2 + x - y + y^2 + 1$
(E) $x^2 + y^2 + 1$

This question tests you on an algebraic topic—that is, how to find the product of two polynomials—and requires knowledge of algebraic principles rather than calculator acumen. You're asked to manipulate variables, not produce a specific value. A calculator would be of no use here.

To solve this problem, you would have to notice that the two polynomials are in the format of what's called the difference of two squares: $(a + b)(a - b) = a^2 - b^2$. In our case, $a = x + y$ and $b = 1$. As a result, $(x + y - 1)(x + y + 1) = (x + y)^2 - 1$. **B** is correct.

Don't Immediately Use Your Calculator

The fact that the test contains all four of these question types means that you shouldn't get trigger-happy with your calculator. Just because you've got an awesome shiny hammer doesn't mean you should try to use it to pound in thumbtacks. Using your calculator to try to answer every question on the test would be just as unhelpful.

Instead of reaching instinctively for your calculator, you should come up with a problem-solving plan for each question. Take a brief look at each question so that you understand what it's asking you to do, and then decide whether you should use a calculator to solve the problem at all. That brief instant of time invested in making such decisions will save you a great deal of time later on. For example, what if you came upon the question:

If $(3, y)$ is a point on the graph of $f(x) = \dfrac{x^2 - 5x + 4}{11x - 44}$, then what is y?

(A) −3
(B) −1.45
(C) 0
(D) .182
(E) 4.87

A trigger-happy calculator user might immediately plug in 3 for x. But the student who takes a moment to think about the problem will probably see that the calculation would be much simpler if the function were simplified first. To start, factor 11 out of the denominator:

$$f(x) = \frac{x^2 - 5x + 4}{11x - 44} = \frac{x^2 - 5x + 4}{11(x - 4)}$$

Then, factor the numerator to its simplest form:

$$f(x) = \frac{x^2 - 5x + 4}{11(x - 4)} = \frac{(x - 4)(x - 1)}{11(x - 4)}$$

The $(x - 4)$ cancels out, and the function becomes $f(x) = (x - 1) \div 11$. At this point you could shift to the calculator and calculate $f(x) = (3 - 1) \div 11 = {}^2/_{11} = .182$, which is answer **D**. If you were very comfortable with math, however, you would see that you don't even have to work out this final calculation. ${}^2/_{11}$ can't work out to any answer other than **D**, since you know that ${}^2/_{11}$ isn't a negative number, won't be equal to zero, and also won't be greater than 1.

Strategy 5: Master Your Approach.

Regardless of the type of question you're up against, there is a standard procedure that you should use to approach any question on the Math Level 2 Test:

1. Read the question without looking at the answers. Determine what the question is asking and come to some conclusion about how to solve it. Do not look at the answers unless you decide that working backward from the answer choice or plugging in your own numbers is the best way to go (we describe how to use these two methods below).
2. If you think you can solve the problem, go ahead. Once you've derived an answer, only then see if your answer matches one of the choices.
3. Once you've decided on an answer, test it quickly to make sure it's correct, and move on.

Working Backward from the Answer Choices

If you run into difficulty while trying to solve a regular multiple-choice problem, you might want to try the process of elimination. On every question the answer is right in front of you, among those five answer choices. So if you can't solve the problem directly, you might be able to plug each answer into the question to see which one works.

Not only can this process help you when you can't figure out a question, there are times when it can actually be faster than setting up an equation, especially if you work strategically. Take the following example:

> A classroom contains 31 chairs, some of which have arms and some of which do not. If the room contains 5 more armchairs than chairs without arms, how many armchairs does it contain?
>
> (A) 10
> (B) 13
> (C) 16
> (D) 18
> (E) 21

Given this question, you could build the following two equations:

$$\text{total chairs } (31) = \text{armchairs } (x) + \text{normal chairs } (y)$$
$$\text{normal chairs } (y) = \text{armchairs } (x) - 5$$

Then, since $y = x - 5$, you can write the following equation, and then solve for x:

$$31 = x + (x - 5)$$
$$31 = 2x - 5$$
$$36 = 2x$$
$$x = 18$$

As you can see, there are 18 armchairs in the classroom.

This approach of building and working out the equations will produce the right answer, but it takes a long time! What if you strategically plugged in the answers instead? Since the numbers ascend in value, let's choose the one in the middle: 16 (**C**). This is a smart strategic move because if we plug in 16 and discover that it was too small a number to satisfy the equation, we can eliminate **A** and **B** along with **C**. Alternatively, if 16 is too big, we can eliminate **D** and **E** along with **C**.

So our strategy is in place. Now let's work it out. If you have 16 armchairs, then you would have 11 normal chairs and the room would contain 27 total chairs. We needed the total numbers of chairs to equal 31, so clearly **C** is not the right answer. But because the total number of chairs was too few, you can also eliminate **A** and **B**, the answer choices with smaller numbers of armchairs. If you then plug in 18, you have 13 normal chairs and 31 total chairs. There's your answer: **D**. In this instance, plugging in the answers takes less time and, in general, just seems easier.

Notice that the last sentence began with the words "in this instance." Working backward and plugging in is not always the best method. For some questions it won't be possible to work backward at all. For the test, you will need to build up a sense of when working backward can most help you. A good rule of thumb for deciding whether to work backward is:

- Work backward when the question describes an equation of some sort and the answer choices are all simple numbers.

If the answer choices contain variables, working backward will often be quite difficult—more difficult than working out the problem would be. If the answer choices are complicated, with hard fractions or radicals, plugging in might prove so complex that it's a waste of time.

Substituting Numbers

Substituting numbers is a lot like working backward, except the numbers you plug into the equation *aren't* in the answer choices. Instead, you have to strategically decide on numbers to substitute into the question to take the place of variables.

For example, take the question:

If p and q are odd integers, then which of the following must be odd?

(A) $p + q$
(B) $p - q$
(C) $p^2 + q^2$
(D) $p^2 \times q^2$
(E) $p + q^2$

It might be hard to conceptualize how the two variables in this problem interact. But what if you chose two odd numbers, let's say 5 and 3, to represent the two variables? Once you begin this substitution it quickly becomes clear that:

(A) $p + q = 5 + 3 = 8$
(B) $p - q = 5 - 3 = 2$
(C) $p^2 + q^2 = 25 + 9 = 34$
(D) $p^2 \times q^2 = 25 \times 9 = 225$
(E) $p + q^2 = 5 + 9 = 14$

By picking two numbers that fit the definition of the variables provided by the question, it becomes clear that the answer has to be $p^2 \times q^2$ (**D**), since it multiplies to 225. By the way, you could have answered this question without doing the multiplication to 225 since two odd numbers, such as 9 and 25, when multiplied, will *always* result in an odd number.

Substituting numbers can help you transform problems from the abstract into the concrete. However, you have to remember to keep the substitution consistent. If you're using a 5 to represent p, don't suddenly start using 3. Also, when picking numbers to use as substitutes, pick wisely. Choose numbers that are easy to work with and that fit the definitions provided by the question.

Math Strategy 6: Guess.

Should you guess on the SAT Math Level 2 Test? We'll begin to answer this question by posing a question of our own:

G. O. Metry is holding five cards, numbered 1–5. Without telling you, he has selected one of the numbers as the "correct" card. If you pick a single card, what is the probability that you will choose the "correct" card?

The answer, of course, is $^1/_5$. But just as important, you should recognize that the question precisely describes the situation you're in when you blindly guess the answer to any SAT Math Level 2 question: you have a $^1/_5$ chance of getting the question right. If you were to guess on ten questions, you would, according to probability, get two questions right and eight questions wrong.

- 2 right answers get you 2 raw points
- 8 wrong answers get you $8 \times -^1/_4$ point $= -2$ raw points

Those ten answers, therefore, net you a total of 0 points. Your guessing was a complete waste of time, which is precisely what ETS wants. They designed the scoring system so that blind guessing is pointless.

Educated Guessing

But what if your guessing isn't blind? Consider the following question:

If $x + 2x = 6$, what is the value of x ?

(A) −2
(B) 0
(C) 1
(D) 2
(E) 3

Let's say you had no idea how to solve this problem, but you did realize that 0 multiplied by any number equals 0 and that $0 + 2 \times 0$ cannot add up to 6. This means that you can eliminate "0" as a possible answer, and now have four choices from which to choose. Is it now worth it to guess? Probability states that if you are guessing between four choices, you will get one question right for every three you get wrong. For that one correct answer you'll get 1 point, and for the three incorrect answers you'll lose a total of $^3/_4$ of a point. $1 - ^3/_4 = ^1/_4$, meaning that if you can eliminate even one answer, the odds of guessing turn in your favor: you become more likely to gain points than to lose points.

Therefore, the rule for guessing on the Math Level 2 is simple: *if you can eliminate even one answer choice on a question, you should definitely guess.* And if you follow the critical thinking methods we described above about how to eliminate answer choices, you should be able to eliminate at least one answer from almost every question.

Guessing as Partial Credit

Some students feel that guessing is similar to cheating, that in guessing correctly credit is given where none is due. But instead of looking at guessing as an attempt to gain undeserved points, you should look at it as a form of partial credit. Take the example of the question above. Most people taking the test will see that adding two zeros will never equal six and will only be able to throw out that choice as a possible answer. But let's say that you also knew that negative numbers added together cannot equal a positive number, 6. Don't you deserve something for that extra knowledge? Well, you do get something: when you look at this question, you can throw out both "0" and "−2" as answer choices, leaving you with a $^1/_3$ chance of getting the question right if you guess. Your extra knowledge gives you better odds of getting this question right, exactly as extra knowledge should.

Now on to the practice tests!

SAT* MATH LEVEL 2
PRACTICE TEST 1

SAT MATH LEVEL 2 PRACTICE TEST 1 ANSWER SHEET

1. Ⓐ Ⓑ Ⓒ Ⓓ Ⓔ	18. Ⓐ Ⓑ Ⓒ Ⓓ Ⓔ	35. Ⓐ Ⓑ Ⓒ Ⓓ Ⓔ
2. Ⓐ Ⓑ Ⓒ Ⓓ Ⓔ	19. Ⓐ Ⓑ Ⓒ Ⓓ Ⓔ	36. Ⓐ Ⓑ Ⓒ Ⓓ Ⓔ
3. Ⓐ Ⓑ Ⓒ Ⓓ Ⓔ	20. Ⓐ Ⓑ Ⓒ Ⓓ Ⓔ	37. Ⓐ Ⓑ Ⓒ Ⓓ Ⓔ
4. Ⓐ Ⓑ Ⓒ Ⓓ Ⓔ	21. Ⓐ Ⓑ Ⓒ Ⓓ Ⓔ	38. Ⓐ Ⓑ Ⓒ Ⓓ Ⓔ
5. Ⓐ Ⓑ Ⓒ Ⓓ Ⓔ	22. Ⓐ Ⓑ Ⓒ Ⓓ Ⓔ	39. Ⓐ Ⓑ Ⓒ Ⓓ Ⓔ
6. Ⓐ Ⓑ Ⓒ Ⓓ Ⓔ	23. Ⓐ Ⓑ Ⓒ Ⓓ Ⓔ	40. Ⓐ Ⓑ Ⓒ Ⓓ Ⓔ
7. Ⓐ Ⓑ Ⓒ Ⓓ Ⓔ	24. Ⓐ Ⓑ Ⓒ Ⓓ Ⓔ	41. Ⓐ Ⓑ Ⓒ Ⓓ Ⓔ
8. Ⓐ Ⓑ Ⓒ Ⓓ Ⓔ	25. Ⓐ Ⓑ Ⓒ Ⓓ Ⓔ	42. Ⓐ Ⓑ Ⓒ Ⓓ Ⓔ
9. Ⓐ Ⓑ Ⓒ Ⓓ Ⓔ	26. Ⓐ Ⓑ Ⓒ Ⓓ Ⓔ	43. Ⓐ Ⓑ Ⓒ Ⓓ Ⓔ
10. Ⓐ Ⓑ Ⓒ Ⓓ Ⓔ	27. Ⓐ Ⓑ Ⓒ Ⓓ Ⓔ	44. Ⓐ Ⓑ Ⓒ Ⓓ Ⓔ
11. Ⓐ Ⓑ Ⓒ Ⓓ Ⓔ	28. Ⓐ Ⓑ Ⓒ Ⓓ Ⓔ	45. Ⓐ Ⓑ Ⓒ Ⓓ Ⓔ
12. Ⓐ Ⓑ Ⓒ Ⓓ Ⓔ	29. Ⓐ Ⓑ Ⓒ Ⓓ Ⓔ	46. Ⓐ Ⓑ Ⓒ Ⓓ Ⓔ
13. Ⓐ Ⓑ Ⓒ Ⓓ Ⓔ	30. Ⓐ Ⓑ Ⓒ Ⓓ Ⓔ	47. Ⓐ Ⓑ Ⓒ Ⓓ Ⓔ
14. Ⓐ Ⓑ Ⓒ Ⓓ Ⓔ	31. Ⓐ Ⓑ Ⓒ Ⓓ Ⓔ	48. Ⓐ Ⓑ Ⓒ Ⓓ Ⓔ
15. Ⓐ Ⓑ Ⓒ Ⓓ Ⓔ	32. Ⓐ Ⓑ Ⓒ Ⓓ Ⓔ	49. Ⓐ Ⓑ Ⓒ Ⓓ Ⓔ
16. Ⓐ Ⓑ Ⓒ Ⓓ Ⓔ	33. Ⓐ Ⓑ Ⓒ Ⓓ Ⓔ	50. Ⓐ Ⓑ Ⓒ Ⓓ Ⓔ
17. Ⓐ Ⓑ Ⓒ Ⓓ Ⓔ	34. Ⓐ Ⓑ Ⓒ Ⓓ Ⓔ	

SAT MATH LEVEL 2 PRACTICE TEST 1

Time—1 hour

For each of the following problems, decide which is the BEST of the choices given. If the exact numerical value is not one of the choices, select the choice that best approximates this value. Then fill in the corresponding oval on the answer sheet.

<u>Notes:</u> (1) A calculator will be necessary for answering some (but not all) of the questions in this test. For each question you will have to decide whether or not you should use a calculator. The calculator you use must be at least a scientific calculator; programmable calculators and calculators that can display graphs are permitted.

(2) For some questions in this test you may need to decide whether your calculator should be in radian or degree mode.

(3) Figures that accompany problems in this test are intended to provide information useful in solving the problems. They are drawn as accurately as possible EXCEPT when it is stated in a specific problem that its figure is not drawn to scale. All figures lie in a plane unless otherwise indicated.

(4) Unless otherwise specified, the domain of any function f is assumed to be the set of all real numbers x for which $f(x)$ is a real number.

REFERENCE INFORMATION

THE FOLLOWING INFORMATION IS FOR YOUR REFERENCE IN ANSWERING SOME OF THE QUESTIONS IN THIS TEST:

Volume of a right circular cone with radius r and height h: $V = \frac{1}{3}\pi r^2 h$

Lateral area of a right circular cone with circumference of the base c and slant height l: $S = \frac{1}{2}cl$

Volume of a sphere with radius r: $V = \frac{4}{3}\pi r^3$

Surface area of a sphere with radius r: $S = 4\pi r^2$

Volume of a pyramid with base area B and height h: $V = \frac{1}{3}Bh$

USE THIS SPACE FOR SCRATCHWORK.

1. If $\dfrac{1}{\sqrt[3]{x^2 - 2}} = 5$, then x could be

(A) −1.42
(B) 0
(C) 1.38
(D) 1.52
(E) 2.01

2. $\dfrac{10!}{2!8!} =$
(A) 50
(B) 45
(C) 40
(D) 35
(E) 30

GO ON TO THE NEXT PAGE

USE THIS SPACE FOR SCRATCHWORK.

3. If a function G is defined on triplets of positive numbers as
    $G(a, b, c) = \sqrt[3]{a \cdot b \cdot c}$, then which of the following is equal to
    $G(1, 2, 3)$?

    (A) $G\left(\dfrac{1}{7}, 6, 12\right)$

    (B) $G\left(\dfrac{1}{3}, 6, 4\right)$

    (C) $G\left(\dfrac{7}{2}, 5, 8\right)$

    (D) $G\left(\dfrac{7}{2}, \dfrac{1}{14}, 24\right)$

    (E) $G\left(\dfrac{7}{2}, \dfrac{1}{7}, 11\right)$

4. In Figure 1, if AB contains the center of the circle, C is any point
    on the circle distinct from A or B, and $\sin s = \dfrac{5}{13}$, then $\sin z =$

    (A) $\dfrac{7}{13}$

    (B) $\dfrac{8}{13}$

    (C) $\dfrac{12}{13}$

    (D) $\dfrac{13}{12}$

    (E) $\dfrac{4}{3}$

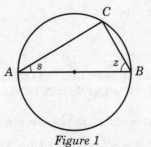

Figure 1

5. If $g(x) = \dfrac{1}{1 + \sqrt{x}}$, then what is the value of $g(g(2))$?

    (A) 2.4
    (B) 1.2
    (C) 0.61
    (D) 0.58
    (E) 0.42

6. $|3 - 4i| =$

    (A) 2.5
    (B) 5
    (C) $5i$
    (D) $\sqrt{7}i$
    (E) 25

GO ON TO THE NEXT PAGE

7. The graph of which of the following is perpendicular to the graph of $y = -\dfrac{x}{5} + \dfrac{2}{5}$?

(A) $y = \dfrac{x}{5} + 3$

(B) $y = 5x + 1$

(C) $y = -5x + \dfrac{2}{5}$

(D) $y = \dfrac{5}{2}x - \dfrac{1}{5}$

(E) $y = \dfrac{2}{5}x + 5$

8. In a class of 120 students, 75 take biology, 60 take chemistry, and 40 take neither biology nor chemistry. What percentage of the class takes both biology and chemistry?

(A) 40.9%
(B) 45.8%
(C) 50%
(D) 55%
(E) Not enough information to tell

9. The graph of $y = ax^2 + bx + c$ cannot have points in the third or fourth quadrants if

(A) $b^2 - 4ac > 0$ and $b > a$
(B) $b^2 - 4ac > 0$ and $b < 0$
(C) $b^2 - 4ac = 0$ and $a < 0$
(D) $b^2 - 4ac < 0$ and $a < 0$
(E) $b^2 - 4ac < 0$ and $a > 0$

10. If $\sec\theta = 7$, then $\tan^2\theta + 1 =$

(A) 49
(B) 48
(C) $\cos^2\theta$
(D) 7
(E) $\sin^2\theta$

GO ON TO THE NEXT PAGE

11. $\dfrac{\dfrac{1}{a} - \dfrac{1}{b}}{\dfrac{1}{a^2} - \dfrac{1}{b^2}} =$

   (A) $\dfrac{a-b}{ab}$

   (B) $\dfrac{a+b}{ab}$

   (C) $\dfrac{ab}{b-a}$

   (D) $\dfrac{ab}{b+a}$

   (E) $\dfrac{1}{a} - \dfrac{1}{b}$

12. In a bag containing 6 oranges and 5 apples, what is the probability of withdrawing, without replacement, 1 orange and then 2 apples?

   (A) $\dfrac{4}{33}$

   (B) $\dfrac{1}{8}$

   (C) $\dfrac{5}{33}$

   (D) $\dfrac{1}{6}$

   (E) $\dfrac{3}{11}$

13. If $m = (z-1)^3$ and $n = \dfrac{1}{z}$, what is m in terms of n ?

   (A) $\left(\dfrac{1-n}{n}\right)^3$

   (B) $\left(\dfrac{n-1}{n}\right)^3$

   (C) $\left(\dfrac{1+n}{n^2}\right)^3$

   (D) $(1-n)^2$

   (E) $(n-1)^3$

14. In Figure 2, if $\theta = 89°$, what is the value of z ?

   (A) 0.03

   (B) .2

   (C) 1.46

   (D) 2

   (E) 114.58

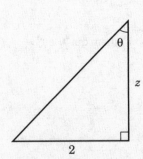

Note: Figure not drawn to scale.

Figure 2

GO ON TO THE NEXT PAGE

15. If Mary makes $25 per hour for the first 30 hours she works, $30 per hour for each additional hour of work up to 40 hours, and $40 per hour for each hour of work over 40 hours, then how many hours must she work in order to make $1,330 ?

(A) 38
(B) 42
(C) 45
(D) 47
(E) 50

16. An operation is defined on two pairs of real numbers by

$(x, y) \oplus (w, t) = \dfrac{x - y}{w + t}$, where $w + t \neq 0$. If

$(2, 1) \oplus (3, t) = (3, 1) \oplus (3, -t)$, then $t =$

(A) −2
(B) −1
(C) 0
(D) 1
(E) 2

17. The probability of event A occurring is $\dfrac{1}{3}$. The probability of event B occurring is $\dfrac{1}{2}$, and the probability of both event A and event B occurring simultaneously is $\dfrac{1}{5}$. What is the probability of either event A or event B occurring?

(A) $\dfrac{19}{30}$

(B) $\dfrac{5}{6}$

(C) $\dfrac{1}{2}$

(D) $\dfrac{3}{4}$

(E) $\dfrac{1}{30}$

GO ON TO THE NEXT PAGE

18. The Golden Mean is defined using the zeros of the function $f(x) = x^2 + x - 1$. Which of the following is the larger of the two zeros?

   (A) −1.618
   (B) 0.618
   (C) 1.618
   (D) 3.241
   (E) 5.011

19. In Figure 3, square $ABCD$ is inscribed within a sphere of radius 2. The center of the sphere, point O, is contained in the square $ABCD$. What is the area of the square?

   (A) $3\sqrt{2}$
   (B) 4
   (C) $4\sqrt{2}$
   (D) 8
   (E) $8\sqrt{2}$

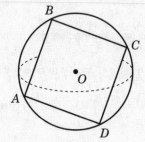

Figure 3

20. If $\log_7(\log_5(\log_3(x))) = 0$, then $x =$

   (A) 243
   (B) 125
   (C) 49
   (D) 25
   (E) 1.4

21. Which of the following are the coordinates of the points at which the hyperbola $\dfrac{x^2}{4} - \dfrac{y^2}{3} = 1$ intersects the graph of the line $y = 1$?

   (A) (−2.31, 0) and (2.31, 0)
   (B) (−2.31, 1) and (2.31, 1)
   (C) (−1.44, 1) and (1.44, 1)
   (D) (−1, 1) and (1, 1)
   (E) (−2.25, 1) and (2.25, 1)

22. The remainder when $3x^5 - 4x^3 + x - 1$ is divided by $x - 2$ is

   (A) 73
   (B) 65
   (C) 31
   (D) 0
   (E) −15

GO ON TO THE NEXT PAGE

USE THIS SPACE FOR SCRATCHWORK.

23. In Figure 4, $\tan\theta =$

    (A) $\dfrac{y}{r}$

    (B) $\dfrac{x}{r}$

    (C) $\dfrac{y}{x}$

    (D) $\dfrac{x}{y}$

    (E) $\dfrac{r}{x+y}$

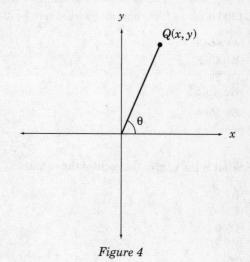

Figure 4

24. The distance between the points $(1, 2, 4)$ and $(-3, 7, 5)$ is approximately

    (A) 1.11
    (B) 4.47
    (C) 5.48
    (D) 6.48
    (E) 10.10

25. What is the area of a parallelogram that has vertices at $(1, 1)$, $(3, 8)$, $(8, 1)$, and $(10, 8)$?

    (A) 64
    (B) 49
    (C) 36
    (D) 25
    (E) 16

26. The circle $x^2 + y^2 = 10$ is symmetric across

    I.   the x-axis
    II. the y-axis
    III. any line that passes through the origin

    (A) I only
    (B) II only
    (C) I and II only
    (D) I, II, and III
    (E) None of the above

GO ON TO THE NEXT PAGE

USE THIS SPACE FOR SCRATCHWORK.

27. A population of birds grows at a rate of 7% per year. If there were 1200 birds in 1990, how many will there be in 2013 ?

    (A) 4643
    (B) 4968
    (C) 5316
    (D) 5688
    (E) 5690

28. What is the sum of the roots of the equation $x^4 - 1 = 0$?

    (A) $-2i$
    (B) -1
    (C) 0
    (D) $4i$
    (E) $6i$

29. Let $\partial f(x)$ be defined as the slope of the graph of $y = f(x)$. For example, if $f(x) = 2x + 1$, then $\partial f(x) = 2$ for all x. Assuming that the graphs of $f(x)$ and $g(x)$ are distinct lines, and that $\partial f(x) = \partial g(x)$, which of the following must be true?

    I. $f(x) = g(x)$
    II. The graph of $f(x)$ is parallel to the graph of $g(x)$
    III. $f(x) - g(x) = k$, where k is a constant

    (A) I only
    (B) II only
    (C) I and II only
    (D) II and III only
    (E) I, II, and III

30. What is the value of $\tan(\sin^{-1}(0.8))$?

    (A) $\dfrac{3}{4}$

    (B) 1

    (C) $\dfrac{4}{3}$

    (D) $\dfrac{5}{3}$

    (E) 2

GO ON TO THE NEXT PAGE

31. An ellipse centered at $(1, 3)$ has a major axis of length 12 and a minor axis of length 8. Which of the following could be the equation of such an ellipse?

    (A) $\dfrac{(x+1)^2}{144} + \dfrac{(y+3)^2}{64} = 1$

    (B) $\dfrac{(x-1)^2}{144} + \dfrac{(y-3)^2}{64} = 1$

    (C) $\dfrac{(x+1)^2}{36} + \dfrac{(y+3)^2}{16} = 1$

    (D) $\dfrac{(x-1)^2}{36} + \dfrac{(y-3)^2}{16} = 1$

    (E) $\dfrac{(x-1)^2}{36} - \dfrac{(y-3)^2}{16} = 1$

32. If $\cos\theta = a\sin\theta$ and $\tan\theta = 4$, then $a =$

    (A) 4
    (B) 0.50
    (C) 0.45
    (D) 0.33
    (E) 0.25

33. A right, circular cone has a slant height of 10 and a base diameter of 12. What is its volume?

    (A) 96π
    (B) 144π
    (C) 384π
    (D) 500π
    (E) 625π

34. If $2\cos^2\theta - 5\cos\theta + 2 = 0$, then θ could be which of the following?

    (A) $\dfrac{\pi}{6}$

    (B) $\dfrac{\pi}{4}$

    (C) $\dfrac{\pi}{3}$

    (D) $\dfrac{5\pi}{6}$

    (E) π

GO ON TO THE NEXT PAGE

USE THIS SPACE FOR SCRATCHWORK.

35. If Figure 5 represents a portion of the graph of
$h(x) = ax^3 + bx^2 + cx + d$, then which of the following must be true?

    I. $a > 0$
    II. $d = 0$
    III. $b = 0$

(A) I only
(B) II only
(C) I and II only
(D) II and III only
(E) I, II, and III

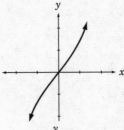

Figure 5

36. The circle $x^2 + y^2 = 4$ is tangent to the circle
$(x - 2\sqrt{2})^2 + (y + 2\sqrt{2})^2 = 4$. What are the coordinates of the point of tangency?

(A) $(\sqrt{2}, -\sqrt{2})$
(B) $(\sqrt{2}, \sqrt{2})$
(C) $(-\sqrt{2}, -\sqrt{2})$
(D) $(2, -2)$
(E) $(2, 2)$

37. Which of the following could be the graph of $g(x) = 2^x - 2^{-x}$ over the interval $[-2, 2]$?

(A)
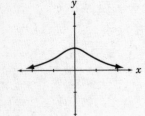

(B)
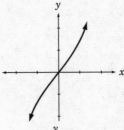

(C)
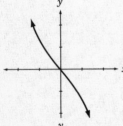

(D)
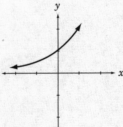

(E)
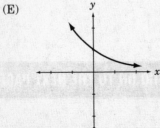

GO ON TO THE NEXT PAGE

10 Practice Exams for the SAT Subject Tests

38. If $\frac{n}{m}$ is a positive odd integer, which of the following must also be

a positive odd integer?

(A) $\frac{m}{n}$

(B) $\frac{n+2}{m}$

(C) $\frac{m}{n+1}$

(D) $\left(\frac{m}{n}\right)^2$

(E) $\left(\frac{n}{m}\right)^2$

39. A function f has the property that $f(x + 2) = f(x)$ for all x in the domain. Which of the following could be a portion of the graph of f?

(A)

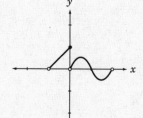

(B)

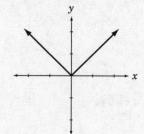

(C)

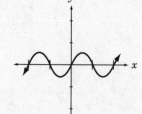

(D)

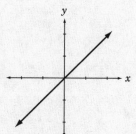

(E)

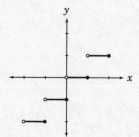

40. What is $\lim\limits_{x \to 1}\dfrac{x^3 + x^2 - 2x}{x^2 - 3x + 2}$?

(A) -4

(B) -3

(C) -2.5

(D) 2

(E) The limit does not exist.

41. If $A = \begin{bmatrix} 4 & -3 \\ 1 & 2 \end{bmatrix}$ and $B = \begin{bmatrix} 3 & 0 \\ 1 & 5 \\ -2 & 4 \end{bmatrix}$, then $AB =$

(A) $\begin{bmatrix} 12 & 0 \\ 1 & 10 \\ -2 & 4 \end{bmatrix}$

(B) $\begin{bmatrix} -12 & 0 \\ 2 & 5 \\ 4 & -8 \end{bmatrix}$

(C) $\begin{bmatrix} 12 & -9 \\ 9 & 7 \\ -4 & 14 \end{bmatrix}$

(D) $\begin{bmatrix} 4 & -12 \\ 5 & 10 \\ -2 & 9 \end{bmatrix}$

(E) $\begin{bmatrix} 12 & 0 \\ 9 & 0 \\ -4 & 0 \end{bmatrix}$

42. What is the minimum value of the function $f(x) = 2x^2 - 4x + 7$?

(A) 5

(B) 4.8

(C) 2.4

(D) 0

(E) -2

GO ON TO THE NEXT PAGE

43. The solution to $\begin{cases} x + y \geq 4 \\ x \leq 4 \\ y \leq 4 \end{cases}$ is represented graphically by

(A)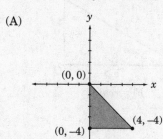

(B)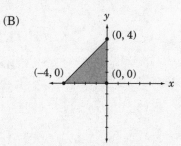

(C)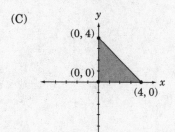

(D)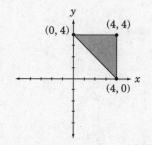

(E)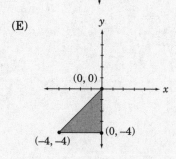

44. The second term of a <u>geometric</u> sequence is 12 and the fourth term is 192. Which of the following could be the sum of the first 6 terms?

(A) 882
(B) 1023
(C) 4095
(D) 5000
(E) 6400

GO ON TO THE NEXT PAGE

USE THIS SPACE FOR SCRATCHWORK.

45. In Figure 6, $\sin(B - A)$ is equal to which of the following?

(A) $\dfrac{a^2 - b^2}{c^2}$

(B) $\dfrac{a^2 - b^2}{a^2 + b^2}$

(C) $\dfrac{b^2 - a^2}{b^2 + a^2}$

(D) $\dfrac{c^2}{b^2 - a^2}$

(E) $\dfrac{c^2}{a^2 - b^2}$

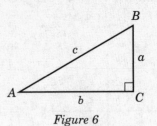

Figure 6

46. What is the least positive integer n for which 2^n has 16 digits?

(A) 48

(B) 49

(C) 50

(D) 51

(E) 55

47. A regular pentagon is inscribed within a circle of radius 1. What is the area of the pentagon?

(A) 1

(B) 1.55

(C) 1.71

(D) 2.20

(E) 2.38

48. If $f(x) = \dfrac{1}{\pi}\log_3(x^5 + 1)$ for $x > -1$, then $f^{-1}(x) =$

(A) $\sqrt[3]{5^{\pi x - 1}}$

(B) $\sqrt[5]{3^{\pi x} - 1}$

(C) $\sqrt[5]{3^{\pi x - 1}}$

(D) $\sqrt[5]{3^{\pi x + 1}}$

(E) $\sqrt[5]{3^{\pi x}} - 1$

GO ON TO THE NEXT PAGE

49. What is the radius of a sphere that has a surface area numerically 20% greater than its volume?

(A) 4
(B) 3.33
(C) 2.67
(D) 2.5
(E) Not enough information to tell

50. A scientific committee must be chosen so that it consists of 2 physicists, 1 mathematician, and 3 biologists. If the pool of candidates is comprised of 15 physicists, 10 mathematicians, and 25 biologists, then how many different committees are possible?

(A) 4,830,000
(B) 2,415,000
(C) 1,610,000
(D) 805,000
(E) 500,000

S T O P

IF YOU FINISH BEFORE TIME IS CALLED, YOU MAY CHECK YOUR WORK ON THIS TEST ONLY.
DO NOT TURN TO ANY OTHER TEST IN THIS BOOK.

SAT MATH LEVEL 2 PRACTICE TEST 1 EXPLANATIONS

MATH LEVEL 2 PRACTICE TEST 1 ANSWERS

Question Number	Answer	Right	Wrong	Question Number	Answer	Right	Wrong
1	A	—	—	26	D	—	—
2	B	—	—	27	D	—	—
3	D	—	—	28	C	—	—
4	C	—	—	29	D	—	—
5	C	—	—	30	C	—	—
6	B	—	—	31	D	—	—
7	B	—	—	32	E	—	—
8	B	—	—	33	A	—	—
9	E	—	—	34	C	—	—
10	A	—	—	35	C	—	—
11	D	—	—	36	A	—	—
12	A	—	—	37	B	—	—
13	A	—	—	38	E	—	—
14	A	—	—	39	C	—	—
15	D	—	—	40	B	—	—
16	B	—	—	41	C	—	—
17	A	—	—	42	A	—	—
18	B	—	—	43	D	—	—
19	D	—	—	44	C	—	—
20	A	—	—	45	B	—	—
21	B	—	—	46	C	—	—
22	B	—	—	47	E	—	—
23	C	—	—	48	B	—	—
24	D	—	—	49	D	—	—
25	B	—	—	50	B	—	—

CALCULATING YOUR SCORE

Your raw score for the SAT Math Level 2 Test is calculated from the number of questions you answer correctly and incorrectly. Once you have determined your composite score, use the conversion table on page 298 of this book to calculate your scaled score. To calculate your raw score, count the number of questions you answered correctly:

_____
A

Count the number of questions you answered incorrectly, and multiply that number by $\frac{1}{4}$:

_____ $\times \frac{1}{4} =$ _____
B   C

Subtract the value in field C from the value in field A:

_____
D

Round the number in field D to the nearest whole number. This is your raw score:

_____
E

MATH LEVEL 2 TEST 1 EXPLANATIONS

1. **A**   Algebra: Equation Solving

This is a straightforward test of your algebraic manipulation skills.

$$\frac{1}{\sqrt[3]{x^2 - 2}} = 5$$

$$\frac{1}{x^2 - 2} = 125$$

$$\frac{1}{125} = x^2 - 2$$

$$\frac{1}{125} + 2 = x^2$$

$$2.008 = x^2$$

$$x = \pm 1.42$$

2. **B**   Statistics: Permutations and Combinations

This question asks you to do a basic calculation with factorials. You should memorize the following formula for calculating a factorial: $n! = n(n-1)(n-2)...(3)(2)(1)$.

$$\frac{10!}{2!8!} = \frac{10 \cdot 9 \cdot 8 \cdot 7 \cdot 6 \cdot 5 \cdot 4 \cdot 3 \cdot 2 \cdot 1}{2 \cdot 1 \cdot 8 \cdot 7 \cdot 6 \cdot 5 \cdot 4 \cdot 3 \cdot 2 \cdot 1}$$

$$= \frac{10 \cdot 9}{2 \cdot 1}$$

$$= 45$$

3. **D**   Functions: Evaluating Functions

The key to this problem is realizing that since $G(a, b, c) = G(1, 2, 3)$, you need to find a triplet of positive numbers such that $a \cdot b \cdot c = 1 \cdot 2 \cdot 3 = 6$. The cube root is not important for finding the correct answer. Among the five answer choices, only **D** supplies a triplet that satisfies this condition.

$$G\left(\frac{7}{2}, \frac{1}{14}, 24\right) = \sqrt[3]{\frac{7}{2} \cdot \frac{1}{14} \cdot 24}$$

$$= \sqrt[3]{6}$$

$$= G(1, 2, 3)$$

4. **C**   Plane Geometry: Triangles, Circles; Trigonometry: Basic Functions

In this question, you have a triangle inscribed within a circle such that the circle's diameter forms one of the triangle's sides. No matter where you draw the two other sides of the triangle to meet at a vertex along the circle's circumference, the sides will form a right angle. The circle's diameter will form the hypotenuse of the right triangle. Since $\angle ACB = 90°$, you can use basic trigonometry to answer this problem.

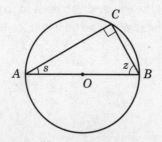

If $\sin s = \dfrac{5}{13}$, you know that, for the angle s, the opposite side (BC) is 5 and the hypotenuse (AB) is 13. Using the Pythagorean Theorem, you can determine that $AC = 12$ and $\sin z = \dfrac{12}{13}$.

5.   **C**   Functions: Evaluating Functions

When you come across a compound expression such as $g(g(2))$, you first need to determine the value of $g(2)$ and then plug that value back into the function $g(x)$.

$$g(2) = \frac{1}{1 + \sqrt{2}}$$

$$g(g(2)) = \frac{1}{1 + \sqrt{\dfrac{1}{1 + \sqrt{2}}}}$$

$$= \frac{1}{1 + 0.6436}$$

$$= 0.61$$

6.   **B**   Miscellaneous Math: Complex Numbers

Most graphing calculators can handle complex number expressions, but you can easily calculate the answer to this question by hand. The absolute value of a complex number of the form $a + bi$ is defined as $|a + bi| = \sqrt{(a + bi)(a - bi)}$.

$$
\begin{aligned}
|3 - 4i| &= \sqrt{(3 - 4i)(3 + 4i)} \\
&= \sqrt{9 - 12i + 12i - 16i^2} \\
&= \sqrt{9 + 16}, \text{ since } i^2 = -1 \\
&= \sqrt{25} \\
&= 5
\end{aligned}
$$

7.   **B**   Coordinate Geometry: Lines

The line $y = mx + b$ is perpendicular to the line $y = Mx + b$ if and only if their slopes have the following relationship: $m = \dfrac{-1}{M}$. You can see that the graph of the line perpendicular to $y = -\dfrac{x}{5} + \dfrac{2}{5}$ must have a slope of:

$$m = -\frac{1}{-\dfrac{1}{5}}$$

$$m = 5$$

B is the only one choice that supplies an equation defining a line with a slope of 5.

8.   **B**   Algebra: Equation Solving

Of the 120 students in the class, 40 take neither biology nor chemistry, so you know that 80 students take one or both of the courses. You need to write an equation that will allow you to solve for the number of students who take both courses: $75 + 60 - x = 80$, where

x represents the overlap in students. You need to subtract x in the equation because you don't want to double count the students who take both biology and chemistry.

$$135 - x = 80$$
$$x = 55$$

Now you can find the percentage of students in the entire class who take both biology and chemistry: $\frac{55}{120} = 0.458$, or 45.8%.

9.   **E**   Functions: Graphing Functions

You can always calculate the roots of a quadratic equation by plugging its coefficients into the quadratic formula. But if you don't need to know the actual values of the roots, you can use the coefficients of the equation to calculate the discriminant, which tells you the type and number of roots the equation has. Given a quadratic of the form $y = ax^2 + bx + c$, the discriminant D is defined as $D = b^2 - ac$. If $D > 0$, the quadratic has 2 distinct real roots and 2 x-intercepts. If $D = 0$, the equation has 1 rational repeated root and touches the x-axis at one point only (think of a parabola with its vertex on the x-axis). If $D < 0$, the equation has no real roots (but 2 complex conjugate ones) and, therefore, never crosses the x-axis.

The question supposes that the graph of the quadratic cannot have points in the third or fourth quadrants, the two quadrants below the x-axis. This means the graph cannot cross below the x-axis, although it can be tangent to the x-axis (the axes are not considered to be part of the quadrants); thus the discriminant must be less than or equal to zero. Since the function can't cross below the x-axis, the coefficient a must be positive so that the graph opens upward. Only **E** completely satisfies these conditions.

10.   **A**   Trigonometry: Pythagorean Identities

You should be prepared to use any of the Pythagorean Identities on this test. The solution to this problem depends on the identity, $\tan^2\theta + 1 = \sec^2\theta$. If $\sec\theta = 7$, then $\sec^2\theta = 7^2 = 49$. When you substitute for $\sec^2\theta$, you get $\tan^2\theta + 1 = 49$.

11.   **D**   Algebra: Algebraic Manipulation

Simplify both the numerator and the denominator fractions by rewriting each as one fraction. Then, simplify the complex fraction by canceling common factors.

$$\frac{\frac{1}{a} - \frac{1}{b}}{\frac{1}{a^2} - \frac{1}{b^2}} = \frac{\frac{b-a}{ab}}{\frac{b^2-a^2}{a^2b^2}}$$

$$= \frac{\frac{b-a}{ab}}{\frac{(b-a) \cdot (b+a)}{a^2b^2}}$$

$$= \frac{\frac{1}{ab}}{\frac{1 \cdot (b+a)}{a^2b^2}}$$

$$= \frac{ab}{b+a}$$

12. A   Statistics: Probability

"Without replacement" means that the number of pieces of fruit in the bag diminishes by 1 each time a piece of fruit is withdrawn. The probability of pulling out an orange first is $\frac{6}{11}$, since initially there are 6 oranges among the 11 pieces of fruit (6 oranges plus 5 apples). Since only 10 pieces of fruit remain after the removal of the orange, the probability of the second fruit being an apple is $\frac{5}{10}$. Finally, the probability of the last piece of fruit also being an apple is $\frac{4}{9}$. Multiply the three probabilities together to find the probability of withdrawing an orange and then 2 apples consecutively: $\frac{6}{11} \cdot \frac{5}{10} \cdot \frac{4}{9} = \frac{4}{33}$.

13. A   Algebra: Systems of Equations

The question asks you to rewrite m in terms of n. Since both m and n are given in terms of z, you should first solve for z in terms of n. If $n = \frac{1}{z}$, then $z = \frac{1}{n}$. Now you can substitute the expression for z in the equation $m = (z-1)^3$.

$$m = (z-1)^3$$
$$= \left(\frac{1}{n} - 1\right)^3$$
$$= \left(\frac{1-n}{n}\right)^3$$

14. A   Trigonometry: Basic Functions

Since the triangle is a right triangle, you know $\tan\theta = \frac{2}{z}$, where 2 is opposite the angle θ and z is adjacent. Plug in $\theta = 89°$, and solve for z.

$$\tan 89° = \frac{2}{z}$$
$$57.29 \approx \frac{2}{z}$$
$$z \approx \frac{2}{57.29}$$
$$z \approx 0.03$$

15. D   Fundamentals: Word Problems

If Mary works 30 hours, she will make $25 \cdot 30 = 750$ dollars, so you know she must work overtime to make a total of \$1,330. If she works 40 hours in total, then she would make $25 \cdot 30 + 10 \cdot 30 = 1,050$ dollars. In order to make 280 dollars more, she has to work an extra 7 hours at \$40/hour. The total amount of time she must work is $30 + 10 + 7 = 47$ hours.

16. B   Functions: Evaluating Functions

The difficult part of solving an arbitrary operation problem is simply unwinding the new definition. Given that $(x, y) \oplus (w, t) = \frac{x - y}{w + t}$, substitute to find $(2, 1) \oplus (3, t) = \frac{2 - 1}{3 + t}$

and $(3, 1) \oplus (3, -t) = \dfrac{3-1}{3+(-t)}$. You can solve for t by setting these two equations equal to each other.

$$\frac{2-1}{3+t} = \frac{3-1}{3-t}$$

$$\frac{1}{3+t} = \frac{2}{3-t}$$

$$3-t = 2(3+t)$$

$$3-t = 6+2t$$

$$-3 = 3t$$

$$t = -1$$

17. **A** Statistics: Probability

You are expected to know the following formula for determining probability. Given the probability of A (denoted $P(A)$), the probability of B (denoted $P(B)$), and the probability of A and B (denoted $P(A \cap B)$), then the probability of A or B (denoted $P(A \cup B)$) can be calculated by $P(A \cup B) = P(A) + P(B) - P(A \cap B)$. Since $P(A)$, $P(B)$, and $P(A \cap B)$ are given in the question, all you need to do is plug them into the formula:

$$P(A \cup B) = \frac{1}{3} + \frac{1}{2} - \frac{1}{5}$$

$$= \frac{19}{30}$$

18. **B** Algebra: Polynomials

This problem asks you to find the larger of the two zeros of the function $f(x) = x^2 + x - 1$. You should use the quadratic formula to find the solutions to $0 = x^2 + x - 1$, where $a = 1$, $b = 1$, and $c = -1$.

$$\frac{-b \pm \sqrt{b^2 - 4ac}}{2a} = \frac{-1 \pm \sqrt{1 - (4 \cdot 1 \cdot (-1))}}{2}$$

$$= \frac{-1 \pm \sqrt{5}}{2}$$

$$= \frac{-1 \pm 2.236}{2}, \text{ which is approximately } -1.618 \text{ or } .618$$

19. **D** Solid Geometry: Solids that Aren't Prisms; Plane Geometry: Polygons

If the center of the sphere is also the center of the square, then you know that the radius of the sphere is half the length of the diagonal of the square (and that the diagonal of the square is equal to the sphere's diameter).

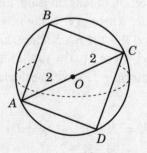

The area of a square can be written as Area $= s^2$, where s is the length of a side, or equivalently as Area $= \frac{1}{2}d^2$, where d is the diagonal of the square. You know $d = 2r$ and $r = 2$, so $d = 4$. Thus Area $= \frac{1}{2} \cdot 4^2 = 8$.

If you didn't memorize this formula for the test, you can always find the length of the square's sides by seeing that the diagonal forms two 45-45-90 triangles. If the hypotenuse of those triangles (the diagonal of the square) is 4, then the lengths of the square's sides are equal to $2\sqrt{2}$, and $(2\sqrt{2})^2 = 8$.

20. **A** Algebra: Equation Solving, Logarithms

A logarithm expresses an exponential relationship. The definition of a logarithm shows that $\log_b y = x$ is equivalent to the expression $b^x = y$. Applying this definition three times to the given equation will allow you to find x by "unwrapping" the logarithms.

$$\log_7(\log_5(\log_3(x))) = 0$$
$$\log_5(\log_3(x)) = 7^0 \text{ and } 7^0 = 1$$
$$\log_3(x) = 5^1$$
$$x = 3^5$$
$$= 243$$

21. **B** Solid Geometry: Hyperbolas

This problem is actually simpler than it appears at first glance. To find the points of intersection between a given hyperbola and the line $y = 1$, you just plug in the value 1 for y and then solve for x.

$$\frac{x^2}{4} - \frac{1^2}{3} = 1$$
$$\frac{x^2}{4} = \frac{4}{3}$$
$$x^2 = \frac{16}{3}$$
$$x = \pm\frac{4}{\sqrt{3}}$$
$$= \pm 2.31$$

Since $y = 1$, you can see that **B** is correct.

22. **B** Algebra: Polynomials

According to the polynomial version of long division, any polynomial $p(x)$ can be written as $p(x) = (x - a) \cdot q(x) + R$, where $p(x)$ is the original polynomial, $(x - a)$ is the divisor, $q(x)$ is the quotient, and R is the remainder. The most efficient way to find the remainder is to plug a into $p(x)$, since $p(a) = (a - a) \cdot (q(a) + R)$, or $p(A) = R$. Since the divisor is $x - 2$, you know that $a = 2$. You can calculate the remainder R by plugging 2 into $p(x)$:

$$R = 3 \cdot (2)^5 - 4(2)^3 + 2 - 1$$
$$= 96 - 32 + 2 - 1$$
$$= 65$$

23. **C** Trigonometry: Basic Functions; Coordinate Geometry: Coordinate Plane

The best way to answer this question is to make a right triangle by drawing a line down from point Q to the x-axis.

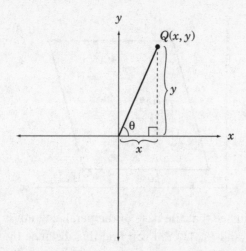

The coordinates of point Q will give you the lengths of two sides of the triangle—the sides opposite and adjacent to the angle θ. Once you have determined the opposite and adjacent sides, you can use simple trigonometry to calculate the value of θ. The side opposite θ has a length equal to the value of the y-coordinate of Q and the adjacent side has a length equal to that of the x-coordinate.

$$\tan\theta = \frac{\text{opposite}}{\text{adjacent}}$$

$$= \frac{y}{x}$$

24. **D** Coordinate Geometry: Lines and Distance

This is a straightforward check to see whether you know the formula for the distance between points in 3-dimensional space. When you have two points in space (x_1, y_1, z_1) and (x_2, y_2, z_2), then the distance between them is given by:

$$d = \sqrt{(x_1 - x_2)^2 + (y_1 - y_2)^2 + (z_1 - z_2)^2}$$

$$d = \sqrt{(1 - (-3))^2 + (2 - 7)^2 + (4 - 5)^2}$$

$$= \sqrt{4^2 + (-5)^2 + (-1)^2}$$

$$= \sqrt{16 + 25 + 1}$$

$$= \sqrt{42}$$

$$= 6.48$$

25. **B** Plane Geometry: Polygons; Coordinate Geometry: Coordinate Plane

This question tells you that the four coordinates form a parallelogram. You should draw a picture of this parallelogram to help you solve this problem.

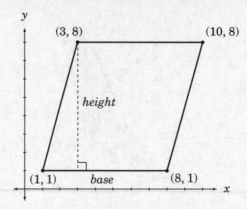

In this picture, you can see that the base of the parallelogram is equal to the distance between points (1, 1) and (8, 1). You can find this distance by finding the difference between the x-coordinates of the points: $8 - 1 = 7$. (The y-coordinates of these points are the same, so you don't need to worry about them.) Because the sides in a parallelogram are parallel, you can find the height by finding the difference between the y-coordinates of points (3, 8) and (1, 1): $8 - 1 = 7$. Since the area of a parallelogram is given by Area $=$ Base $\cdot$ Height, for this parallelogram the Area $= 7 \cdot 7 = 49$.

26. **D** Functions: Transformations and Symmetry

The given equation describes a circle of radius $\sqrt{10}$ centered at the origin of the coordinate plane. Looking at the figure below, you can see that any line that passes through the origin will divide the circle symmetrically in half. Since both the x- and y-axes are specific lines through the origin, you can see that I, II, and III must be true.

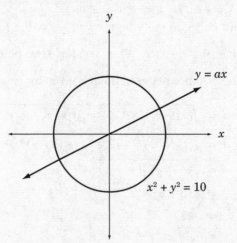

27. **D** Algebra: Equation Solving, Exponential Growth and Decay

The formulas for growth and decay are fair game on the Math Level 2 Test. Given an original population P, a percentage rate of growth or decay r (written as a decimal) and a length of time t, you can use the following formula to calculate the population after an amount of time, t.

$$P(t) = P(1 \pm r)^t$$

Since the length of time is 2013 − 1990 = 23 years, plug in 23 for t:

$$
\begin{aligned}
P(23) &= 1200(1 + 0.07)^{23} \\
&= 1200(1.07)^{23} \\
&= 1200 \cdot 4.74053 \\
&\approx 5688
\end{aligned}
$$

28. C Algebra: Polynomials

There are two approaches to this problem. The first is to factor this quartic equation and then add together its roots:

$$
\begin{aligned}
x^4 - 1 &= (x^2 - 1)(x^2 + 1) \\
&= (x - 1)(x + 1)(x - i)(x + i) = 0
\end{aligned}
$$

The roots are $1, -1, i, -i$. You can add them together to find the answer:

$$
1 + (-1) + i + (-i) = 0
$$

The second approach is to recall that for an equation in the form $0 = ax^4 + bx^3 + cx^2 + dx + e$, the sum of the roots must equal $-\dfrac{b}{a}$. In the equation $x^4 - 1 = 0$, the coefficient b is equal to 0, so the sum of the roots is equal to $-\dfrac{0}{1}$, or 0.

29. D Coordinate Geometry: Lines and Distance

If the graph of $f(x)$ is a line, then $f(x)$ must be in the form of $f(x) = m_1 x + b_1$. Similarly, $g(x)$ must be of the form $g(x) = m_2 x + b_2$. The question states that $\partial f(x) = m_1$ and $\partial g(x) = m_2$. If $\partial f(x) = \partial g(x)$, then $m_1 = m_2$. The lines must be parallel because their slopes are equal. Additionally, if $m_1 = m_2$, then:

$$
\begin{aligned}
f(x) - g(x) &= m_1 x + b_1 - (m_2 x + b_2) \\
&= (m_1 - m_2)x + b_1 - b_2 \\
&= 0x + b_1 - b_2 \\
&= b_1 - b_2, \text{ which is a constant}
\end{aligned}
$$

Statement I is false because the lines can have different y-intercepts. But II and III are always true, and the correct answer is **D**.

30. C Trigonometry: Inverse Trigonometric Functions

The fastest way to solve this question is to use a calculator. First find $\sin^{-1}(0.8)$, and then plug the result into $\tan x$.

$$
\begin{aligned}
\sin^{-1}(0.8) &\approx 53.130° \\
\tan(53.130°) &\approx 1.333 \\
&= \frac{4}{3}
\end{aligned}
$$

31. D Coordinate Geometry: Ellipses

You should arrange the information given in the question as an equation for an ellipse.

The general equation for an ellipse centered at the point (h, k) is $\dfrac{(x - h)^2}{a^2} + \dfrac{(y - k)^2}{b^2} = 1,$

where the length of the major axis is either $2a$ or $2b$ and the length of the minor axis is accordingly either $2b$ or $2a$. Assume for the moment that the major axis is $2a$ (in other words, that the major axis is horizontal), and see whether you can fit the given data to one of the answer choices. If $2a = 12$, then $a = 6$ and $a^2 = 36$. Similarly, if $2b = 8$, then $b = 4$ and $b^2 = 16$. (h, k), the center of the ellipse, is given in the question as $(1, 3)$. Thus the equation could be:

$$\frac{(x-1)^2}{36} + \frac{(y-3)^2}{16} = 1, \text{ which is } \textbf{D}.$$

32. **E** Trigonometry: Basic Functions

A trigonometric equation of this sort always requires some form of manipulation. You want to see if you can rewrite $\cos\theta = a \cdot \sin\theta$ in a simpler form. Since you're solving for a, isolate a on one side of the equation. Divide both sides by $\cos\theta$ and then divide by a to obtain:

$$\frac{1}{a} = \frac{\sin\theta}{\cos\theta}$$

$$\frac{1}{a} = \tan\theta$$

You're told that $\tan\theta = 4$, so you can write the following equation:

$$\frac{1}{a} = 4$$

$$a = \frac{1}{4} \text{ or } 0.25$$

33. **A** Solid Geometry: Prisms

The formula for the volume of a cone requires the cone's radius and height. The question tells you that the base diameter of the cone is 12, so you know that the radius is 6. To find the height of the cone, draw a picture, including the radius and slant height.

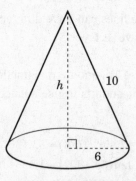

A right triangle is formed by the radius of the cone's base, the slant height of the cone, and the height of the cone. You can solve for the height of the cone using the Pythagorean Theorem, where the slant height of the cone is the hypotenuse of the triangle and the radius of the cone is one of the triangle's legs.

$$h = \sqrt{10^2 - 6^2}$$

$$= \sqrt{100 - 36}$$

$$= \sqrt{64} \text{ or } 8$$

Now that you have the cone's height, you can find its volume:

$$V = \frac{1}{3}\pi r^2 h$$

$$= \frac{1}{3}\pi \cdot 36 \cdot 8$$

$$= 96\pi$$

34.   C   Algebra: Equation Solving; Trigonometry: Inverse Trigonometric Functions

This problem may seem daunting until you realize that the expression involving $\cos\theta$ is really only a quadratic equation in which $\cos\theta$ takes the place of x. You should factor the equation because factoring often reveals solutions to seemingly complicated problems on the Math Level 2 Test.

$$2\cos^2\theta - 5\cos\theta + 2 = 0$$
$$(2\cos\theta - 1)(\cos\theta - 2) = 0$$

If $\cos\theta - 2 = 0$, then $\cos\theta = 2$, which has no real solutions. If $2\cos\theta - 1 = 0$, then $\cos\theta = \frac{1}{2}$ and $\theta = \frac{\pi}{3}, \frac{5\pi}{3}$. **C**, which is $\frac{\pi}{3}$, is correct.

35.   C   Algebra: Polynomials

This question asks you for information on the coefficients of the function and provides you with the function and a portion of its graph. From the graph, you can determine that the roots of this cubic polynomial are $r_1 = -2$, $r_2 = 0$, and $r_3 = 1$.

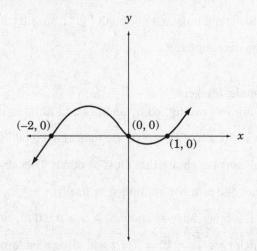

You can rewrite the polynomial as $h(x) = a(x - r_1)(x - r_2)(x - r_3)$, which becomes $h(x) = a(x + 2)(x - 0)(x - 1)$ when you substitute the values of the roots. Multiply this out to get $h(x) = a(x^3 + x^2 - 2x)$. Since, as you can see from the graph, overall the function increases as x increases, $a > 0$. Also, d must be equal to zero since there is no constant term in the function, and b is *not* equal to zero since there is an x^2 term.

36.   A   Coordinate Geometry: Circles

You are looking for the point where these two circles are tangent—in other words, where their (x, y) coordinates are equal. Since the equations of the two circles both equal 4—

$x^2 + y^2 = 4$ and $(x - 2\sqrt{2})^2 + (y + 2\sqrt{2})^2 = 4$, you can simply set these expressions equal to each other to solve for x and y.

$$x^2 + y^2 = (x - 2\sqrt{2})^2 + (y + 2\sqrt{2})^2$$
$$x^2 + y^2 = x^2 - 4\sqrt{2}x + 8 + y^2 + 4\sqrt{2}y + 8$$

When you rearrange and cancel terms, you get:

$$x = 2\sqrt{2} + y$$

Plug this expression for x back into $x^2 + y^2 = 4$ in order to solve for y.

$$(2\sqrt{2} + y)^2 + y^2 = 4$$
$$8 + 4\sqrt{2}y + 2y^2 = 4$$
$$2y^2 + 4\sqrt{2}y + 4 = 0, \text{ which is a perfect square}$$
$$2(y + \sqrt{2})^2 = 0$$

Now you know $y = -\sqrt{2}$. Plug this value for y into $x = 2\sqrt{2} + y$ to get $x = \sqrt{2}$. The point of tangency is $(\sqrt{2}, -\sqrt{2})$.

37. **B**   Functions: Graphing Functions

You can graph the function $g(x) = 2^x - 2^{-x}$ on your calculator to find the correct answer. You can also answer this question without a calculator. Since $g(0) = 1 - 1 = 0$, you know the graph must pass through $(0, 0)$, ruling out **A**, **D**, and **E**. Additionally, $g(1) = 2 - \frac{1}{2}$ means the graph must pass through $\left(1, \frac{3}{2}\right)$, so you can eliminate **C**, leaving you with the correct answer choice, **B**.

38. **E**   Fundamentals: Integers

The result of an odd number multiplied by another odd number must be odd; thus an odd number raised to any positive integer power must remain odd (for example, $3^3 = 27$ and $3^4 = 81$). The only answer choice that must be odd is **E** because it is the square of a positive odd integer (an odd number multiplied by itself).

You can rule out the other answer choices. **A** is a fraction, not an integer (except where $m = n$, in which case $\frac{n}{m} = \frac{m}{n} = 1$); n will always be larger than m if $\frac{n}{m}$ is an integer, because the reverse, $\frac{m}{n}$, will always be a fraction. If, for example, $n = 6$ and $m = 2$, then $\frac{n}{m} = 3$, but $\frac{m}{n} = \frac{1}{3}$.

C is a fraction because it simply increases the denominator of $\frac{m}{n+1}$. **D** squares **A**; thus it is also either 1 or a fraction. **B** can be either odd or even. If $\frac{n}{m} = \frac{6}{2} = 3$, then $\frac{n+2}{m} = \frac{8}{2} = 4$.

39. **C**   Functions: Graphing Functions

When you see something like $f(x + 2) = f(x)$, you should instantly realize you're dealing with a periodic function, where the value of y repeats at a regular interval. The period of this function is 2 because the value of $f(x)$ repeats itself when x increases by 2.

You need to find a graph with a period of 2 (in other words, a graph which repeats itself over every interval of length 2). Algebraically you can see that $f(-2 + 2) = f(-2)$, so $f(0) = f(-2)$, and $f(0 + 2) = f(0)$, so $f(2) = f(0)$. The only answer choice that satisfies these conditions is **C**.

40. **B**   Miscellaneous Math: Limits

There will almost certainly be a limit question on the Math Level 2 Test. To answer this question, you must reduce the function into its most basic form; otherwise, the function will appear to be undefined at the point it approaches (try plugging 1 into the original version, and you'll end up with the undefined quantity $\frac{0}{0}$). Remember to factor and to cancel like terms before plugging in 1.

$$\lim_{x \to 1} \frac{x^3 + x^2 - 2x}{x^2 - 3x + 2} = \lim_{x \to 1} \frac{x(x+2)(x-1)}{(x-2)(x-1)}$$

$$= \lim_{x \to 1} \frac{x(x+2)}{(x-2)}$$

Now you can plug in $x = 1$:

$$= \frac{1(1+2)}{1-2}$$

$$= -3$$

41. **C**   Numbers and Operations: Matrices

The number of rows in A equals the number of columns in B. Accordingly, to form product matrix AB, multiply each row of B by each column of A, arranging the six resulting entries in a 3-row, 2-column matrix as follows:

$$\begin{bmatrix} (B \text{ row } 1)(A \text{ col. } 1) = & (B \text{ row } 1)(A \text{ col. } 2) = \\ (3)(4) + (0)(1) = 12 & (3)(-3) + (0)(2) = -9 \\ (B \text{ row } 2)(A \text{ col. } 1) = & (B \text{ row } 2)(A \text{ col. } 2) = \\ (1)(4) + (5)(1) = 9 & (1)(-3) + (5)(2) = 7 \\ (B \text{ row } 3)(A \text{ col. } 1) = & (B \text{ row } 3)(A \text{ col. } 2) = \\ (-2)(4) + (4)(1) = -4 & (-2)(-3) + (4)(2) = 14 \end{bmatrix}$$

$$\text{Matrix } AB = \begin{bmatrix} 12 & -9 \\ 9 & 7 \\ -4 & 14 \end{bmatrix}$$

42. **A**   Functions: Graphing Functions

You can use your graphing calculator to solve this question, or you can do the calculation by hand. Since the graph of this quadratic equation is an upward-opening parabola, the y-coordinate of the vertex must be the minimum value of the function. Your first step should be to calculate the vertex of this function. You can do this by rewriting the equation as $y = a(x - h)^2 + ky$, where (h, k) is the vertex of the parabola:

$$y = 2x^2 - 4x + 7$$

$$= 2(x^2 - 2x) + 7$$

Now you need to change $(x^2 - 2x)$ so that it factors into the form $(x - h)^2$. You can do this by "completing the square"—adding a constant to both sides of the equation. In this case, add 2 to each side to complete the square:

$$y + 2 = 2(x^2 - 2x + 1) + 7$$
$$y = 2(x - 1)^2 + 5$$

So the vertex is the point $(1, 5)$, and the minimum value must be 5.

43. **D**   Coordinate Geometry: Linear Inequalities, Graphing

To find the graph of the set of equations, you first need to graph the equations individually; then you can find the intersection of the three graphs. The graph of $x + y \geq 4$ is equivalent to the graph of $y \geq 4 - x$, which is shown below.

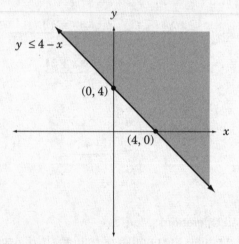

The graphs of $x \leq 4$ and $y \leq 4$ look like this:

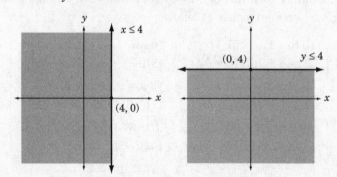

The intersection of all these graphs is given by **D**.

44. **C**   Miscellaneous Math: Sequences and Series

The Math Level 2 Test will probably include a question on sequences, so you should memorize the sequence formulas. The formula for a general term of a geometric sequence $\{a, ar, ar^2, ...\}$ is given by $a \cdot r^{n-1} = a_n$, where a is the first term in the sequence, a_n is the nth term, and the ratio r is a constant. The sum of the first n terms in a geometric series is given by $S = \dfrac{a(1 - r^n)}{1 - r}$. In order to determine the sum of the first 6 terms in this geometric series, you will need to find the values of a and r first. Using the formula for a general term in the sequence, you have:

$$12 = a \cdot r^1, \text{ since 12 is the second term.}$$

$$192 = a \cdot r^3, \text{ since 192 is the fourth term.}$$

Dividing the bottom equation by the top equation, you get:

$$\frac{192}{12} = \frac{ar^3}{ar^1}$$

$$16 = r^2$$

$$r = \pm 4$$

If $r = -4$, then $a = -3$. And if $r = 4$, then $a = 3$.

Plug the sets of numbers into the formula for S. When you try the positive pair of numbers, you'll see that:

$$S = \frac{3(1 - 4^6)}{1 - 4}$$

$$S = 4095$$

45. **B**   Trigonometry: Sum and Difference Formulas
This question tests you on angle addition/subtraction. You should definitely memorize the sum and difference formulas for both sine and cosine. To answer this question, recall that $\sin(A - B) = \sin A \cos B - \cos A \sin B$. Apply this formula to the triangle in the figure below:

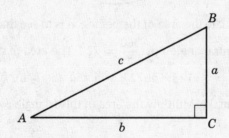

$$\sin(A - B) = \frac{a}{c} \cdot \frac{a}{c} - \frac{b}{c} \cdot \frac{b}{c}$$

$$= \frac{a^2 - b^2}{c^2}$$

$$= \frac{a^2 - b^2}{a^2 + b^2} \text{ because } a^2 + b^2 = c^2$$

46. **C**   Fundamentals: Logarithms, Inequalities
Since this problem asks you to solve for n when n is an exponent, you need to use logarithms in your solution. Your first step, though, should be to set up an inequality. The smallest positive integer with 16 digits is 10^{15}, since it is a 1 followed by 15 zeros. Since

2^n must be equal to or greater than the smallest positive 16-digit integer, you can set up the following inequality:

$$2^n \geq 10^{15}$$

Now take the logarithm of each side:

$$\log 2^n \geq \log 10^{15}$$

Apply the power rule of logarithms to the inequality to get:

$$n \cdot \log 2 \geq \log 10^{15}$$

$$n \geq \frac{\log 10^{15}}{\log 2}$$

$$n \geq 49.83$$

Thus the least positive integer n is 50.

47.   **E**   Plane Geometry: Polygons

The figure below shows a regular pentagon inscribed within a circle of radius 1.

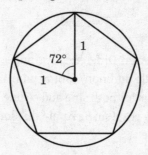

The easiest way to calculate the area of the pentagon is to see that the pentagon consists of 5 triangles whose central angle θ is $\frac{360}{5} = 72°$. The area of one of these triangles is given by $A = \frac{1}{2}ab\sin\theta = \frac{1}{2} \cdot 1 \cdot 1 \cdot \sin 72°$, where a and b are two sides of the triangle and θ is the angle they make. Multiply the area of this triangle by 5 to get the area of the pentagon.

$$\text{Area} = 5 \cdot \frac{1}{2} \cdot 1 \cdot 1 \cdot \sin 72°$$

$$= 2.38$$

346

48. B   Functions: Inverse Functions

Solving for the inverse function of $f(x)$ requires three steps. First, replace $f(x)$ with y. Second, switch x and y. Third, solve for y. The expression you get for y is the inverse function of f.

$$f(x) = \frac{1}{\pi}\log_3(x^5 + 1)$$

$$y = \frac{1}{\pi}\log_3(x^5 + 1)$$

$$x = \frac{1}{\pi}\log_3(y^5 + 1)$$

$$\pi x = \log_3(y^5 + 1)$$

$$3^{\pi x} = y^5 + 1, \text{ since } 3^x \text{ is the inverse of } \log_3 x$$

$$3^{\pi x} - 1 = y^5$$

$$\sqrt[5]{3^{\pi x} - 1} = y$$

$$\sqrt[5]{3^{\pi x} - 1} = f^{-1}(x)$$

49. D   Solid Geometry: Solids that Aren't Prisms

Given a sphere of radius r, the volume and surface area of the sphere are calculated by the formulas $V = \frac{4}{3}\pi r^3$ and $SA = 4\pi r^2$, respectively. The question states that the surface area is numerically 20% larger than the volume; this relationship can be expressed as $SA = 1.2V$, where 120% is the decimal 1.2.

$$4\pi r^2 = 1.2 \cdot \frac{4}{3}\pi r^3$$

$$\frac{5}{2} = r$$

50. B   Statistics: Permutations and Combinations

The Math Level 2 writers expect you to know the formulas for permutations and combinations. In this problem, the order of selection is not important, since you are choosing undifferentiated committees. When you choose r objects out of a total of n objects, the formula for the number of possible choices is $\binom{n}{r} = \frac{n!}{r!(n-r)!}$. (In many textbooks and on many calculators $\binom{n}{r}$ is denoted nCr.) Since you are choosing 2 physicists out of 15, 1 mathematician out of 10, and 3 biologists out of 25, you can write the following:

$$\binom{15}{2} \cdot \binom{10}{1} \cdot \binom{25}{3} = \frac{15!}{2!13!} \cdot \frac{10!}{1!9!} \cdot \frac{25!}{3!22!}$$

$$= \frac{15 \cdot 14}{2 \cdot 1} \cdot \frac{10}{1} \cdot \frac{25 \cdot 24 \cdot 23}{3 \cdot 2 \cdot 1}$$

$$= \frac{28,980,000}{12}$$

$$= 2,415,000$$

SAT* MATH LEVEL 2 PRACTICE TEST 2

SAT MATH LEVEL 2 PRACTICE TEST 2 ANSWER SHEET

1. Ⓐ Ⓑ Ⓒ Ⓓ Ⓔ	18. Ⓐ Ⓑ Ⓒ Ⓓ Ⓔ	35. Ⓐ Ⓑ Ⓒ Ⓓ Ⓔ
2. Ⓐ Ⓑ Ⓒ Ⓓ Ⓔ	19. Ⓐ Ⓑ Ⓒ Ⓓ Ⓔ	36. Ⓐ Ⓑ Ⓒ Ⓓ Ⓔ
3. Ⓐ Ⓑ Ⓒ Ⓓ Ⓔ	20. Ⓐ Ⓑ Ⓒ Ⓓ Ⓔ	37. Ⓐ Ⓑ Ⓒ Ⓓ Ⓔ
4. Ⓐ Ⓑ Ⓒ Ⓓ Ⓔ	21. Ⓐ Ⓑ Ⓒ Ⓓ Ⓔ	38. Ⓐ Ⓑ Ⓒ Ⓓ Ⓔ
5. Ⓐ Ⓑ Ⓒ Ⓓ Ⓔ	22. Ⓐ Ⓑ Ⓒ Ⓓ Ⓔ	39. Ⓐ Ⓑ Ⓒ Ⓓ Ⓔ
6. Ⓐ Ⓑ Ⓒ Ⓓ Ⓔ	23. Ⓐ Ⓑ Ⓒ Ⓓ Ⓔ	40. Ⓐ Ⓑ Ⓒ Ⓓ Ⓔ
7. Ⓐ Ⓑ Ⓒ Ⓓ Ⓔ	24. Ⓐ Ⓑ Ⓒ Ⓓ Ⓔ	41. Ⓐ Ⓑ Ⓒ Ⓓ Ⓔ
8. Ⓐ Ⓑ Ⓒ Ⓓ Ⓔ	25. Ⓐ Ⓑ Ⓒ Ⓓ Ⓔ	42. Ⓐ Ⓑ Ⓒ Ⓓ Ⓔ
9. Ⓐ Ⓑ Ⓒ Ⓓ Ⓔ	26. Ⓐ Ⓑ Ⓒ Ⓓ Ⓔ	43. Ⓐ Ⓑ Ⓒ Ⓓ Ⓔ
10. Ⓐ Ⓑ Ⓒ Ⓓ Ⓔ	27. Ⓐ Ⓑ Ⓒ Ⓓ Ⓔ	44. Ⓐ Ⓑ Ⓒ Ⓓ Ⓔ
11. Ⓐ Ⓑ Ⓒ Ⓓ Ⓔ	28. Ⓐ Ⓑ Ⓒ Ⓓ Ⓔ	45. Ⓐ Ⓑ Ⓒ Ⓓ Ⓔ
12. Ⓐ Ⓑ Ⓒ Ⓓ Ⓔ	29. Ⓐ Ⓑ Ⓒ Ⓓ Ⓔ	46. Ⓐ Ⓑ Ⓒ Ⓓ Ⓔ
13. Ⓐ Ⓑ Ⓒ Ⓓ Ⓔ	30. Ⓐ Ⓑ Ⓒ Ⓓ Ⓔ	47. Ⓐ Ⓑ Ⓒ Ⓓ Ⓔ
14. Ⓐ Ⓑ Ⓒ Ⓓ Ⓔ	31. Ⓐ Ⓑ Ⓒ Ⓓ Ⓔ	48. Ⓐ Ⓑ Ⓒ Ⓓ Ⓔ
15. Ⓐ Ⓑ Ⓒ Ⓓ Ⓔ	32. Ⓐ Ⓑ Ⓒ Ⓓ Ⓔ	49. Ⓐ Ⓑ Ⓒ Ⓓ Ⓔ
16. Ⓐ Ⓑ Ⓒ Ⓓ Ⓔ	33. Ⓐ Ⓑ Ⓒ Ⓓ Ⓔ	50. Ⓐ Ⓑ Ⓒ Ⓓ Ⓔ
17. Ⓐ Ⓑ Ⓒ Ⓓ Ⓔ	34. Ⓐ Ⓑ Ⓒ Ⓓ Ⓔ	

SAT MATH LEVEL 2 PRACTICE TEST 2

Time—1 hour

For each of the following problems, decide which is the BEST of the choices given. If the exact numerical value is not one of the choices, select the choice that best approximates this value. Then fill in the corresponding oval on the answer sheet.

<u>Notes:</u> (1) A calculator will be necessary for answering some (but not all) of the questions in this test. For each question you will have to decide whether or not you should use a calculator. The calculator you use must be at least a scientific calculator; programmable calculators and calculators that can display graphs are permitted.

(2) For some questions in this test you may need to decide whether your calculator should be in radian or degree mode.

(3) Figures that accompany problems in this test are intended to provide information useful in solving the problems. They are drawn as accurately as possible EXCEPT when it is stated in a specific problem that its figure is not drawn to scale. All figures lie in a plane unless otherwise indicated.

(4) Unless otherwise specified, the domain of any function f is assumed to be the set of all real numbers x for which $f(x)$ is a real number.

REFERENCE INFORMATION

THE FOLLOWING INFORMATION IS FOR YOUR REFERENCE IN ANSWERING SOME OF THE QUESTIONS IN THIS TEST:

Volume of a right circular cone with radius r and height h: $V = \frac{1}{3}\pi r^2 h$

Lateral area of a right circular cone with circumference of the base c and slant height l: $S = \frac{1}{2}cl$

Volume of a sphere with radius r: $V = \frac{4}{3}\pi r^3$

Surface area of a sphere with radius r: $S = 4\pi r^2$

Volume of a pyramid with base area B and height h: $V = \frac{1}{3}Bh$

USE THIS SPACE FOR SCRATCHWORK.

1.   If x is an integer, then which of the following is the least value of x that satisfies $3^x > 240$?

(A) 3
(B) 4
(C) 5
(D) 6
(E) 7

GO ON TO THE NEXT PAGE

USE THIS SPACE FOR SCRATCHWORK.

2. If $\dfrac{1}{z} = \dfrac{x+y}{2}$, what is x in terms of y and z ?

(A) $\dfrac{2}{z} + y$

(B) $\dfrac{2}{z} - y$

(C) $\dfrac{2-y}{z}$

(D) $\dfrac{2+y}{z}$

(E) $\dfrac{2}{z-y}$

3. Figure 1 shows the graph of which of the following equations?

(A) $y = \dfrac{4}{3}x + 2$

(B) $y = \dfrac{4}{3}x + \dfrac{9}{4}$

(C) $y = \dfrac{3}{4}x + 2$

(D) $y = \dfrac{3}{4}x + \dfrac{9}{4}$

(E) $y = \dfrac{3}{4}x + 3$

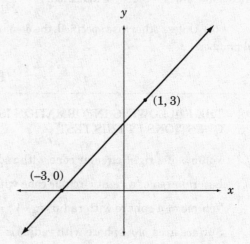

(1, 3)

(−3, 0)

<u>Note:</u> Figure not drawn to scale.
Figure 1

4. $\dfrac{3!}{2! + 3!} =$

(A) $\dfrac{1}{7}$

(B) $\dfrac{1}{5}$

(C) $\dfrac{1}{2}$

(D) $\dfrac{2}{3}$

(E) $\dfrac{3}{4}$

5. If $h(x) = \dfrac{x^2 + x + 1}{2}$ and $f(x) = x \cdot h(x)$, what is $f(2)$?

(A) $\dfrac{7}{2}$

(B) 7

(C) 8

(D) $\dfrac{17}{2}$

(E) 20

GO ON TO THE NEXT PAGE

USE THIS SPACE FOR SCRATCHWORK.

6. Let f be a function defined on pairs of positive integers as
$f(a, b) = a^b$. For which of the following does $f(a, b) = f(b, a)$?

(A) $a = 1, b = 2$
(B) $a = 2, b = 4$
(C) $a = 2, b = 3$
(D) $a = 3, b = 4$
(E) $a = 3, b = 5$

7. How many vertical asymptotes does the graph of
$f(x) = \dfrac{x - 3}{(x + 2)(x^2 - 9)}$ have?

(A) None
(B) One
(C) Two
(D) Three
(E) Four

8. $\dfrac{\sin^2\theta}{\cos^2\theta} - \dfrac{1}{\cos^2\theta} =$

(A) -1

(B) 0

(C) $\dfrac{1}{2}$

(D) 1

(E) $\sec^2\theta$

9. In Figure 2, if $\cos(\theta) = \dfrac{2}{7}$, then $\tan(\tau) =$

(A) 0.8
(B) 0.6
(C) 0.5
(D) 0.4
(E) 0.3

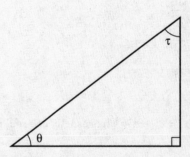

10. If $f(x) = \dfrac{3}{\sqrt{x^3 + 8}}$ and $f(a) = 3$, then $a =$

(A) 2.73
(B) 1.91
(C) -1.85
(D) -1.91
(E) -2.13

Note: Figure not drawn to scale.
Figure 2

GO ON TO THE NEXT PAGE

USE THIS SPACE FOR SCRATCHWORK.

11. Line l intersects plane P perpendicularly at point p. How many lines in plane P pass through p <u>and</u> are perpendicular to l ?

(A) None
(B) One
(C) Two
(D) Infinitely many
(E) Not enough information to tell

12. In a certain game the probability that John wins is $\frac{2}{7}$ and, independently, the probability that Robert wins is $\frac{1}{3}$. What is the probability that Robert wins and John loses?

(A) $\frac{2}{21}$

(B) $\frac{5}{21}$

(C) $\frac{2}{7}$

(D) $\frac{1}{3}$

(E) $\frac{13}{21}$

13. If the surface area of a cube is 1, what is its volume?

(A) $\frac{1}{2}$

(B) $\frac{\sqrt{6}}{6}$

(C) $\frac{\sqrt{6}}{36}$

(D) $\frac{\sqrt{6}}{216}$

(E) $\frac{1}{216}$

14. If $f(x) = x^2 - 6x + k$ has exactly one real root, then $k =$

(A) 9
(B) 8
(C) 7
(D) 6
(E) 0

GO ON TO THE NEXT PAGE

USE THIS SPACE FOR SCRATCHWORK.

15. If y varies inversely with x, and $y = 45$ when $x = \frac{1}{3}$, what is the value of x when $y = 30$?

(A) $\frac{1}{8}$

(B) $\frac{1}{4}$

(C) $\frac{1}{2}$

(D) $\frac{2}{3}$

(E) $\frac{3}{4}$

16. If $(x, h(x))$ is a point on the graph of $h(x) = x^2 + 1$, what is the slope of the line between the points $(-1, h(-1))$ and $(4, h(4))$?

(A) -4

(B) -3

(C) 1

(D) 2

(E) 3

17. Given the triangles in Figure 3, what is the value of $\sin(a + b)$?

(A) $\frac{57}{65}$

(B) $\frac{56}{65}$

(C) $\frac{55}{65}$

(D) $\frac{54}{65}$

(E) $\frac{12}{39}$

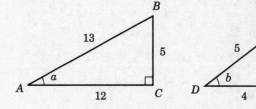

Note: Figure not drawn to scale.

Figure 3

18. How many even integers between 100 and 200 are divisible by 3 ?

(A) 17

(B) 16

(C) 15

(D) 14

(E) 13

GO ON TO THE NEXT PAGE

USE THIS SPACE FOR SCRATCHWORK.

19. What is the range of the function $f(x) = \dfrac{7}{x} - 3$?

    (A) All real numbers except −7
    (B) All real numbers except −3
    (C) All real numbers except 7
    (D) All real numbers except 0
    (E) All real numbers

20. The cost of shipping a package in terms of its weight is given by the formula $C = 3.00 + 0.76\lceil x - 1 \rceil$ where C is the cost (in dollars), x is the weight (in lbs.) and $\lceil x \rceil$ is the greatest integer less than or equal to x. What is the cost of shipping a $25\frac{1}{2}$-lb. package?

    (A) $19.76
    (B) $20.76
    (C) $21.24
    (D) $22.00
    (E) $22.24

21. If $x + 3$ is a factor of $x^3 + x^2 - 4cx + 1$, what is the value of c ?

    (A) 5
    (B) $\dfrac{17}{4}$
    (C) $\dfrac{17}{15}$
    (D) $\dfrac{17}{12}$
    (E) $\dfrac{17}{13}$

22. A line has parametric equations $x = 2t + 1$ and $y = t - 3$, where t is the parameter. What is the slope of the line?

    (A) 0
    (B) $\dfrac{1}{2}$
    (C) $\dfrac{2}{3}$
    (D) 2
    (E) 3

GO ON TO THE NEXT PAGE

USE THIS SPACE FOR SCRATCHWORK.

23. The shaded area in Figure 4 could be the solution set to which of the following pairs of inequalities?

(A) $\begin{cases} y \le 1-x^2 \\ y \le x \end{cases}$

(B) $\begin{cases} y \le 1-x^2 \\ y < x \end{cases}$

(C) $\begin{cases} y \le 1-x^2 \\ y \ge x \end{cases}$

(D) $\begin{cases} y \ge 1-x^2 \\ y \le x \end{cases}$

(E) $\begin{cases} y \ge 1-x^2 \\ y \ge x \end{cases}$

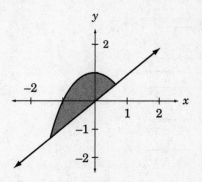

Figure 4

24. Which of the following equations produces an infinite set of points that are 3 units from the origin?

(A) $y^2 - x^2 = 3$
(B) $y^2 - x^2 = 9$
(C) $x^2 - y^2 = 3$
(D) $x^2 + y^2 = 3$
(E) $x^2 + y^2 = 9$

25. If $(x+y)^3 = 64$ and $\sqrt{x-y} = 4$, then $x =$

(A) 10
(B) 11
(C) 12
(D) 13
(E) Not enough information to tell

26. What is the maximum value of $f(x) = 3 - \sqrt{x-4}$ if $x \ge 4$?

(A) 4
(B) 3
(C) 2
(D) 0
(E) –3

GO ON TO THE NEXT PAGE

USE THIS SPACE FOR SCRATCHWORK.

27. In Figure 5, which of the following expressions is equal to $\sec(\theta)$?

(A) $\dfrac{h^2 - y^2}{h}$

(B) $\dfrac{h^2 + y^2}{h}$

(C) $\sqrt{\dfrac{h}{h^2 - y^2}}$

(D) $\dfrac{h}{\sqrt{h^2 - y^2}}$

(E) $\dfrac{h}{\sqrt{h^2 + y^2}}$

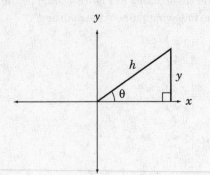

Figure 5

28. If $f(x) = 3^x$ and $f(g(x)) = x$, then $g(x) =$

(A) $\sqrt[3]{x}$

(B) $\dfrac{1}{3^x}$

(C) $\log_3 x$

(D) $\ln x$

(E) $\log_x 3$

29. If $f(x, y) = \begin{cases} x^2, \ x \le y \\ 1 - x, \ x > y \end{cases}$, what is the value of $f(2, 1) - f(1, 2)$?

(A) -2
(B) -1
(C) 0
(D) 2
(E) 6

30. A triangle has 2 vertices at the points $(2, 3)$ and $(2, 6)$. The third vertex lies somewhere on the line $x = -4$. The area of this triangle is

(A) 8
(B) 9
(C) any number less than 9
(D) any number greater than 9
(E) Not enough information to tell

GO ON TO THE NEXT PAGE

31. If vector $\vec{v} = (1, 3)$ and vector $\vec{w} = (2, -7)$, then which of the following is equal to $2\vec{v} - 3\vec{w}$?

    (A) $(-8, 18)$
    (B) $(8, -18)$
    (C) $(2, 27)$
    (D) $(-4, 27)$
    (E) $(-4, -27)$

32. If $x_0 = 1$ and $x_{n+1} = (x_n - 1)^2$, what is the value of x_3 ?

    (A) -3
    (B) -2
    (C) -1
    (D) 0
    (E) 1

33. Distribution D contains five real numbers, a, b, c, d, and e, where $a < b < c < d < e$. Which of the following changes, each considered individually, would increase the standard deviation of Distribution D?

    I.   Increase a by 1
    II. Increase c by 1
    III. Increase e by 1

    (A) I only
    (B) III only
    (C) I and II only
    (D) II and III only
    (E) I, II, and III

GO ON TO THE NEXT PAGE

34. Which of the following could be a portion of the graph of

$$\frac{x^2}{9} - \frac{y^2}{16} = 1?$$

(A)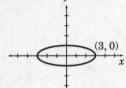

(B)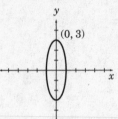

(C)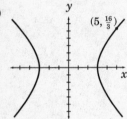

(D)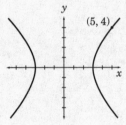

(E)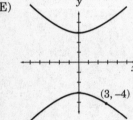

35. $(-i)^k$ is a negative integer if $k =$

(A) 1021
(B) 1022
(C) 1023
(D) 1024
(E) 1025

36. What is the value of $\lim\limits_{x \to \infty} \dfrac{2x^2 + 3x + 1}{5x^2 - 2x + 3}$?

(A) $-\infty$

(B) $-\dfrac{2}{5}$

(C) 0

(D) $\dfrac{2}{5}$

(E) $-\infty$

GO ON TO THE NEXT PAGE

USE THIS SPACE FOR SCRATCHWORK.

37. $f(x) = ax + b$ and $f^{-1}(x) = f(x)$ for all real x. If $f(0) = 3$, then what is the value of $f^{-1}(1)$?

   (A) 2

   (B) 1

   (C) $\dfrac{1}{2}$

   (D) 0

   (E) –2

38. What is the area of the circle defined by the equation
    $x^2 - 4x + y^2 - 6y - 212 = 0$?

   (A) 144π
   (B) 169π
   (C) 196π
   (D) 225π
   (E) 256π

39. Which of the following could be a portion of the graph $y = \dfrac{1}{2}e^{-x^2}$?

   (A) 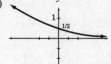   (B)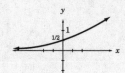

   (C) 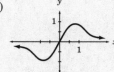   (D)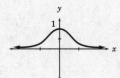

   (E)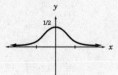

40. What is the measure of the largest angle in a triangle with sides of lengths 12, 17, and 24 ?

    (A) 109.7°
    (B) 110.5°
    (C) 112.1°
    (D) 112.8°
    (E) 112.9°

41. Which of the following is the polar coordinate representation for the point $(2\sqrt{3}, 2)$ in the (x, y) plane?

    (A) $(4, 60°)$
    (B) $(4, 30°)$
    (C) $(4, 25°)$
    (D) $(2, 60°)$
    (E) $(2, 30°)$

42. How many possible rearrangements can one make using all of the letters in the word COFFEE, including the arrangement COFFEE ?

    (A) 960
    (B) 720
    (C) 240
    (D) 190
    (E) 180

43. If $0 \le \theta \le 2\pi$ and the tangent of θ is equal to the sine of θ, then which of the following must be true?

    (A) $\cos\theta = \dfrac{\sqrt{2}}{2}$ or $\cos\theta = \dfrac{-\sqrt{2}}{2}$

    (B) $\cos\theta = \dfrac{\sqrt{3}}{2}$

    (C) $\cos\theta = -1$ or $\cos\theta = 1$

    (D) $\cos\theta = 1$ only

    (E) $\cos\theta = \dfrac{\sqrt{2}}{2}$ only

GO ON TO THE NEXT PAGE

44. If the volume of a sphere is tripled, then its surface area will grow by a factor of

    (A) $\sqrt[2]{3}$
    (B) $\sqrt[2]{9}$
    (C) $\sqrt[3]{3}$
    (D) $\sqrt[3]{9}$
    (E) $\sqrt[3]{18}$

45. If the graph of $f(x) = 2(x-4)^3 - 7$ is translated 7 units up and 4 units left, what is the y-value of the transformed graph at $x = 2$?

    (A) −23
    (B) 14
    (C) 16
    (D) 18
    (E) 20

46. $3x$, $2x + 1$, and $4x - 3$ (where x is a real number) form the first three terms of a geometric sequence. Which of the following could be the value of x ?

    (A) 2.12
    (B) 1.70
    (C) 1.01
    (D) 0.07
    (E) −1.2

47. An indirect proof of the statement "if x is a member of set P, then x is a member of set Q" could begin with the assumption that

    (A) x is not a member of Q
    (B) x is a member of Q
    (C) x is a member of P
    (D) x is not a member of P
    (E) x is neither a member of P nor Q

GO ON TO THE NEXT PAGE

USE THIS SPACE FOR SCRATCHWORK.

48. Figure 6 shows the intersection of a rhombus and a circle. What is the ratio of the area of the shaded region to the area of the rhombus?

    (A) 0.81
    (B) 0.75
    (C) 0.66
    (D) 0.60
    (E) 0.51

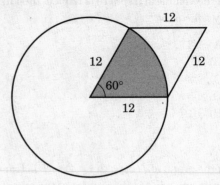

Figure 6

49. Water is leaking out of a right circular cone of radius 7 and height 15, as shown in Figure 7. What volume of water, in cubic units, will remain in the cone when the height of the water is 9 ?

    (A) 167.8
    (B) 166.3
    (C) 156.3
    (D) 151.2
    (E) 140.5

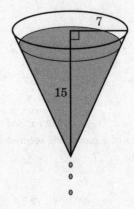

Figure 7

50. If $\left(2x - \dfrac{2}{x}\right)^2 + \left(3x - \dfrac{3}{x}\right) = 0$, then x could equal which of the following?

    (A) −2
    (B) −1
    (C) 0
    (D) 2
    (E) 7.2

S T O P

IF YOU FINISH BEFORE TIME IS CALLED, YOU MAY CHECK YOUR WORK ON THIS TEST ONLY.
DO NOT TURN TO ANY OTHER TEST IN THIS BOOK.

SAT MATH LEVEL 2 PRACTICE TEST 2 EXPLANATIONS

MATH LEVEL 2 PRACTICE TEST 2 ANSWERS

Question Number	Answer	Right	Wrong	Question Number	Answer	Right	Wrong
1	C	—	—	26	B	—	—
2	B	—	—	27	D	—	—
3	D	—	—	28	C	—	—
4	E	—	—	29	A	—	—
5	B	—	—	30	B	—	—
6	B	—	—	31	D	—	—
7	C	—	—	32	D	—	—
8	A	—	—	33	B	—	—
9	E	—	—	34	C	—	—
10	D	—	—	35	B	—	—
11	D	—	—	36	D	—	—
12	B	—	—	37	A	—	—
13	C	—	—	38	D	—	—
14	A	—	—	39	E	—	—
15	C	—	—	40	B	—	—
16	E	—	—	41	B	—	—
17	B	—	—	42	E	—	—
18	A	—	—	43	C	—	—
19	B	—	—	44	D	—	—
20	C	—	—	45	C	—	—
21	D	—	—	46	B	—	—
22	B	—	—	47	A	—	—
23	C	—	—	48	D	—	—
24	E	—	—	49	B	—	—
25	A	—	—	50	B	—	—

CALCULATING YOUR SCORE

Your raw score for the SAT Math Level 2 Test is calculated from the number of questions you answer correctly and incorrectly. Once you have determined your composite score, use the conversion table on page 298 of this book to calculate your scaled score. To calculate your raw score, count the number of questions you answered correctly:

_____
A

Count the number of questions you answered incorrectly, and multiply that number by $\frac{1}{4}$:

_____ $\times \frac{1}{4} =$ _____
B   C

Subtract the value in field C from the value in field A:

_____
D

Round the number in field D to the nearest whole number. This is your raw score:

_____
E

MATH LEVEL 2 TEST 2 EXPLANATIONS

1. C Algebra: Inequalities

The simplest way to solve this problem is to plug the answer choices into the inequality. Since the choices are given in increasing order, you should start with **C**. If **C** produces a value greater than 240, you'll know to try a smaller number for x. If **C** produces a value less than 240, you'll know to try a larger number. **C** says that $x = 5$. Plug 5 into the inequality: $3^5 = 243$ and $243 > 240$. Now try $x = 4$: $3^4 = 81$ and $81 < 240$. **C** is correct.

You can also solve this problem using logarithms. Take the log of both sides of the inequality:

$$\log 3^x > \log 240$$
$$x \log 3 > \log 240$$
$$x > \frac{\log 240}{\log 3}$$
$$x > 4.99$$

Since x is the smallest integer that's greater than 4.99, you know that x equals 5.

2. B Algebra: Equation Solving

This is a straightforward algebra question that asks you to solve for x. To isolate x, start by multiplying both sides by 2:

$$\frac{1}{z} = \frac{x+y}{2}$$
$$\frac{2}{z} = x+y$$

Subtract y from both sides:

$$\frac{2}{z} - y = x$$

3. D Coordinate Geometry: Lines

The question asks you to find the equation of the line shown in Figure 1. Since the answer choices are given in slope-intercept form ($y = mx + b$), you know you need to calculate the slope and y-intercept of the line. First use the two points shown in the figure to determine the slope:

$$m = \frac{\Delta y}{\Delta x}$$
$$= \frac{3-0}{1-(-3)}$$
$$= \frac{3}{4}$$

Now plug the slope into the slope-intercept equation:

$$y = \frac{3}{4}x + b$$

You can solve for the y-intercept, b, by plugging the point $(-3, 0)$ into the equation:

$$0 = \frac{3}{4}(-3) + b$$

$$\frac{9}{4} = b$$

You end up with the equation $y = \frac{3}{4}x + \frac{9}{4}$.

4. **E**   Statistics: Factorials

For the Math Level 2 Test, you definitely need to know how to solve factorials:

$$n! = n \cdot (n-1) \cdot (n-2)\dots(1)$$

Apply this definition to each of the factorials in the expression:

$$\frac{3!}{2! + 3!} = \frac{3 \cdot 2 \cdot 1}{2 \cdot 1 + 3 \cdot 2 \cdot 1}$$

$$= \frac{6}{2 + 6}$$

$$= \frac{6}{8}$$

$$= \frac{3}{4}$$

5. **B**   Functions: Evaluating Functions

The question tells you that $f(x) = x \cdot h(x)$ and that $h(x) = \frac{x^2 + x + 1}{2}$. Find $f(x)$ by multiplying $h(x)$ by x:

$$f(x) = x \cdot \left(\frac{x^2 + x + 1}{2}\right)$$

$$= \frac{x^3 + x^2 + x}{2}$$

Now find $f(2)$ by plugging 2 into $f(x)$:

$$f(2) = \frac{2^3 + 2^2 + 2}{2}$$

$$= 7$$

6. **B**   Functions: Evaluating Functions

If $f(a, b) = a^b$, then $f(b, a) = b^a$. The question asks you for the values of a and b when $f(a, b) = f(b, a)$, which is the same as $a^b = b^a$. The easiest way to solve this problem is to go through the answer choices plugging in the possible values for a and b. **B** is the correct answer since $2^4 = 4^2$.

7. **C**   Functions: Graphing Functions

Vertical asymptotes and holes occur at points where $f(x)$ is undefined—in other words, whenever one of the factors in the denominator of $f(x)$ equals zero. To find the vertical asymptotes of $f(x)$, first factor the function into its simplest form:

$$f(x) = \frac{x - 3}{(x + 2)(x^2 - 9)}$$

$$= \frac{x - 3}{(x + 2)(x + 3)(x - 3)}$$

Cancel $x - 3$ from the numerator and the denominator of the function. At $x = 3$, the function has a hole. The simplified function is:

$$f(x) = \frac{1}{(x + 2)(x + 3)}$$

The function is undefined at $x = -3$ and $x = -2$ because both of those values make the denominator equal to zero. Thus $f(x)$ has two vertical asymptotes: at $x = -3$ and at $x = -2$.

8. **A** Trigonometry: Pythagorean Identities
The Pythagorean Trigonometric Identities will help you simplify seemingly complicated trigonometry problems on the Math Level 2 Test. The most useful such identity is $\sin^2\theta + \cos^2\theta = 1$. You can see how this identity will help you out if you rewrite the expression as a single fraction:

$$\frac{\sin^2\theta}{\cos^2\theta} - \frac{1}{\cos^2\theta} = \frac{\sin^2\theta - 1}{\cos^2\theta}$$

By rearranging the identity, you find that $\sin^2\theta - 1 = -\cos^2\theta$. Plug $-\cos^2\theta$ into the equation:

$$= \frac{-\cos^2\theta}{\cos^2\theta}$$
$$= -1$$

9. **E** Trigonometry: Basic Functions
The question asks you to find $\tan(\tau)$. Since you know that $\cos\theta = \frac{2}{7}$, you can label the triangle's sides like this:

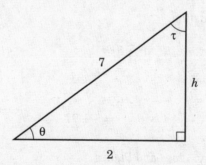

$\tan(\tau)$ is equal to the opposite side, 2, over the adjacent side, h. You can find the side h using the Pythagorean Theorem:

$$7^2 = h^2 + 2^2$$
$$45 = h^2$$
$$3\sqrt{5} = h$$

Now plug this value for h into the equation $\tan(\tau) = \frac{2}{h}$:

$$\tan(\tau) = \frac{2}{3\sqrt{5}}$$
$$= 0.3$$

You can also solve this problem by first finding the angle θ. Since $\cos(\theta) = \frac{2}{7}$, you know that $\theta = \cos^{-1}\left(\frac{2}{7}\right)$. Plug this inverse function into your calculator, and you'll find that $\theta = 73.4°$. Since the three angles in a triangle add up to $180°$, you can find the angle τ by subtracting θ and the right angle from $180°$:

$$\tau = 180 - 90 - \theta$$
$$= 180 - 90 - 73.4$$
$$= 16.6°$$

Now plug this angle into $\tan(\tau)$: $\tan(16.6°) = 0.3$.

10. D   Functions: Evaluating Functions

If $f(x) = \dfrac{3}{\sqrt{x^3 + 8}}$, then $f(a) = \dfrac{3}{\sqrt{a^3 + 8}}$. Since the question states that $f(a) = 3$, you can set up the following equation:

$$\frac{3}{\sqrt{a^3 + 8}} = 3$$

Use this equation to solve for a:

$$3 = \frac{3}{\sqrt{a^3 + 8}}$$
$$1 = \frac{1}{\sqrt{a^3 + 8}}$$
$$\sqrt{a^3 + 8} = 1$$

Square each side of the equation:

$$a^3 + 8 = 1$$
$$a^3 = -7$$
$$a = \sqrt[3]{-7}$$
$$= -1.91$$

11. D   Plane Geometry: Lines and Planes

This problem is difficult because you need to visualize a three-dimensional intersection. The perpendicular intersection of the line and the plane looks like this:

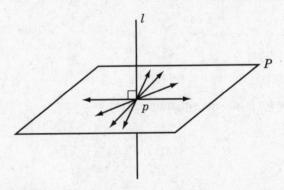

From this picture, you should see that any line in the plane P that passes through the point p is perpendicular to the line l. Plane P contains an infinite amount of lines passing through point p, so the correct answer is **D**.

12. **B**   Statistics: Probability

If you have two independent events A and B, the probability of both of them happening is the product of their independent probabilities: $P(A \text{ and } B) = P(A) \cdot P(B)$. The question tells you that the probability of Robert winning is $\frac{1}{3}$ and that the probability of John winning is $\frac{2}{7}$. In order to solve the problem, though, you need to find the probability of John *losing*. The probability of John losing is equal to 1 minus the probability of his winning:

$$
\begin{aligned}
P(\text{Robert wins and John loses}) &= P(\text{Robert wins}) \cdot P(\text{John loses}) \\
&= P(\text{Robert wins})[1 - P(\text{John wins})] \\
&= \frac{1}{3}\left(1 - \frac{2}{7}\right) \\
&= \frac{1}{3}\left(\frac{5}{7}\right) \\
&= \frac{5}{21}
\end{aligned}
$$

13. **C**   Solid Geometry: Prisms

In order to find the volume of a cube, you need to find the length s of the cube's sides. The question tells you that the surface area of the cube is equal to 1. Since the surface area of a cube is $6s^2$, you can solve for s by setting $6s^2 = 1$.

$$
\begin{aligned}
6s^2 &= 1 \\
s^2 &= \frac{1}{6} \\
s &= \frac{1}{\sqrt{6}}
\end{aligned}
$$

Now plug this value for s into the volume formula, $V = s^3$:

$$
\begin{aligned}
V &= \left(\frac{1}{\sqrt{6}}\right)^3 \\
&= \frac{1}{6\sqrt{6}} \\
&= \frac{\sqrt{6}}{36}
\end{aligned}
$$

14. **A**   Functions: Roots

The question tells you that $x^2 - 6x + k$ has exactly one real root. If this root is at $x = a$, you know that $x^2 - 6x + k = (x - a)^2$ must be true. Multiply out $(x - a)^2$ to get:

$$
x^2 - 6x + k = x^2 - 2ax + a^2
$$

Since the coefficients of the x term must be equal, you can set up the equation $-6x = -2ax$, which tells you that $a = 3$. Since $k = a^2$, you know that $k = 9$.

You could also have used the discriminant to solve this problem. If a function has only one real root, then its discriminant equals zero: $b^2 - 4ac = 0$. In this function, $a = 1$, $b = -6$, and $c = k$. Plug these numbers into the discriminant: $36 - 4k = 0$ so $k = 9$.

15. **C**   Algebra: Writing Equations, Variation

The statement "y varies inversely with x" means that y decreases as x increases and that y increases as x decreases. You can express this relationship as $y = \dfrac{k}{x}$ (or $yx = k$), where the constant k indicates that y isn't necessarily equal to $\dfrac{1}{x}$. You can find k by plugging $y = 45$ and $x = \dfrac{1}{3}$ into the expression:

$$k = 45 \cdot \dfrac{1}{3}$$
$$= 15$$

The question asks you to solve for x when $y = 30$:

$$k = yx$$
$$15 = 30 \cdot x$$
$$x = \dfrac{1}{2}$$

16. **E**   Coordinate Geometry: Lines; Functions: Evaluating Functions

Before you can find the slope between these two points, you first need to figure out what the points are by evaluating $h(x)$ at $x = -1$ and $x = 4$.

If $h(x) = x^2 + 1$, then $h(-1) = (-1)^2 + 1 = 2$ and $h(4) = 4^2 + 1 = 17$. Now find the slope between $(-1, 2)$ and $(4, 17)$ by dividing the change in the y-value by the change in the x-value:

$$\dfrac{\Delta y}{\Delta x} = \dfrac{17 - 2}{4 - (-1)}$$
$$= \dfrac{15}{5}$$
$$= 3$$

17. **B**   Trigonometry: Sum and Difference Formulas

You should memorize the angle addition formulas for $\sin\theta$ and $\cos\theta$. This question requires that you use the addition formula for $\sin\theta$: $\sin(a + b) = \sin a \cos b + \cos a \sin b$. In $\triangle ABC$, $\sin a = \dfrac{5}{13}$ and $\cos a = \dfrac{12}{13}$. In $\triangle DEF$, $\sin b = \dfrac{3}{5}$ and $\cos b = \dfrac{4}{5}$. Plug these values into the formula:

$$\sin(a + b) = \sin a \cos b + \cos a \sin b$$
$$= \dfrac{5}{13} \cdot \dfrac{4}{5} + \dfrac{12}{13} \cdot \dfrac{3}{5}$$
$$= \dfrac{4}{13} + \dfrac{36}{65}$$
$$= \dfrac{56}{65}$$

18.   A   Fundamentals: Integers

Even numbers are divisible by 2. If an even number is also divisible by 3, then the number must be a multiple of 6, since 6 is the least integer divisible by both 2 and 3. The smallest multiple of 6 greater than 100 is 102 (17×6) and the largest multiple of 6 less than 200 is 198 (33×6). The number of multiples of 6 between 100 and 200 is equal to the inclusive difference between 33 and 17: $33 - 17 + 1 = 17$.

19.   B   Functions: Domain and Range

The range of a function $f(x)$ is the set of all possible values of $f(x)$. An easy way to solve for the range of a function is to replace $f(x)$ with y in the equation and then solve for x:

$$y = \frac{7}{x} - 3$$

$$\frac{7}{x} = y + 3$$

$$\frac{7}{y+3} = x$$

You can see from this equation that y cannot be equal to -3, since x is undefined when $y = -3$ (because the denominator of the expression is equal to 0). Thus the range of $f(x)$ is all real numbers except -3.

20.   C   Functions: Evaluating Functions

This question looks complicated because of the unfamiliar operation, but answering it is mostly a matter of plugging $x = 25\frac{1}{2}$ into the provided formula:

$$C = 3.00 + 0.76 \lceil x - 1 \rceil$$

$$= 3.00 + 0.76 \left\lceil 25\frac{1}{2} - 1 \right\rceil$$

$$= 3.00 + 0.76 \left\lceil 24\frac{1}{2} \right\rceil$$

Here's the tricky part. The question says that whatever is inside the operation $\lceil \ \rceil$ should be rounded down to the nearest integer. So you end up with:

$$= 3.00 + 0.76(24), \text{ since the greatest integer less than or equal to } 24\frac{1}{2} \text{ is } 24$$

$$= 21.24$$

21.   D   Algebra: Polynomials

The question tells you that $(x + 3)$ is a factor of the polynomial $x^3 + x^2 - 4cx + 1$, practically begging you to solve the problem using polynomial long division. The polynomial version of long division says that any polynomial $P(x)$ can be written $P(x) = (x - a) \cdot Q(x) + R$, where $(x - a)$ is the divisor, $Q(x)$ is the quotient, and R is the remainder. The remainder R can be found by plugging a into $P(x)$, since $P(a) = (a - a) \cdot Q(a) + R = R$.

There are two unknown variables in this question: x and c. Since you want to solve for c, you need to make it the only unknown in an equation. You can do this by plugging in a value for x that will give you a value you've already determined for $P(x)$, such as

$P(a) = R$. In this question, $a = -3$, since $(x + 3)$ is the divisor $(x - a)$. Because $(x + 3)$ is a factor of $P(x)$, it divides $P(x)$ evenly, leaving no remainder. Since $R = 0$, you know $P(a) = 0$. You can solve for c by setting $P(a) = 0$ and plugging in $a = -3$:

$$P(a) = a^3 + a^2 - 4ca + 1 = 0$$
$$P(-3) = (-3)^3 + (-3)^2 - 4c(-3) + 1 = 0$$

Now you have an equation in which c is the only variable:

$$-27 + 9 + 12c + 1 = 0$$
$$12c = 17$$
$$c = \frac{17}{12}$$

22. **B** Coordinate Geometry: Parametric Equations, Lines and Distance

A simple way to solve this problem is to find two (x, y) points on the line and then use these points to determine the slope. You can find two points by plugging two values for t into the parametric equations for x and y. If $t = 0$, then $x = 1$, and $y = -3$, giving you the point $(1, -3)$. If $t = 1$, then $x = 3$, and $y = -2$, giving you the point $(3, -2)$. Find the slope of the line by dividing the change in the y-value by the change in the x-value:

$$\frac{\Delta y}{\Delta x} = \frac{-3 - (-2)}{1 - 3} = \frac{1}{2}$$

23. **C** Coordinate Geometry: Graphing Linear Inequalities

Since the answer choices give the same equations for the two lines, all you need to do is figure out the correct inequality signs. Since the lines in the figure are solid, the inequalities must be inclusive; in other words, they must look like $\leq$ or $\geq$. To figure out the direction of the inequality signs, start by graphing the curve $y = 1 - x^2$ and the line $y = x$ on your calculator:

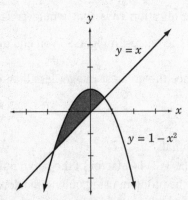

The shaded area is above $y = x$ and below $y = 1 - x^2$, and you can represent the area as the intersection of the inequalities $y \geq x$ and $y \leq 1 - x^2$.

24. **E** Plane Geometry: Circles

The infinite set of points 3 units from the origin is a circle of radius 3 centered at the origin. The equation for a circle centered at the origin is $x^2 + y^2 = r^2$. Plug in $r = 3$ to solve the problem: $x^2 + y^2 = 9$.

25. **A** Algebra: Systems of Equations

You should start by getting rid of the exponent and root in these two equations. Simplify the first equation by taking the cube root of both sides:

$$(x + y)^3 = 64$$
$$x + y = 64^{1/3}$$
$$x + y = 4$$

Now simplify the second equation by squaring both sides:

$$\sqrt{x - y} = 4$$
$$x - y = 4^2$$
$$x - y = 16$$

If you add the equations $x + y = 4$ and $x - y = 16$, you can cancel out y, leaving you with:

$$2x = 20$$
$$x = 10$$

26. **B** Functions: Evaluating Functions

In order to maximize the value of $f(x)$ over the domain $x \geq 4$, you need to make $\sqrt{x - 4}$ as small as possible. If $x \geq 4$, then the smallest value of $\sqrt{x - 4}$ is zero, which you get when $x = 4$. Thus the maximum value of $f(x)$ is 3, since $3 - \sqrt{4 - 4} = 3$. If x is greater than 4, the number under the square root will be positive, so you'll end up subtracting a positive number from 3.

You could also answer this problem by graphing $f(x)$ on your calculator and finding the maximum value of y.

27. **D** Trigonometry: Basic Functions

$\sec \theta$ is equal to $\dfrac{1}{\cos \theta}$ or $\dfrac{\text{hypotenuse}}{\text{adjacent}}$. The figure shows you that the triangle's hypotenuse is h and that the side opposite θ is y.

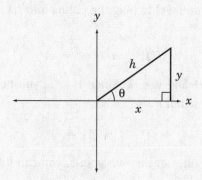

In order to find the adjacent leg, x, you need to use the Pythagorean Theorem:

$$x^2 + y^2 = h^2$$
$$x^2 = h^2 - y^2$$
$$x = \sqrt{h^2 - y^2}$$

Now you can solve for $\sec\theta$:

$$\sec\theta = \frac{1}{\cos\theta}$$

$$= \frac{h}{x}$$

$$= \frac{h}{\sqrt{h^2 - y^2}}$$

28. **C**   Functions: Compound Functions, Logarithms

When you see $f(g(x)) = x$, you've got an inverse function on your hands. $f(g(x)) = x$ means the same thing as $g(x) = f^{-1}(x)$. There are three main steps to solving an inverse function: first, replace $f(x)$ with y; second, switch the places of x and y; third, solve for y. Apply these steps to $f(x) = 3^x$:

$$y = 3^x$$

$$x = 3^y$$

Use a logarithm to get y out of the exponent.

$$\log_3 x = \log_3 3^y$$

Since $\log_A A^x = x$, you have:

$$\log_3 x = y$$

Finally, since $y = f^{-1}(x) = g(x)$, you end up with: $\log_3 x = g(x)$.

29. **A**   Functions: Piecewise Functions

Piecewise functions have different definitions for different intervals in their domains. The function in this question is a piecewise function with two input values: x and y. The question asks you to find the difference between two points on the function. Your first step should be to figure out the values of $f(2, 1)$ and $f(1, 2)$. At the point $f(2, 1)$, $x = 2$ and $y = 1$. Since $2 > 1$, you need to plug the points into $f(x, y) = 1 - x$, which is true when $x > y$:

$$f(2, 1) = 1 - 2 = -1$$

At the point $f(1, 2)$, $x = 1$ and $y = 2$. Since $1 < 2$, you need to plug the point into $f(x, y) = x^2$, which is true when $x \le y$:

$$f(1, 2) = (1)^2 = 1$$

Now that you know the values of the two points, you can find the difference between them:

$$f(2, 1) - f(1, 2) = -1 - 1$$

$$= -2$$

30. B Plane Geometry: Triangles; Coordinate Geometry: Coordinate Plane

Draw a picture of the situation described in the question:

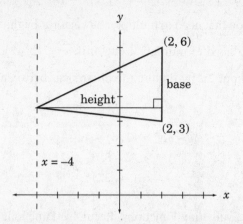

In order to find the area of the triangle, you need to know the triangle's base and height. The base of the triangle is the vertical distance between the points $(2, 6)$ and $(2, 3)$: $6 - 3 = 3$. As you can see from the picture, no matter where you draw the triangle's third vertex along the line $x = -4$, the height of $\triangle ABC$ will be 6. Plug these values for the base and height into the triangle area formula:

$$\text{Area } \triangle ABC = \frac{1}{2}bh$$

$$= \frac{1}{2}(3)(6)$$

$$= 9$$

31. D Coordinate Geometry: Vectors

Vectors are fair game on the Math Level 2 Test, so you need to be prepared for them. A vector has both magnitude and direction. The magnitude of a vector is its length, and the direction is the counterclockwise angle the vector makes with the positive x-axis. Below, the figure on the left shows a vector defined by its magnitude and direction. The figure on the right shows the same vector broken into its x- and y-components:

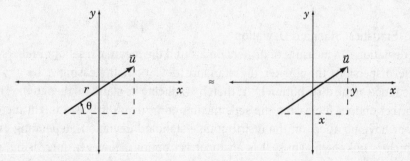

As you can see from this figure, a vector can be defined either by its length r and direction θ or by its x- and y-components. Usually, questions involving vectors will ask you to do simple calculations, such as multiplication by scalars (nonvector numbers) or vector addition. These questions are easy to answer using the x- and y-components. When multiplying a vector $\vec{u}$ by the scalar a, simply multiply the x- and y-components of $\vec{u}$ by a:

$a(x, y) = (ax, ay)$. When adding two vectors, simply add together their x-components, and then add together their y-components: $(x_1, y_1) + (x_2, y_2) = ((x_1 + x_2), (y_1 + y_2))$.

For this question, you first need to multiply the vector $\vec{v}$ by the scalar 2: if $\vec{v} = (1, 3)$, $2\vec{v} = (2, 6)$. Then you need to multiply $\vec{w}$ by 3: if $\vec{w} = (2, -7)$, $3\vec{w} = (6, -21)$. Now you can subtract $3\vec{w}$ from $2\vec{v}$ by finding the differences between the two x-values and the two y-values:

$$\begin{aligned}
2\vec{v} - 3\vec{w} &= (2, 6) - (6, -21) \\
&= (2 - 6, 6 - (-21)) \\
&= (-4, 27)
\end{aligned}$$

32. D   Functions: Evaluating Functions, Recursive Functions

An easy way to find the value of x_3 is to find first the values of x_1 and x_2. You can use $x_0 = 1$ to find the value of x_1:

$$\begin{aligned}
x_{0+1} &= (x_0 - 1)^2 \\
x_1 &= (1 - 1)^2 \\
&= 0
\end{aligned}$$

Now use $x_1 = 0$ to find x_2:

$$\begin{aligned}
x_2 &= (x_1 - 1)^2 \\
&= (0 - 1)^2 \\
&= 1
\end{aligned}$$

Now you can solve for x_3 since you have x_2:

$$\begin{aligned}
x_3 &= (x_2 - 1)^2 \\
&= (1 - 1)^2 \\
&= 0
\end{aligned}$$

33. B   Statistics: Standard Deviation

Standard deviation is a measure of dispersion around the mean of a set of numbers. The greater the dispersion, the greater the standard deviation. Increasing a by 1 would reduce the range of the distribution by 1, thereby reducing its standard deviation. Thus, I is an incorrect option. Increasing the set's median term (c in this case) might increase, decrease, or have no affect on the distribution's standard deviation, depending on the mean, which is unknown. Thus, II is an incorrect option. However, increasing e, the greatest of the five numbers, by 1 would increase the distribution's range by 1, thereby increasing its standard deviation. III is the only correct option.

34. C   Coordinate Geometry: Hyperbolas

Hyperbola and ellipse questions are fair game on the Math Level 2 Test. So, you should know the equations for both, and you should be able to tell the difference between their equations. The equation of a hyperbola is $\dfrac{(x-h)^2}{a^2} - \dfrac{(y-k)^2}{b^2} = 1$ or $\dfrac{(y-k)^2}{b^2} - \dfrac{(x-h)^2}{a^2} = 1$, where

380

(h, k) is the center of the hyperbola. The equation of an ellipse is $\frac{(x+h)^2}{a^2} + \frac{(y+k)^2}{b^2} = 1$, where (h, k) is the center of the ellipse. The equation in the question has a minus sign, so you should instantly recognize it as the equation of a hyperbola. You can rule out **A** and **B**, since they show the graphs of ellipses. Try plugging some points from the other three graphs into the equation. Both **C** and **D** contain the point $(3, 0)$. When you plug this point into the equation, you get $1 = 1$, so you know that point is on the graph. Because **E** doesn't include that point, you can rule it out as an answer. Now plug in the point $(5, \frac{16}{3})$:

$$\frac{5^2}{9} - \frac{\left(\frac{16}{3}\right)^2}{16} = \frac{25}{9} - \frac{16}{9}$$

$$= \frac{9}{9}$$

$$= 1$$

C is correct because it contains the point $(5, \frac{16}{3})$.

35. **B**   Miscellaneous Math: Complex Numbers

For the Math Level 2 Test, you need to know the effect of raising i to different powers. There are four possible results:

$$i^1 = i$$
$$i^2 = -1$$
$$i^3 = -i$$
$$i^4 = 1$$

When you raise i to an exponent larger than 4, you can figure out the value of the expression by dividing the exponent by 4 and looking at the remainder. If 4 divides the exponent evenly, leaving a remainder of 0, then the expression is equivalent to $i^4 = 1$. If the division leaves a remainder of 1, then the expression is equivalent to $i^1 = i$. If you get a remainder of 2, then the expression is equivalent to $i^2 = -1$. If the remainder is 3, then the expression is equivalent to $i^3 = -i$.

Use the law of exponents to rewrite $(-i)^k$ as $(-1)^k(i)^k$. The question tells you that $(-i)^k$ equals a negative integer, so you know that k must be an even number, since even exponents produce the integers 1 or –1. If k is even, then $(-1)^k = 1$ and $(-1)^k(i)^k = (i)^k$. In order for $(i)^k$ to equal –1, k must leave a remainder of 2 when divided by 4. Divide each of the answer choices by 4 and see what remainder each division produces. Only **B**, 1022, leaves a remainder of 2, so it is the correct answer.

36. **D**   Miscellaneous Math: Limits

The question asks you to find the limit of the function as x approaches infinity—in other words, to determine the value of the function as the value of x gets close to infinity.

When finding the limit at infinity, you should first find the terms with the highest degrees (or exponents) in the numerator and denominator of the function. In this case, $2x^2$ is the term with the highest degree in the numerator, and $5x^2$ is the term with the highest degree in the denominator. At infinity, the function essentially reduces to these highest terms, $\frac{2x^2}{5x^2}$, since the lower degree terms become insignificantly small compared to the highest degree terms as x grows infinitely large. The x^2 terms in the numerator and denominator of $\frac{2x^2}{5x^2}$ cancel out, leaving you with $\frac{2}{5}$, which is the value of the limit at infinity.

37.   A   Functions: Inverse Functions

You need to solve for the three unknowns: a, b, and x. The question tells you that $f(0) = 3$, so you know that $a(0) + b = 3$, or $b = 3$. Now you have two unknowns left. In order to solve for them, you need to write another equation. Your next step should be to find $f^{-1}(x)$. Finding an inverse function requires three steps. First, replace $f(x)$ with y, so that $y = ax + 3$. Second, switch x and y, so that $x = ay + 3$. Third, solve for y:

$$x = ay + 3$$
$$x - 3 = ay$$
$$y = \frac{x-3}{a}$$
$$f^{-1}(x) = \frac{x-3}{a}$$

Because $f(x) = f^{-1}(x)$, you know that $f^{-1}(0) = 3$. Plug $x = 0$ into $f^{-1}(x)$:

$$f^{-1}(0) = \frac{0-3}{a} = 3$$
$$-3 = 3a$$
$$a = -1$$

Now you have the inverse function $f^{-1}(x) = -\frac{x-3}{1}$. Plug $x = 1$ into this function to solve the problem: $f^{-1}(1) = -\frac{1-3}{1} = 2$.

38.   D   Coordinate Geometry and Plane Geometry: Circles

In order to find the area of the circle, you need to know the circle's radius. To find the radius, rewrite the given equation in the standard form for a circle: $(x - h)^2 + (y - k)^2 = r^2$, where (h, k) is the center and r is the radius. Complete the squares of x and y:

$$x^2 - 4x + y^2 - 6y - 212 = 0$$
$$x^2 - 4x + y^2 - 6y = 212$$
$$(x^2 - 4x + 4) + (y^2 - 6y + 9) = 212 + 9 + 4$$
$$(x - 2)^2 + (y - 3)^2 = 225$$

According to the standard form of a circle's equation, $225 = r^2$. Since the area of a circle is πr^2, you don't need to solve for r.

$$\text{Area}_{\text{circle}} = \pi r^2$$
$$= 225\pi$$

39. E   Functions: Graphing Functions

The best way to answer this problem is to graph the function on your calculator. The graph of $y = \frac{1}{2}e^{-x^2}$ should look like this:

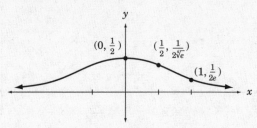

D and **E** both resemble the graph above, but **E** has the correct y-intercept: $(0, \frac{1}{2})$. You can double check that **E** is correct by plugging $x = 0$ into $y = \frac{1}{2}e^{-x^2}$:

$$y = \frac{1}{2}e^{-(0)^2}$$

$$= \frac{1}{2}(1)$$

$$= \frac{1}{2}$$

40. B   Trigonometry: Solving Non-Right Triangles

When you're given the three sides of a non-right triangle, you can use the law of cosines to determine the angles in the triangle. According to the law of cosines, $c^2 = a^2 + b^2 - 2ab\cos C$ in $\triangle ABC$:

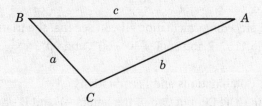

As you can see from the picture, the largest angle of a triangle is opposite the largest side. Since you're looking for the largest angle in a triangle with sides 12, 17, and 24, you should let $c = 24$. Plug the triangle's sides into the law of cosines:

$$24^2 = 12^2 + 17^2 - 2(12)(17)\cos C$$

$$24^2 - 12^2 - 17^2 = -408\cos C$$

$$-\frac{143}{408} = \cos C$$

$$C = \cos^{-1}\left(-\frac{143}{408}\right)$$

$$= 110.5°$$

41. B   Coordinate Geometry: Polar Coordinates

Polar coordinate questions rarely appear on the Math Level 2 Test. When they do, the

question will most likely ask you to convert an (x, y) point into polar coordinate form,

(r, θ). You should memorize the conversion before you take the test; fortunately, it's pretty straightforward: $r = \sqrt{x^2 + y^2}$ and $\theta = \tan^{-1}\left(\frac{y}{x}\right)$.

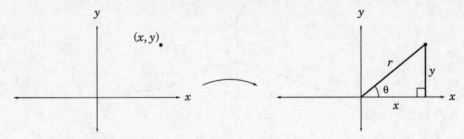

As you can see from the figure, r is the hypotenuse of a right triangle formed by the lengths x and y, so you can find r using the Pythagorean Theorem:

$$r = \sqrt{x^2 + y^2}$$
$$= \sqrt{(2\sqrt{3})^2 + 2^2}$$
$$= \sqrt{16}$$
$$= 4$$

Since the triangle is a right triangle, you can solve for θ using inverse tangent:

$$\theta = \tan^{-1}\left(\frac{y}{x}\right)$$
$$= \tan^{-1}\left(\frac{2}{2\sqrt{3}}\right)$$
$$= 30°$$

You can shortcut the preceding calculations if you see that the triangle is a special right triangle with side ratio $1:\sqrt{3}:2$ and angles 30°, 60°, and 90°.

42. **E**   Statistics: Combinations and Permutations
There are six letters in COFFEE, but two of the letters—F and E—are duplicated. When figuring out the number of possible arrangements, you need to take these duplicated letters into account so you don't double count any arrangements. Divide the number of possible arrangements of six letters by the number of arrangements of EE and FF:

$$\frac{(\text{total number of letters})!}{(\text{number of Es})!(\text{number of Fs})!} = \frac{6!}{2!2!}$$
$$= 180$$

43. **C**   Trigonometry: Basic Functions
When you see $\tan\theta$ in a trigonometry problem, you can often spot the solution by rewriting $\tan\theta$ as $\frac{\sin\theta}{\cos\theta}$.

$$\tan\theta = \sin\theta$$
$$\frac{\sin\theta}{\cos\theta} = \sin\theta$$
$$0 = \sin\theta - \frac{\sin\theta}{\cos\theta}$$
$$0 = \sin\theta\left(1 - \frac{1}{\cos\theta}\right)$$

According to this equation, either $\sin\theta = 0$ or $1 - \dfrac{1}{\cos\theta} = 0$.

$$\sin\theta = 0, \text{ and } 0 \le \theta \le 2\pi$$
$$\theta = 0, \pi, 2\pi$$

If $\theta = 0, \pi, 2\pi$, then $\cos\theta = 1, -1$.

$$1 - \dfrac{1}{\cos\theta} = 0$$
$$\cos\theta = 1$$

C is the correct answer because it says that $\cos\theta$ equals either 1 or –1.

44. D   Solid Geometry: Solids that Aren't Prisms

The question asks you what happens to the surface area of a sphere when its volume is tripled. Since a sphere's volume and surface area depend on its radius, you should first figure out what happens to the radius when the volume triples. Call the original radius r and the new radius R. The original volume of the sphere is:

$$V = \dfrac{4}{3}\pi r^3$$

The new volume of the sphere is:

$$3V = \dfrac{4}{3}\pi(R)^3$$
$$3\left(\dfrac{4}{3}\pi r^3\right) = \dfrac{4}{3}\pi R^3$$
$$3r^3 = R^3$$

Take the cube root of both sides:

$$\sqrt[3]{3}\,r = R$$

This equation tells you that the sphere's radius increases by $\sqrt[3]{3}$ when the volume triples. The sphere's original surface area is $4\pi r^2$, and the new surface area is $4\pi R^2$. Replace R with $\sqrt[3]{3}\,r$ to see how the surface area changes:

$$4\pi R^2 = 4\pi\left(\sqrt[3]{3}\,r\right)^2$$
$$= 4\pi\sqrt[3]{9}\,r^2$$
$$= \sqrt[3]{9}(4\pi r^2)$$
$$= \sqrt[3]{9}(SA)$$

The new surface area is $\sqrt[3]{9}$ times as large as the original surface area.

45. C   Functions: Graphing Functions

A "translated" graph moves to a different position in the coordinate plane, but doesn't change its shape. Call the graph of the function in the question $y = f(x)$. When you move the graph vertically, you're changing its y-value. To move the function in the question up by 7 units, add 7 to $f(x)$: $y = f(x) + 7$. When you move the graph horizontally, you're changing its x-value. To move the function 4 units to the left, you need to add 4 to x: $y = f(x + 4)$. Now combine these translations:

$$y = f(x + 4) + 7$$
$$= 2((x + 4) - 4)^3 - 7 + 7$$
$$= 2x^3$$

Your new function is $h(x) = 2x^3$. The question asks you for the y-value of the transformed graph at $x = 2$. To find this value, simply plug $x = 2$ into $h(x)$.

$$h(2) = 2(2)^3$$
$$= 2(8)$$
$$= 16$$

46. B   Miscellaneous Math: Sequences and Series

In a geometric sequence, the ratio of successive terms is constant. For example, the ratio of a_1 to a_2 is equal to the ratio of a_2 to a_3. In this question, $a_1 = 3x$, $a_2 = 2x + 1$, and $a_3 = 4x - 3$. You can write the following equation with the ratios of these terms:

$$\frac{a_1}{a_2} = \frac{a_2}{a_3}$$
$$\frac{3x}{2x + 1} = \frac{2x + 1}{4x - 3}$$

Cross multiply to get:

$$12x^2 - 9x = 4x^2 + 4x + 1$$
$$8x^2 - 13x - 1 = 0$$

You can plug the coefficients into the quadratic formula to solve for x:

$$x = \frac{13 \pm \sqrt{169 + 32}}{16}$$
$$\approx -0.07, 1.70$$

Since **B** is $x = 1.70$, it's the correct answer.

47. A   Miscellaneous Math: Logic

Occasionally, Math Level 2 questions will ask what assumption is made by the indirect proof of a statement. These questions sound more complicated than they are. All you need to know is how to find the assumption of an indirect proof; you don't need to know how to find the indirect proof itself. In an indirect proof of "if p, then q," you assume the negative of the conclusion q; in other words, you start out the proof with the assumption that you have "not q." In this case, you have the statement "if x is a member of set P, then x is a member of set Q." The assumption the indirect proof makes is the negative of "x is a member of set Q." So **A**, which states that "x is *not* a member of set Q," is correct.

48. D Plane Geometry: Polygons, Sectors; Fundamentals: Ratios

In order to solve this problem, you need to find the area of the rhombus and the area of the shaded region. The area of a rhombus is the product of its base and height.

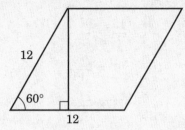

The base of the rhombus is 12. Its height h is equal to $12 \sin 60°$. Plug the base and height into the area formula: $\text{Area}_{\text{rhombus}} = 12 \times 12 \sin 60° = 72\sqrt{3}$. Now you need to find the area of the shaded region. As you can see from this picture, the shaded region is a sector:

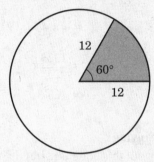

The formula for the area of a sector is: $\text{Area}_{\text{sector}} = \dfrac{n}{360} \times \pi r^2$, where n is the central angle of the sector and r is the radius of the circle. The central angle of the sector is the same as the angle of the rhombus: $60°$. The radius of the circle is the same as the side of the rhombus: 12. Plug these values into the formula to find the sector's area:

$$\text{Area}_{\text{sector}} = \frac{60}{360} \times \pi(12)^2$$
$$= 24\pi$$

Now you can find the ratio of the area of the sector to the area of the rhombus:

$$\frac{\text{Area}_{\text{sector}}}{\text{Area}_{\text{rhombus}}} = \frac{24\pi}{72\sqrt{3}}$$
$$= 0.60$$

49. B Solid Geometry: Solids that Aren't Prisms

The volume of a cone depends on its radius, so you need to figure out the radius of the cone that's formed when the water is at a height of 9. Redraw the figure to show the sunken water level:

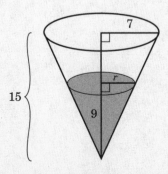

As you can see from this picture, you have two similar right triangles: one with base 7 and height 15, and the other with base r and height 9. Because these triangles are similar, you can find r using the following ratio of height to base:

$$\frac{15}{7} = \frac{9}{r}$$

$$r = \frac{7(9)}{15}$$

$$= \frac{21}{5}$$

Now you can plug r into the formula for the volume of a cone:

$$\text{Volume}_{cone} = \frac{1}{3}\pi r^2 h$$

$$= \frac{1}{3}\pi\left(\frac{21}{5}\right)^2(9)$$

$$= \frac{1323}{25}\pi$$

$$= 166.3$$

50. **B**   Algebra: Equation Solving

You may be tempted to multiply out this equation, but if you do, you'll end up with some really messy math. The trick to answering this question is to factor a constant out of each of the expressions, so you end up with a constant number multiplied by $\left(x - \frac{1}{x}\right)$:

$$\left(2x - \frac{2}{x}\right)^2 + \left(3x - \frac{3}{x}\right) = 0$$

$$2^2\left(x - \frac{1}{x}\right)^2 + 3\left(x - \frac{1}{x}\right) = 0$$

Since both of the expressions contain $\left(x - \frac{1}{x}\right)$, you can factor again:

$$\left(x - \frac{1}{x}\right)\left[4\left(x - \frac{1}{x}\right) + 3\right] = 0$$

This equation's solution is either $x - \frac{1}{x} = 0$ or $x - \frac{1}{x} = -\frac{3}{4}$. If $x - \frac{1}{x} = 0$, then $x^2 - 1 = 0$ and $x = \pm 1$. You don't need to solve $x - \frac{1}{x} = -\frac{3}{4}$ since **B** says that x can equal -1.

THE SAT
U.S. HISTORY
TEST

INTRODUCTION TO THE SAT U.S. HISTORY TEST

IMAGINE TWO CHILDREN, ELOISE AND BARTHOLOMEW, RACING in the forest. Who will win—Eloise, who never stumbles because she knows the placement of every tree and all the twists and turns and hiding spots, or Bartholomew, who keeps falling down and tripping over roots because he doesn't pay any attention to the landscape? The answer is obvious. Even if Bartholomew is a little faster and more athletic, Eloise will win because she knows how to navigate the landscape and use it to her advantage.

This example of a race in the forest illustrates a point: in the metaphor, the forest is the structure of the SAT U.S. History Test, and the competition is taking the test. In this chapter we're going to describe the "landscape" of the SAT U.S. History Test: what topics the questions cover, what the questions look like, and how the questions are organized. In the next chapter, we'll show you some strategies that will allow you to navigate and use the landscape to get the best score you can.

CONTENT OF THE SAT U.S. HISTORY TEST

The SAT U.S. History Test covers 600 years of United States history, beginning with the period before Columbus's discovery of the New World and continuing to the present. There are two ways to organize and think about the 600 years of U.S. history covered on the test: by chronological eras, and by different aspects of history, such as political, social, or economic history.

Chronological Eras

ETS breaks down the content of the test into three chronological eras, and tells us how much of each the test covers:

Era	Approximate % of the Test	Approximate No. of Questions
Pre-Columbian to 1789	20	18
1790–1898	40	36
1899–present	40	36

Unfortunately, these categories are too broad to be very helpful—the Pre-Columbian to 1789 category alone contains three distinct historical periods, each with its own characteristics: the Pre-Columbian period, the Colonial Period, and the American Revolution.

Below, we've created a test breakdown of smaller, more manageable categories.

Era	Approximate % of the Test	Approximate No. of Questions
Pre-Columbian	2	2
Colonial Period	10	9
American Revolution and Constitution	8	7
First Years of the New Nation	7	6
Age of Jackson and Jacksonian Democracy	5	4
Westward Expansion and Sectional Strife	7	6
Civil War and Reconstruction	5	5
Industrial Revolution	14	13
American Imperialism	2	2
Progressive Era	5	4
World War I	4	4
The Roaring Twenties	4	4
The Great Depression and the New Deal	8	7
World War II	6	5
1950s: Cold War, Civil Rights	7	6
1960s: Vietnam, Civil Rights, Social Movements	5	5
1970s–Present	1	1

Each question in the practice tests has been categorized according to this breakdown so that when you take practice tests, you can very precisely identify your weaknesses and then use this book to address them.

Types of History

The second way to think about the content covered by the SAT U.S. History Test is in terms of different aspects of history, regardless of time period. The test targets five types of historical knowledge:

Types	Approximate % of the Test	Approximate No. of Questions
Political history	35	31
Economic history	19	17
Social history	21	19
Intellectual, cultural history	11	10
Foreign policy	14	12

In our opinion, this categorization is not as helpful as the chronological breakdown. For example, studying the economic history of the Industrial Revolution would be pointless without knowing any political history of the period. You can't really understand one without the other. Instead, use this breakdown to get a sense of where you need to focus while studying a chronological era. This list is a good reminder that you need to do more than just memorize key facts; you must really understand the context in which each piece of history fits.

FORMAT OF THE SAT U.S. HISTORY TEST

The SAT U.S. History Test is a one-hour-long test composed of 90–95 multiple-choice questions. The instructions for the test are very simple. You should memorize them so you don't waste time reading them on the day of the test.

> <u>Directions:</u> Each of the questions or incomplete statements below is followed by five suggested answers or completions. Select the one that is best in each case and then fill in the corresponding oval on the answer sheet.

Have you read the directions? Have you memorized them? (Don't lie to us.) Have you *really* memorized them? Good.

Basically, the instructions inform you of two simple things: all the questions on the test are five-choice multiple-choice questions, and you will have an answer sheet on which to mark down your answers.

But we want to give you the lowdown on some aspects of the test the instructions *don't* mention.

- The questions on the test aren't organized by time period or difficulty. For example, a difficult question about the Sherman Antitrust Act during the Industrial Revolution might be followed by an easy question about the causes of the War of 1812.
- You can skip around while taking the test. If, for some reason, you have a yearning to answer question 90 first, then question 1, then question 67, then 22 . . . well, you can do that. However, if you do plan to skip questions and return to them later, remember it's important to pace yourself, and make sure you fill out the answer sheet correctly.
- All questions are worth the same number of points, whether easy or difficult.

All of these facts can greatly affect your approach to taking the test, as we will explain in the next chapter, on strategy.

Question Types

Each multiple-choice question on the SAT U.S. History Test falls into one of the following four categories:

1. Fact Questions
2. Trend Questions
3. EXCEPT Questions
4. Cartoons/Charts/Maps Questions

If you familiarize yourself with each question type, you'll be much less likely to be surprised by anything you encounter on the test.

Fact Questions

Fact questions test your knowledge of names and definitions, as well as your ability to recognize, describe, and explain specific events and the people associated with them. In this type of question, you might be asked about the ramifications of one particular act, rather than the effects of a general legislative policy. The questions will cover all time periods and themes—everything from presidents to social revolutionaries, from the Great Awakening to Jimmy Carter's foreign policy.

Here's an example fact question:

> The Haymarket Riot of 1886
>
> (A) helped rouse public support and sympathy for unions
> (B) contributed to the Knights of Labor's success in demanding higher wages and shorter work days
> (C) effectively ruined the Knights of Labor, temporarily crippling the labor movement
> (D) was violent but effective, as it forced the police to give strikers more liberty to express their grievances
> (E) had little effect, since "scabs" went to work in place of those striking

Answer: **C**. In the Haymarket Riot of 1886, laborers met in Chicago to protest police brutality against strikers. The riot turned violent when a member of the Knights of Labor threw a bomb, killing a police officer. In all, nine people were killed and close to sixty were injured. Many leaders of the Knights of Labor were convicted of inciting the riot, and public support plummeted, effectively destroying the union. In the aftermath, a general anti-union hysteria spread through the American public, portraying unions as violent and lawless.

Just in case you can't get enough, here's another example:

> The first immigrants to be blocked from entering the U.S. were
>
> (A) Polish
> (B) Italians
> (C) Irish
> (D) Russians
> (E) Chinese

Answer: **E**. The Chinese Immigration Act was passed in 1882, preventing the Chinese from immigrating for the next six decades.

Trend Questions

Trend questions cover basic themes regarding groups, movements, and time periods. These questions test your ability to draw connections between the facts that you know and to display a more nuanced understanding of U.S. history. For example, you might be asked to spot connections between three listed acts or to identify key issues during a listed span of years. Some Trend questions will include quotations, asking you to identify a speaker's attitude and to fit that speaker into a larger historical context by associating him or her with a relevant political or social movement.

Here's an example of a regular trend question:

> Which of the following best characterizes the Transcendentalists?
>
> (A) They aimed to transcend nature and overcome man's inherent flaws.
> (B) They believed that, through the church, man could unite with God and achieve perfection.
> (C) They urged enlightenment through reason and the close study of scripture.
> (D) They believed that man could personally connect with God through oneness with nature.
> (E) They preached church reform and encouraged women to join the clergy.

Answer: **D**. Transcendentalists called for an individualistic approach to faith, shunning the institutional church and its restrictive disciplines. They urged instead that people commune with God through nature, through personal and emotional responses rather than an intellectualization of faith.

Here's an example of a quote trend question:

> "With malice toward none; with charity for all; with firmness in the right, as God gives us to see the right, let us strive on to finish the work we are in; to bind up the nation's wounds; to care for him who shall have borne the battle, and for his widow and his orphan—to do all which may achieve and cherish a just and lasting peace among ourselves."
>
> These words from 1864 best describe which of the following political agendas?
>
> (A) A war relief program to help Civil War veterans and their loved ones
> (B) A moderate Republican plan, known as the Ten Percent Plan, to ease Reconstruction and reunite the nation
> (C) A religious plan to unite the nation through faith in God
> (D) A Southern appeasement plan, drafted by Southern Congressmen, to help rehabilitate the South without military supervision or Northern intervention
> (E) The aims of the Radical Republicans to reunite the nation through a long and punishing reform of the South

Answer: **B**. Abraham Lincoln finished his second inaugural address with these words, expressing his desire to reunite the nation quickly and without conflict. The moderate Ten Percent Plan allowed the southern states to reenter the Union so long as ten percent of their voters pledged an oath of loyalty to the Union. Radical Republicans condemned the plan as too lenient; they wanted to punish the South for seceding.

"EXCEPT" Questions

"EXCEPT" questions can be either fact- or trend-related and are characterized by the use of the words *except*, *not*, *least*, *incorrect*, *inconsistent*, or something similar. These words will always appear in all caps.

"EXCEPT" questions can be tricky because the right answer is actually the *wrong* answer; it is the one answer among the five that doesn't fit. Though the idea is simple, it's easy to get confused as you're moving quickly through the test. If you are careful not to fall into a trap, though, the format of the question can actually help you. On other question types, if you aren't sure of the answer, you have to eliminate four answer choices in order to find the right one. On "EXCEPT" questions, all you have to do is eliminate one, and you've found your answer.

Here's an example of an "EXCEPT" question:

> The Populist Party supported all of the following EXCEPT
>
> (A) a graduated income tax
> (B) immigration restriction
> (C) public ownership of railroads, telephone, and telegraph systems
> (D) maintaining the gold standard, countering inflation
> (E) an eight-hour work day

Answer: **D**. The Populist Party vehemently opposed the gold standard, which served to limit the money in circulation and further aggravated farmers' debts and poverty. William Jennings Bryan, the Populist and Democratic candidate in the 1896 presidential election, condemned the gold standard as oppressive, declaring that the people (farmers and laborers in particular) should not be "crucified on this cross of gold." Bryan and the Populists pushed for a silver standard, which would cause inflation and raise prices. They argued that increasing the money supply would help boost the struggling economy (and make farmers' debts worth less).

And another:

> Of the following, which was NOT a factor in the Panic of 1837 ?
>
> (A) Overspeculation
> (B) Inflation, followed by a tight contraction of credit
> (C) The successful recharter of the Second National Bank
> (D) Recall of loans and Jackson's issuance of the Specie Circular
> (E) Possible bank mismanagement

Answer: **C**. Andrew Jackson vetoed the recharter of the Second National Bank, considering it corrupt and unconstitutional.

Cartoons / Charts / Maps Questions

These questions present you with an image and ask you to interpret it. Since charts and maps tend to hold more information than a single question can test, read the question first so you know what to look for in the image. Pay close attention to any text, title, or date within the image. These things can help you place the image in a historical context, making it easier to decipher the question. There are usually 5 to 7 questions of this type on the test. Here's an example:

THE SPANISH BRUTE—ADDS MUTILATION TO MURDER.
By Hamilton in "Judge."

The above cartoon suggests that

(A) the Spaniards used cruel guerilla tactics in the Spanish-American War
(B) the Spanish tried to demoralize Americans by desecrating their grave sites
(C) a disproportionate number of soldiers killed in the Spanish-American War were from Maine
(D) Spain was a brutish colonial power that had to be punished for sinking the *Maine*
(E) Americans attributed Spain's victory in the Spanish-American War to Spaniards' brutish, subhuman nature

Answer: **D**. The cartoon shows Spain as a savage power hovering over a grave site for "Maine soldiers"—that is, for the 256 soldiers killed in the explosion of the U.S. naval ship, the *Maine*, off the coast of Havana in 1898. A 1976 investigation revealed that a fire onboard the ship caused the blast, but in 1898 the U.S. government and general public were convinced that an underwater Spanish mine was to blame. Soon after the incident, the U.S. declared war on Spain to avenge both the loss of the *Maine* and Spain's well-publicized cruelty against Cuban nationalists, who had been fighting for independence from Spanish rule since 1895. The U.S. won the war within two months, securing Cuban independence.

SCORING THE SAT U.S. HISTORY TEST

Scoring on the SAT U.S. History Test is the same as scoring for all other SAT Subject Tests: for every right answer, you earn one point; for every wrong answer, you lose $1/4$ of a point; for every blank answer, you earn no points. These points combined equal your raw score. ETS then converts your raw score to a scaled score according to a special curve table tailored to the particular test you take. We have included a generalized version of that table on the next page. (Note that because ETS changes the curve slightly for each edition of the test, the table will be close to, but not exactly the same as, the table used by ETS.) You should use this chart to convert your raw scores on practice tests into a scaled score.

In addition to its function as a conversion table, this chart contains crucial information: it tells you that you can do very well on the SAT U.S. History Test without answering every question correctly. In fact, you could skip some questions and get other questions wrong and still earn a "perfect" score of 800.

For example, in a test of 90 questions, you could score:

- 800 if you answered 83 right, 4 wrong, and left 3 blank
- 750 if you answered 74 right, 8 wrong, and left 8 blank
- 700 if you answered 67 right, 12 wrong, and left 11 blank
- 650 if you answered 61 right, 20 wrong, and left 9 blank
- 600 if you answered 53 right, 24 wrong, and left 13 blank

This chart should prove that when you're taking the test, you shouldn't imagine your score plummeting with every question you can't confidently answer. You can do very well on this test without knowing or answering everything. The key is to follow a strategy that ensures that you will get to see and answer all the questions you can answer correctly, and then intelligently guess on those questions about which you are a little unsure. We will discuss these strategies in the next section.

Raw Score	Scaled Score	Raw Score	Scaled Score	Raw Score	Scaled Score
90	800	55	650	21	450
89	800	54	640	20	440
88	800	53	640	19	440
87	800	52	630	18	430
86	800	51	630	17	430
85	800	50	620	16	420
84	800	49	610	15	420
83	800	48	600	14	410
82	800	47	600	13	410
81	790	46	590	12	400
80	790	45	590	11	400
79	790	44	580	10	390
78	780	43	570	9	390
77	780	42	570	8	380
76	770	41	560	7	380
75	770	40	560	6	370
74	760	39	550	5	370
73	760	38	540	4	360
72	750	37	540	3	360
71	740	36	530	2	350
70	740	35	530	1	340
69	730	34	520	0	340
68	720	33	520	−1	330
67	720	32	510	−2	320
66	710	31	510	−3	320
65	700	30	500	−4	310
64	700	29	490	−5	310
63	690	28	490	−6	300
62	690	27	480	−7	300
61	680	26	480	−8	290
59	670	25	470	−9	290
58	670	24	470	−10	280
57	660	23	460		
56	660	22	460		

STRATEGIES FOR TAKING THE SAT U.S. HISTORY TEST

To really kick SAT U.S. History Test butt, you not only need to be an expert SAT Subject Test-taker generally, but you also need to know how to dominate the SAT U.S. History Test specifically. Here's your two-pronged strategy: read over the general test-taking strategies. Learn them; live them. Then bone up on specific test-taking strategies covered in this chapter. And don't worry: you're gonna do just fine.

Strategy 1: Know How the SAT U.S. History Exam Tests History.

Often, students think that studying history means memorizing lots of dates, names, and events. This sort of thinking will not serve you well on the SAT U.S. History Test. While you do need to memorize facts, you also need to understand them within their larger contexts.

Thinking Contextually Helps You Study

Thinking about history in unifying terms like eras, movements, and trends helps you organize the information you learn. To demonstrate our point, imagine we had a box of 100 tacks, and we threw the tacks on the floor. Then we let you look at the tacks for 5 minutes. After that time, we asked you to go into another room and draw, on a piece of paper, where all of the tacks were. You probably wouldn't do a very good job of it, would you? But if you noticed that the tacks were organized into geometric shapes—27 of the tacks were in a circle, 19 formed a triangle, another 28 formed a squiggly line, and 26 formed a hexagon—drawing them later would be much easier. The same idea applies to history: always be aware of the context the facts fit into.

Thinking contextually also ensures that you remain engaged with the material you're studying. You might read over a list of facts and think you've "memorized" them, only to find you've forgotten everything on test day. But if you constantly try to fit what you learn into an era or trend, you give yourself an active grip on the material. This will make your studying more efficient and fruitful.

Thinking Contextually Helps You Answer SAT U.S. History Questions

Many questions on the SAT U.S. History Test are "big picture" questions. These test your general knowledge of an era or movement, and just knowing straight facts isn't going to help you much. For example, look at the question below:

> Which of the following best characterizes American foreign policy during the first half of the Progressive Era, 1900 to 1910 ?
>
> (A) Aggressive intervention, through both military involvement and capitalist investment
> (B) Strict isolationism
> (C) Minimal diplomacy, as the U.S. focused almost exclusively on domestic reform
> (D) Primarily business-minded, aimed at expanding markets overseas
> (E) Alarmist and reactionary in nature, as the Red Scare swept the nation

This question doesn't ask you for names or dates. Instead, it tests to see if you understand the overall character of a particular era. Now, it is true that in order to understand an era you have to know certain facts, but you don't have to know *everything*. There are a number of ways you could figure out the answer to the question. If you know that the U.S. won the Spanish-American War in 1898 and in the process became a world power, you could infer that the U.S. was heavily involved in foreign nations in the early 1900s, sometimes through military means. The answer has to be **A**. Alternately, you might have known that Teddy Roosevelt, president during that time period, advocated "big stick" diplomacy. Again, that implies military intervention, giving you the answer **A**. Note that, to get the question right, you didn't need to know detailed facts, such as the fact that one of the territories the U.S. gained in the Spanish-American war was the Philippines or that Roosevelt helped engineer a revolt in Panama. Instead, all you needed to know were the broad trends and developments during the era that was the question's focus.

Fact Questions Are Trend Questions in Disguise

But what about the more nitpicky questions that test you on precise facts and names? First, we've already discussed how thinking about history in terms of eras, movements, and trends will help you to remember individual facts. But there's an additional advantage: even if you aren't sure about a particular fact, understanding historical trends can help you answer a question that covers that fact. Let's say, for example, you are asked the following question:

> John Calhoun most bitterly opposed Andrew Jackson's policies regarding
>
> (A) American involvement in Europe
> (B) slavery
> (C) income taxes
> (D) the nullification crisis
> (E) the Supreme Court

If you approach the SAT U.S. History Test as if it's testing only a collection of facts, you might panic if you don't know who John Calhoun was. In fact, you might very well skip this question and move on, assuming you can't answer it.

But if you approach the test with the understanding that all facts fit into trends, then not knowing who John Calhoun was becomes less ominous. Based on the question, you know that Calhoun opposed Andrew Jackson on an issue. You know that this issue took place during Jackson's presidency, and, if you studied well, you should know the general trends of Jackson's presidency: an emerging two-party system that vastly increased popular interest and participation in government; the development of a strong executive branch that included a spoils system in which a party rewarded its followers with political posts; sectional strife over tariffs that led to the nullification crisis; and the removal of the Cherokee Indians from Georgia. With a basic understanding of the policies of the Jacksonian era, you can see that the answer to this question must be **D**.

The SAT U.S. History Test will ask questions in ways you won't expect, forcing you to be flexible with your knowledge of history. While studying, always try to fit what you're learning into the larger picture. Studying for the SAT U.S. History Test should be like reading a great story, in which all details are connected by the story's plot.

Strategy 2: Understand Multiple-Choice Questions.

When you look at an SAT U.S. History Test question, the answer is always right there in front of you, hidden among a selection of incorrect answer choices. There are two methods you can use to answer the question correctly:

1. Go directly to the right answer.
2. Eliminate wrong answers until there's only one answer left.

In a perfect world, you would always know the right answer. And for many of the questions on the test, this will probably be the case. But for questions you're uncertain about you can also work backwards, crossing out choices you know *can't* be right.

Eliminating Wrong Answers

We've already explained how thinking contextually can help your studying, and help you spot correct answers. It can also help you eliminate wrong answers. Let's say you come across this question:

> Between the 1860s and 1890s, the United States changed in all of the following ways EXCEPT:
>
> (A) It became increasingly urban.
> (B) Labor unions became a powerful force, gaining widespread popular support.
> (C) Immigration significantly boosted the supply of workers.
> (D) Big corporations and monopolies thrived, often unchecked by the government.
> (E) More women began to work outside of the home.

What if you look at this question and just don't know the answer? Take a step back: first identify the era the question covers to help you put the question into some historical context. In this case, knowing that "Between the 1860s and 1890s" roughly corresponds to the Industrial Revolution will help you remember the themes of that time period. What comes to mind when you think of industrialization? Perhaps big business and a rise in urbanization and immigration? If so, you can proceed to check off **A** and **C**, since they're both true. (Remember, for these "EXCEPT" questions, you are looking for the answer that *doesn't* belong, so eliminate all the answers that are true.) The Industrial Revolution also created an increase in available jobs, which likely drew many women out of the home and into factories, allowing you to eliminate answer **E**. Answer choice **D** might be a little trickier. Half of the answer is true—this period (also known as the "Era of Big Business") spawned huge corporations like Carnegie's steel company and Rockefeller's oil company—but what about government regulation? If you can't remember what government did about business during the Industrial Revolution, you can't decide if **D** is true or false. As for **B**, you may not know precisely what went on with unions during those years, so you can't say for sure whether that answer is right or wrong either.

Left with two possible answer choices, **B** and **D**, how do you choose? You should be able to see that **B** and **D** are at odds with one another. If **B** were true, and unions held such power, they probably would have pushed for government to strictly regulate business in order to check the tyranny of monopolies (that is, the poor treatment of workers and the high prices of goods). If this were the case, then the Industrial Revolution would hardly be known as the "Era of Big Business," would it? Think again about what you remember about the trends of industrialization: big business was definitely a major one; unions, on the other hand, don't stand out in your memory. Armed with this knowledge, take a little leap of faith and guess that **B** is the correct answer.

Guess what? You guessed right!

Questions for Which You Can't Eliminate All Answers

Not all questions on the SAT U.S. History Test will work out quite as well as our last example. You might not always be able to use your knowledge of trends and eras to eliminate four answer choices, ensuring that you get the question right. But for almost every question you *will* probably be able to eliminate *at least one* answer, and that can help a lot. Let's move on to the next section to find out why.

Strategy 3: Guess.

Should you guess on the SAT U.S. History Test? We'll begin to answer this question by posing a question of our own:

> Franklin Delano Roosevelt is holding five cards, numbered 1–5. Without telling you, he has selected one of the numbers as the "correct" card. If you pick a single card, what is the probability that you will choose the "correct" card?

The answer, of course, is 1 in 5. But the answer is only important if you recognize that this question precisely describes the situation you're in when you blindly guess on any SAT U.S. History Test question—you have a 1 in 5 chance of getting the question right. If you were to blindly guess on ten questions in a row, you would (according to probability) get two questions right and eight questions wrong.

- 2 right answers get you 2 raw points
- 8 wrong answers get you $8 \times \frac{1}{4}$ points $= -2$ raw points

Those ten answers, therefore, net you a total of zero points. ETS designed the scoring system in such a way that random guessing is pointless. They want to ensure you have to *think*.

Educated Guessing

Suppose you're faced with this question:

> The religious revivalism that swept across the American colonies in the 1730s was known as
>
> (A) the Enlightenment
> (B) the Glorious Revolution
> (C) Antinomianism
> (D) Bacon's Rebellion
> (E) the Great Awakening

The correct answer is **E**; but if you didn't have a clue, you could still improve your odds by eliminating any choice that doesn't sound like a plausible name for a religious revival. Certainly, a "rebellion" seems an unlikely such name, doesn't it? Once you've eliminated **D** as a likely answer, you have four remaining choices. Is it worth it to guess? Yes. Probability states that if you are guessing between four choices you will get one question right for every three you get wrong. For that one correct answer you'll get 1 point, and for the three incorrect answers you'll lose a total of $3/4$ of a point.

$$1 - \frac{3}{4} = \frac{1}{4}$$

The math indicates that if you can eliminate one answer, the odds of guessing are in your favor: you become more likely to gain points than to lose points.

The rule for guessing on the SAT U.S. History Test, therefore, is simple: *if you can eliminate even one answer choice on a question, you should definitely guess.*

If You're Stumped

If you cannot eliminate even one answer choice and find yourself staring at a certain question with mounting panic, throw a circle around that nasty question and move on. Return to it later if you have time. Remember, answering a hard question correctly doesn't earn you any more points than answering an easy question correctly. You want to be sure to hit every question you *can* answer instead of running out of time by fixating on the really tough questions. While taking five minutes to solve a particularly difficult question might strike you as a moral victory when you're taking the test, you possibly could have used that same time to answer six other questions that would have vastly increased your score. Instead of getting bogged down on individual questions, you will do better if you learn to skip and leave for later the very difficult questions that either you can't answer or that will take an extremely long time to figure out.

Now on to the practice tests!

SAT* U.S. HISTORY PRACTICE TEST 1

SAT U.S. HISTORY PRACTICE TEST 1 ANSWER SHEET

1. Ⓐ Ⓑ Ⓒ Ⓓ Ⓔ	31. Ⓐ Ⓑ Ⓒ Ⓓ Ⓔ	61. Ⓐ Ⓑ Ⓒ Ⓓ Ⓔ
2. Ⓐ Ⓑ Ⓒ Ⓓ Ⓔ	32. Ⓐ Ⓑ Ⓒ Ⓓ Ⓔ	62. Ⓐ Ⓑ Ⓒ Ⓓ Ⓔ
3. Ⓐ Ⓑ Ⓒ Ⓓ Ⓔ	33. Ⓐ Ⓑ Ⓒ Ⓓ Ⓔ	63. Ⓐ Ⓑ Ⓒ Ⓓ Ⓔ
4. Ⓐ Ⓑ Ⓒ Ⓓ Ⓔ	34. Ⓐ Ⓑ Ⓒ Ⓓ Ⓔ	64. Ⓐ Ⓑ Ⓒ Ⓓ Ⓔ
5. Ⓐ Ⓑ Ⓒ Ⓓ Ⓔ	35. Ⓐ Ⓑ Ⓒ Ⓓ Ⓔ	65. Ⓐ Ⓑ Ⓒ Ⓓ Ⓔ
6. Ⓐ Ⓑ Ⓒ Ⓓ Ⓔ	36. Ⓐ Ⓑ Ⓒ Ⓓ Ⓔ	66. Ⓐ Ⓑ Ⓒ Ⓓ Ⓔ
7. Ⓐ Ⓑ Ⓒ Ⓓ Ⓔ	37. Ⓐ Ⓑ Ⓒ Ⓓ Ⓔ	67. Ⓐ Ⓑ Ⓒ Ⓓ Ⓔ
8. Ⓐ Ⓑ Ⓒ Ⓓ Ⓔ	38. Ⓐ Ⓑ Ⓒ Ⓓ Ⓔ	68. Ⓐ Ⓑ Ⓒ Ⓓ Ⓔ
9. Ⓐ Ⓑ Ⓒ Ⓓ Ⓔ	39. Ⓐ Ⓑ Ⓒ Ⓓ Ⓔ	69. Ⓐ Ⓑ Ⓒ Ⓓ Ⓔ
10. Ⓐ Ⓑ Ⓒ Ⓓ Ⓔ	40. Ⓐ Ⓑ Ⓒ Ⓓ Ⓔ	70. Ⓐ Ⓑ Ⓒ Ⓓ Ⓔ
11. Ⓐ Ⓑ Ⓒ Ⓓ Ⓔ	41. Ⓐ Ⓑ Ⓒ Ⓓ Ⓔ	71. Ⓐ Ⓑ Ⓒ Ⓓ Ⓔ
12. Ⓐ Ⓑ Ⓒ Ⓓ Ⓔ	42. Ⓐ Ⓑ Ⓒ Ⓓ Ⓔ	72. Ⓐ Ⓑ Ⓒ Ⓓ Ⓔ
13. Ⓐ Ⓑ Ⓒ Ⓓ Ⓔ	43. Ⓐ Ⓑ Ⓒ Ⓓ Ⓔ	73. Ⓐ Ⓑ Ⓒ Ⓓ Ⓔ
14. Ⓐ Ⓑ Ⓒ Ⓓ Ⓔ	44. Ⓐ Ⓑ Ⓒ Ⓓ Ⓔ	74. Ⓐ Ⓑ Ⓒ Ⓓ Ⓔ
15. Ⓐ Ⓑ Ⓒ Ⓓ Ⓔ	45. Ⓐ Ⓑ Ⓒ Ⓓ Ⓔ	75. Ⓐ Ⓑ Ⓒ Ⓓ Ⓔ
16. Ⓐ Ⓑ Ⓒ Ⓓ Ⓔ	46. Ⓐ Ⓑ Ⓒ Ⓓ Ⓔ	76. Ⓐ Ⓑ Ⓒ Ⓓ Ⓔ
17. Ⓐ Ⓑ Ⓒ Ⓓ Ⓔ	47. Ⓐ Ⓑ Ⓒ Ⓓ Ⓔ	77. Ⓐ Ⓑ Ⓒ Ⓓ Ⓔ
18. Ⓐ Ⓑ Ⓒ Ⓓ Ⓔ	48. Ⓐ Ⓑ Ⓒ Ⓓ Ⓔ	78. Ⓐ Ⓑ Ⓒ Ⓓ Ⓔ
19. Ⓐ Ⓑ Ⓒ Ⓓ Ⓔ	49. Ⓐ Ⓑ Ⓒ Ⓓ Ⓔ	79. Ⓐ Ⓑ Ⓒ Ⓓ Ⓔ
20. Ⓐ Ⓑ Ⓒ Ⓓ Ⓔ	50. Ⓐ Ⓑ Ⓒ Ⓓ Ⓔ	80. Ⓐ Ⓑ Ⓒ Ⓓ Ⓔ
21. Ⓐ Ⓑ Ⓒ Ⓓ Ⓔ	51. Ⓐ Ⓑ Ⓒ Ⓓ Ⓔ	81. Ⓐ Ⓑ Ⓒ Ⓓ Ⓔ
22. Ⓐ Ⓑ Ⓒ Ⓓ Ⓔ	52. Ⓐ Ⓑ Ⓒ Ⓓ Ⓔ	82. Ⓐ Ⓑ Ⓒ Ⓓ Ⓔ
23. Ⓐ Ⓑ Ⓒ Ⓓ Ⓔ	53. Ⓐ Ⓑ Ⓒ Ⓓ Ⓔ	83. Ⓐ Ⓑ Ⓒ Ⓓ Ⓔ
24. Ⓐ Ⓑ Ⓒ Ⓓ Ⓔ	54. Ⓐ Ⓑ Ⓒ Ⓓ Ⓔ	84. Ⓐ Ⓑ Ⓒ Ⓓ Ⓔ
25. Ⓐ Ⓑ Ⓒ Ⓓ Ⓔ	55. Ⓐ Ⓑ Ⓒ Ⓓ Ⓔ	85. Ⓐ Ⓑ Ⓒ Ⓓ Ⓔ
26. Ⓐ Ⓑ Ⓒ Ⓓ Ⓔ	56. Ⓐ Ⓑ Ⓒ Ⓓ Ⓔ	86. Ⓐ Ⓑ Ⓒ Ⓓ Ⓔ
27. Ⓐ Ⓑ Ⓒ Ⓓ Ⓔ	57. Ⓐ Ⓑ Ⓒ Ⓓ Ⓔ	87. Ⓐ Ⓑ Ⓒ Ⓓ Ⓔ
28. Ⓐ Ⓑ Ⓒ Ⓓ Ⓔ	58. Ⓐ Ⓑ Ⓒ Ⓓ Ⓔ	88. Ⓐ Ⓑ Ⓒ Ⓓ Ⓔ
29. Ⓐ Ⓑ Ⓒ Ⓓ Ⓔ	59. Ⓐ Ⓑ Ⓒ Ⓓ Ⓔ	89. Ⓐ Ⓑ Ⓒ Ⓓ Ⓔ
30. Ⓐ Ⓑ Ⓒ Ⓓ Ⓔ	60. Ⓐ Ⓑ Ⓒ Ⓓ Ⓔ	90. Ⓐ Ⓑ Ⓒ Ⓓ Ⓔ

SAT U.S. HISTORY PRACTICE TEST 1

Time—1 hour

> **Directions:** Each of the questions or incomplete statements below is followed by five suggested answers or completions. Select the one that is best in each case and then fill in the corresponding oval on the answer sheet.

1. Which of the following was NOT a provision of the Federal Reserve Act of 1913 ?

    (A) Only the Federal Reserve can lend money to individuals.
    (B) The Federal Reserve banks are authorized to distribute currency.
    (C) The Federal Reserve banking system consists of twelve regional districts.
    (D) Private bankers own the Federal Reserve System banks.
    (E) The Federal Reserve controls the discount rate.

2. The Stamp Act of 1765 was primarily intended to

    (A) punish the colonies for protesting the Sugar Act
    (B) suppress the distribution of propaganda pamphlets
    (C) shut down colonial newspapers critical of the Crown
    (D) increase British revenues to offset Britain's mounting debt after the French and Indian War
    (E) thwart the colonial mercantile practice of triangular trade

3. In introducing the Kansas-Nebraska Bill, Stephen Douglas sought primarily to

    (A) bring the issue of slavery to a final resolution
    (B) facilitate the building of a transcontinental railroad
    (C) ensure that slavery would be excluded in the territories
    (D) thwart the efforts of the Free Soil Party
    (E) increase the value of his land holdings in the West

4. Which of the following most accurately characterizes society in the United States during the so-called "baby boom" era of the 1950's and early 1960's?

    (A) An increased emphasis on the two-income household in which both spouses held paying jobs
    (B) A great influx of new immigrants, especially from Europe
    (C) An exodus of Caucasian Americans from urban centers to newly developed suburbs
    (D) The retirement of a large segment of the population from the workforce
    (E) Increasingly liberal attitudes toward gender roles and sexual behavior

5. The New Deal resulted in all of the following EXCEPT

    (A) the institution of collective bargaining
    (B) insurance for Americans' savings accounts
    (C) a constitutional amendment requiring a balanced budget
    (D) government involvement in public utilities
    (E) an expansion in the size and power of the federal government

6. From the end of the Civil War to the end of the nineteenth century, America's expanding economy was fostered by

    (A) agricultural consolidation
    (B) the breakup of the railroad monopoly
    (C) the decentralization of the banking system
    (D) the growth of large-scale, heavy industry
    (E) increasingly stringent tariff policies

GO ON TO THE NEXT PAGE

7. The cartoon above criticizes American involvement in the League of Nations on the grounds that involvement would result in

    (A) the exploitation of American military power by other nations
    (B) the inability of the United States to adequately secure its own borders
    (C) a reduction in protective tariffs needed to strengthen the U.S. economy
    (D) American obligation to participate in wars under the collective security clause
    (E) further hostilities with Germany after the signing of the Treaty of Versailles

GO ON TO THE NEXT PAGE

8. Which of the following was an advantage that the Confederacy had over the Union during the Civil War?

   (A) Better organized leadership
   (B) Stronger military tradition
   (C) Larger military forces
   (D) Greater wealth
   (E) More abundant food crops

9. Which of the following best explains why Alexander Hamilton was pleased with the outcome of the Whiskey Rebellion?

   (A) The rebels were successful in evading the Whiskey tax.
   (B) Anti-federalists lost the backing of the rebels, who then became supporters of the Federalists.
   (C) The defeat of the rebels demonstrated the power of the federal government.
   (D) He profited financially from the suppression of the revolt
   (E) The rebels' victory weakened Thomas Jefferson's political support.

10. Which of the following led most directly to the near annihilation of the native population of Spanish America during the 1500's and 1600's?

   (A) Wars with Spain over the acquisition and control of land
   (B) Importation of agricultural pests that destroyed crops the natives relied on for food
   (C) Enslavement of the natives by the Spanish and relocation in Europe
   (D) The introduction of gunpowder, which native tribes used in wars amongst themselves
   (E) Human diseases brought from Europe and spread among the native population

11. The only immigrants to face governmental immigration restriction in the United States prior to the twentieth century were the

   (A) Chinese
   (B) Irish
   (C) Jews
   (D) Russians
   (E) Germans

12. "Now, the typical American citizen is the business man. The typical business man is a bad citizen; he is busy. If he is a 'big business man' and very busy, he does not neglect, he is busy with politics, oh, very busy and very businesslike. . . . He is a self-righteous fraud, this big business man. He is the chief source of corruption, and it were a boon if he would neglect politics. But he is not the business man that neglects politics."

   The sentiments expressed in this quotation are most characteristic of which of the following groups?

   (A) Muckrakers
   (B) Marxists
   (C) Republicans
   (D) New Dealers
   (E) Single taxers

13. The Atlantic Charter, co-written by Franklin D. Roosevelt and Winston Churchill and adopted in 1941, provided for all of the following EXCEPT

   (A) the unconditional surrender by the Axis powers as a prerequisite for peace
   (B) freedom of the seas
   (C) the establishment of an institution for collective world security after the war
   (D) a division of labor for the British, Russian, and American armies
   (E) the self-determination of nations after the war

GO ON TO THE NEXT PAGE

14. Of the following, which book was most responsible for the passage of the Pure Food and Drug Act of 1906 ?

    (A) *The Octopus*
    (B) *The Jungle*
    (C) *The Rise of Silas Lapham*
    (D) *The Promise of American Life*
    (E) *The Age of Innocence*

15. "Now finding I had arrived to man's estate, and was a slave, and these revelations being made known to me, I began to direct my attention to this great object, to fulfill the purpose for which, by this time, I felt assured I was intended. Knowing the influence I had obtained over the minds of my fellow servants . . . I now began to prepare them for my purpose, by telling them something was about to happen that would terminate in fulfilling the great promise that had been made to me."

    The statement above was most likely made by a(n)

    (A) former indentured servant planning a way to end his poverty
    (B) abolitionist recalling his efforts to help former slaves during the antebellum period
    (C) former slave remembering his role in a plot to rise up against a plantation owner
    (D) mill worker recounting the events leading to the invention of the cotton gin
    (E) slave pondering the danger of worshiping God openly in violation of his slaveholder's rules

16. Part of the New Deal, the Public Works Administration was established in order to

    (A) stabilize the banking industry
    (B) ensure that all legislation was approved by public referendum
    (C) guarantee labor's collective bargaining rights
    (D) create jobs for unemployed citizens
    (E) integrate African Americans into American industries

17. The first human inhabitants of North America came from

    (A) Asia
    (B) South America
    (C) Africa
    (D) Europe
    (E) Australia

18. Under the Marshall Plan, the United States pledged to

    (A) place limits on immigration to the United States
    (B) contain Communism in Eastern Europe by military force
    (C) provide government jobs for unemployed workers during the Great Depression
    (D) join the Allied powers in World War II
    (E) provide financial assistance to European nations

19. In the *McCulloch v. Maryland* decision of 1819, the Supreme Court ruled

    (A) that federal power had supremacy over the power of the states
    (B) that the Bank of the United States was unconstitutional
    (C) to overturn congressional authorization for internal improvements
    (D) to renounce the doctrine of judicial review
    (E) to affirm the states' right to tax federal property

GO ON TO THE NEXT PAGE ➡

20. Although John F. Kennedy won the Democratic presidential nomination in 1960, many political analysts believed that he would NOT be elected because he

    (A) was an aggressive anti-communist
    (B) was opposed to civil rights
    (C) was a Roman Catholic
    (D) was fiscally liberal
    (E) chose Lyndon B. Johnson as his running mate

21. Abraham Lincoln's Reconstruction plan was designed to

    (A) facilitate the quick return of the southern states to the Union
    (B) punish the southern states for secession and impose harsh economic penalties on them
    (C) give African Americans complete civil and political equality
    (D) provide former slaves with "forty acres and a mule"
    (E) rebuild cities in the South devastated by the Civil War

22. In general, political appointments during the second half of the nineteenth century were

    (A) rigidly controlled by strict rules at the national, state, and local levels
    (B) decided by state elections
    (C) difficult to make because of employment opportunities offered by industry
    (D) governed by property qualifications as they had been since the Constitution was first adopted
    (E) subject to patronage practices at all levels of government

23. During World War I, Americans increasingly viewed Germany as inhumane because of all of the following EXCEPT the

    (A) sinking of the *Lusitania*
    (B) Zimmerman Telegram
    (C) invasion of Belgium
    (D) construction of concentration camps
    (E) use of submarine warfare

24. Within the context of American social reform in the nineteenth century, Dorothea Dix was primarily associated with which of the following?

    (A) Harsher prison sentences for violent criminals
    (B) The development of public common schools
    (C) Improved treatment for the mentally ill
    (D) The abolition of slavery
    (E) Suffrage and other women's rights

25. Which of the following would have been INCONSISTENT with the Republican Party political platform of 1856?

    (A) The Homestead Act
    (B) A central route for the transcontinental railroad
    (C) The expansion of slavery into the territories
    (D) High protective tariffs
    (E) Liberal immigration policies

26. Lyndon B. Johnson was given unlimited authority to protect American interests in Vietnam under

    (A) the War Powers Act
    (B) Article II of the U.S. Constitution
    (C) the collective security agreement reached by NATO
    (D) the Gulf of Tonkin Resolution
    (E) a peacekeeping resolution passed in the United Nations Security Council

GO ON TO THE NEXT PAGE

27. "We shall not realize our objectives, however, unless we are willing to help free peoples to maintain their free institutions and their national integrity against aggressive movements that seek to impose upon them totalitarian regimes. This is no more than a frank recognition that totalitarian regimes imposed on free peoples, by direct or indirect aggression, undermine the foundations of international peace and hence the security of the United States."

The speaker quoted above would most likely agree with which of the following policies?

(A) NATO-sponsored collective security
(B) Containment
(C) Deference to the United Nations
(D) Isolationism
(E) Massive retaliation

28. The enforcement of the Navigation Acts in the late 1800's marked the end of

(A) reciprocal trade as between Britain and the American colonies
(B) the mercantilist era for the British economy
(C) Britain's toleration of certain trading practices on the part of the American colonies
(D) a lenient policy of taxation on goods imported to the American colonies from Britain
(E) free exploration of the open seas by all countries

29. The main issue debated during the Scopes Monkey Trial was

(A) the teaching of evolution in Tennessee schools
(B) scientific experimentation on animals
(C) the legality of the Ku Klux Klan
(D) the constitutionality of a Tennessee law banning the American Civil Liberties Union
(E) the validity of creationism

30. Which of the following contributed LEAST to the end of Reconstruction in the South?

(A) Factions within the Democratic Party
(B) Corruption in the Ulysses S. Grant administration
(C) The rise of the Liberal Republicans
(D) A stock market crash
(E) The waning influence of Radical Republicans in Congress

31. The War Hawks supported the War of 1812 for all of the following reasons EXCEPT they

(A) thought that peace with Britain would result in the disgrace of the United States
(B) saw war with England as a way to end the recession in the southern and western regions of the United States
(C) advocated the continuation of impressment
(D) saw war with England as a way to annex Canada
(E) feared the British alliance with Native Americans

32. Students at Kent State University in Ohio were shot by the national guard in May 1970 as they were

(A) protesting Richard Nixon's Cambodian incursion
(B) attempting to desegregate the university's dormitories
(C) protesting against an increase in tuition
(D) attempting to close an army recruiting office located on campus
(E) rioting against the U.S. military draft policy

33. In keeping with his stance on big business, Woodrow Wilson supported

(A) measures that would strip organized labor of power
(B) the complete privatization of the banking system
(C) raising protective steel tariffs
(D) the principles of laissez-faire economics
(E) federal regulation of interstate trade and business monopolies

GO ON TO THE NEXT PAGE

34. Which political party did John Calhoun and Henry Clay establish in opposition to the Jacksonian Democrats?

    (A) The Republicans
    (B) The Whigs
    (C) The Federalists
    (D) The Populists
    (E) The Nationalists

35. On which of the following grounds did President Harry Truman justify his decision to use the atomic bomb?

    (A) A massive American ground invasion of Japan would result in millions of Japanese and American casualties.
    (B) It was an appropriate retaliatory action after the attack on Pearl Harbor.
    (C) Japan was rapidly developing its own bomb.
    (D) The American electorate was growing tired of the war and demanded action.
    (E) The British and Russian allies supported his action.

36. All of the following were contributing causes of the stock market crash in 1929 EXCEPT

    (A) the expansion of credit and installment buying
    (B) overproduction by American industries
    (C) the lack of purchasing power among American consumers
    (D) farm production falling beneath government quotas
    (E) stock-market speculation on the parts of banks

37. The Puritans left England for the New World primarily because they

    (A) lost their land and homes in England
    (B) intended to purify the Anglican Church of its Catholic rituals
    (C) were opposed to England's involvement in the African slave trade
    (D) believed the taxes they were required to pay were unjust
    (E) adhered to the concept of the separation of church and state

38. "Our greatest danger is that in the great leap from slavery to freedom we may overlook the fact that the masses of us are to live by the productions of our hands, and fail to keep in mind that we shall prosper in proportion as we learn to dignify and glorify common labour and put brains and skill into the common occupations of life; . . . No race can prosper till it learns that there is as much dignity in tilling a field as in writing a poem. It is at the bottom of life we must begin, and not at the top."

    This statement most accurately reflects the philosophy of which of the following individuals?

    (A) Frederick Douglass
    (B) Booker T. Washington
    (C) W.E.B. Du Bois
    (D) Marcus Garvey
    (E) A. Philip Randolph

39. The Spanish Empire was interested in the Americas primarily as a

    (A) source of raw materials
    (B) marketplace for finished products
    (C) mechanism to ease overcrowding
    (D) source of gold and silver
    (E) penal colony for convicted criminals

GO ON TO THE NEXT PAGE

40. Which of the following statements about the Hartford Convention of 1814 is most accurate?

    (A) Its primary purpose was to address the U.S. military's unpreparedness for the War of 1812.
    (B) The delegates argued that states did not possess the right to nullify federal law.
    (C) The resolutions of the Convention resulted in the end of the War of 1812.
    (D) The Convention significantly weakened the Federalist party by making it appear unpatriotic.
    (E) Republicans and Federalists were generally in agreement about the resolutions offered by the Convention.

41. In 1767, John Dickinson published *Letters from a Pennsylvania Farmer* in response to which of the following acts?

    (A) Stamp Act
    (B) Declaratory Act
    (C) Townshend Acts
    (D) Tea Act
    (E) Intolerable Acts

42. "The soul is the perceiver and revealer of truth. We know truth when we see it, let skeptic and scoffer say what they choose. Foolish people ask you, when you have spoken what they do not wish to hear, 'How do you know it is truth, and not an error of your own?' We know truth when we see it, from opinion, as we know when we are awake that we are awake."

    This discussion of knowledge and truth is characteristic of which intellectual movement?

    (A) The Enlightenment
    (B) The Great Awakening
    (C) Deism
    (D) Transcendentalism
    (E) Antinomianism

43. In Congress, which of the following served to undermine Lyndon B. Johnson's Great Society plan?

    (A) A Republican filibuster, which prevented the plan's enactment into law
    (B) The failure of Johnson's "war on poverty" to gain the support of Democratic leaders
    (C) Corporate lobbying against the proposed reform programs
    (D) The federal government's increasing focus on the war in Vietnam
    (E) The freedom rides, which turned prominent politicians against the civil rights movement

44. Roger Williams was banished from the Massachusetts Bay Colony for

    (A) denouncing the Church of England
    (B) trying to establish the rival colony of Rhode Island
    (C) marrying a Native American woman
    (D) advocating the separation of church and state
    (E) assisting Native Americans in resisting the colonists' efforts to seize the Natives' land

45. During the late 1800's, the U.S. railroad industry adopted the practice of giving rebates

    (A) in order to avoid costly lawsuits from customers
    (B) because Congressional law mandated them in 1881
    (C) in order to increase its overall profit
    (D) in exchange for stock in other companies
    (E) as favors to its largest customers

46. Which of the following was ruled unconstitutional by the Supreme Court in the *Dred Scott v. Sandford* case?

    (A) The "separate but equal" doctrine
    (B) The denial of civil rights for African Americans
    (C) Slavery throughout the United States
    (D) The extension of slavery into the territories
    (E) Popular sovereignty

GO ON TO THE NEXT PAGE

THE WORLD'S CONSTABLE

47. The image of the United States as "The World's Constable" (as portrayed above) refers specifically to

(A) the Open Door policy
(B) the Roosevelt corollary to the Monroe Doctrine
(C) the Panama Canal crisis
(D) U.S. suppression of the Boxer Rebellion
(E) the annexation of Hawaii

GO ON TO THE NEXT PAGE

48. The Northwest Ordinance of 1787 called for the

    (A) deportation of Native Americans to the west of the Mississippi River
    (B) prohibition of slavery north of the Ohio River
    (C) division of the Northwest Territory into townships
    (D) regulation of commerce in the territories
    (E) creation of a central government for the Northwest Territory

49. The Interstate Commerce Commission, created in 1887, sought to regulate railroads by mandating all of the following EXCEPT the

    (A) publication of all railroad rates
    (B) consolidation of competing railroads into a single government-regulated industry
    (C) elimination of different rate structures depending on the level of competition
    (D) end of the practice of pooling of business by the railroads
    (E) elimination of freight-charge rebates to freight-line customers

50. The *Brown v. Board of Education* (1954) decision relied most heavily on which of the following in overturning the constitutionality of segregation in public schools?

    (A) The elastic clause
    (B) Habeas corpus
    (C) The First Amendment
    (D) The "Supreme Law of the Land" clause
    (E) The Fourteenth Amendment

51. Which of the following best expresses the philosophy of manifest destiny, prominently employed as a justification for America's westward expansion in the nineteenth century?

    (A) The United States had a God-given right to settle all the land in North America.
    (B) Farmlands needed to be settled so that America could fulfill its destiny of feeding Europe.
    (C) American capitalism was the best system of trade and commerce for developing new territories.
    (D) Slavery was the best means of employing labor and required room to expand.
    (E) Native American tribes should be permitted to remain on their lands while Americans settled the vacant lands to the west of the reservations.

52. The National Origins Act of 1924 sought specifically to limit the number of immigrants arriving annually to the United States from

    (A) Ireland
    (B) western Europe
    (C) southern and eastern Europe
    (D) Latin America
    (E) Asia

53. Among the following justifications for the continuation of slavery in the United States, which one most accurately reflects the prevailing position of white slaveholders after 1831?

    (A) The American economy was expanding tremendously due to slavery and that the North and West would soon use slaves as their main source of labor.
    (B) Slavery was superior to free labor in terms of sheer profits.
    (C) Slavery afforded whites the leisure time befitting their elite status and was thus central to southern culture.
    (D) The total absence of slave rebellions indicated that the system was the best possible way to maintain a labor force.
    (E) Slavery served an important function in civilizing "inferior" people who could not survive in American society on their own.

54. The mass production of war materials for use in World War II resulted domestically in

    (A) a decline in real wages
    (B) a series of strikes by organized labor
    (C) the end of an economic depression
    (D) renewed stock speculation and margin buying
    (E) the re-emergence of the Republican Party

GO ON TO THE NEXT PAGE

55. The cartoon above satirizes the political contest in which

    (A) Henry Clay deprived Andrew Jackson of the presidency in 1824
    (B) Andrew Jackson destroyed the Second Bank of the United States
    (C) John Calhoun defied the 1828 tariff legislation
    (D) Andrew Jackson vetoed the Maysville Road bill passed by Congress
    (E) Peggy Eaton was humiliated by members of Jackson's cabinet

GO ON TO THE NEXT PAGE →

56. The United States gained access to the land through which the Panama Canal was built by

    (A) purchasing it outright from Panama for $10 million
    (B) trading several battleships to Panama for the land
    (C) promoting the Panamanian Revolution against Colombia
    (D) defeating Spain in 1898
    (E) negotiating with the British Empire for the rights to the land

57. Shays' Rebellion worried some American political leaders, including George Washington, because

    (A) it demonstrated that the central government could not respond effectively to upheavals by the lower classes
    (B) they feared that their slaves would be emancipated should such a rebellion occur in Virginia
    (C) they suspected a similar uprising could overthrow the central government
    (D) no one was putting an end to Native American attacks in the West
    (E) the British supported the revolt and were seeking to reclaim the colonies

58. During Reconstruction, the Radical Republicans supported which of the following in opposition to President Andrew Johnson?

    (A) Abraham Lincoln's "ten percent plan" for southern states' readmission to the Union
    (B) Banning powerful plantation owners from participating in government
    (C) The ratification of the Thirteenth Amendment, which outlawed slavery in the United States
    (D) Southern states' imposition of Black Codes, which placed restrictions on the actions of African Americans
    (E) The passage of the Fourteenth Amendment, which guaranteed citizenship to all people born or naturalized in the United States

59. In the 1890's, the federal government often used the Sherman Antitrust Act to

    (A) stop railroads from practicing price discrimination
    (B) prevent workers from striking
    (C) bust corrupt trusts, while regulating "good" ones
    (D) impose protective tariffs
    (E) raise the rate of inflation

60. A proprietary colony was a colony that was

    (A) controlled by a small corporation that received a charter from the Crown
    (B) established after settlers arrived in America and settled on previously unclaimed land
    (C) created when the king gave a huge land grant to a wealthy subject who controlled how the colony would be settled
    (D) developed according to precise religious tenets to ensure that tolerance would be practiced and that all religions would be welcome
    (E) prohibited from establishing slavery or any form of indentured servitude

GO ON TO THE NEXT PAGE

61. Which of the following was a major difference between the Pilgrims and the Puritans?

(A) Puritans were separatists, while Pilgrims welcomed all worshippers.
(B) Puritans left the Anglican Church, while Pilgrims remained attached to it.
(C) Pilgrims left the Anglican Church, while Puritans hoped to reform it.
(D) Puritans held slaves, and Pilgrims did not.
(E) Puritans were Catholics, and Pilgrims were Protestants.

62. Which of the following was the main issue of debate at the Constitutional Convention of 1787 ?

(A) The method by which slaves would be counted in the U.S. population
(B) Whether the nation's capital should be Washington, D.C., or Philadelphia
(C) The establishment of two competing political parties
(D) How to strike a balance between the needs of large and small states
(E) The first presidential election and George Washington's candidacy

63. Franklin D. Roosevelt's New Deal measures achieved all of the following EXCEPT:

(A) They raised spending by the federal government.
(B) They created Social Security.
(C) They won Democrats the support of African-American voters.
(D) They strengthened white southerners' support for the Democratic Party.
(E) They cast the Democratic Party as the political representative of the poor.

64. In *Progress and Poverty* (1879), Henry George called for a solution to the disparity of wealth created by industrialization by proposing

(A) the dissolution of all trusts and the restoration of free trade
(B) socialist revolution to give workers control of the means of production
(C) a popular referendum on the issue of antitrust legislation
(D) that the government use tax income to fund social programs
(E) enforcement of the Sherman Antitrust Act

65. Bacon's Rebellion resulted from

(A) tensions between the rich and poor in the Virginia colony
(B) a dispute over tariffs
(C) harsh working conditions in the Virginia tobacco fields
(D) southern colonists' outrage at the triangular trade, which primarily benefited northern colonists
(E) tensions between slaves and their owners on plantations around Jamestown

GO ON TO THE NEXT PAGE

66. The shaded countries illustrated on the map above represent the

    (A) Allied powers during World War II
    (B) members of the League of Nations
    (C) original members of NATO
    (D) members of the Warsaw Pact
    (E) partners in the Peace Corps

GO ON TO THE NEXT PAGE

67. For which of the following reasons did Woodrow Wilson call on the leaders who met at Versailles at the end of World War I to create "peace without victory"?

    (A) The United States stood to gain economically from helping to rebuild Europe.
    (B) The imposition of a harsh settlement on Germany would create resentment.
    (C) No country had actually won the war, and resumption of the status quo was the best remaining alternative to continued fighting.
    (D) That policy would ensure freedom of the seas, about which Wilson was passionate.
    (E) He wanted to return to his progressive reform agenda and not worry any longer about foreign affairs.

68. Plantation owners in the antebellum South often required their slaves to attend Sunday church services because

    (A) the owners felt guilty for enslaving the slaves and sought atonement
    (B) the services taught obedience and urged slaves to be content with their fate
    (C) southern law required religious worship for all adults
    (D) the owners were attempting to deflect antislavery criticism
    (E) some slaves demanded that they be allowed to attend

69. The Reagan Doctrine is widely considered to have prompted all of the following ventures EXCEPT

    (A) the U.S. Marines' invasion of Grenada
    (B) American support for the contras in Nicaragua
    (C) the U.S. invasion of Cambodia
    (D) the deployment of U.S. Marines to Lebanon
    (E) the American bombing of Libya

70. Which of the following statements about the Molasses Act of 1733 is LEAST accurate?

    (A) It was enacted after complaints from British sugar planters in the West Indies.
    (B) It resulted in widespread smuggling by American colonists, who intended to avoid the tax.
    (C) British sugar planters were supportive of the act and were pleased that the government had listened to them.
    (D) It was rigidly enforced and led to bitter feelings in the American colonies.
    (E) It was intended to further the policy of salutary neglect.

71. Warren Harding's election to the presidency in 1920 reflected Americans'

    (A) interest in supply-side economic policies
    (B) willingness to be actively engaged in world affairs
    (C) desire to isolate themselves from war-torn Europe
    (D) determination to fight communism after the Russian Revolution
    (E) support for women's right to vote

72. During the Spanish-American War, U.S. foreign policy consistently sought to maintain Cuba's independence rather than making it a colony because

    (A) Americans were uneasy about communism
    (B) no economic advantage would be gained by annexation
    (C) McKinley did not want the responsibility for assisting Cuba financially
    (D) many Americans saw similarities between the Cuban and American revolutions
    (E) slavery still existed in Cuba, which would raise fundamental constitutional issues

GO ON TO THE NEXT PAGE

73. Theodore Roosevelt's progressive philosophy addressed the problem of corporate corruption and political interference by

    (A) seeking to bust all trusts and restore free competition to the economic marketplace
    (B) dissolving corrupt corporations and regulating the others
    (C) adopting a laissez-faire governmental approach based on corporate goodwill
    (D) mandating that the Supreme Court regulate the trusts
    (E) nationalizing all industry under full government control

74. *The Narrative of the Life of Frederick Douglass* (1845) was an important part of the abolitionist movement for all of the following reasons EXCEPT that it

    (A) presented a picture of slavery as a harsh and oppressive system
    (B) motivated Nat Turner to rebel in Virginia
    (C) complemented the work being done by northern abolitionists
    (D) was written by an escaped slave who had become an abolitionist
    (E) called for complete political and economic equality

75. Which of the following men promoted the Gospel of Success?

    (A) Horatio Alger
    (B) Herbert Hoover
    (C) Ralph Waldo Emerson
    (D) Brigham Young
    (E) Horace Mann

76. Indentured servants were brought to the American colonies primarily in order to

    (A) replace expensive slave labor
    (B) decrease the size of the working class in England
    (C) secure an initial workforce for the colonies
    (D) increase the workforce in the South after regulations were placed on the slave trade
    (E) defend colonial settlements from Native American attacks

77. During his administration, Andrew Jackson came into direct conflict with the Supreme Court when he

    (A) vetoed the recharter of the Second Bank of the United States
    (B) refused to strike down the "Tariff of Abominations"
    (C) ordered the removal of Native Americans in order to clear land for American settlement
    (D) formed a "Kitchen Cabinet" composed of his supporters and political allies
    (E) signed the Force Bill, which authorized the use of the military to collect customs duties

78. "The wealth of this land is tied up in a few hands. It makes no difference how many years the laborer has worked, nor does it make any difference how many dreary rows the farmer has plowed. The wealth he has created is in the hands of the manipulators. They have not worked any more than many people who have nothing. Now we do not propose to hurt these very rich persons. We simply say that when they reach the place of millionaires they have everything they can use and they ought to let somebody else have something. The people cannot ever come to light unless we share our wealth."

    The author of this quotation would be most likely to oppose which of the following?

    (A) Efforts of the American Federation of Labor to organize unskilled assembly-line workers
    (B) The concept of rugged individualism espoused by Herbert Hoover during his presidency
    (C) Strict enforcement and application of the Sherman Act
    (D) Franklin D. Roosevelt's initial approach to solving problems caused by the Great Depression
    (E) The recognition of tribal ownership with respect to Native American reservation lands

GO ON TO THE NEXT PAGE

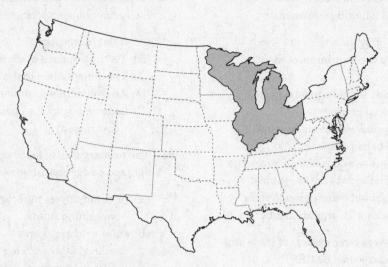

79. The shaded area on the map represents land that was

    (A) under French control after the American Revolution
    (B) part of the original thirteen colonies
    (C) governed by the Northwest Ordinances
    (D) sold to the United States as part of the Louisiana Purchase
    (E) set aside for the expansion of slavery

GO ON TO THE NEXT PAGE

80. Andrew Carnegie probably would have agreed most strongly with which of the following statements?

    (A) The wealthy have an obligation to create opportunities to help the poor improve their situations.
    (B) The federal government should support the arts through direct financial grants.
    (C) Taxes on corporations and wealthy individuals should be increased to help finance wars.
    (D) The federal government should zealously prosecute large corporations that violate antitrust laws.
    (E) Industrial magnates should enter into collective bargaining agreements with organized labor.

81. All of the following cities were large centers of trade and commerce in the American colonies EXCEPT

    (A) Philadelphia
    (B) New York
    (C) Boston
    (D) Chicago
    (E) Charleston

82. A small farmer from Texas in the 1890's would most likely have supported which of the following?

    (A) A flat income tax
    (B) The free coinage of silver
    (C) The deregulation of the transportation industry
    (D) An end to immigration restrictions
    (E) Loans made by the business sector to the federal government

83. The primary goal of labor strikes during Andrew Jackson's administration was to

    (A) force employers to recognize workers' collective bargaining rights
    (B) raise workers' wages
    (C) demand better working conditions in factories
    (D) petition Congress to restrict further immigration of Irish workers
    (E) advance the antislavery movement

GO ON TO THE NEXT PAGE

**Votes of Delegates to Connecticut, Pennsylvania, and New Hampshire
Ratifying Conventions, by Occupation**

	Federalist	*Antifederalist*
Merchants, manufacturers, doctors, lawyers, ministers, large landholders	84%	16%
Artisans, innkeepers, surveyors	64%	36%
Farmers	46%	54%

84. According to the chart above, which of the following groups of people would most likely support a loose interpretation of the U.S. Constitution?

(A) Lawyers
(B) Farmers
(C) Innkeepers
(D) Politicians
(E) Not enough information to tell

GO ON TO THE NEXT PAGE

85. In 1948, Harry Truman invoked the Smith Act to prosecute

    (A) communists in the United States
    (B) Joseph McCarthy for his witch-hunting tactics
    (C) members of organized labor who engaged in violence
    (D) members of the Student Non-violent Coordinating Committee
    (E) war criminals from World War II

86. The Black Power movement advocated

    (A) the integration of African Americans into all aspects of American life
    (B) gradualism in African Americans' acquiring of basic civil rights
    (C) a decrease in interracial cooperation
    (D) economic opportunity instead of voting rights for African Americans
    (E) the creation of a civil rights act

87. The First Great Awakening can best be described as a movement that

    (A) advocated immediate repentance and rejection of material comforts
    (B) called for the separation of church and state
    (C) praised human reason and encouraged skepticisim
    (D) supported the abolition of slavery and the granting of citizenship rights to former slaves
    (E) encouraged introspection and a return to nature

88. The America First Committee sought to influence American politics by which of the following means?

    (A) Campaigning against American involvement in World War II prior to Pearl Harbor
    (B) Lobbying for tax reductions in order to stimulate the U.S. economy
    (C) Providing relief aid to American troops overseas
    (D) Supporting Franklin D. Roosevelt's decision to make precautionary preparations for war in 1939
    (E) Campaigning actively in support of the Lend-Lease Act

89. During the post-war Reconstruction era, the practice of sharecropping in the South

    (A) revived the southern economy and helped rebuild its infrastructure
    (B) provided African Americans with the economic stake they needed to migrate north
    (C) mired African Americans in a cycle of debt and turned them into second-class citizens
    (D) was declared unconstitutional
    (E) was Booker T. Washington's method of making African Americans economically useful to the southern economy

90. Which of the following motivated the formal announcement of the Monroe Doctrine in 1823 ?

    (A) James Monroe's desire to build a political platform for reelection
    (B) John Quincy Adams's fears that Russia and Spain were interested in colonizing parts of North America
    (C) A general feeling in the United States that England would once again attempt to regain her former colonies
    (D) An economic need to stimulate trade with foreign countries
    (E) A Republican attempt to destroy the Federalist party

S T O P

IF YOU FINISH BEFORE TIME IS CALLED, YOU MAY CHECK YOUR WORK ON THIS TEST ONLY.
DO NOT TURN TO ANY OTHER TEST IN THIS BOOK.

SAT U.S. HISTORY PRACTICE TEST 1 EXPLANATIONS

U.S. HISTORY PRACTICE TEST 1 ANSWERS

Question Number	Answer	Right	Wrong	Question Number	Answer	Right	Wrong
1	A	___	___	46	E	___	___
2	D	___	___	47	B	___	___
3	B	___	___	48	B	___	___
4	C	___	___	49	B	___	___
5	C	___	___	50	E	___	___
6	D	___	___	51	A	___	___
7	D	___	___	52	C	___	___
8	B	___	___	53	E	___	___
9	C	___	___	54	C	___	___
10	E	___	___	55	B	___	___
11	A	___	___	56	C	___	___
12	A	___	___	57	A	___	___
13	D	___	___	58	E	___	___
14	B	___	___	59	B	___	___
15	C	___	___	60	C	___	___
16	D	___	___	61	C	___	___
17	A	___	___	62	D	___	___
18	E	___	___	63	D	___	___
19	A	___	___	64	D	___	___
20	C	___	___	65	A	___	___
21	A	___	___	66	C	___	___
22	E	___	___	67	B	___	___
23	D	___	___	68	B	___	___
24	C	___	___	69	C	___	___
25	C	___	___	70	D	___	___
26	D	___	___	71	C	___	___
27	B	___	___	72	D	___	___
28	C	___	___	73	B	___	___
29	A	___	___	74	B	___	___
30	A	___	___	75	A	___	___
31	C	___	___	76	C	___	___
32	A	___	___	77	C	___	___
33	E	___	___	78	D	___	___
34	B	___	___	79	C	___	___
35	A	___	___	80	A	___	___
36	D	___	___	81	D	___	___
37	B	___	___	82	B	___	___
38	B	___	___	83	B	___	___
39	D	___	___	84	A	___	___
40	D	___	___	85	A	___	___
41	C	___	___	86	C	___	___
42	D	___	___	87	A	___	___
43	D	___	___	88	A	___	___
44	D	___	___	89	C	___	___
45	E	___	___	90	B	___	___

CALCULATING YOUR SCORE

Your raw score for the SAT U.S. History Test is calculated from the number of questions you answer correctly and incorrectly. Once you have determined your composite score, use the conversion table on page 399 of this book to calculate your scaled score. To calculate your raw score, count the number of questions you answered correctly:

_____
A

Count the number of questions you answered incorrectly, and multiply that number by $\frac{1}{4}$:

$$\underline{\hspace{2cm}}_{B} \times \frac{1}{4} = \underline{\hspace{2cm}}_{C}$$

Subtract the value in field C from the value in field A:

_____
D

Round the number in field D to the nearest whole number. This is your raw score:

_____
E

U.S. HISTORY TEST 1 EXPLANATIONS

1. **A** The Progressive Era
The Federal Reserve lends money to commercial banks in the United States. It does not deal directly with individuals.

2. **D** Revolution & Constitution
After mounting a large debt during the French and Indian War, Britain imposed the Stamp Act on the American colonies in order to raise revenue. The 1765 act required colonists to buy special watermarked paper for legal documents, newspapers, and playing cards. The act also placed a tax on licenses and liquor.

3. **B** Westward Expansion & Sectional Strife
Douglas wanted the government to build a transcontinental railroad between Chicago and the Pacific coast. Douglas tried to facilitate the building of this railroad by settling Nebraska as a U.S. territory under the Kansas-Nebraska Act.

4. **C** Cultural Trends—1950 to 1969
This time period saw a major exodus, mainly on the part of the Caucasian (white) population, from the cities to new houses built in outlying areas called suburbs. This trend came to be known as "white flight."

5.   **C**   The Great Depression & New Deal

A balanced budget was not part of the New Deal measures, which used deficit spending to relieve the depression. FDR hoped that federal spending would revive the U.S. economy by increasing individuals' purchasing power.

6.   **D**   Industrial Revolution

The growth of large-scale, heavy industry spurred the country's economic growth during the second half of the nineteenth century. Its impact accounted for a tripling of America's gross national product and an enormous rise in exports by the turn of the century.

7.   **D**   The Roaring Twenties

The cartoon shows a helpless Uncle Sam (the United States) with his hands tied behind his back and tugged in different directions by foreign countries. The binds that attach the United States to the other countries are labeled "The League of Nations." The message of the cartoon is that membership in the League of Nations will bind the United States to the interests of other countries, and these binds will render the United States powerless. This suspicion of the League of Nations was shared by many senators at the time. Under the leadership of Henry Cabot Lodge, the Senate rejected membership in the League of Nations, fearing that a collective security measure would force Americans into future wars that did not necessarily involve the United States.

8.   **B**   Civil War & Reconstruction

From the outset of the Civil War, the Union held an advantage over the Confederacy in terms of resources, population, and wealth. One of the Confederacy's main advantages, though, was a strong military tradition. The Confederate military leaders tended to have more battle experience than their counterparts in the North, and the fact that fewer Confederate troops than Northern troops defected suggests that the Confederate troops had higher morale.

9.   **C**   A New Nation

The federal government quickly raised an army and quelled the Whiskey Rebellion. Hamilton approved of the government's response, since it demonstrated the strength of the federal government and the new Constitution. The defeat of the rebels was especially important, since the government had come under fire for failing to respond effectively to Shays' Rebellion in Massachusetts.

10.   **E**   Pre-Colonial America

Europeans brought new diseases to the Americas. Because Native Americans had never built up immunity to these diseases, they succumbed quickly to illness. In the end, these imported diseases decimated the native population in Spanish America.

11.   **A**   Industrial Revolution

The Chinese Exclusion Act of 1882 prohibited Chinese immigrants from entering the United States over the following ten-year period. The act was passed in response to rising anti-immigration sentiment in the United States.

12. A   The Progressive Era

The muckraker Lincoln Steffens penned this critique of big business's corrupt practice of using politics for its own purposes. Calling for reform, Steffens and other muckrakers published newspaper articles that reviled industry for its corrupt and exploitative practices.

13. D   World War II

Using Woodrow Wilson's fourteen points as a model, Churchill and Roosevelt drafted the Atlantic Charter, which presented their vision of the ideal postwar world. This ideal included unconditional surrender by the Axis powers **A**, freedom of the seas **B**, the establishment of an international security institution **C**, and self-determination for all nations **E**. Although the United States had not yet entered the war in August 1941, when the Charter was created, these goals would become a major focus for the Allies throughout the war. The Charter did not propose the division of labor among armies.

14. B   The Progressive Era

In *The Jungle*, Upton Sinclair depicted the unhealthy conditions that prevailed in American meatpacking plants. In response to the novel's popularity and influence, the government passed the Pure Food and Drug Act and a Meat Inspection Act in 1906.

15. C   Westward Expansion & Sectional Strife

The first sentence tells us that the speaker is either a current or former slave. As a whole, the quotation strongly suggests that the speaker senses a "purpose" to prepare fellow slaves for an important event. A rebellion against their slaveholder would certainly constitute such an event. (In fact, this quotation is from Nat Turner's "confessions," in which he explained how he prepared his fellow slaves for the rebellion in Southampton County, Virginia, in 1831. Believing that he had been divinely inspired, Turner gathered a small band of slaves to revolt against his owner and white neighbors.)

16. D   The Great Depression & New Deal

The Public Works Administration gave jobs to unemployed Americans during the depression. In keeping with the New Deal's commitment to increasing purchasing power without increasing production, the PWA employed people on building schools, post offices, bridges, and other pieces of infrastructure. These construction jobs gave workers income without flooding the domestic market with new consumer goods.

17. A   Pre-Colonial America

The first humans arrived in the Americas from Asia, crossing over a land bridge that connected Siberia (in modern-day Russia) to Alaska.

18. E   The 1950s

Created in 1948, the Marshall Plan pledged American financial assistance to European nations recovering from the war. The United States hoped that this financial aid would prevent communist expansion into Europe by eliminating political instability and economic insecurity. The Marshall Plan was the financial counterpart to the Truman Doctrine, which established the United States in the role of global policeman.

19. A A New Nation

In the *McCulloch* ruling, the Supreme Court prohibited the state of Maryland from taxing a local branch of the First Bank of the United States. This decision affirmed the supremacy of the federal government over the states and demonstrated that the Supreme Court would carefully monitor state laws in order to ensure their constitutionality.

20. C The 1960s

Until Kennedy, no American president had been Catholic. Anti-Catholicism was rampant in political and social arenas, and many people believed that Kennedy would not win the election because of his religion.

21. A Civil War & Reconstruction

Lincoln wanted to return the southern states to the Union as quickly as possible. His plan required ten percent of the voters in each state to take an oath of allegiance to the Union. Once a state obtained this ten percent, it could create a new government and elect representatives to send to Congress.

22. E Industrial Revolution

Government jobs were viewed as rewards for party loyalty, for elected officials offered them to important supporters. Accordingly, with the election of a new administration, there were wholesale changes in the governmental workforce.

23. D World War I

Germany did not use concentration camps during World War I. At the time, anti-German sentiment in the United States resulted from Germany's aggressive tactics, such as the sinking of the *Lusitania* **A**, the Zimmerman Telegram **B**, the invasion of Belgium **C**, and the use of submarine warfare **E**.

24. C Cultural Trends—1781 to 1860

Dix's main concern was the treatment of the insane in American poorhouses and prisons. She worked diligently to reform the care given to the mentally ill and to improve their living conditions. Her efforts helped create mental institutions, where the mentally ill could receive humane treatment.

25. C Westward Expansion & Sectional Strife

The Republicans formed between 1854 and 1855 as a northern-based party opposed to the extension of slavery into the territories. The party formed as a coalition of groups with disparate aims: some Republicans supported the complete abolition of slavery, while others believed that slavery should be allowed where it already existed. Despite these differences, the Republicans were united in their support of free-soil territories, and in the 1856 election, they were the main opposition to the pro-slavery Democrats.

26. D The 1960s

After North Vietnamese gunboats attacked American destroyers in the Tonkin Gulf, Johnson requested congressional authorization to use whatever power he deemed necessary to protect American interests in Vietnam. The Gulf of Tonkin Resolution gave Johnson the authority he needed to send ground troops to Vietnam in 1965.

27. **B**   World War II

The quotation is essentially a statement of Truman's policy of containment. Believing that the Soviet Union would continue to expand its influence, Truman asked Congress to give financial assistance to the democratic governments in Greece and Turkey in order to suppress "totalitarian regimes." The Truman Doctrine was a major aspect of American policy during the late 1940s.

28. **C**   Revolution & Constitution

The Navigation Acts, passed between 1651 and 1673, were designed to secure a favorable balance of trade for England at the expense of the colonies in part by forbidding colonists from exporting sugar and tobacco to countries other than England. The acts were not rigorously enforced, though, until the late eighteenth century, when England began to enforce the Navigation Acts because it needed to pay off its debts from the French and Indian War. This enforcement represented a shift in England's colonial policies, away from salutary neglect toward tighter regulation.

29. **A**   The Roaring Twenties

In 1925, the Tennessee legislature banned the teaching of evolution in schools. In response, the American Civil Liberties Union offered to defend any Tennessee teacher willing to break this law and teach his students evolution. John Scopes accepted this offer, and Clarence Darrow defended him at his trial. Although Scopes was found guilty, Darrow managed to humiliate the anti-evolution proponents, significantly weakening the anti-evolution cause in the U.S.

30. **A**   Civil War & Reconstruction

During Reconstruction, the Democratic Party was united in its efforts to return the South to Democratic control. A combination of other factors, including the ones stated in choices **B**, **C**, **D**, and **E**, contributed to the end of Reconstruction.

31. **C**   A New Nation

The War Hawks, a group of westerners and southerners, pushed for a war against Britain in 1812, partially because they objected to Britain's policy of impressment. Under the leadership of John Calhoun and Henry Clay, they argued that a peace settlement with Britain would embarrass and weaken the new American government.

32. **A**   1970–2000

During the Vietnam War, Nixon decided to expand the fighting into Cambodia in an effort to root out North Vietnamese soldiers who were hiding there. His decision prompted widespread antiwar protests on college campuses across the United States. At Kent State University, the confrontation turned violent, as national guardsmen fired on student demonstrators and bystanders, killing four of them.

33. **E**   The Progressive Era

A Progressive, Woodrow Wilson pushed through an agenda of corporate reform. He supported lowering tariffs, creating a publicly controlled centralized bank, workers' rights, and government regulation of trade and trusts. The Federal Trade Commission Act of 1914 created an agency that would investigate violations of interstate trade regulations, and the Clayton Antitrust Act of 1914 built on the vaguely worded Sherman Antitrust Act by defining illegal business practices.

34. B The Age of Jackson

John Calhoun and Henry Clay established the Whig Party in opposition to Jackson's Democrats. Calhoun and Clay objected to Jackson's policies and his frequent use of the veto. Taking their name from the British party that sought to reduce the power of the Crown, the Whigs first ran a candidate for president in 1836.

35. A World War II

Truman's military advisors estimated that one million Americans and millions of Japanese could die during a ground invasion of Japan. Truman thought that dropping an atomic bomb would result in fewer casualties and a quicker end to the war than invading Japan would.

36. D The Great Depression & New Deal

The stock market crash resulted from a combination of overproduction and underconsumption. Underproduction on American farms was not a cause of the crash. In fact, one of FDR's New Deal measures after the crash was designed to encourage farmers to reduce production. The Agricultural Adjustment Administration provided subsidies to farmers who were willing to lower production levels; the AAA hoped that reduced production would result in increased prices for farm products.

37. B The Colonial Period

The Puritans left for Massachusetts Bay, hoping to purify the Anglican Church of its Catholic trappings. In 1630, under the leadership of John Winthrop, the Puritans settled in modern-day Boston, establishing a community they hoped would be a beacon of religious righteousness.

38. B Industrial Revolution

This excerpt is from Booker T. Washington's Atlanta Exposition Address, in which Washington presented a blueprint for African-American advancement in the South. Washington emphasized vocational education and manual skills, which he claimed would make African Americans economically useful in the rebuilding of the South. Other civil rights leaders, such as W.E.B. Du Bois, criticized Washington for not demanding immediate political and social rights.

39. D The Colonial Period

The Spanish Empire was interested in its American colonies primarily as a source of gold and silver. Because Spain had no manufacturing or agricultural base, it relied on the acquisition of precious metals to buy needed products from other European countries.

40. D A New Nation

At the 1814 Hartford Convention, Federalists gathered to complain about the policies of the ruling Republican Party. The New England–based Federalists accused the Republicans of neglecting the needs of New England commerce, which was hurt by the trade restrictions imposed during the War of 1812. The Republicans, of course, did not agree with the Federalists on this point. The rest of the country reacted hostilely to the Convention, which precipitated the near demise of the Federalist Party.

41. **C** Revolution & Constitution

In *Letters from a Pennsylvania Farmer*, Dickinson argued against the legality of the Townshend Acts, which established taxes on glass, lead, paint, paper, and tea entering the colonies.

42. **D** Cultural Trends—1781 to 1860

This quotation from Ralph Waldo Emerson is characteristic of transcendentalism. In the 1830s, a period marked by growing consumption, transcendentalists like Emerson preached self-reliance and self-knowledge. They believed that people could acquire knowledge through emotional openness, intuition, and the senses.

43. **D** The 1960s

Johnson's Great Society plan called for extensive legislation to promote social welfare and civil rights. While achieving many legislative successes, Johnson ultimately lost support for the plan, primarily due to the government's shifting focus from domestic to foreign policy, as the situation in Vietnam worsened. The program's poor design and its enormous scope also contributed to its failure.

44. **D** The Colonial Period

Williams was banished from Massachusetts for advocating the complete separation of church and state. He argued that without complete separation, the state would eventually corrupt the church. In the colony of Rhode Island, which Williams established in 1647, the government broke from the Church of England and permitted religious freedom.

45. **E** Industrial Revolution

The railroad industry's largest customers, such as Rockefeller's Standard Oil, demanded rebates in return for doing exclusive business with railroad companies. Rockefeller reasoned that Standard Oil would give a railroad company so much business that he was entitled to a financial kickback.

46. **E** Westward Expansion & Sectional Strife

In the *Dred Scott* ruling, the Supreme Court declared that popular sovereignty was unconstitutional because it violated the Fifth Amendment, which stated that a citizen's property, including slaves, could not be taken away without due process. According to the Court's interpretation of the amendment, any attempt to prohibit slavery was unconstitutional. Popular sovereignty fell into this category, since it could potentially result in the prohibition of slavery in the territories. The Court also ruled that no African American, even if free, could become a citizen of the United States.

47. **B** The Age of Imperialism

The cartoon shows Theodore Roosevelt as a policeman, swinging a "big stick" labeled "The New Diplomacy." The Roosevelt corollary to the Monroe Doctrine stated that the United States had the right to monitor and intervene in the affairs of Latin America. The corollary did not express any expansionist desires, but it did help create the image of the United States as the world's policeman.

48. **B**   Revolution & Constitution

The 1787 Northwest Ordinance prohibited slavery north of the Ohio River. The ordinance also created a settler's bill of rights and established the process through which territories became states.

49. **B**   Industrial Revolution

The main function of the Interstate Commerce Commission was to stop railroad companies from practicing price discrimination. The ICC did not consolidate the railroad companies into a single industry regulated by the government.

50. **E**   The 1950s

In the *Brown* case, the Supreme Court ruled that segregation deprived African Americans of their rights under the Fourteenth Amendment, which guaranteed citizenship rights to all people born or naturalized in the United States. By ruling in this manner, the Court created an important precedent of using the Fourteenth Amendment to attack racial discrimination.

51. **A**   Westward Expansion & Sectional Strife

Americans explained westward expansion by stating that they had a divine right to settle the continent. This sense of manifest destiny allowed the government to justify land acquisition and its policy toward Native Americans, and it sparked the Mexican War over the territory of Texas.

52. **C**   The Roaring Twenties

The National Origins Act restricted the number of immigrants from southern and eastern Europe during the 1920s. At the time, southern and eastern Europeans were considered "inferior races," and they were also suspected of holding radical political views that threatened American stability.

53. **E**   Cultural Trends—1781 to 1860

After the Nat Turner insurrection of 1831, southerners changed their defense of slavery from the "necessary evil" justification to the "positive good" justification. According to the "positive good" justification, the institution of slavery functioned like a school, caring for and educating slaves. This justification implied that slaves were inferior people who depended on whites for survival.

54. **C**   World War II

When the United States began production of war materials, many formerly unemployed citizens were hired to work in the defense industry. Since the goods produced were shipped to Europe, the United States saw a rise in consumer purchasing power without the burden of additional supply. The United States emerged from the economic depression as demand rose while supply remained constant.

55. **B**   The Age of Jackson

After vetoing the recharter of the Second Bank of the United States, Andrew Jackson began removing government funds from that bank and placing them in state banks. As the cartoon suggests, Jackson's actions effectively destroyed the Second Bank and its directors, who are seen running from the bank's ruins.

56. C   The Age of Imperialism

After negotiations between Theodore Roosevelt and Colombia stalled, the United States fomented a revolution that resulted in Panamanian independence. Panama then signed a treaty that gave the United States perpetual use of what became the Canal Zone.

57. A   Revolution & Constitution

During Shays' Rebellion, western Massachusetts farmers violently attacked a federal arsenal in Springfield, Massachusetts, hoping to prevent the foreclosure of their farms. Politicians believed the rebellion was an expression of lower class discontent and worried that the newly formed government was too weak to control such outbreaks.

58. E   Civil War & Reconstruction

In 1864, Johnson, a Southern Democrat, became president after Lincoln's assassination. Although he pushed through a slightly modified version of Lincoln's Reconstruction plan, he was quite lenient, particularly in the opinion of the Radical Republicans, on the former Confederate states. He pardoned many powerful pro-slavery southerners and allowed southern governments to be dominated by pro-slavery groups. After gaining control of Congress in 1866, the Radical Republicans began to implement their own Reconstruction plans, which Johnson opposed but was unable to stop. The Fourteenth Amendment, which gave citizenship rights to all people born or naturalized in the United States, was one of the measures the Radical Republicans passed despite Johnson's opposition.

59. B   Industrial Revolution

Although the Sherman Antitrust Act was intended to outlaw trusts, which prohibited free trade, the pro-business government of the 1890s frequently used the act to stop workers from striking, claiming that strikes were "in restraint of trade." In the early 1900s, the Progressive government, under Theodore Roosevelt, began using the act to bust corrupt trusts and to regulate other ones.

60. C   The Colonial Period

Proprietary colonies were large land grants given by the British government to wealthy individuals who governed the land and reported directly to the king. The largest proprietary colonies in North America were Pennsylvania, Maryland, and Delaware.

61. C   The Colonial Period

The Pilgrims were a Separatist group who came to America to escape religious persecution and split from the Anglican Church. The Puritans, on the other hand, came to America intent on reforming and "purifying" the Anglican Church but did not want to break from it.

62. D   Revolution & Constitution

Delegates at the Constitutional Convention debated how to balance the competing needs of large and small states. Small states secured protection in the Senate, where each state was equally represented by two senators. In the House of Representatives, the number of representatives from each state was in proportion to the state's population.

63. **D**   The Great Depression & New Deal

The New Deal measures redefined the Democratic and Republican parties. African Americans, who consistently voted Republican ("the party of Lincoln") until the 1930s, shifted their votes to the Democrats as FDR turned the Democrats into the party of the underprivileged. Farmers and urban workers also flocked to the Democratic Party at this time. In the meantime, the Democrats lost the support of the white South, which switched its allegiance to the Republicans.

64. **D**   Industrial Revolution

George wrote *Progress and Poverty* in response to the growing gap between the rich and the poor. In his book, he argued that the government should use tax income to pay for social programs for the poor.

65. **A**   The Colonial Period

Bacon's Rebellion is an example of the tensions between the rich and the poor in colonial America. In 1676, Nathaniel Bacon accused the governor of Virginia of failing to protect poor farmers from Native American attacks. Bacon rallied a large group of poor farmers, who then attacked the Native Americans. When the governor branded them rebels, Bacon and his men attacked and looted the colonial city of Jamestown.

66. **C**   The 1950s

The shaded countries were charter members of the North Atlantic Treaty Organization, which formed in 1949. NATO was designed to contain communism, and it included a collective security provision to protect all member-nations.

67. **B**   World War I

Wilson correctly perceived that a punitive settlement against Germany would create resentment and animosity, so he called instead for a peace without victory. The other Allied countries ignored Wilson's suggestion, and his fears were confirmed when Germany rearmed and World War II exploded throughout Europe.

68. **B**   Cultural Trends—1781 to 1860

Slave owners sent their slaves to church on Sunday, hoping that the services would teach the slaves obedience and contentment. The sermons made no reference to liberation and emphasized that slaves should be content with their fate and faithful to their masters.

69. **C**   1970–2000

The Reagan Doctrine emphasized a renewed American presence and active engagement in third world countries. The Cambodian incursion occurred in 1970, before Reagan became president in 1980.

70. **D**   The Colonial Period

The Molasses Act had little real impact on the American colonies, since it was laxly enforced and since the colonists could avoid the tax by smuggling **B**. The act was passed primarily to assuage the grievances of British sugar planters in the West Indies **A**, and these sugar planters supported its passage **C**. The British did not vigorously enforce the act, though, in keeping with its policy of salutary neglect, which stated that trade laws that hurt the colonial economy would not be enforced **E**.

440

71. C   The Roaring Twenties

During his campaign, Harding promised what he called a "return to normalcy." After the upheavals of industrialization, modernization, and especially World War I, most Americans longed for a period of tranquillity and relative isolation from war-torn Europe. Harding capitalized on that desire in order to win the election.

72. D   The Age of Imperialism

Cuba's revolt against the Spanish Empire reminded many Americans of their own colonial struggle against England. The similarity between those two events led prominent politicians to support Cuban independence, and the Senate passed the Teller Amendment, which stated that America would not annex Cuba.

73. B   The Progressive Era

Roosevelt was determined to break up corrupt trusts that restrained trade or commerce. He did not want to break up all trusts, though. He allowed good trusts to remain in business as long as they adhered to government regulations.

74. B   Cultural Trends—1781 to 1860

The Turner Rebellion occurred in 1831, fourteen years before Douglass wrote his *Narrative*. The rebellion inspired many abolitionists to begin their crusade against slavery.

75. A   Industrial Revolution

Alger was a proponent of the Gospel of Success, which claimed that any man could achieve wealth through hard work. To illustrate his beliefs, Alger wrote fictional stories about young men who went from rags to riches based on their determination and talent.

76. C   The Colonial Period

Indentured servants provided the American colonies with their initial labor force. In exchange for passage to the colonies, indentured servants agreed to work for free for a certain period of time (often seven years). At the end of this period, their masters gave them some clothing, seed, and perhaps a little plot of land for farming.

77. C   The Age of Jackson

Jackson and the Supreme Court clashed over the Indian Removal Act of 1830. The act granted Jackson the authority to remove Native Americans to assigned western regions. Jackson wanted to clear the land that tribes occupied in order to make room for American settlers. In 1832, the Supreme Court ruled in *Worcester v. Georgia* that the Cherokee were a "domestic dependent nation" with a right to be protected from forced migration and other harassment. Jackson scoffed at this ruling, reportedly saying, "John Marshall has made his decision; now let him enforce it." The Supreme Court was powerless to enforce its decision, and the Cherokee removal continued unchecked.

78. D   The Great Depression & New Deal

The author of this statement, Huey Long, proposed the "share our wealth" plan as a way of redistributing income and correcting the great imbalance of wealth in the country. As one of the New Deal's harsher critics, Long pushed FDR to act boldly during the planning of the Second New Deal.

79. **C**   Revolution & Constitution

The shaded states were created under the Northwest Ordinances of 1784 and 1787. The Ordinances prohibited slavery in all of the shaded states, which lie north of the Ohio River, and they established the process by which regions in the territories could become states in the Union.

80. **A**   Industrial Revolution

Carnegie believed that as a steward of society, he had an obligation to give back to his society the fortunes he had accumulated as a private industrialist. Rather than give money directly to the poor, he chose to build educational institutions that could teach the poor to compete on their own in society.

81. **D**   The Colonial Period

Chicago was not founded until after the colonial period. Philadelphia, New York, Boston, and Charleston were the principal centers of economic and political activity in the colonies.

82. **B**   Industrial Revolution

Small farmers struggled financially throughout the late eighteenth century, as crop prices fell and land prices rose. Farmers' groups, such as the Grange and the Farmers' Alliance, lobbied for political reform that would help small farms. In 1892, members of the Farmers' Alliance formed the Populist Party. The Populists' agenda focused on policies that would improve the situations of small farmers and urban laborers. One of the major items of this agenda was the free coinage of silver, which would create inflation, easing debt repayment and raising crop prices.

83. **B**   The Age of Jackson

During Jackson's administration, most strikes were about the issue of wages. Suffering from the period's frequent economic downturns, workers wanted to increase their wages in order to meet their everyday needs.

84. **A**   A New Nation

Federalists advocated a loose reading of the Constitution. They supported a strong federal government with the power to create all laws beneficial to the country. Anti-federalists, or strict constructionists, believed that the federal government's powers should be confined to those enumerated in the Constitution in order to prevent a tyrannical centralized government from developing. According to the chart, lawyers tended to vote with the Federalists, suggesting that lawyers tended to support a loose reading of the Constitution.

85. **A**   The 1950s

During the presidential campaign of 1948, Truman invoked the Smith Act to prosecute eleven leaders of the Communist Party in the United States. This prosecution was supposed to demonstrate his aggressive stance against communism.

86. **C**   The 1960s

Black Power was the name given to militant civil rights groups in the late 1960s. Advocates of Black Power argued for separation from white society and sometimes preached violence against whites in order to achieve equality "by any means necessary."

87. **A**   The Colonial Period
The First Great Awakening was a religious revival movement that gained support during the 1730s and 1740s. Revival ministers urged their listeners to repent immediately in order to avoid divine punishment and to renounce material trappings. Their sermons, such as Jonathon Edwards's "Sinners in the Hands of an Angry God," often terrified audiences to near hysteria with stories of human corruption and sin. The Great Awakening was a response to Enlightenment thought, which encouraged skepticism and logical reasoning.

88. **A**   World War II
The America First Committee, which consisted of industrialists, senators, and influential owners of media outlets, opposed American involvement in World War II. Supported by large segments of the Republican Party, the committee frequently criticized FDR's prewar measures. The committee endorsed Wendell Willkie for the presidency in 1940 because of his isolationist position.

89. **C**   Industrial Revolution
The sharecropping system kept African Americans in debt and tied to the land. The system prevented African Americans from making enough money to pay their bills and migrate north; as a result, they were forced to remain in the South, where they provided a cheap labor force for whites.

90. **B**   A New Nation
During Monroe's presidency, Secretary of State John Quincy Adams wrote the Monroe Doctrine, which stated that the United States was the dominant power in the western hemisphere. Adams wrote this doctrine out of fear that Russia was interested in establishing colonies in the Northwest and that Spain would try to regain its North American colonies.

SAT* U.S. HISTORY PRACTICE TEST 2

SAT U.S. HISTORY PRACTICE TEST 2 ANSWER SHEET

1. Ⓐ Ⓑ Ⓒ Ⓓ Ⓔ	31. Ⓐ Ⓑ Ⓒ Ⓓ Ⓔ	61. Ⓐ Ⓑ Ⓒ Ⓓ Ⓔ
2. Ⓐ Ⓑ Ⓒ Ⓓ Ⓔ	32. Ⓐ Ⓑ Ⓒ Ⓓ Ⓔ	62. Ⓐ Ⓑ Ⓒ Ⓓ Ⓔ
3. Ⓐ Ⓑ Ⓒ Ⓓ Ⓔ	33. Ⓐ Ⓑ Ⓒ Ⓓ Ⓔ	63. Ⓐ Ⓑ Ⓒ Ⓓ Ⓔ
4. Ⓐ Ⓑ Ⓒ Ⓓ Ⓔ	34. Ⓐ Ⓑ Ⓒ Ⓓ Ⓔ	64. Ⓐ Ⓑ Ⓒ Ⓓ Ⓔ
5. Ⓐ Ⓑ Ⓒ Ⓓ Ⓔ	35. Ⓐ Ⓑ Ⓒ Ⓓ Ⓔ	65. Ⓐ Ⓑ Ⓒ Ⓓ Ⓔ
6. Ⓐ Ⓑ Ⓒ Ⓓ Ⓔ	36. Ⓐ Ⓑ Ⓒ Ⓓ Ⓔ	66. Ⓐ Ⓑ Ⓒ Ⓓ Ⓔ
7. Ⓐ Ⓑ Ⓒ Ⓓ Ⓔ	37. Ⓐ Ⓑ Ⓒ Ⓓ Ⓔ	67. Ⓐ Ⓑ Ⓒ Ⓓ Ⓔ
8. Ⓐ Ⓑ Ⓒ Ⓓ Ⓔ	38. Ⓐ Ⓑ Ⓒ Ⓓ Ⓔ	68. Ⓐ Ⓑ Ⓒ Ⓓ Ⓔ
9. Ⓐ Ⓑ Ⓒ Ⓓ Ⓔ	39. Ⓐ Ⓑ Ⓒ Ⓓ Ⓔ	69. Ⓐ Ⓑ Ⓒ Ⓓ Ⓔ
10. Ⓐ Ⓑ Ⓒ Ⓓ Ⓔ	40. Ⓐ Ⓑ Ⓒ Ⓓ Ⓔ	70. Ⓐ Ⓑ Ⓒ Ⓓ Ⓔ
11. Ⓐ Ⓑ Ⓒ Ⓓ Ⓔ	41. Ⓐ Ⓑ Ⓒ Ⓓ Ⓔ	71. Ⓐ Ⓑ Ⓒ Ⓓ Ⓔ
12. Ⓐ Ⓑ Ⓒ Ⓓ Ⓔ	42. Ⓐ Ⓑ Ⓒ Ⓓ Ⓔ	72. Ⓐ Ⓑ Ⓒ Ⓓ Ⓔ
13. Ⓐ Ⓑ Ⓒ Ⓓ Ⓔ	43. Ⓐ Ⓑ Ⓒ Ⓓ Ⓔ	73. Ⓐ Ⓑ Ⓒ Ⓓ Ⓔ
14. Ⓐ Ⓑ Ⓒ Ⓓ Ⓔ	44. Ⓐ Ⓑ Ⓒ Ⓓ Ⓔ	74. Ⓐ Ⓑ Ⓒ Ⓓ Ⓔ
15. Ⓐ Ⓑ Ⓒ Ⓓ Ⓔ	45. Ⓐ Ⓑ Ⓒ Ⓓ Ⓔ	75. Ⓐ Ⓑ Ⓒ Ⓓ Ⓔ
16. Ⓐ Ⓑ Ⓒ Ⓓ Ⓔ	46. Ⓐ Ⓑ Ⓒ Ⓓ Ⓔ	76. Ⓐ Ⓑ Ⓒ Ⓓ Ⓔ
17. Ⓐ Ⓑ Ⓒ Ⓓ Ⓔ	47. Ⓐ Ⓑ Ⓒ Ⓓ Ⓔ	77. Ⓐ Ⓑ Ⓒ Ⓓ Ⓔ
18. Ⓐ Ⓑ Ⓒ Ⓓ Ⓔ	48. Ⓐ Ⓑ Ⓒ Ⓓ Ⓔ	78. Ⓐ Ⓑ Ⓒ Ⓓ Ⓔ
19. Ⓐ Ⓑ Ⓒ Ⓓ Ⓔ	49. Ⓐ Ⓑ Ⓒ Ⓓ Ⓔ	79. Ⓐ Ⓑ Ⓒ Ⓓ Ⓔ
20. Ⓐ Ⓑ Ⓒ Ⓓ Ⓔ	50. Ⓐ Ⓑ Ⓒ Ⓓ Ⓔ	80. Ⓐ Ⓑ Ⓒ Ⓓ Ⓔ
21. Ⓐ Ⓑ Ⓒ Ⓓ Ⓔ	51. Ⓐ Ⓑ Ⓒ Ⓓ Ⓔ	81. Ⓐ Ⓑ Ⓒ Ⓓ Ⓔ
22. Ⓐ Ⓑ Ⓒ Ⓓ Ⓔ	52. Ⓐ Ⓑ Ⓒ Ⓓ Ⓔ	82. Ⓐ Ⓑ Ⓒ Ⓓ Ⓔ
23. Ⓐ Ⓑ Ⓒ Ⓓ Ⓔ	53. Ⓐ Ⓑ Ⓒ Ⓓ Ⓔ	83. Ⓐ Ⓑ Ⓒ Ⓓ Ⓔ
24. Ⓐ Ⓑ Ⓒ Ⓓ Ⓔ	54. Ⓐ Ⓑ Ⓒ Ⓓ Ⓔ	84. Ⓐ Ⓑ Ⓒ Ⓓ Ⓔ
25. Ⓐ Ⓑ Ⓒ Ⓓ Ⓔ	55. Ⓐ Ⓑ Ⓒ Ⓓ Ⓔ	85. Ⓐ Ⓑ Ⓒ Ⓓ Ⓔ
26. Ⓐ Ⓑ Ⓒ Ⓓ Ⓔ	56. Ⓐ Ⓑ Ⓒ Ⓓ Ⓔ	86. Ⓐ Ⓑ Ⓒ Ⓓ Ⓔ
27. Ⓐ Ⓑ Ⓒ Ⓓ Ⓔ	57. Ⓐ Ⓑ Ⓒ Ⓓ Ⓔ	87. Ⓐ Ⓑ Ⓒ Ⓓ Ⓔ
28. Ⓐ Ⓑ Ⓒ Ⓓ Ⓔ	58. Ⓐ Ⓑ Ⓒ Ⓓ Ⓔ	88. Ⓐ Ⓑ Ⓒ Ⓓ Ⓔ
29. Ⓐ Ⓑ Ⓒ Ⓓ Ⓔ	59. Ⓐ Ⓑ Ⓒ Ⓓ Ⓔ	89. Ⓐ Ⓑ Ⓒ Ⓓ Ⓔ
30. Ⓐ Ⓑ Ⓒ Ⓓ Ⓔ	60. Ⓐ Ⓑ Ⓒ Ⓓ Ⓔ	90. Ⓐ Ⓑ Ⓒ Ⓓ Ⓔ

SAT U.S. HISTORY PRACTICE TEST 2

Time—1 Hour

Directions: Each of the questions or incomplete statements below is followed by five suggested answers or completions. Select the one that is best in each case and then fill in the corresponding oval on the answer sheet.

---

1. In *On the Road*, Jack Kerouac depicted the

    (A) attitudes of the Beat Generation
    (B) building of the interstate highway system
    (C) phenomenon of family car trips in the 1950's
    (D) relocation of city dwellers to the suburbs
    (E) devastation caused by environmental pollution

2. England established its first permanent colony in North America at

    (A) New York
    (B) Philadelphia
    (C) Jamestown
    (D) Plymouth
    (E) Roanoke

3. A member of the Progressive Party would have been most likely to support which of the following policies?

    (A) Non-involvement by the U.S. in the internal affairs of other countries
    (B) Increased government regulation of private industry
    (C) Increased efforts by the Supreme Court to check the excesses of both government and big business
    (D) Desegregation and antilynching legislation
    (E) The integration of social Darwinism into the public school curricula

4. The decision by the United States to join the North American Treaty Organization in 1949 was

    (A) met with strong opposition by several charter member countries of the organization
    (B) motivated primarily by a desire to increase trade with Europe
    (C) an attempt to continue the Good Neighbor Policy in Latin America
    (D) contradictory to the country's prior wariness of collective security
    (E) a requirement of the Marshall Plan

5. From 1860 to 1890, which of the following was the largest group of immigrants to the United States?

    (A) Africans
    (B) Chinese
    (C) English
    (D) Northern and western Europeans
    (E) Southern and eastern Europeans

6. Which of the following best expresses Abraham Lincoln's intent in issuing the Emancipation Proclamation?

    (A) To declare that he would free all slaves at the end of the war
    (B) To let the Confederate states know that their return to the Union depended on emancipation
    (C) To free slaves in the western territories only
    (D) To free slaves in the Union
    (E) To free slaves in areas under Confederate control

GO ON TO THE NEXT PAGE

JOIN, or DIE.

7. This political cartoon, which appeared in 1754, emphasizes the necessity for the American colonies to unite in response to the

   (A) Sugar Act
   (B) Stamp Act
   (C) Coercive Acts
   (D) French and Indian War
   (E) Navigation Acts

GO ON TO THE NEXT PAGE

8. Which of the following developments led to the passage of the Embargo Act in 1807 ?

   (A) The failure of the Non-Intercourse Act to stop trade with foreign ports
   (B) An alliance between Britain and France
   (C) Tripoli's practice of demanding payment from American sea crews passing through the Mediterranean Sea
   (D) British harassment of U.S. seamen, culminating in an attack on a U.S. ship
   (E) Britain's abolition of slavery

9. In 1951, General Douglas MacArthur was relieved from duty because he

   (A) failed to defeat North Korea in the Korean War
   (B) was denounced as a communist by Senator Joseph McCarthy
   (C) publicly criticized the Truman administration's policies
   (D) refused to lead the American occupation of Japan
   (E) flouted regulations established by the United Nations

10. Which of the following was NOT a factor in the United States' decision to support the Allies in World War I?

    (A) Germany's use of submarine warfare
    (B) Anti-German propaganda
    (C) A fear that Germany would help Mexico regain Texas, Arizona, and New Mexico
    (D) Germany's alliance with Russia
    (E) The sinking of the *Lusitania*

11. Which of the following was the primary cause of the Great Depression?

    (A) The stock market crash in 1929
    (B) Overseas investment by American corporations
    (C) The Stimson Doctrine
    (D) Strikes organized by the American Federation of Labor
    (E) An imbalance in supply and demand of goods in the domestic market

Union Troops Available for Duty

1862	527,204
1863	698,808
1864	611,250
1865	620,924

12. Which of the following best accounts for the rise in the number of Union troops in 1863 ?

    (A) Disheartened by Confederate losses, many Confederate troops decided to defect to the Union.
    (B) In support of Lincoln and his policy on slavery, Britain and France sent reinforcements to the Union army.
    (C) At the end of 1862, Nebraska became a state in the Union, and its citizens joined the Union troops.
    (D) After the Emancipation Proclamation, the Union began to enlist freed slaves in conquered Confederate territories.
    (E) In 1863, Maryland and West Virginia, which had seceded, decided to rejoin the Union.

13. In one of its first efforts to exert control over the colonies, Britain issued the Proclamation of 1763, which

    (A) levied a series of heavy internal taxes
    (B) prohibited the colonies from engaging in internal trade
    (C) took away all the corporate charters and replaced them with royal governors
    (D) drew a line at the Appalachian mountains beyond which only Native Americans could live
    (E) abolished slavery in New England

GO ON TO THE NEXT PAGE

14. Which of the following was a central feature of the economic program enacted by the Reagan administration in the 1980's?

    (A) The lowering of interest rates in order to raise inflation
    (B) Government subsidies for working class families
    (C) An increase in federal spending on education and public transportation
    (D) Increased government regulation of industry
    (E) Tax cuts designed for the wealthy and intended to "trickle down" to lower classes

15. Congress created the Civil Service Commission in 1883 in order to

    (A) give official support to the "spoils system"
    (B) train bureaucrats
    (C) give the civil service authority to regulate industry
    (D) create a civil service
    (E) minimize the practice of patronage in government jobs

16. After the United States entered World War II, the Allied powers collectively decided to do which of the following?

    (A) Focus their attention on defeating Japan
    (B) Focus their attention on defeating Germany
    (C) Divide responsibilities, with Britain and the United States fighting Japan, while Russia dealt with Germany
    (D) Immediately force Italy's surrender
    (E) Expel the Germans from Latin America

17. John Calhoun made all of the following arguments in support of nullification EXCEPT:

    (A) States' rights are supreme.
    (B) Tariffs levied by Congress must benefit all states equally.
    (C) The central government is sovereign.
    (D) Protective tariffs raised in 1816, 1824, and 1828 damaged the Southern economy.
    (E) States have the authority to decide the constitutionality of laws that affect their citizens.

18. The philosophy of transcendentalism

    (A) instructed individuals to turn inward in order to escape the materialism of the world
    (B) argued that the poor could overcome poverty through hard work
    (C) advocated westward expansion
    (D) supported the women's rights movement
    (E) rekindled religious fervor and prompted many Americans to attend church

19. In the Freeport Doctrine, Stephen Douglas asserted which of the following about slavery?

    (A) It could be prohibited in the territories if the new states did not pass protective slave codes.
    (B) It was inevitable and therefore Congress should allow it to expand into the western territories.
    (C) It would soon end because it was growing increasingly unprofitable.
    (D) It should not impede the development of a transcontinental railroad.
    (E) It was too difficult a political issue for quick resolution and a five-year moratorium for debate over it was needed.

20. Passed in 1933, the Twenty-first Amendment to the Constitution

    (A) outlawed communism in the United States
    (B) mandated that presidents balance the federal budget
    (C) repealed prohibition
    (D) set a two-term limit on the presidency
    (E) gave states new powers to regulate commerce

GO ON TO THE NEXT PAGE

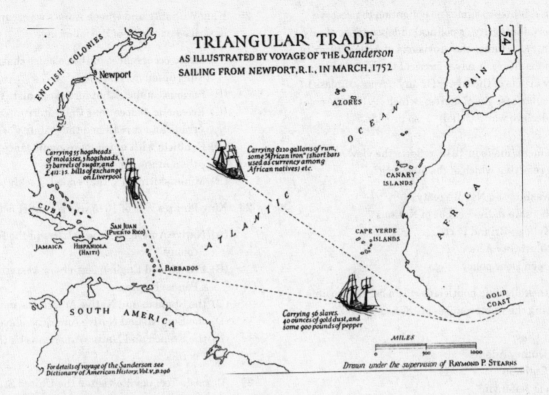

TRIANGULAR TRADE

AS ILLUSTRATED BY VOYAGE OF THE *Sanderson*

SAILING FROM NEWPORT, R.I., IN MARCH, 1752

21. The map pictured above illustrates the economic policy known as

(A) supply-side economics
(B) free trade
(C) export focused economics
(D) mercantilism
(E) protective tariffs

GO ON TO THE NEXT PAGE

22. "The United States assumes no obligation to preserve the territorial integrity or political independence of any other country . . . under the provisions of Article 10, or to employ the military or naval forces of the United States under any article of the treaty for any purpose, unless in any particular case the Congress, which . . . has the sole power to declare war . . . shall . . . so provide."

    This statement, made in 1919, reflects the view of the Senate in rejecting which of the following?

    (A) The Washington Naval Treaty
    (B) Membership in the League of Nations
    (C) The Kellogg-Briand Pact
    (D) The Neutrality Acts
    (E) The Open Door policy

23. Which of the following politicians was most responsible for designing the Compromises of 1833 and 1850?

    (A) Henry Clay
    (B) John Quincy Adams
    (C) John Calhoun
    (D) Thomas Jefferson
    (E) James Monroe

24. During the 1950's and 1960's, American politicians who believed in the "domino theory" argued

    (A) for a gradual transition from tariff barriers to free trade
    (B) that if a foreign country fell to communism, neighboring countries would likely become communist as well
    (C) that two-year terms in the House of Representatives would create instability
    (D) that the civil rights protests were creating public support for integration
    (E) that the exploration of outer space would give the United States an advantage over the Soviet Union during the Cold War

25. King William's and Queen Anne's wars can best be described as which of the following?

    (A) Major occurrences in the colonies that totally disrupted normal life
    (B) Serious conflicts that forced colonists to choose sides
    (C) Economic dislocations that interrupted colonial trade and threatened the stability of the colonies
    (D) Conflicts with much more significance in Europe than in the colonies
    (E) Minor skirmishes that ended quickly

26. King Philip's War of 1675 was a conflict between

    (A) Native Americans and settlers in the Plymouth colony
    (B) French and English settlers in western Pennsylvania
    (C) the Spanish and Native Americans in Florida
    (D) the English and Native American slaves in Virginia
    (E) the French and Native Americans on the Canadian border

27. Alexis de Tocqueville visited the United States in the 1830's in an attempt to

    (A) study the concept and practice of American democracy
    (B) join the utopian community at Oneida
    (C) advocate for women's rights
    (D) determine whether slaves were well treated
    (E) become involved in prison reform

GO ON TO THE NEXT PAGE

28. Which of the following statements about the Suffolk Resolves is LEAST accurate?

    (A) They declared the Intolerable Acts invalid.
    (B) They called for a boycott of English goods until the Intolerable Acts were repealed.
    (C) King George viewed them as a serious threat that could result in war with the American colonies.
    (D) The American colonists used them to signal their desire for independence.
    (E) They indicated that the colonies were still loyal to the king.

29. Which of the following people was nicknamed the "Wizard of Menlo Park"?

    (A) J. P. Morgan
    (B) Cornelius Vanderbilt
    (C) John D. Rockefeller
    (D) Thomas Edison
    (E) Alexander Graham Bell

30. African Americans and women entered the American workforce in record numbers during

    (A) Reconstruction
    (B) industrialization
    (C) World War I
    (D) the New Deal
    (E) the 1950's

31. Which of the following statements best reflects Enlightenment thought in eighteenth-century America?

    (A) Religion is the most important aspect of daily life, and it guarantees eternal happiness.
    (B) The universe was created rationally, and humans can use reason to determine how it operated.
    (C) Involvement in the slave trade is a fundamental sin against God.
    (D) English control is retarding economic growth in the American colonies.
    (E) All residents of the American colonies should be able to participate in the political process.

32. "It is emphatically the province and duty of the judicial department to say what the law is. Those who apply the rule to particular cases, must of necessity expound and interpret that rule. If two laws conflict with each other, the courts must decide on the operation of each. So if a law be in opposition to the constitution; if both the law and the constitution apply to a particular case, so that the court must either decide that case conformably to the law, disregarding the constitution; or conformably to the constitution, disregarding the law; the court must determine which of these conflicting rules governs the case. This is of the very essence of judicial duty."

The author of this statement from 1803 would probably have agreed that

    (A) state nullification laws violate the Constitution
    (B) the Supreme Court has the power of judicial review
    (C) the abolition of slavery is unconstitutional
    (D) Congress should control interstate commerce
    (E) the president has the authority to interpret the Constitution

33. During his presidency, William Howard Taft argued that global stability could be achieved through which of the following means?

    (A) Gunboat diplomacy
    (B) American investment abroad
    (C) Isolationism
    (D) Free trade
    (E) Peace without victory

GO ON TO THE NEXT PAGE

34. The growth of journalism in the 1840's had important consequences for American society primarily because

    (A) politicians exploited newspapers as a new means to campaign for office
    (B) newspapers exposed the conflicting views of the North and the South over the issue of slavery
    (C) newspapers played an important role in expanding religious evangelicalism
    (D) journalists promoted traditional family values
    (E) newspapers fostered literacy, in turn leading to the advent of public school systems

35. In the early 1870's, Granger organizations transformed from being predominantly social and cultural to being political because

    (A) their membership was declining as farmers abandoned their homes and moved to cities
    (B) other farm organizations began to compete for members by offering farm education lectures and events
    (C) of their grievances against the railroads
    (D) they were ridiculed in the eastern press for being old-fashioned
    (E) of their increasing support for segregation

36. During the Civil War, England refrained from entering into an alliance with the Confederacy for all of the following reasons EXCEPT:

    (A) Mill owners in England wanted to replace southern cotton with Egyptian cotton.
    (B) England relied more heavily on wheat from the North than on cotton from the South.
    (C) France had already allied with the North, and England did not want to start a war against another European nation.
    (D) Antislavery sentiment in England was strong.
    (E) The North's victory at Antietam convinced Britain that the South could not win the war.

37. Which of the following prompted the meeting of the First Continental Congress?

    (A) The Battle of Saratoga
    (B) The Battle of Lexington and Concord
    (C) The Coercive Acts
    (D) The Stamp Act
    (E) The Intolerable Acts

38. William Randolph Hearst contributed to the Spanish-American War by

    (A) practicing yellow journalism
    (B) providing Cuban nationalists with financial backing
    (C) winning public support for the Spanish after publishing articles that cast the Cubans in a negative light
    (D) lobbying President William McKinley to support the Spanish
    (E) representing the United States in negotiations with Spain

39. Settlement houses, such as Jane Addams's Hull House in Chicago, were designed to

    (A) offer religious services to the homeless
    (B) help immigrants adjust to urban life
    (C) provide mortgages for the purchase of new homes
    (D) rehabilitate alcoholics and drug users
    (E) clean up the political corruption of municipal government

40. Through the Monroe Doctrine, the United States was

    (A) asserting its intention to dominate its hemisphere without European interference
    (B) advocating the settlement of the West
    (C) announcing its desire to be actively involved in European political affairs
    (D) reacting to an economic downturn by trying to increase trade
    (E) hoping to avoid costly wars with Native American tribes in the West

GO ON TO THE NEXT PAGE

41. The Tuskegee Institute was established in order to provide African Americans with which of the following?

   (A) A lobbying group
   (B) Liberal arts education
   (C) Practical education
   (D) An archive of the African-American experience
   (E) Healthcare in the rural south

42. Which of the following provided the initial source of wealth in the Jamestown colony?

   (A) Gold and precious metals
   (B) The slave trade
   (C) Timber
   (D) Tobacco
   (E) Cotton

43. For which of the following reasons was Franklin D. Roosevelt unsuccessful in his attempt to pack the Supreme Court in 1937 ?

   (A) His brain trust was ineffective in persuading Congress to support the idea.
   (B) His identification with organized labor damaged his image.
   (C) Packing the court was unconstitutional.
   (D) The Depression was receding and no one was focused on politics.
   (E) Most Americans did not want to alter the balance of power in government.

44. All of the following were examples of American nativism and xenophobia in the post–World War I era EXCEPT the

   (A) Palmer Raids
   (B) National Origins Act
   (C) rebirth of the Ku Klux Klan
   (D) Chinese Exclusion Act
   (E) executions of Sacco and Vanzetti

45. Social Darwinists in the United States argued that Americans who suffered financially and socially from industrialization

   (A) required the assistance of the federal government through welfare programs
   (B) should be assisted by their churches
   (C) should be exempt from taxes
   (D) would not survive and should be left alone to face extinction
   (E) only required some luck and honest effort to succeed in society

46. "We hold these truths to be self-evident: that all men and women are created equal; that they are endowed by their Creator with certain inalienable rights; that among these are life, liberty, and the pursuit of happiness; that to secure these rights governments are instituted, deriving their just powers from the consent of the governed. . . . The history of mankind is a history of repeated injuries and usurpations on the part of man toward woman, having in direct object the establishment of an absolute tyranny over her."

   At which of the following events was the statement above most likely to have been made?

   (A) Washington Conference
   (B) Hartford Convention
   (C) Seneca Falls Convention
   (D) Annapolis Convention
   (E) Potsdam Conference

47. The Northwest Ordinances of 1784 and 1787 resolved which of the following issues?

   (A) Regulation of Native American affairs
   (B) Competing colonial land claims
   (C) Control of interstate trade
   (D) Design of a uniform currency
   (E) Organization of national armed forces

GO ON TO THE NEXT PAGE

REAR VIEW.
—Orr in the Chicago *Tribune.*

48. What does the 1919 cartoon above suggest about Woodrow Wilson as a diplomat?

(A) He successfully reconciled the differences between World War I combatants.

(B) His peace plan received careful consideration because the United States had been invaluable in winning the war.

(C) He was politically sophisticated and knew how to deal with each combatant's desires within the structure of world peace.

(D) His former allies were turning against him and planning to break all diplomatic relations with the United States.

(E) His peace plan was destined to fail because it conflicted with the Allies' hidden agendas.

GO ON TO THE NEXT PAGE

49. By protesting in 1965 at Selma, Alabama, Martin Luther King Jr. hoped to

    (A) extend the 1964 Civil Rights Act into the private sector
    (B) secure voting rights for African Americans
    (C) support an economic "bill of rights" for African Americans
    (D) stop the extensive drafting of African Americans to fight in Vietnam
    (E) promote racial harmony in the AFL-CIO

50. Which of the following was the main reason for European exploration of the New World during the 1400's and early 1500's?

    (A) A land isthmus between Asia and North America had been discovered, allowing land access to the New World.
    (B) The Spanish monarchy wanted to convert all people of the world to Christianity.
    (C) Europeans wished to find alternative trade routes to the Far East.
    (D) Earlier explorers were unsuccessful in finding new lands in Africa suitable for agriculture.
    (E) Europeans sought to escape religious persecution in their own countries.

GO ON TO THE NEXT PAGE

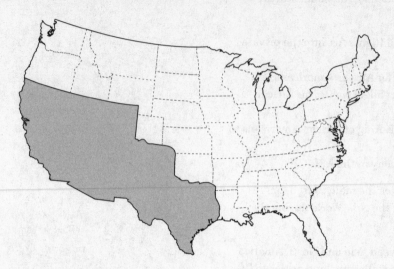

51. The shaded area on the map above indicates the land

   (A) in which slavery was permitted by the Missouri Compromise
   (B) that was purchased from the French in 1803
   (C) that was the focus of the Wilmot Proviso
   (D) that was set aside for Native American reservations
   (E) in which slavery was prohibited by the Compromise of 1850

52. Huey Long opposed the New Deal, arguing that it did not sufficiently address which of the following?

    (A) The plight of banks
    (B) Demands of labor unions
    (C) Complaints raised by the American Liberty League
    (D) Conservation of the Tennessee Valley
    (E) Suffering of the poor

53. According to English mercantile theory, the American colonies were

    (A) not a relevant priority
    (B) a source of raw materials and a marketplace for finished goods
    (C) a hindrance that needed to be controlled
    (D) a potential source of cheap labor
    (E) a good military base for impeding the commerce of other nations

54. Pursuant to his policy of social and economic policy of "dynamic conservatism," Dwight Eisenhower proposed all of the following measures EXCEPT

    (A) reducing the defense budget
    (B) the desegregation of public education
    (C) government-funded public works projects
    (D) farm subsidies
    (E) an increase in Social Security

55. To which of the following does the "Era of Good Feelings" refer?

    (A) James Monroe's presidency
    (B) The period following the establishment of the First Bank of the United States
    (C) The period immediately following the Treaty of Ghent between the U.S. and Great Britain
    (D) The period immediately following the adoption of the Constitution
    (E) The period following the Louisiana Purchase

56. Which of the following has led historians to refer to 1866 as "the critical year" in the process of Reconstruction?

    (A) Andrew Johnson took control of Reconstruction after Abraham Lincoln's assassination.
    (B) All of the southern states had returned to the Union under Abraham Lincoln's ten percent plan.
    (C) All former Confederate states ratified the Fourteenth Amendment.
    (D) Radical Republicans won enormous majorities in the congressional elections.
    (E) The Supreme Court declared the Black Codes unconstitutional.

57. The Specie Circular of 1836 mandated that

    (A) government lands could be purchased only with gold or silver
    (B) all citizens pay an income tax
    (C) slave sales be confined to major slave markets in Washington, D.C., and Charleston
    (D) the Second Bank of the United States pay all government debts immediately
    (E) paper money was no longer legal currency in the United States

58. In the 1840's, American nativists accused new immigrants of all of the following EXCEPT

    (A) creating slums in urban areas
    (B) taking jobs away from American citizens
    (C) bringing dangerous revolutionary ideas into the country
    (D) conspiring to give the Catholic Church influence in American politics
    (E) trying to replace slaves as a free labor force in the South

GO ON TO THE NEXT PAGE

59. Which of the following was the most serious weakness of the government created by the Articles of Confederation?

    (A) The lack of a president
    (B) Insufficient attention to foreign policy
    (C) Congress's inability to coin money
    (D) Congress's inability to tax
    (E) Land policy restrictions

60. With which of the following statements would a nineteenth-century advocate of the Social Gospel most likely have agreed?

    (A) A return to evangelical religion was necessary to cure the immorality that resulted from industrialization.
    (B) Christians, through their churches, were obligated to help the poor.
    (C) The wealthy deserved their success and should not be condemned for it.
    (D) Industrialists had an obligation to provide educational opportunities for other Americans.
    (E) Hard work, honesty, and some luck could make anyone wealthy and successful.

61. Which of the following best characterizes Malcolm X's contribution to the civil rights movement?

    (A) He urged African Americans to take pride in their heritage, and he extolled the virtues of self-defense and community action.
    (B) Throughout his life, he maintained a virulent racist attitude toward whites and advocated violent rebellion.
    (C) He supported the major civil rights organizations and their campaign to integrate African Americans fully into American society.
    (D) He was a prominent speaker at the March on Washington and advocated the passage of the 1964 Civil Rights Act.
    (E) He was the architect of the voting rights drive in Alabama, which the Student Non-violent Coordinating Committee undertook in the early 1960's.

62. In *Schenck v. The United States* (1919), the Supreme Court ruled that

    (A) socialism was unconstitutional and should be banned
    (B) civil liberties could be restricted in times of national crisis
    (C) prohibiting women from voting violated the Fourteenth Amendment
    (D) the League of Nation's collective security clause violated the Senate's enumerated power to declare war
    (E) Congress did not have the authority to regulate immigration

63. The Haymarket riot of 1886 carried which of the following results?

    (A) Waning public support for unions
    (B) A prolonged strike by factory workers
    (C) The formation of the Knights of Labor
    (D) Passage of the Sherman Anti-trust Act
    (E) The imprisonment of several prominent farm owners

GO ON TO THE NEXT PAGE

64. "If a nation shows that it knows how to act with reasonable efficiency and decency in social and political matters, if it keeps order and pays its obligations, it need fear no interference from the United States. Chronic wrongdoing, or an impotence which results in a general loosening of the ties of civilized society, may in America, as elsewhere, ultimately require intervention by some civilized nation, and in the Western Hemisphere the adherence of the United States to the Monroe Doctrine may force the United States, however reluctantly, in flagrant cases of such wrongdoing or impotence, to the exercise of an international police power."

Which of the following aspects of American imperialist thought does this quoted statement best reflect?

(A) The search for new economic markets
(B) The white man's burden
(C) The Open Door policy
(D) Dollar diplomacy
(E) Manifest destiny

65. The adoption of the Three-fifths clause during the framing of the Constitution settled the issue of how

(A) to select delegates to the electoral college
(B) new states would enter the Union
(C) slaves would be counted in the population
(D) the Supreme Court would be represented
(E) to pay state debts

66. The War for "Bleeding Kansas" had all of the following repercussions EXCEPT

(A) John Brown's murder of a group of pro-slavery settlers
(B) the drafting of the Lecompton Constitution, which proposed establishing slavery in Kansas
(C) an attack by a pro-slavery groups from Missouri on an antislavery group in Lawrence, Kansas
(D) Kansas's entrance to the Union as a slave state in 1861
(E) interference in the Kansas election by "border ruffians" from Missouri

67. The efforts of the Agricultural Adjustment Administration during the New Deal resulted in

(A) the strict enforcement of farm production quotas under threat of imprisonment
(B) a decrease in the price of farm products
(C) an increase in the production of staple crops
(D) the migration of many poor farmers from the dust bowl to California
(E) the increasing importation of staple crops from overseas

68. Which of the following was NOT an outcome of the 1763 French and Indian War?

(A) Britain took Florida from Spain.
(B) France gave Louisiana to Spain.
(C) Britain had amassed a substantial war debt.
(D) The American colonies became self-governing.
(E) France gave Canada to Britain.

69. The Montgomery Bus Boycott helped shape future civil rights strategies because it

(A) was the first time nonviolent protest had been employed in the cause of civil rights
(B) relied on extensive media exposure
(C) combined direct action protest with litigation in the courts
(D) convinced most white southerners to change their attitudes toward African Americans
(E) met with no hostility from local southern authorities or townspeople in Montgomery

GO ON TO THE NEXT PAGE

70. Which of the following served to enhance the pace of industrialization in post–Civil War America?

    (A) The consolidation of the railroads
    (B) Technological innovations
    (C) The utilization of steam power
    (D) Southern focus on factory building
    (E) The Granger movement

71. To which of the following does the Harlem Renaissance refer?

    (A) Urban renewal in New York City's largest African-American ghetto
    (B) Civil rights activity stressing desegregation
    (C) The emerging political power of African Americans on the municipal level
    (D) An African-American literary and cultural awakening
    (E) Marcus Garvey's desire to separate the African-American community from the white community and to create independent African-American institutions

72. In response to the Supreme Court's decision to integrate public schools, one hundred southern Congressmen

    (A) swore to uphold the new law despite criticism from their constituents
    (B) filed an appeal in the federal courts
    (C) issued a southern "manifesto" that urged defiance of the ruling
    (D) requested federal funds to facilitate the integration process
    (E) agreed to follow the law, but only if it could be implemented gradually

73. The strike by the American Railway Union against the Pullman Sleeping Car Company was organized and led by

    (A) John Altgeld
    (B) Samuel Gompers
    (C) Terrence Powderly
    (D) Eugene Debs
    (E) A. Philip Randolph

74. Before entering the war in 1941, the United States contributed to the Allied effort by

    (A) starting work on the Manhattan Project
    (B) establishing the Committee to Defend America First
    (C) providing lend-lease aid
    (D) signing the Tripartite Pact
    (E) selling arms to rebels in Italy

75. Helen Hunt Jackson wrote *A Century of Dishonor* (1881) in order to

    (A) encourage people to attend church
    (B) argue for women's rights
    (C) raise support for the abolition of slavery
    (D) attack the actions of the American government since the end of colonial rule
    (E) describe the suffering of Native Americans at the hands of the government

76. Which of the following was a result of the Cuban Missile Crisis of 1962?

    (A) The Bay of Pigs invasion
    (B) The Soviet Union's agreement to remove its missiles from Cuba
    (C) The beginning of strategic arms limitations talks between Khruschev and Kennedy
    (D) The building of nuclear missiles aimed at Cuba
    (E) Fidel Castro's alliance with the United States

77. The American Federation of Labor was established in order to

    (A) organize factory workers nationwide into one large powerful union
    (B) lead a socialist revolution that would put workers in control of factories
    (C) create a powerful interracial union that would fight race discrimination in southern factories
    (D) unionize only skilled workers who could deal with employers from a position of strength
    (E) shut down the Knights of Labor, which Gompers considered anti-Catholic

GO ON TO THE NEXT PAGE

78. Which of the following was a point of contention between strict constructionists and loose constructionists?

    (A) The establishment of political parties
    (B) The elastic clause of the Constitution
    (C) The balance of power between large states and small states
    (D) The morality of slavery
    (E) The central government's response to the Whiskey Rebellion

79. Which of the following events was a major catalyst in the secession of southern states from the Union in 1860 and 1861?

    (A) Abraham Lincoln's election to the presidency
    (B) The Tariff of Abominations
    (C) Northerners' condemnation of slavery
    (D) The South's relative poverty compared to the North
    (E) The Supreme Court's ruling that popular sovereignty was unconstitutional

80. Which of the following was a primary cause of the Gulf War?

    (A) Iraq's invasion of Kuwait
    (B) A communist threat to expand into Iraq
    (C) Israel's invasion of Iraq
    (D) An Iraqi threat to attack the United States
    (E) Retaliation for Iraq's treatment of American hostages

81. The Quaker belief that individuals could experience the "inner light" of God for themselves made Quakers

    (A) controlling and nonreligious
    (B) abandon the concept of priests and ministers
    (C) critical of Puritans and Pilgrims
    (D) advocates of slavery because slaves were heathens
    (E) unwilling to allow women to worship with men

82. "We meet in the midst of a nation brought to the verge of moral, political and material ruin. Corruption dominates the ballot-box.... The people are demoralized ... public opinion silenced ... homes covered with mortgages, labor impoverished, and the land concentrating in the hands of capitalists. The fruits of the toils of millions are boldly stolen to build up colossal fortunes for a few, unprecedented in the history of mankind.... From the same prolific womb of governmental injustice we breed the two great classes—tramps and millionaires."

    This statement best represents the political philosophy of which of the following groups?

    (A) Anti-federalists
    (B) Progressives
    (C) Populists
    (D) The New Deal coalition
    (E) Mugwumps

83. The Supreme Court decision in *Plessy v. Ferguson* (1896) gave constitutional legitimacy to

    (A) industrial rebates
    (B) Jim Crow laws
    (C) women's right to vote
    (D) sharecropping
    (E) trusts and monopolies

84. When it was formed between 1854 and 1855, the Republican Party was united in its stance

    (A) against immigration
    (B) against the existence of slavery
    (C) against the extension of slavery
    (D) in favor of the Kansas-Nebraska Act
    (E) in favor of popular sovereignty

GO ON TO THE NEXT PAGE

85. Which of the following developments best explains why the women's suffrage movement gained enough support to culminate in the passage of the Nineteenth Amendment, which enfranchised women?

    (A) The Supreme Court ruled that women's disenfranchisement was unconstitutional.
    (B) Women's contributions in World War I convinced Americans that they deserved to vote.
    (C) The Republican Party had always supported women's suffrage and backed the amendment.
    (D) Nativists wanted to increase the number of native voters in order to keep political power out of the hands of foreigners.
    (E) A sufficient number of women had been elected to Congress to push the amendment to a vote.

86. Supporters of the eugenics movement would most likely call for

    (A) aggressive foreign policy focused on colonization and economic imperialism
    (B) states' rights
    (C) improvements in secondary education
    (D) an end to immigration
    (E) political and corporate reform

87. The federal government's approach to business during the 1880's can be best described as

    (A) hostile
    (B) regulatory
    (C) laissez-faire
    (D) exploitative
    (E) nonexistent

88. For which of the following reasons was the Bill of Rights added to the Constitution?

    (A) Prominent critics of the Constitution demanded more civil rights protections as a condition for ratification.
    (B) Federalists wanted to emphasize the importance of civil liberties by describing them in a separate document.
    (C) The framers of the Constitution wanted to test the efficiency of the amendment process.
    (D) The Bill of Rights effectively balanced the power of the federal government with that of the states.
    (E) Pro-slavery forces wanted to distinguish free people from slaves.

89. William Lloyd Garrison argued that slavery should be

    (A) gradually abolished over a ten-year period
    (B) continued until slaves could purchase their freedom
    (C) subject to a political referendum regarding abolition
    (D) abolished immediately without compensation to slaveowners
    (E) subject to judicial review by the Supreme Court

GO ON TO THE NEXT PAGE

AFTER THE FEAST.
THE WORKING MAN GETS WHAT IS LEFT!

90. Which of the following best summarizes the point of the cartoon above?

    (A) The wealthy earn their success through hard work, whereas the poor are lazy and wait for handouts.
    (B) Working men are not fit to survive in society, so they will die from starvation.
    (C) In the United States, wealthy robber barons outnumber workers.
    (D) In American society, the wealthy control all the money and leave nothing for the average working man.
    (E) The wealthy are stealing from the poor, who are left with nothing.

S T O P

IF YOU FINISH BEFORE TIME IS CALLED, YOU MAY CHECK YOUR WORK ON THIS TEST ONLY.
DO NOT TURN TO ANY OTHER TEST IN THIS BOOK.

U.S. HISTORY PRACTICE TEST 2 ANSWERS

SAT U.S. HISTORY PRACTICE TEST 2 EXPLANATIONS

U.S. HISTORY PRACTICE TEST 2 ANSWERS

Question Number	Answer	Right	Wrong	Question Number	Answer	Right	Wrong
1	A	——	——	46	C	——	——
2	C	——	——	47	B	——	——
3	B	——	——	48	E	——	——
4	D	——	——	49	B	——	——
5	D	——	——	50	C	——	——
6	E	——	——	51	C	——	——
7	D	——	——	52	E	——	——
8	D	——	——	53	B	——	——
9	C	——	——	54	B	——	——
10	D	——	——	55	A	——	——
11	E	——	——	56	D	——	——
12	D	——	——	57	A	——	——
13	D	——	——	58	E	——	——
14	E	——	——	59	D	——	——
15	E	——	——	60	B	——	——
16	B	——	——	61	A	——	——
17	C	——	——	62	B	——	——
18	A	——	——	63	A	——	——
19	A	——	——	64	B	——	——
20	C	——	——	65	C	——	——
21	D	——	——	66	D	——	——
22	B	——	——	67	D	——	——
23	A	——	——	68	D	——	——
24	B	——	——	69	C	——	——
25	D	——	——	70	B	——	——
26	A	——	——	71	D	——	——
27	A	——	——	72	C	——	——
28	D	——	——	73	D	——	——
29	D	——	——	74	C	——	——
30	C	——	——	75	E	——	——
31	B	——	——	76	B	——	——
32	B	——	——	77	D	——	——
33	B	——	——	78	B	——	——
34	B	——	——	79	A	——	——
35	C	——	——	80	A	——	——
36	C	——	——	81	B	——	——
37	E	——	——	82	C	——	——
38	A	——	——	83	B	——	——
39	B	——	——	84	C	——	——
40	A	——	——	85	B	——	——
41	C	——	——	86	D	——	——
42	D	——	——	87	C	——	——
43	E	——	——	88	A	——	——
44	D	——	——	89	D	——	——
45	D	——	——	90	D	——	——

CALCULATING YOUR SCORE

Your raw score for the SAT U.S. History Test is calculated from the number of questions you answer correctly and incorrectly. Once you have determined your composite score, use the conversion table on page 399 of this book to calculate your scaled score. To calculate your raw score, count the number of questions you answered correctly:

_____
A

Count the number of questions you answered incorrectly, and multiply that number by $\frac{1}{4}$:

$$\frac{\rule{3cm}{0.4pt}}{B} \times \frac{1}{4} = \frac{\rule{3cm}{0.4pt}}{C}$$

Subtract the value in field C from the value in field A:

_____
D

Round the number in field D to the nearest whole number. This is your raw score:

_____
E

U.S. HISTORY TEST 2 EXPLANATIONS

1. **A**   The 1950s
Many people consider *On the Road* to be the bible of the Beat Generation. Kerouac's novel centers on a group of traveling youths who rebel against the conformity and conservatism of American life in the 1950s.

2. **C**   The Colonial Period
England's first permanent colony in North America was established at Jamestown in 1607. England's earlier attempt to settle Roanoke failed when storms and a dearth of supplies forced the settlers to abandon the colony around 1590.

3. **B**   The Progressive Era
Progressives demanded an interventionist government on all levels—national, state, and local. They also believed that the government should hold big business accountable for its corrupt practices. The Progressive Era lasted roughly from 1901 to 1917.

4. **D**   World War II
America's participation in NATO represented a shift in the nation's foreign policy. At the end of World War I, the Senate rejected membership in the League of Nations on the grounds that the collective security clause in the League's charter could force the United States into future wars. After World War II, however, the fear of communism began to dominate foreign policy, and the United States decided to join NATO as part of its strategy of containment.

5.   D   The Industrial Revolution

From 1860 to 1890, most immigrants to the United States came from northern and western Europe. In the mid-nineteenth century, there was also significant Chinese immigration to the West, but in 1882, the government excluded Chinese immigration for a ten-year period, after anti-immigrant sentiments (often directed against the Chinese) arose among the public. During the 1890s, "new" immigrants, southern and eastern Europeans, began arriving in the United States in large numbers, and many of them settled in the Northeast.

6.   E   Civil War & Reconstruction

The Emancipation Proclamation freed slaves under Confederate control. It did not free slaves in the Union or in parts of the Confederacy that were under Union control. Because the Confederacy did not acknowledge Lincoln's authority, the proclamation in fact freed almost no slaves.

7.   D   The Colonial Period

This cartoon depicts a snake divided into eight sections. The abbreviations stand for South Carolina, North Carolina, Virginia, Maryland, Pennsylvania, New Jersey, New York, and the New England colonies. The slogan "Join, or Die" refers to Benjamin Franklin's 1754 Albany Plan, which advocated the unification of the colonies in the face of French and Native American threats. The Albany Plan proposed the creation of a single government that would rule all the colonies, but the colonies, not ready for unification, rejected the plan.

8.   D   A New Nation

In 1807, the British HMS *Leopard* first attacked and then boarded the American USS *Chesapeake*. On board, the British hanged four men they accused of deserting the Royal Navy. Thomas Jefferson responded to this event by passing the Embargo Act, which put an end to American importation and exportation. He hoped that the act would end Britain's continual violation of American neutrality at sea, but instead the act's primary effect was to damage the American economy.

9.   C   The 1950s

MacArthur was relieved from duty for publicly criticizing the Truman administration. Frustrated by the military stalemate in Korea, MacArthur wanted to bomb North Korean munitions reserves in Manchuria, but Truman refused to grant him permission. In response, MacArthur criticized Truman's effectiveness as commander-in-chief of the Army. This criticism outraged Truman's military advisors, who then urged Truman to fire the general.

10.   D   World War I

Russia did not enter into an alliance with Germany during World War I. After the Russian Revolution, Russia dropped out of the war and signed a punitive peace treaty with Germany.

11.   E   The Great Depression & New Deal

Overproduction and underconsumption were the fundamental causes of the Great Depression. Corporations continued to produce goods, but American consumers were unable to purchase them because wages did not keep up with rising prices. The stock market crash in 1929 was a symptom of the depression—not its cause.

12.   D   Civil War & Reconstruction

Lincoln's Emancipation Proclamation of 1863 freed slaves in Confederate-held territories. Because the Confederacy refused to recognize the Union's authority, the proclamation in practice freed very few slaves at the time it was issued. But as the Union troops conquered Confederate territories, they began to enlist the freed slaves in those areas. By the end of the war, African-American soldiers made up almost ten percent of the Union troops.

13.   D   Revolution & Constitution

The Proclamation of 1763 was part of England's policy on Native Americans. The proclamation was made in the wake of Pontiac's Rebellion, which demonstrated that Native Americans on the frontier posed a significant danger to English settlers. England hoped to prevent further bloodshed by drawing a line separating English lands from the Native American lands.

14.   E   1970–2000

Reagan cut taxes for the very wealthy, hoping that these tax cuts would have a "trickle-down" effect. This policy was based on supply-side economics, which held that tax cuts for the very rich would trickle down to the poor, since tax cuts would free up more money for the rich to invest in the economy. Reagan's tax cuts resulted in a major recession in the middle of the 1980s and in an increase in the federal deficit.

15.   E   Industrial Revolution

Congress created the Civil Service Commission under the Pendleton Act in order to create a meritocratic civil service. Until the creation of the Civil Service Commission, government jobs were distributed to the administration's supporters and allies. The commission was created in order to restrict this practice of patronage and to prevent the massive turnover in government jobs that occurred with each new presidential administration.

16.   B   World War II

The Allies agreed that Germany posed the greatest threat in World War II. Accordingly, they resolved to defeat Germany before dealing with Japan.

17.   C   The Age of Jackson

Calhoun, a native of South Carolina, was outraged by the protective tariffs Congress levied in 1816, 1824, and 1828. In response to the 1828 "Tariff of Abominations," Calhoun argued that the tariffs were unconstitutional because they protected regional interests, and he urged southern states to nullify the tariffs within their borders. The nullification argument depended on the argument that states' rights were supreme. The supporters of nullification did not believe that the central government was sovereign.

18.   A   Cultural Trends—1781 to 1850

A challenge to rationalism and materialism, transcendentalism was a spiritual movement that focused on the individual. Transcendentalists believed that individuals could acquire an understanding of God by turning inward; they emphasized intuition and emotion. Ralph Waldo Emerson and Henry David Thoreau were leading figures in the transcendentalist movement.

19. **A** Westward Expansion & Sectional Strife
In the *Dred Scott* decision, the Supreme Court ruled that popular sovereignty was unconstitutional because it violated the Fifth Amendment. Douglas, a supporter of popular sovereignty, devised the Freeport Doctrine as a way of getting around the Supreme Court's ruling. Douglas suggested that territories could effectively abolish slavery by not enacting slave codes. He argued that slaveholders would not risk bringing their slaves into areas without laws that protected their slaveholding rights.

20. **C** The Great Depression & New Deal
The Twenty-First Amendment, ratified in 1933, repealed prohibition.

21. **D** The Colonial Period
Copying Britain's successful practice of mercantilism, the American colonies used triangular trade routes to increase their profits and create a favorable balance of trade. This cartoon illustrates the triangular trade between the United States, Africa, and the West Indies. New England rum was shipped to Africa, where it was traded for slaves. Then the slaves were shipped to the West Indies, and they were traded for sugar and molasses. The sugar and molasses were brought back to New England, where they were traded for rum. This cycle continued, bringing in substantial profits, particularly for New England tradesmen.

22. **B** The Roaring Twenties
The quotation is from a statement made by Henry Cabot Lodge to the Senate when it was deliberating joining the League of Nations. Lodge opposed participation because he thought the collective security clause (Article 10 of the League's charter) would commit the United States to fighting its allies' wars. The Senate agreed with Lodge and rejected membership in the League of Nations.

23. **A** A New Nation
Henry Clay, a congressman from Kentucky, designed the Compromise of 1833 and the Compromise of 1850. Known as the "Great Compromiser," Clay also helped negotiate the Missouri Compromise of 1820 and resolve many sectional tensions in Congress.

24. **B** The 1960s
According to the domino theory, if a nation falls to communism, the nations surrounding it will likely fall to communist rule as well. This theory played a crucial role in justifying the policy of containment that the U.S. government employed in the 1950s and 1960s. Dwight Eisenhower relied on this theory when deciding to intervene in Vietnam. He believed that if communists took over Vietnam, they would soon control most of Southeast Asia.

25. **D** The Colonial Period
Both wars were fought primarily in Europe. Although each involved some fighting in the colonies, the conflict did not disrupt colonial life. Most American colonies were not directly affected by either war.

26.   A   The Colonial Period

Metacomet, called King Philip by the colonists, led Native Americans in an attack on Plymouth in 1675, after Plymouth colonists had executed several members of Metacomet's tribe for the murder of a settler. Metacomet and many of his followers were killed during the war.

27.   A   Cultural Trends

De Tocqueville was intrigued by the practice of democracy in America and wanted to compare it to the practice of democracy in France. He wrote his monumental work, *Democracy in America*, based on his studies of American democracy in the 1830s.

28.   D   Revolution & Constitution

The colonists issued the Suffolk Resolves as a strong protest against the Intolerable Acts, but they refrained from demanding independence. Instead, the colonists pledged continued loyalty to the king. The main purpose of the Suffolk Resolves was to state the colonists' intention of boycotting British goods until the British government repealed the acts. Despite the pledge of loyalty, King George viewed the resolves as a serious threat to peace and feared that violence would ensue.

29.   D   Industrial Revolution

In his research laboratory in Menlo Park, New Jersey, Thomas Edison invented the phonograph, the moving picture projector, and the incandescent light bulb, thus earning him the nickname of the "Wizard of Menlo Park."

30.   C   World War I

African Americans and women entered the workforce in record numbers during World War I. The war stimulated the domestic economy, increasing factory output. In order to meet new production levels, the workforce swelled by a million people.

31.   B   The Colonial Period

Enlightenment thought, which spread through Europe and the United States in the eighteenth century, promoted the idea that the universe was grounded in rationalism and logic. Enlightenment thinkers revised traditional religious beliefs and advised looking to science and logic for proof of religion. Most of these rational thinkers believed that the world's natural order implied the existence of a rational creator. Benjamin Franklin and Thomas Jefferson are two examples of famous American rationalists.

32.   B   A New Nation

The quotation is from the Supreme Court's 1803 decision in *Marbury v. Madison*. This decision established the principle of judicial review, extending the power given to the Supreme Court by the Constitution. The principle of judicial review holds that the Supreme Court has the authority to declare an act of Congress unconstitutional.

33.   B   The Progressive Era

Taft advocated a foreign policy of "dollar diplomacy." According to Taft, American investment abroad would promote global stability in addition to aiding American economic interests. Dollar diplomacy was a marked contrast to Theodore Roosevelt's "big stick" policies, which called for an aggressive approach to international affairs. Taft's efforts at investment failed in China and met with little success elsewhere in the world. Eventually, he was forced to use military force in Nicaragua in order to suppress a revolt.

34. **B**   Civil War & Reconstruction

During the 1840s, newspapers played a key role in publicizing the growing conflict between the North and the South over slavery. They reported on the marked differences between life in the slaveholding states and life in the free states, and northern papers published abolitionist editorials, which exacerbated tensions.

35. **C**   Industrial Revolution

The Grange was formed by midwestern farmers in 1867. It hosted biweekly social functions where farmers could get an education, bond, and voice their complaints. The organization became increasingly political as the railroad companies began to hike up prices for short-distance shipments. In response to the railroads' practices, the Grangers lobbied Congress, and the Interstate Commerce Act was passed in 1887.

36. **C**   Civil War & Reconstruction

France did not enter into an alliance with the North. For a brief time, the Confederacy flirted with the idea of allying with France or England, but neither of these alliances came to fruition.

37. **E**   Revolution & Constitution

The Intolerable Acts of 1774 provoked the colonies into unified action for the first time and led directly to the meeting of the First Continental Congress in Philadelphia in 1775.

38. **A**   The Age of Imperialism

Hearst's newspaper, the *New York Journal*, engaged in yellow journalism, exaggerating and sometimes inventing accounts of Spanish atrocities against the Cuban rebels. Responding to these sensationalist reports, the American public gave increasing support to the Cuban nationalists and called for American intervention in the revolt.

39. **B**   Industrial Revolution

In the late nineteenth century, settlement houses tried to help recently arrived immigrants cope with unfamiliar and often hostile urban surroundings. They provided education, childcare, and room and board.

40. **A**   A New Nation

The Monroe Doctrine asserted U.S. supremacy in the western hemisphere and warned foreign nations against colonization or interference in that region. In exchange, the United States promised to refrain from interfering in European political affairs.

41. **C**   The Progressive Era

Booker T. Washington founded the Tuskegee Institute in order to provide African Americans with an education. The institute focused on providing a practical rather than a liberal arts education. Washington believed practical education would help African Americans achieve economic independence from whites.

42. **D**   The Colonial Period

The original settlers in Jamestown hoped to find gold and precious metals, but the colony's initial source of wealth came from tobacco. After several years of disease, starvation, and death, the colony began to flourish when John Rolfe, who later married Pocahontas, introduced a strain of West Indian tobacco to the colony. The crop grew well, and the Virginia Company made a huge profit exporting tobacco.

43. E   The Great Depression & New Deal
The Court Packing scheme tarnished FDR's reputation. In 1937, FDR attempted to reform the Supreme Court by introducing a bill that would allow the president to appoint an additional justice for each sitting justice over seventy years old. Many Americans accused FDR of trying to change the system of checks and balances by diluting the power of conservative justices on the Supreme Court.

44. D   The Roaring Twenties
The Chinese Exclusion Act, which banned Chinese immigration for ten years, was passed in 1882, not in the post–World War I era.

45. D   Industrial Revolution
Social Darwinists applied Charles Darwin's "survival of the fittest" theory to human society. They argued that the very poor were not "fit" to survive and that the government should not prolong their misery by giving them relief.

46. C   Cultural Trends—1781 to 1860
This excerpt is from the Declaration of Sentiments, which stated that men and women are created equal. The Declaration was issued in 1848 at the Seneca Falls Convention, where the members of the women's rights movement met under the leadership of Lucretia Mott and Elizabeth Cady Stanton.

47. B   Revolution & Constitution
By establishing a system for admitting new states to the Union, the Northwest Ordinances resolved the competing land claims held by existing states. The ordinances created the states of Michigan, Illinois, Wisconsin, Indiana, and Ohio from the Northwest territory.

48. E   World War I
Although his former allies paid attention to Wilson out of respect for the United States' contribution to World War I, each allied country had its own agenda which conflicted with Wilson's peace plan. The cartoon depicts each nation holding a secret gun that reflects its intentions and prevents "everlasting peace."

49. B   The 1960s
At Selma, King protested for voting rights, which previous civil rights legislation had not obtained for African Americans. Although historians disagree about the impact his protest had on reform, that same year Lyndon B. Johnson proposed a law that became the Voting Rights Act of 1965.

50. C   Age of Exploration
European exploration during the 1400s arose from a desire to find an all-water route to the Far East for the purpose of trading goods. Italy had blocked other Europeans from gaining access to the Mediterranean Sea for this purpose.

51. C   Westward Expansion & Sectional Strife
The shaded area on the map represents the land the United States acquired during the Mexican War. This territory was the subject of the Wilmot Proviso, which proposed banning slavery in all lands acquired during the war. The proviso failed to win support in the House of Representatives.

52. **E**   The Great Depression & New Deal

A champion of the lower classes, Huey Long criticized the New Deal for failing to alleviate conditions for the poor. Long proposed an alternative to the New Deal, called the Share Our Wealth program, which would focus on income redistribution and benefits for the poor.

53. **B**   The Colonial Period

Mercantilist theory held that a country could amass great wealth by increasing exports and collecting raw and precious materials in exchange. The American colonies were important to England because they provided both a marketplace for finished English products and a source for raw materials used by English manufacturers.

54. **B**   The 1950s

Although Eisenhower criticized many aspects of the New Deal, he continued some of its most important programs and practices, including the public works projects and farm subsidies. He also approved an increase in Social Security, while trimming the defense budget after the Korean War. While he upheld the Supreme Court's decision in *Brown v. Board of Education*, desegregation was not a component of his dynamic conservatism, and he considered the *Brown* ruling to be a mistake.

55. **A**   A New Nation

The Era of Good Feelings centers on Monroe's presidency (1817 to 1825). From the end of the War of 1812 to the rise of Andrew Jackson in 1828, the American political scene was dominated by a one-party system, with little opposition or controversy.

56. **D**   Civil War & Reconstruction

The 1866 election was an overwhelming success for Radical Republicans. The huge majorities they won in both houses of Congress allowed them to override presidential vetoes and to control the Reconstruction process.

57. **A**   The Age of Jackson

The Specie Circular was an executive order issued by Andrew Jackson in order to cool down the rampant speculation that threatened to destabilize the economy. The order required that government lands be purchased with only gold or silver instead of with credit or paper currency. Financial panic and economic depression gripped the country, as speculators who could not pay their government debts were forced into bankruptcy.

58. **E**   Cultural Trends—1871 to 1860

Nativists did not believe that immigrants were trying to replace slave labor in the south. Their main fear was that continued immigration would swamp and destroy "American" values and culture. Nativist groups, such as the Know-Nothings, gained support in northern cities during the 1840s and 1850s in response to increasing levels of immigration during those decades.

59. **D**   Revolution & Constitution

The Articles of Confederation did not give Congress the authority to tax. As a result, the central government could not raise operating funds or afford to raise an army. In order to raise funds, the government continued to print paper money, thus lowering the currency's value and creating serious economic problems.

60. B Industrial Revolution
The Social Gospel preached the idea that Christians had a moral duty to assist the poor. Poverty, they believed, was the result of unbridled capitalism. Those individuals neglected by the process deserved help from others more fortunate.

61. A The 1960s
Malcolm X urged African Americans to take pride in their heritage and history, and to look to Africa as their ancestral home. He stressed the necessity of self-defense and called for the African-American community to unite. Although he was frequently depicted as a violent racist, he never advocated violence. Near the end of his life, he came to understand that racism, in any form, grew out of ignorance.

62. B World War I
In the *Schenck* decision, the Supreme Court ruled that Americans' civil liberties, such as the right to free speech, could be denied or curtailed by the government in time of "clear and present danger." This precedent-setting case brought into question the applicability of the Bill of Rights in times of war and national crisis.

63. A The Industrial Revolution
In 1886, workers in Chicago protested the use of police brutality against strikers. The protest became violent when a member of the Knights of Labor threw a bomb, and the police retaliated. The police arrested several leaders of the Knights of Labor, who were then convicted for inciting the riot. Public support for the unions quickly fell afterward, and the Knights of Labor were effectively destroyed.

64. B The Age of Imperialism
The statement strongly suggests that the speaker claims adherence to the Monroe Doctrine and proposes to invoke the doctrine in a new circumstance. In fact, the statement expresses the Roosevelt corollary to the Monroe Doctrine, which functioned on the assumption of the "white man's burden." Roosevelt believed that many nations in the western hemisphere were hanging on to the "ties of civilized society" and that these countries needed the United States to keep them "civilized." The corollary proposed that the United States intervene whenever "inferior" people proved themselves unfit to govern their own nations.

65. C Revolution & Constitution
During the framing of the Constitution, southern states argued for the inclusion of slaves in population counts to determine the number of representative seats a state would have in Congress. Northern delegates objected to this inclusion, since it would give the South an unfair advantage. In the end, the delegates compromised and agreed on the Three-fifths clause, which would count slaves as three-fifths of a free person for representation and taxation purposes.

66. **D** Westward Expansion & Sectional Strife

Kansas was not a slave state. It entered the Union as a free state in 1861 after the crisis over "Bleeding Kansas."

67. **D** The Great Depression & New Deal

The Agricultural Adjustment Administration was designed to regulate farm production in the United States. Its goal was to decrease farm production and increase farm prices by paying subsidies to farmers who agreed to produce under certain quotas. While the AAA benefited many large farmers, its efforts hurt landless laborers and tenant farmers in the rural Midwest. As a result of the efforts of the AAA, as well as a severe drought in the American heartland, many of these farmers ended up migrating west, hoping to find employment in California.

68. **D** The Colonial Period

The American colonies did not become self-governing as a result of the French and Indian War. Trying to raise revenue to pay its large debt from the war, the British government began to levy harsh taxes on the colonies after 1763, and Britain moved away from its former policy of salutary neglect to one of tight control.

69. **C** The 1950s

The boycott successfully used two civil rights strategies: community protest and litigation. The Montgomery Improvement Association, led by Martin Luther King Jr., organized a boycott that crippled the Montgomery City Lines bus company. At the same time, the National Association for the Advancement of Colored People sought legal redress through the courts. The combination of direct action and litigation led to success in Montgomery and provided a useful model for future civil rights protests.

70. **B** Industrial Revolution

Rapid technological innovation throughout the nineteenth century fueled industrial development in the United States and expanded the American labor force.

71. **D** The Roaring Twenties

The Harlem Renaissance refers to African-American cultural production during the 1920s. The Renaissance was a predominantly urban phenomenon in which African-American writers, painters, artists, and intellectuals produced new forms of cultural expression that reflected the African-American experience.

72. **C** The 1950s

One hundred southern congressmen signed a southern "manifesto" condemning the *Brown v. Board of Education* ruling, which called for the integration of public schools, and urging states to nullify it. The call for nullification recalled the struggle in the nineteenth century between the states and the federal government. By issuing the manifesto, the congressmen demonstrated that integration would not proceed smoothly in the South.

73. **D** Industrial Revolution

Debs organized the railway workers' strike after Pullman ordered a twenty-five percent cut in the workers' wages. The strike was unsuccessful. It destroyed the union and resulted in Debs's incarceration for failure to obey court procedure.

74. C   World War II

Although FDR wanted to wait for public support before entering World War II, he assisted the Allies through other means before 1941. Several months before the United States entered the war, FDR passed the Lend-Lease Act, which gave the president the authority to lend or lease supplies to nations if he deemed them "vital to the defense of the United States." FDR started by providing lend-lease aid to Britain and later extended the aid to the Soviet Union.

75. E   Westward Expansion & Sectional Strife

Jackson wrote *A Century of Dishonor* in order to raise public awareness of the Native American situation. In the book, she blames the plight of the Native Americans on the U.S. government and on American citizens.

76. B   The 1960s

When the United States discovered Soviet missile bases on Cuba, Kennedy threatened to quarantine Cuba with a naval blockade and to dismantle the bases by force. For several days, the United States and the USSR seemed on the brink of nuclear war, but finally Soviet Premier Krushchev sent a proposal to Kennedy: the Soviets would dismantle the bases if the Americans promised never to invade Cuba. Kennedy agreed, and the USSR removed its missiles from Cuba.

77. D   Industrial Revolution

Samuel Gompers founded the AFL as a union for skilled craftsmen. He believed that skilled workers had an advantage in labor negotiations, since employers could not easily replace them if they went on strike.

78. B   Revolution & Constitution

Strict constructionists and loose constructionists disagreed over the elastic clause. Strict constructionists believed that the powers of the federal government should be confined to those expressly stated in the Constitution. Loose constructionists favored a strong central government that could do anything not expressly forbidden by the Constitution. The elastic clause gave Congress the power to create all laws "necessary and proper" in order to keep the country operating. Strict constructionists argued that the elastic clause gave the federal government too much power, but loose constructionists believed the clause was necessary in order to have an effective central government.

79. A   Westward Expansion & Sectional Strife

In 1828, South Carolina threatened to secede from the Union after the passage of the "Tariff of Abominations," but the southern slaveholding states viewed Lincoln's election as a much greater threat, even though Lincoln promised not to interfere with slavery in the South. Shortly after his election in 1860, a South Carolina convention unanimously agreed to secede. A year later, six other states followed suit. These seven states formed the Confederate States of America and elected Jefferson Davis their president. In 1861, four other slaveholding states seceded and joined the Confederacy.

80. A   1970–2000

In August 1990, Iraq invaded Kuwait. George H.W. Bush called for a counterattack to force out the invading Iraqis. In January 1991, the United States started the Gulf War by launching air assaults on Iraqi troops, military bases, and supply lines. Many people believe that the United States got involved in the war to protect American oil interests in Kuwait and Saudi Arabia.

81. **B**   The Colonial Period

The Quakers did not have priests or ministers because they believed that people communicated on an individual level with God.

82. **C**   Industrial Revolution

This quotation is from the preamble to the Populist Party platform of 1892. The Populists distrusted big business and the wealthy. Their platform called for the nationalization of the railroads, secret ballot box laws, and regulation of industry.

83. **B**   Industrial Revolution

In the 1896 *Plessy* decision, the Court stated that Jim Crow laws, which institutionalized segregation in the South, were constitutional as long as the facilities available to whites and Africans Americans were equal. The "separate but equal" doctrine established in this decision was overturned in 1954 in the *Brown v. Board of Education* case.

84. **C**   Westward Expansion & Sectional Strife

The Republican Party formed as a coalition of groups opposed to the extension of slavery. Although the groups that formed the Republicans had disparate aims, they were united in their stance against slavery's extension into the Western territories. Their "free soil" campaign sought to ban slavery in the territories, but it did not seek to ban slavery where it already existed.

85. **B**   The Roaring Twenties

Women's contribution to the war effort during World War I won them the respect of many Americans and ultimately helped them win the right to vote. During the war, women worked as volunteers in the armed forces, performing clerical duties and serving as nurses. Many women worked in defense industries, filling in vacancies left by men who were fighting overseas.

86. **D**   The Progressive Era

The eugenics movement represented an extreme form of progressivism. Supporters of eugenics wanted to turn the United States into a white, Protestant nation, completely free of the "impurities" of other races and religions. The eugenics movement was virulently anti-immigration, and a eugenics supporter would have wholeheartedly wished for an end to immigration.

87. **C**   Industrial Revolution

During the 1880s, the government took a hands-off approach to business. According to the government's laissez-faire approach, the market should be free of any government intervention because free markets would produce competition, which would in turn produce goods of fair quality at fair prices. Regulatory legislation that was passed during this period was only laxly enforced.

88. **A**   Revolution & Constitution
The Bill of Rights was added to the Constitution because critics, such as Thomas Jefferson and James Madison, worried that the Constitution did not adequately protect individual civil liberties. Those critics, who were generally Anti-federalists, demanded the addition of civil liberties protections in exchange for ratification of the Constitution.

89. **D**   Cultural Trends
Garrison, the most famous white abolitionist in the 1830s, advocated the immediate abolition of slavery, arguing that slavery was an unjustifiable and immoral system.

90. **D**   Industrial Revolution
This cartoon highlights the disparity of wealth between the wealthy and the working class during the "Gilded Age." On the right, luxuriously dressed and well-fed men enjoy their cigars, while a skinny working man timidly stands in the room on the left. The caption says, "After the feast, the working man gets what is left," but what's left is nothing— just the skeleton of the bird that the rich men devoured for dinner. The cartoon criticizes the wealthy for growing fat off their wealth while leaving nothing behind for the poor workers.